The Constitution of Agency

D1745197

The Constitution of Agency

Essays on Practical Reason and Moral Psychology

Christine M. Korsgaard

OXFORD
UNIVERSITY PRESS

OXFORD

UNIVERSITY PRESS

Great Clarendon Street, Oxford OX2 6DP

Oxford University Press is a department of the University of Oxford.
It furthers the University's objective of excellence in research, scholarship,
and education by publishing worldwide in

Oxford New York

Auckland Cape Town Dar es Salaam Hong Kong Karachi
Kuala Lumpur Madrid Melbourne Mexico City Nairobi
New Delhi Shanghai Taipei Toronto

With offices in

Argentina Austria Brazil Chile Czech Republic France Greece
Guatemala Hungary Italy Japan Poland Portugal Singapore
South Korea Switzerland Thailand Turkey Ukraine Vietnam

Oxford is a registered trade mark of Oxford University Press
in the UK and in certain other countries

Published in the United States
by Oxford University Press Inc., New York

© Christine M. Korsgaard 2008

British Library Cataloguing in Publication Data

Data available

Library of Congress Cataloging in Publication Data

Data available

Typeset by Laserwords Private Limited, Chennai, India
Printed in Great Britain
on acid-free paper by
CPI Antony Rowe, Chippenham

ISBN 978–0–19–955273–3 (Hbk)
978–0–19–955274–0 (Pbk)

10 9 8 7 6 5 4 3 2 1

For Bernard Williams,

for questions

For John Rawls,

for answers

Contents

Acknowledgments

This collection was assembled and its introduction written under the auspices of a grant from the Mellon Foundation, to whom I am deeply grateful. I would also like to thank Japa Pallikkathayil, who helped me to prepare the collection, and Peter Momtchiloff for his assistance and his patience.

Each essay in the volume is followed by acknowledgments to the many individuals and audiences who have helped me to write them, and I will not try to repeat all of them here. Instead, I would like especially to thank the following friends and students, all of whom have helped my work, past and present, in ways that they may not suspect: through their own work, their conversation, their responses to my work, their encouragement, their interest, and through their friendship, philosophical and personal:

Carla Bagnoli, Melissa Barry, Selim Berker, Matt Boyle, Charlotte Brown, Mary Clayton Coleman, Charles Crittenden, Kyla Ebels Duggan, Kate Elgin, Steve Engstrom, Luca Ferrero, Micki Fistioc, Ana Marta González, Barbara Herman, Tom Hill, Louis-Philippe Hodgson, Peter Hylton, Arthur Kuflik, Tony Laden, Doug Lavin, Dick Moran, Sara Olack, Japa Pallikkathayil, Andy Reath, Arthur Ripstein, Faviola Rivera-Castro, Amélie Rorty, Tim Scanlon, Tamar Schapiro, Jay Schleusener, Sally Sedgwick, Sharon Street, Gisela Striker, and Dave Sussman.

Abbreviations for Frequently Cited Works

References to and citations of frequently cited works are given parenthetically in the text, using the abbreviations cited below. For the editions and translations quoted, please see the Bibliography.

1. Aristotle

References to Aristotle's works will be given by the standard Bekker page, column, and line numbers, using the following abbreviations.

NE   *Nicomachean Ethics*
M   *Metaphysics*
MA   *Movement of Animals*
PHY   *Physics*
OS   *On the Soul*
EE   *Eudemian Ethics*
POL   *Politics*
RHE   *Rhetoric*

2. Hume

References to Hume's *Treatise* will be given by book, part, section and page number, and to Hume's *Enquiries* using the section and page number, using the following abbreviations.

T   *A Treatise of Human Nature*
1E   *Enquiry Concerning Human Understanding*
2E   *Enquiry Concerning the Principles of Morals*

3. Kant

References to Kant's works will be given by the page numbers of the relevant volume of *Kants gesammelte Schriften*, which appear in the margins of most translations. The *Critique of Pure Reason*, however, is cited in its own standard way, by the page numbers of both the first (A) and second (B) editions. The abbreviations used follow.

ANTH	*Anthropology from a Pragmatic Point of View*
C1	*Critique of Pure Reason*
C2	*Critique of Practical Reason*
CBHH	"Conjectures on the Beginning of Human History"
G	*Groundwork of the Metaphysics of Morals*
IUH	"Idea for a Universal History with a Cosmopolitan Purpose"
LE	*Lectures on Ethics*
MM	Prefaces and Introduction to *The Metaphysics of Morals* and Part 2, *The Metaphysical Principles of Virtue*
MPJ	*The Metaphysical Principles of Justice* (Part I of the Metaphysics of Morals)
OQ	"An Old Question Raised Again: Is the Human Race Constantly Progressing?"
PP	*Perpetual Peace*
REL	*Religion within the Limits of Reason Alone*
TP	"On the Common Saying: 'This May Be True in Theory but It Does not Apply in Practice'"
WE	"What is Enlightenment?"

4. Plato

References to Plato's works are inserted into the text, using the standard Stephanus numbers inserted into the margins of most editions and translations of Plato's works.

R	*Republic*

Other works are indicated by title.

5. My own works

CKE	*Creating the Kingdom of Ends*
SN	*The Sources of Normativity* (cited by section and page number)

Introduction

What constitutes an agent? I believe that we—that is, we rational beings—constitute ourselves as agents, by choosing our actions in accordance with the principles of practical reason, especially moral principles.[1] It sounds paradoxical, I know. How can we constitute ourselves, or choose our actions one way or another, unless we are already agents? How can we take control of our movements, unless we are already in control of them? In the essays in this book, completed with one exception between 1993 and 2003, I develop the Kantian conceptions of practical reason and agency that have led me to this view, and I try to explain how it works.[2] I also sketch and defend an Aristotelian account of the role of our passions, reactions, and emotions in action that I believe coheres well with these Kantian conceptions. And, in Part 3, I discuss some related issues in moral philosophy and philosophical methodology.

The essays are reprinted here with only minor changes, to ensure consistency in style, and in the translations of philosophical classics that I cite. For these essays, while they are primarily constructive rather than interpretive, work with and from the classics of the history of philosophy. In them, I try to think about agency, rationality, and virtue, in the company of Plato, Aristotle, Kant, and Hume, in effect asking them what they think about these issues, and trying to work with the answers that they give. This way of working reflects my deep conviction that the way to make progress in philosophy is to build on the achievements of our predecessors. I do not mean by treating their works as authoritative sources of the truth, of course, but rather by engaging with them in the confidence that real illumination on these topics is there to be found. Where the apparently different views of these philosophers, once properly understood, prove to embody strikingly similar insights—and I believe that this happens far more often than most philosophers suppose—I think we've

---

[1] This idea is also explored in my book *Self-Constitution: Agency, Identity, and Integrity* (Oxford University Press, 2009). One of the essays in this collection, "Self-Constitution in the Ethics of Plato and Kant" (Essay 3) provides a very short version of the ideas developed in the book.

[2] The one exception is "Aristotle on Function and Virtue," first published in 1986. I planned "Aristotle's Function Argument" as a companion piece to this essay, but never published the earlier version that I wrote of the latter.

found as good a place as we could possibly find to go digging for the truth.[3] Where their differences appear to be deep and genuine, we cannot do better than to try to discover and articulate the sources of those differences.

In this introduction, I will explain the main ideas I argue for in the three parts of this book.

1. The Principles of Practical Reason

1.1 *Reason and Rationality*

The essays in the first part of the book are devoted to the principles of practical reason. Before discussing the more specific conclusions I reach in them, it will be helpful to say what I mean by "reason."

When we talk about reason, we seem to have three different things in mind. In the philosophical tradition, Reason—I'll use the capitalized form to refer to the general faculty of Reason—refers to the active rather than the passive or receptive aspect of the mind. Reason in this sense is opposed to perception, sensation, and perhaps emotion, which are forms of, or at least involve, passivity or receptivity. Reason has also traditionally been identified with either the employment of, or simply conformity to, certain principles, rational principles, which may include the rules of logical inference, the principles that Kant identified as principles of the understanding, canons for the assessment of evidence, mathematical principles, and the principles of practical reason. A person is called "reasonable" or "rational" when her beliefs and actions conform to the dictates of those principles, or when she consciously and deliberately guides her thoughts and actions by them. And then finally, there are the particular, substantive, considerations, counting in favor of belief or action, that we call "reasons."[4]

What are the relations among these three things? I suppose one might think that they, or some of them, are completely separate things, which have related names more or less by accident.[5] To me it seems more natural to see them as aspects of a single human capacity, and so to relate them somehow, but how? According to one theory, the primary item here is the third thing I mentioned, the reason, a substantive consideration that counts in favor of something—some belief, action, or attitude—and that has normative force.

---

[3] See, in particular, "Self-Constitution in the Ethics of Plato and Kant" (Essay 3 in this volume) and "From Duty and for the Sake of the Noble: Kant and Aristotle on Morally Good Action" (Essay 6 in this volume), for essays that most strongly represent this conviction.

[4] This paragraph is more or less lifted from Essay 7, "Acting for a Reason," pp. 207–8.

[5] John Broome is one example of a philosopher who doubts whether these notions are connected. See, for example, his paper "Does Rationality Give Us Reasons?"

In the case of reasons for action, for example, the fact that an action will bring you pleasure is a reason to do it; the fact that it will harm another person is a reason not to do it; the fact that you promised to do it is a reason to do it, and so on. The principles of reason are simply identified as principles that direct us to act on those considerations, telling us what to count in favor of what. Perhaps they also tell us how to weigh and balance reasons against one another, or in some way how to adjudicate between them when they conflict. And then we call a person "rational" or "reasonable"—that is, we ascribe the faculty of Reason to her—in virtue of the fact that she recognizes and responds appropriately to reasons.

In my own view, there are two related problems with this conception of the relations among the various aspects of reason. First, on this conception the substantive reasons come first, so we cannot appeal to the nature of Reason or to the principles of rationality to help us to identify the substantive reasons. How then are we to identify them, except possibly through the use of intuition?[6] And that brings me to my second objection, which is that this conception does not do justice to the idea that Reason is the active dimension of the mind. Rather, those who favor it envision Reason as a receptive faculty that functions something like a sense, except that what it senses is normative rather than empirical facts.

In the Kantian conception of rationality that I favor, the order of the three aspects of reason goes the other way. Reason—the faculty of reason—is identified first, as the active dimension of the mind, and rational principles are identified as those that describe or constitute rational activity. When those principles are applied to facts and cases, they pick out the substantive considerations that we then regard as reasons.

Taking it more slowly:

The source of Reason is a particular form of self-consciousness that characterizes the human mind. Human beings are conscious of the potential grounds of our beliefs and actions *as potential grounds*. Let me explain what I mean by this. Any conscious animal is guided through her environment by means of her perceptions and her desires or instinctive impulses. Her perceptions constitute her representation of her environment and her desires and instinctive impulses tell her what to do in response to what she finds there. Indeed I believe that for the other animals perceptual representation and desire are not strictly separate. Either through original instinct or as a result

---

[6] Of course some philosophers who think that the substantive reason is the primary item here think that they can be identified without recourse to intuition. For one example, see T. M. Scanlon's discussion in *What We Owe to Each Other*, chapter 1, section 12, pp. 64–72.

of learning, an animal represents the world to herself as a world that is, as we might put it, already normatively interpreted, in the sense that she perceives things in terms of her own interests. She lives in a world that consists of things perceived *as* food or prey, *as* danger or predator, *as* potential mate, *as* child: that is to say, as to-be-eaten, to-be-avoided, to-be-mated-with, to-be-cared-for, and so on. These "normatively loaded" perceptions serve as the grounds of her actions—where a ground is a representation that causes the animal to do what she does.

The exact way in which these perceptions or representations operate on an animal's mind to produce her actions may, I now believe, differ in ways that can be ranged along a scale, depending on what sort of consciousness the animal has of her own representations. Primitive animals may respond more or less mechanically to these perceptions; more sophisticated animals may operate with something more like concepts or categories of "food" or "predator" or "threat" to which they respond intelligently; and yet more sophisticated animals may even be aware *that* they and their fellows experience, say, desire or fear. These differences affect the degree of control that the animal has, both over herself and, correlatively, over her environment. Exactly how any given kind of animal's representations give rise to his or her actions is a matter to be investigated empirically. But however it may be with the other animals, there is no question that we human beings are aware, not only that we perceive or desire or fear certain things, but also that we are inclined to believe and to act in certain ways on the basis of these perceptions or desires or fears. We are aware not only of our representations and desires as such but also of the way in which they tend to operate on us. That is what I mean by saying that we are aware of the potential grounds of our beliefs and actions *as potential grounds*.

And this awareness is the source of Reason. For once we are aware that we are inclined to believe on the ground of a certain perception, or to act on the ground of a certain desire, we find ourselves faced with a decision, namely, whether we should do that—whether we should draw the conclusion, or perform the action, on the ground in question, or not. Once the space of awareness—of reflective distance, as I like to call it—opens up between the potential ground of a belief and the belief itself, or between the potential ground of an action and the action itself, we must step across that distance with some awareness that we are doing so, and so must be able to endorse the operation of that ground as the basis for what we believe or do. And a ground of belief or action whose operation on us as a ground is one that we can endorse is a reason. This means that the space of reflective distance presents us with both the possibility and the necessity of exerting a kind of control over our beliefs and actions that the other animals probably do not have. We are active, self-directing, with respect to our beliefs and actions to a greater extent than they are. And it is the same fact that we now both can have, and absolutely require, *reasons* to believe and act as we do.[7]

Where are we to find these reasons? How are we to determine whether our perceptions and desires are adequate grounds for the beliefs and actions to which they incline us? To identify reasons we need principles, principles that we can apply to facts and cases in order to decide whether our impulses to believe and to act count as reasons or not. But as the philosophical tradition shows us, there are many contenders to serve as our rational principles. And this would seem to set us off on a regress. For it appears that we need a reason to conform to one proposed principle rather than another, and, if that is so, there must be a further principle behind every principle, to give us a reason for conforming to it. However—to anticipate my conclusion—there need be no such regress if there are principles that are *constitutive* of the very rational activities that we are trying to perform when we take control of our beliefs and of our actions, in the way that rationality requires of us.[8, 9]

1.2 *Rational Principles*

In the tradition of moral philosophy, three kinds of principles have been proposed as requirements of practical reason.

First, there is the principle of instrumental reason. According to this principle, practical rationality requires us to take the means to our ends. Here there is little dispute about how to formulate the requirement, except that some philosophers regard the ends in question as things desired, while others, such as Kant, argue that a rational requirement can apply only to things willed.

Second, there are versions of what I will call the principle of prudence or rational self-interest, usually understood to require that we maximize the satisfaction of our own desires or interests over time, or something along those lines. It is difficult to give an uncontroversial formulation of this principle, because here there are many disputes. Some philosophers think we are required to maximize the satisfaction only of the desires we have in the present. Others think we must take future desires into account but may discount for the fact

[7] This account of the nature of reason is taken with some modifications from *The Sources of Normativity*, especially 3.2.1, pp. 92–4, and "Fellow Creatures: Kantian Ethics and Our Duties to Animals," pp. 85–7.

[8] The ancestor of this argument is to be found in "Morality as Freedom" (CKE essay 6), pp. 164–7.

[9] For another version of constitutivism, see the work of David Velleman, found primarily in his books *Practical Reflection*, *The Possibility of Practical Reason*, and *Self to Self*. Velleman focuses on the idea that action has a constitutive aim, rather than on the idea that it has a constitutive principle. A more crucial difference between us is that he usually identifies that aim as self-knowledge, whereas when I think in terms of an aim, I identify it as autonomy.

that they are future. Most agree that any "pure" preference for the present over the future (any preference not based on extraneous factors like the greater uncertainty that attaches to future events) is irrational, but differ about what kinds of items the principle must take into account: all desires, all reasons? The common element in these views is that there is *some* principle requiring us to take the effects on our other ends into account when we reason about how to realize any particular end.

Third, many philosophers have believed that moral requirements are requirements of practical reason. Here, the main distinction is between philosophers who think that the basic moral requirement is formal, like a universalizability principle, and those who think that certain substantive moral principles, like the prescriptions that we should tell the truth and keep our promises, are self-evident rational requirements.

In the first three essays in the book, I take up these three kinds of principles in turn, asking in virtue of what the proposed type of principle is normative—that is, binding upon us—and thereby what qualifies it to count as a rational principle.

In "The Normativity of Instrumental Reason," and (more implicitly) in "The Myth of Egoism," I contrast three possible accounts of the normativity of practical principles generally. According to an empiricist account, the normativity of the principles of practical reason rests primarily in the capacity of those principles to motivate us—in their effects on the will. On this account, the principle of instrumental reason is normative (or, perhaps, does not need to be normative) because we are reliably motivated to take the means to our ends once we know what those are, and the principle of prudence is normative because we reliably prefer the action that leads to our greater good once we see clearly that it does so. The role of reason in action, on this view, is not strictly practical: it is only to clear up mistakes. According to a rationalist or realist account, by contrast, the normativity of practical principles is not something that can be further explained. Certain principles or reasons simply have normative force, as a kind of property. According to this view, reason is supposed to be practical. But, as I mentioned at the beginning, to say that we are practically rational is just to say that we recognize and respond to these normative requirements, in essentially the same way that (according to this theory) we respond to theoretical reasons.

In "The Normativity of Instrumental Reason," I criticize these two accounts. I argue that the empiricist account, while it may explain how we are motivated by rational principles, cannot explain how we can be guided by them, or more generally how they can bind us. A principle that moves us inevitably cannot serve as a guide, for it is not possible to be guided unless it is also possible to fail to be guided. (For these arguments see especially "The Normativity of Instrumental Reason," section 2; and "The Myth of Egoism," section 1.1.) The rationalist account, by contrast, cannot explain why rational principles necessarily motivate us. So long as bindingness or normativity is conceived of as a fact external to the will, and therefore external to the person, it seems possible to conceive of a person who is indifferent to it. But this throws doubt on whether such principles can be binding after all. For what is amiss with a person who is indifferent to his reasons and obligations? He fails to *apply* certain principles to his actions, but then why should he do so? We cannot say that he has a reason to act on his reasons, or an obligation to meet his obligations, without manifest circularity. We can *say* that what is amiss with such a person is that he is irrational, of course, but according to the rationalist theory, that is just to repeat that he does not respond appropriately to reasons. (For these arguments, see "The Normativity of Instrumental Reason," section 3; "The Myth of Egoism, section 1.5; and also "Acting for a Reason," section 3, and "Realism and Constructivism in Twentieth-Century Moral Philosophy," section 4.) If we are to explain the normative force of the principles of practical reason, we cannot just regard them as principles that we are free to apply or not. Instead, like the rules of logical inference, they must be principles *in accordance* with which we operate—either well or badly.

So in place of these unsatisfactory conceptions, I offer a different kind of account of the normativity of the principles of practical reason, according to which the principles of practical reason are constitutive principles of action. I explain how this works in the case of the instrumental principle in "The Normativity of Instrumental Reason," and in the case of the formal principles of morality championed by Plato and Kant in "Self-Constitution in the Ethics of Plato and Kant."[10] I will describe this view of instrumental and moral reasoning more generally before returning to the vexed fate of the principle of prudence or rational self-interest.

1.3 *Constitutive Principles*

But before I go on I must say what I mean by a constitutive principle. First, what I will here call a constitutive *standard* (in the essays, I sometimes use "internal" for "constitutive") is one that arises from the very nature of the object or activity to which it applies. It belongs to the nature of the object or activity that it both ought to meet, and in a sense is trying to meet, that standard. Constitutive

---

[10] Plato's account of justice in the *Republic* is formal because he regards justice as that principle that unifies or harmonizes the soul, whatever it might be. See R 443e–444a and "Self-Constitution in the Ethics of Plato and Kant," Essay 3 of this volume, pp. 119–20.

standards apply most obviously to objects that have some standard use or function or purpose. If it is the function of a house to provide shelter from the weather, then it is a constitutive standard for houses that they should be waterproof. If it is the function of an encyclopedia to provide information to those who consult it, then it is a constitutive standard for encyclopedias that their statements should be true. Constitutive standards are opposed to external standards, which mention desiderata for an object that are not essential to its being the kind of thing that it is. Of course there is often room for contention about which desiderata are essential, but generally speaking one might suppose it is an external standard for a house that it should have a swimming pool or for an encyclopedia that it should be written in elegant prose.

Two things are important to notice about standards of this kind. First of all, constitutive standards are at once normative and descriptive. They are descriptive because an object must meet them, or at least aspire to meet them, in order to be what it is. And they are normative because an object to which they apply can fail to meet them, at least to some extent, and is subject to criticism if it does not. This double nature finds expression in the fact that we can criticize such objects either by saying that they are poor objects of their kind ("That's a poor encyclopedia, it isn't up to date."), or by saying that they are not such objects at all ("That's not an encyclopedia: it's just a compendium of nineteenth-century opinion!"). Second, constitutive standards meet challenges to their normativity with ease: someone who asks why a house should have to be waterproof, or an encyclopedia should record the truth, shows that he just doesn't understand what these objects are for, and therefore, since they are functional objects, what they are.

An especially important instance of the constitutive standard is what I will call the constitutive *principle*, a constitutive standard applying to an activity. In the case of essentially goal-directed activities, constitutive principles arise from the constitutive standards of the goals to which they are directed. A house-builder is, as such, trying to build an edifice that will keep the rain and weather out; the writer of an encyclopedia article is, as such, trying to convey the truth. But all activities—as opposed to mere sequences of events or processes—are, by their nature, directed, self-guided, by those who engage in them, even if they are not directed or guided with reference to external goals. And the principles that describe the way in which an agent engaged in an activity directs or guides himself are the constitutive principles for that activity. So it is a constitutive principle of walking that you put one foot in front of the other, a constitutive principle of swimming that you make movements that will impel you forward through the water, a constitutive principle of intelligible linguistic expression that your sentences include both a subject and a verb, a constitutive principle of typing that you hit the letters that you wish to appear on the page, and so on. And in all these cases, we can say that unless you are following the principle in question, you are not performing that activity at all.

Constitutive principles, like constitutive standards more generally, are normative and descriptive at the same time. They are normative, because in performing the activities of which they are the principles, we are guided by them, and yet we can fail to conform to them. But they are also descriptive, because they describe the activities we perform when we are guided by them. Sometimes people are puzzled by the idea that you can fail to conform to a constitutive principle—if following the principle is constitutive of the activity, and you fail to conform to it, then aren't you failing to engage in the activity after all? In one sense that is right, but in another it cannot be, for if you were not engaging in the activity after all, then your failure to conform to its constitutive principle would not be a failure at all. If I am not swimming, but just cooling myself by splashing about in the water, then my failure to make headway through the water is no failure at all. But if I am trying to swim—suppose there is a shark headed towards me—and all I succeed in doing is splashing around in the water, then my failure to make headway is a failure indeed. And this sort of thing does happen—people trying to walk can trip over their feet, people trying to type can hit the wrong letter, and people trying to write can fail to make themselves intelligible for want of a verb. And again, the double nature of the constitutive principle here is reflected in the language we use to describe failures to conform to them. As I watch your inefficient flailing about in the water I can say, with equal force, and meaning the same thing, "You're swimming very poorly" or "You aren't swimming, you're just splashing around." One way to put the point I am trying to make here is to say that the correct account of the metaphysics of activities is a Platonic one. An activity is the activity that it is by virtue of its imperfect *participation* in the perfect Platonic *form* of that activity.

The principles of practical reason, I propose, are constitutive principles of rational activity: they are the principles by which we take control of our beliefs and actions. Or rather, since these terms may already be taken to imply control, perhaps I should say that they are the principles by which we take control of our representations or conceptions of the world, and of our own movements—using "movement" as a general term for the various ways, physical and mental, that we bring about states of affairs in the world.[11]

---

[11] I think that some of the disagreement about whether non-human animals have beliefs or count as agents results from the fact that they have different, and lesser, kinds of control over their

Before I go on, let me notice one complication that arises from my view of reason. I have characterized reason *in general* as a faculty by virtue of which we are active. Of course many philosophers would disagree with that. Some philosophers think that arriving at beliefs is somehow a more passive process than arriving at decisions to act. They think that we cannot help believing the evidence of our senses or the conclusions of our theoretical arguments in some way that we always can help doing what we decide we have most reason to do. Other philosophers, in particular the ones I mentioned earlier, who think that rationality is a matter of responding appropriately to substantive reasons, might deny that there is any such difference, but they would deny it because they think practical reasoning is no *more* active than theoretical reasoning. Both are just a form of responsiveness to the reasons that are there. I disagree with both of those camps, but I will not attempt to engage these large issues here. Since I believe that reason is essentially an active faculty, I regard "action" in the special sense relevant to practical reason as one among several forms of "rational activity." As I am thinking of it, "acting" in the sense relevant to practical reason is that activity that is directed to producing some state of affairs in the world.[12] So action is taking control of the movements by means of which we produce states of affairs in the world. Obviously, any adequate account of action, in this perhaps narrower sense, should also capture the core idea of being active that is common to all forms of rational activity. But for now I will focus on action in this more specific sense. The question, what the principles of practical reason are, is then the question what the constitutive principles of action are: what counts as taking control of our own movements?

1.4 *Agency*

Many of the problems that are now discussed under the rubric of "the philosophy of action" were once discussed under the rubric of "freedom of the will," and this is no accident. Agency is almost as mysterious as freedom of the will, and for the same reasons—with this important difference: that it

representations and movements than human beings do. One can grant that, and still think there is no argument worth having about how much control entitles us to call a representation a belief or a representation-directed movement an action.

[12] Of course someone who tries to reason his way to the truth is also trying to bring about a state of affairs in the world—that he has true beliefs about the subject at hand—and to that extent he is acting. But I do not think this thought captures the full sense in which belief is an active state, for this much is common to reasoning your way to true beliefs and manipulating yourself into them, and those are different. Theoretical reasoning has rules of its own. As if probably clear from the text, I am a bit puzzled about how exactly to characterize the relation between action and rational activity more generally.

is much harder for skeptics, even those with "scientific" pretensions, to deny that agency exists. Since I take an action to be a movement that is attributable to an agent, I take agency to be the central notion in the philosophy of action. In virtue of what, then, is a movement attributable to an agent? When can we say that an agent has determined her own movements, and so that those movements are actions? We want to say that a movement is attributable to an agent if the agent is its cause, but this may seem, at first blush, to be in tension with the belief that every event is caused by some other event. How can an agent determine her own movements, if her movements are determined by certain events, which in turn are determined by other events, and so on?

Part of the answer is that there is surely a difference between a case in which the event most immediately determining your movements is, say, that you are pushed from behind, and a case in which the event most immediately determining your movements is a thought of your own. To take the most obvious case: most people do not feel that their freedom or power of self-determination is threatened by the possibility that their movements are determined by their own thoughts about what they ought to do. Rather, they feel that their freedom or power of self-determination is threatened by the possibility that this may *not* be the case. So perhaps we should claim that we are active to the extent that our movements are caused by our conceptions of what we ought to do.[13]

Now I can imagine two possible and opposed reactions to this claim. On the positive side you might react by thinking that it is intuitively plausible: how could we be more in control of our own movements than we are when they are caused by our very own reflections about what we ought to do? But on the more skeptical side you might want to argue that, even granting this kind of mental causation, there is no reason to suppose that thoughts with one sort of content—thoughts about what we ought to do—cause movements that are any more "self-determined" than thoughts with any other sort of content. After all, why should the *content* of the thought make any difference to the degree to which the person moved by that thought counts as a self-determining agent?

Kant's theory of autonomy, I believe, addresses this problem. The will, Kant famously argues, is a kind of causality, and as such, it must operate in

---

[13] On my view there are actually degrees of activity or agency, and the phrase "conceptions of what we ought to do" is meant to cover all of them, ranging from a non-human animal's instinctive normative perceptions to a reflective human being's explicit practical deliberations. The argument I go on to give in the text, however, most obviously applies to that last thing: the way we are active when we reflect on what to do. Here again I want to take a Platonic line: other forms of action or self-determination count as forms of action or self-determination because of the extent to which they imperfectly participate in the perfect self-determination that is represented by being determined by explicitly practical deliberation.

accordance with laws.[14] A free will—a fully self-determining will—would be one that is not moved by any *alien* cause. That is, it would not be subject to determination by any law that is outside of itself. Since a free will must operate in accordance with laws, and yet must not be determined by any law outside of itself, the free will must be determined by a law that it gives to itself—a law that it legislates to govern its own movements. The free will, that is, must be an autonomous will. In other words, to be free is to be motivated by the thought that the principle in accordance with which you propose to act is one that you would will as a law. But of course Kant also believed that the moral law is the law of acting on a maxim that you yourself, on your own deepest reflection, would will to be a law—either one that *qualifies* to be a law (when the action is permissible), or one that you *must* will as a law (when the action is required). This means that in Kant's theory autonomy is linked, on the one hand, to the very idea of action—that is, of self-determination—and, on the other hand, to thoughts about what we ought to do. According to Kant, then, to think thoughts about what you ought to do is at the same time to think thoughts about what you would do were you a fully self-determining being.[15] And if it is possible for us to act as we would act if we were fully self-determining beings, then we are, for practical purposes, fully self-determining beings (G 4:446–448). This is why the content of the thoughts that move us can make a difference to the degree of self-determination we exhibit when our movements are caused by our thoughts.[16] The categorical imperative, on this view, is not just the principle of morality. It is also the constitutive principle of action.

More precisely, I believe that the principle of governing oneself by universal laws is the constitutive principle of rational activity generally. For the require-ment of universalizability governs every aspect of rational thought. To believe on the basis of a rational consideration is to believe on the basis of a consider-ation that could govern the beliefs of any rational believer, and still be a belief about the public, shared world. To act on the basis of a rational consideration is to act on the basis of a consideration that could govern the choices of any rational chooser, and still be *efficacious* in the public, shared world. This is

[14] For an explanation of the connection between action and laws see "Self-Constitution in the Ethics of Plato and Kant," Essay 3 in this volume, pp. 120–4.

[15] Take that as a very rough reading of Kant's claim that "*the world of understanding contains the ground of the world of sense and so too of its laws,* and is therefore immediately lawgiving with respect to my will" (G 4:454).

[16] I intend this argument to address the question how we can conceive of ourselves as agents. I do not intend it to address the question of the grounds on which we hold one another responsible. I do not think that attributions of responsibility are directly tied to attributions of freedom or agency in that way. For my views on this matter see "Creating the Kingdom of Ends: Reciprocity and Responsibility in Personal Relations," CKE essay 7.

what I have elsewhere called the "practical contradiction" interpretation of the categorical imperative test.[17] The notion of efficacy brings in the other element of Kant's account of action, the principle of instrumental reason. For if to act is to engage in practical activity that is directed to producing some state of affairs in the world, then the agent must also seek to be efficacious, that is, to work with the natural causal mechanisms that he can use to make things happen in the world. He must use the means. And this means that the maxim or principle on which he proposes to act must serve as a universal *practical* law. It is the universalizability principle in that specific sense—the law of acting only on universal *practical* laws, which is constitutive of action in the more specific sense.

Let me put the point another way. To be an agent is to be, at once, autonomous and efficacious—it is to have effects on the world that are determined by yourself. By following the categorical imperative we render ourselves autonomous and by following the principle of instrumental reason, we render ourselves efficacious. So by following these principles we constitute ourselves as agents: that is, we take control of our movements.

1.5 *Self-Constitution*

If the idea of self-constitution still seems paradoxical, it may be helpful to compare the human agent with another sort of agent whose claims to self-constitution are perhaps less assailable: the political state. In "Self-Constitution in the Ethics of Plato and Kant," I follow Plato in using this comparison to tease out the conditions under which a complex entity can, in Plato's words, "achieve anything as a unit" (R 352a). A state is like an individual human being insofar as all of its actions supervene on other, so to speak smaller, events: in the case of the state, on the decisions and actions of various citizens and office-holders. What makes a certain event or set of events count as an action attributable to the state is that the state has a set of deliberative procedures—a constitution—of which these smaller events can be seen as parts. For example, the constitution might specify that the majority vote of certain citizens who are taken to represent other citizens counts as the enactment of a law. The outcomes of following those procedures, the laws and the execution of the laws, are the actions of the state. Thus the function of the constitution of the state is to unify a diverse group of citizens into a single agent, whose movements count as its actions when they are in accordance with its laws. And so the citizens, by adopting these deliberative procedures, can be said to

---

[17] See "Kant's Formula of Universal Law" (CKE essay 3), pp. 93–102.

constitute themselves as a unified agent. In the same way, an individual human being constitutes himself as an agent, by adopting a procedure for the making of laws—a procedure that he requires because of the reflective distance that makes it necessary for him to act for reasons, and therefore on principles.

As Plato argued, however, while there is a formal or procedural sense in which *any* deliberative procedure—any constitution—can unify a diverse group of citizens into a state, there is also a substantive sense in which only a certain kind of constitution—a just constitution—can do so successfully. According to Plato, a just constitution must be one in which the class of the wisest citizens, in the state—or reason, in the soul—rules over the other parts. A state that is ruled, not by the wise, but by the soldiers or by the wealthy or by the common people contains the seeds of civil war within it, because none of these groups can be relied on to govern, as the wisest do, for the good of the whole. And if civil war occurs, then the state can no longer act as a unit. So only a just constitution truly unifies the citizenry into a state. And, for the same reason, Plato thought that a soul ruled by the principle of one of its inferior parts—by appetite or spirit—was in danger of losing the unity that is required for "achieving anything as a unit." Only a just person has the integrity that is essential to agency.

A similar distinction can be found in Kant, for we can distinguish between a maxim that is universal in a merely formal or procedural sense—a maxim that an agent may tell himself, perhaps with insufficient reflection, that he is prepared to will as a law—and a maxim that is actually, substantively, universalizable. A substantively universal maxim is one that an agent really could, with all due reflection, will to be in effect, and to govern his own conduct, in all relevantly similar circumstances. Thus, according to both Plato and Kant, just as the agency of the state is constituted by the adoption of deliberative procedures whose perfect realization depends upon political justice, so the agency of the soul, of the human individual, is constituted by the adoption of deliberative procedures whose perfect realization depends upon personal justice or morality. The unity that is essential to agency and moral integrity are one and the same thing.

1.6 *The Problem of Prudence*

I now return to the other proposed rational principle, the principle of prudence or self-interest. In "The Myth of Egoism," I argue that some common assumptions about this principle cannot be right. The principle is not, as many social scientists seem to assume, either identical to, or a mere application of, the principle of instrumental reason. For if there is a rational requirement of prudence, it does not merely require us to take the means to some end that we already or inevitably have. Rather, it requires us to *have* a certain end—one in which our more particular ends are somehow harmoniously combined—and to always prefer that end to all of those more particular ends themselves. The principle of prudence, if it exists, is therefore a principle of pure practical reason. How is such a normative principle then to be established? Part of the difficulty is that the idea of prudence, as usually conceived, is trying to do a double job. Prudence is usually supposed to require us to take into account all of the ends we have reason to promote, including those we will have in the future, whenever we deliberate. But it is also supposed to require us to be (especially? exclusively?) attentive to what is in some difficult-to-define sense our own personal good or interest. I call those two elements of the principle the requirements of balancing and of particularity, respectively. In the essay I argue that no intelligible account can be given of the requirement of particularity (see especially sections 2.1–2.3). More generally, it seems obvious to me that a requirement of self-interested prudence could not possibly be established in the way that I believe the principle of instrumental reason and the categorical imperative can. That is, it could not be a constitutive principle of action that we pursue our own overarching good. If acting is determining yourself to be a *cause* of some state of affairs, then you are *just not acting* unless you take the means to that state of affairs. If acting is determining *yourself* to be a cause of some state of affairs, then you are *just not acting* unless your movements are determined by a law that you give to yourself. But we certainly cannot argue that you are *just not acting* unless you pursue your own overarching good.

However, I believe that perhaps this kind of foundation may be given for the requirement of balancing, taken separately from any thought about particularity or self-interest, although I do not now see my way to an argument to this effect. I believe this partly because the requirement of balancing does seem to me to be a requirement of practical reason, and indeed one without which the theory of practical reason is radically incomplete. And I believe it partly because it seems plausible to say that our unity as agents depends on our conformity to such a requirement. If that is right, then the principle of balancing may also be a constitutive principle of agency, and so a principle of practical reason.

2. Moral Virtue and Moral Psychology

Our agency depends in important ways on the character of our more passive or receptive faculties. Human action partakes of *reaction* at least to this extent: something must make it occur to us that we might perform a certain action. And this means that our ability to do what reason demands also depends on these faculties. In the examples used to illustrate the duty of beneficence in the *Groundwork*, Kant envisions someone to whom it occurs to help, but who doesn't wish to: he tests the maxim of *not* helping, and finds that he cannot will it as a universal law (G 4:423). But suppose that he has so little sympathy that the thought of helping doesn't even come into his mind? A Kantian agent with the most determined resolution to test all of his maxims by the categorical imperative would not succeed in meeting all of the requirements of duty if certain things never occurred to him. And more generally when we are formulating our maxims, with a view to testing them, we need to know what features of our situation are relevant to the question whether we have good reason to act as we propose to do or not. Our attention must be directed in the right ways, and this depends on our receptive faculties—on what we feel and what we notice. Kant himself noticed at least the first of these problems. In *The Metaphysical Principles of Virtue*, after quoting the universal law formulation of the categorical imperative, he remarks:

Maxims are here regarded as subjective principles which merely *qualify* for a giving of universal law, and the requirement that they so qualify is only a negative principle (not to come into conflict with law as such).—How can there be, beyond this principle, a law for the maxims of actions? (MM 6:389)[18]

By a law for the maxims of actions, Kant means a law making it necessary to have certain maxims. And he takes this problem as the point of entry for his own account of virtue.

The term "virtue" may be used broadly to refer to one's moral condition in general, or more narrowly to refer to the possession of certain dispositions that make one *receptive* to the demands of reason. And for the reasons I have just sketched, these will include dispositions of our desires and emotions, as well as of reason and will. The first three essays in the second part of this book, taken together, sketch a reading of Aristotle's *Nicomachean Ethics*, which I take to be centrally concerned with the question of virtue in this sense. I do not believe that Aristotle's is a "virtue ethics," if that is supposed to mean that he believes that the fact that something would be chosen by the virtuous person, or by the practically wise person, is what *makes* it right. What makes

---

[18] Both Mary Gregor and James Ellington (in his translation of the *Metaphysical Principles of Virtue* in *Ethical Philosophy*) translate the parenthetical remark with the phrase "a law"—as in Gregor's "not to come into conflict with a law as such." I have deleted the "a." What Kant means is not that the maxim is not supposed to conflict with some particular law; he means that the maxim is not supposed to conflict with the very idea—the form—of law. See "Kant's Analysis of Obligation: The Argument of Groundwork I" (CKE essay 2), pp. 61–2.

an action right in Aristotle's theory, I think, is that it is both an expression of, and promotes, the successful performance of the human function, which is rational activity. Aristotle thinks that the person of practical wisdom, being most susceptible to the demands of reason, is best able to *identify* the action that is right in this sense. I believe that this account of virtue is available to the Kantian as well. Aristotle certainly gives a greater role to receptivity and a lesser role to ratiocination in identifying the right than Kant does, but these are matters of degree, and do not render the two views incompatible. And if you substitute "autonomy" for "rational activity" in the account of what makes an action right that I just ascribed to Aristotle, their views about what makes actions right look fairly similar as well.

As I've already hinted, my reading of the *Nicomachean Ethics* turns on Aristotle's famous "function argument" in 1.7, and the first of the three essays, "Aristotle's Function Argument," is a defense of that argument. Aristotle argues that in order to ascertain the good for human beings, we must first identify the human function, and he settles on rational activity as the answer (NE 1.7 1097b22–1098a17). There are many evident objections to this argument (which I review and reply to in the essay) and as a result some philosophers have apparently thought that the reader of Aristotle should simply set it aside. But the argument plays an essential structural role in the project of the *Nicomachean Ethics*. The Greek philosophers recognized a conceptual connection between function (*ergon*) and virtue (*arete*). A thing's virtues are the properties that make it good at performing its function. It is an essential part of Aristotle's project to show that the qualities that are ordinarily considered moral virtues are really virtues in this more technical sense, since the desirability of the virtuous life turns on the fact that virtues make us good at performing our function.

That point sets up the project of the second essay in Part 2, "Aristotle on Function and Virtue," which is to ask how exactly having certain emotional reactions *could* contribute to rational activity, and to examine the merits of various possible answers suggested by the text of the *Nicomachean Ethics*. This essay, unlike the others in the volume, is an older essay (1986), and there are many things in it that I would not now say, or would say in different ways. But I still endorse its conclusions, both as an interpretation of Aristotle and, at least to a large extent, as an account of virtue. Aristotle seems to suggest, at different moments, that the emotions contribute to rational activity by giving way to reason, by harmonizing with its demands, by making the agent susceptible to its influence, by promoting rational activity in the way that good physical habits promote physical activity, or by enabling us to perceive what is good. The conclusion I reach combines several of those ideas: that the emotions constitute a kind of *perception* of the good, or of reason, that at once makes us susceptible to reason's influence and helps us to form and act on correct *conceptions* of the good.

Now let me return to the question what all this might have to do with Kant's theory of rational agency. My views about the compatibility of Kant and Aristotle are somewhat unorthodox, and defending them sets the project of the third essay in Part 2, "From Duty and For the Sake of the Noble: Kant and Aristotle on Morally Good Action." Here I argue that Kant and Aristotle share an important view about the locus of moral value, and a related thesis in moral psychology, which sets them apart from most other moral philosophers. In order to describe this view here I will use some technical terminology that I set out most plainly in the fourth essay in Part 2, "Acting for a Reason," especially section 4. The thesis is that moral value does not attach to mere *acts* (to use a couple of Kant's examples: making a lying promise, committing suicide) but rather to what I call *actions*: an act performed for the sake of a certain end (making a lying promise for the sake of personal gain, committing suicide in order to escape your troubles). A Kantian maxim, the sort of thing tested by the categorical imperative test, and an Aristotelian *logos*, its analog, always include (at least) both an act and an end, and it is *these* formulations that describe the locus of moral value, the objects that we deem to be obligatory or forbidden, noble or base. What's forbidden or base is not, for example, telling a lie, but telling a lie for the sake of personal gain. The associated thesis in moral psychology is that these formulations also describe the objects of human choice. According to both Aristotle and Kant, human beings do not just choose acts, motivated by ends that are foisted upon us by natural forces (e.g. desires). Rather, the object of a rational choice is a certain act performed for the sake of a certain end, and we decide whether to do that by asking whether the whole action described by that formulation is a thing worth doing for its own sake. According to Kant, we ask whether a certain act performed for a certain end is required by duty, permissible, or forbidden; according to Aristotle, we ask whether it is noble, not ignoble, or base.

I believe that the main disagreement between these two philosophers, concerning the role of the emotions, does not spring from their moral theories, but rather from their views about the nature of the emotions. Aristotle's theory of the virtues, as I interpret it in "Aristotle on Function and Virtue," is predicated upon his view that pleasure and pain—and therefore the emotions that always involve them—are perceptions of good and bad, or as we might say of reasons. To feel fear, for instance, is to feel oneself in the presence of a reason to flee. But Kant does not believe that pleasure and pain, and with them the emotions, are perceptions: he considers them to be mere feelings, which, as he puts it, express nothing at all in the object but simply a relation to the subject (MM 6:211–212). So when he famously denies, in the first section of the *Groundwork*, that there is any moral worth in action motivated by sympathy (G 4:398), it is important to keep in mind that he is thinking of sympathy, not as an inchoate perception of the fact that there is reason for helping, but rather as something like a *taste* for helping. His sympathetic man *likes* helping, the way one might like chocolate. If we think of the sympathetic man's sympathy instead as an inchoate perception that there is reason for helping, we will disagree with Kant about this example. But this will not make it necessary to disagree with the conclusions Kant draws about the moral law, for what sympathy perceives is a normative demand that is grounded in the other's humanity. On Kant's view of the emotions, they could at most be instrumental aids to moral choice, accidentally pointing us in the right direction, whereas on Aristotle's they are a more intrinsic part of our grasp of our reasons to act.

Is Kant stuck with the view that emotions are mere feelings or tastes? One might suppose that only a substantive realist about reasons could treat them as objects of perception, and so only a realist about reasons could interpret the emotions as perceptions of reasons.[19] But I do not think this is true. Any animal, in perceiving the world, perceives it through the lens of her own cognitive requirements and interests, perceives it in a way that enables that particular animal to find her way around. And as I mentioned earlier, I think it is the nature of every animal to have normative perceptions—to see the world through the lens of her own concerns and interests, or, as we might say, her values. And this is true of us as well. The implication for rational beings is that the development of rationality requires the acquisition of a second nature—a set of emotional responses and an accompanying normative view of the world that conforms to the demands of reason. The acquisition of virtue, a condition of the receptive faculties that makes us sensitive to the demands of reason, is therefore essential to the perfection of our moral nature, and to the integrity that makes agency possible.

In the last essay in Part 2, "Acting for a Reason," I put Aristotle and Kant's view about the locus of moral value and the object of human choice to work, using it to address some contemporary issues about the ontology of reasons and the nature of rational motivation. I start from the debate between those who think that desires and other mental states are reasons for action and those who think that only certain facts—facts about what is good about the action

---

[19] See "Realism and Constructivism in Twentieth-Century Moral Philosophy," Essay 10 in this volume, for the difference between realism and Kant's constructivist account.

or its effects—can provide us with reasons for doing it. I argue that reasons have an essentially reflexive structure not captured by either of these accounts. The person who acts for a reason must be motivated by certain facts about the action, but he must at the same time be motivated by the awareness that these facts constitute a reason. An account of rational motivation must show how these two elements in an agent's motivational state can be combined. The issue is similar to that presented by the Kantian idea that good moral agents do the right thing from duty. Many readers criticize this idea because they think that acting from duty must be an *alternative* to acting for the sake of some concrete end such as the welfare of others. They think it is intelligible to ask whether someone acted from duty, or because the other person's welfare was his end. No one thinks it is similarly intelligible to ask whether someone acted for a reason, or because the other person's welfare was his end. Yet the problem is the same: to show that these two elements in motivation are not alternatives, but can be combined. Aristotle and Kant's view that value and choice attach to whole "actions" rather than mere "acts" solves this problem, for they show that acting "from duty" or "for the sake of the noble" is not an alternative to acting for the sake of certain ends. Rather, for example, the agent who helps from the motive of duty judges that it is his duty to make the welfare of another his end. More generally, on their theory the choice of an action has the required reflective structure: the maxim or *logos* specifies what is good about the act—say, that the act realizes a certain end—and the agent chooses the whole action on the basis of an assessment of its value as a whole. Only theories of this kind, therefore, can give a satisfactory account of what it means to act for a reason.

3. Other Reflections

The three essays in Part 3 of the book are admittedly miscellaneous; in these remarks I will focus on their links to the major themes of the book. In "Taking the Law into Our Own Hands: Kant on the Right to Revolution," I take on the problem posed by Kant's paradoxical attitude towards revolution. Kant's personal enthusiasm for the French Revolution earned him the nickname "the Old Jacobin," but in the *Metaphysical Principles of Justice* he argues that political revolution is always wrong (MPJ 6:320). I defend this last conclusion on the grounds that the political state must function as a unified agent, whose constitution makes its government the voice of its general will. Given Kant's view that justice requires that we regard ourselves as citizens of the political state, we must regard ourselves as subject to the general will. But I argue that in certain circumstances a virtuous person might nevertheless be morally motivated to instigate or participate in revolution. Here the distinction between procedural and substantive justice to which I appealed in "Self-Constitution in the Ethics of Plato and Kant" again plays a role. For the argument I've just gestured at depends on a procedural conception of justice, and there can be circumstances in which what is procedurally just is not substantively so. In these cases an individual with the virtue of justice is divided against himself, and must make a judgment about what to do which is not governed by any principle that we share with others and therefore may not be justifiable to them. The case vindicates Plato's view that we cannot be fully unified as individuals if the state in which we live is unjust and therefore is itself disunified.

To the extent that that is true, our efforts at self-constitution may be affected, even limited, by what goes on in the world around us. This is an aspect of the subject about which I have written little. The second essay in Part 3, "The General Point of View: Love and Moral Approval in Hume's Ethics" touches on a view that carries this thought to the opposite extreme, for on Hume's view, our agency is entirely constituted in the eyes of those around us. This conclusion naturally follows from Hume's view that causality in general is something that exists in the eyes of beholders—that is, those who observe the constant conjunction of certain events—together with the fact that to be an agent is to be a cause.

The question of how we conceive of agency in Hume's theory arises obliquely in the essay, which is directed to a question about Hume's doctrine of the general point of view. In Hume's theory moral virtue depends on moral approval rather than the reverse: a moral virtue is, essentially, a quality of which spectators approve. And Hume argues that moral approval, in turn, is a calm form of love we feel when we view someone from the general point of view. To view someone from the general point of view is to view him sympathetically from the point of view of his usual associates, and to consider the general effects of his conduct rather than the specific effects of his actions in this or that case. My own argument starts from the question why we should take up the general point of view in the first place. Given that it is from this point of view that the very idea of virtue arises, it cannot be that we take up the general point of view in order to observe someone's virtues more clearly. If we did not take up the general point of view, we would not see people as having virtues at all. Nor, I argue, does Hume's own account of why we take up the general point of view—in order to reach agreement with others and make consistent judgments within ourselves—work. For again there is no virtue to reach agreement *about* until after we take up the general point of view. On Hume's behalf I construct an argument to the effect that our capacity to view another as a regular cause and so as an agent depends on taking up the general point of view. I trace our motivation for taking up that point of view to the demands of love, which seeks to view its object as a person with a character, and so as an agent. The resulting view gives us an account of why we view the world morally that I think can be motivated by Hume's theory even if it was not his own. It also gives us a picture of how agency might be constituted from the outside in. While I don't share Hume's view that our characters exist primarily in the eyes of beholders, I do believe in a more moderate implication of his view: that sympathy with others shapes and limits our powers of self-constitution in important ways.

In the final essay in the volume, "Realism and Constructivism in Twentieth-Century Moral Philosophy," I turn to more methodological issues. The essay was written as a lecture for (as it turned out) two occasions on which I was asked to speak about the issues and achievements of moral philosophy at the turn of the century. In it I try to describe the difference between a realist and a constructivist moral theory. I have long believed that it is unhelpful to characterize moral realism as a view about whether moral statements are true or false. This makes it seem as if realism and early non-cognitivist theories—views according to which moral statements are the expressions of attitudes rather than truth-apt assertions—are the only available options. That in turn lumps together as "realist" theories that are different in important and systematic ways. In *The Sources of Normativity*, I tried to capture this thought by distinguishing "substantive" from "procedural" realism (SN 1.4.4, pp. 34–7). Here, I argue that the difference between a realist and a constructivist theory rests in the way the two views understand the function of concepts, rather than in their views about the truth-value of sentences.[20] A realist believes that the function of concepts is to describe the world, to mark out the entities we find there, while a constructivist believes that the function of (at least some) concepts is to mark out, in a schematic way, the solution to some problem that we face. The task of the philosopher is then to identify the content of such a concept by working out the solution to the problem, thus providing a particular *conception* of whatever the concept names.

John Rawls's work provides an example of what I have in mind. In his philosophy, the concept of justice schematically names the solution to a problem: "justice" names whatever solves the problem of how we are to distribute the benefits and burdens of social cooperation. We have the concept of justice *because* we face the problem, not because justice is something we have encountered in the world. Rawls's own two principles of justice are a

---

[20] For a remarkably similar view, but in an expressivist context, see Allan Gibbard, *Thinking How to Live*, e.g., pp. 79–82, 102–5. For instance, Gibbard says, "There is no contrast to be drawn between ethical and natural properties. The contrast is between ethical and naturalistic concepts" (p. 105).

conception of justice, worked out by imagining the way a suitably situated group of people who are actually faced with the task of choosing principles of justice—people in the original position—would reason about what their principles should be.

Once we have identified the correct or best conception for a given concept, there is no reason to deny that sentences involving the use of that concept can be true, for the concept is applied correctly when it is applied in accordance with the correct or best conception. For a Rawlsian to say that some policy is just, is, unpacked, to say that it is in accord with the principles that would be chosen in the original position and that those principles represent the correct or best solution to the distribution problem. There is nothing there that is not truth-apt, for anyone who disagrees is disagreeing about something real—either about whether the justice of the policy does follow from those principles or about whether those principles represent the correct solution to the problem that gives us the concept of justice. Yet moral philosophy as conceived by constructivism is a practical enterprise, an enterprise of working out the solutions to problems, not a mysteriously non-empirical theoretical enterprise aimed at identifying normative facts that are somehow part of the external world. The difference between substantive realists and constructivists does then not rest in a disagreement about the truth-value of sentences deploying normative terms; rather, it rests in a larger difference of approach to the subject: the constructivist regards moral philosophy as a form of practical thinking all the way down.

I see my own view as constructivist in this sense, and the remarks I made in the first part of this introduction, in particular about how we might reason from the nature of agency to the principles of practical reason, are intended as a constructivist argument. I could perhaps make that structure clearer if I put the argument this way: The reflective distance produced by the awareness of the potential grounds of our actions as grounds confronts us with a problem, a problem we face as rational agents. That is the problem of how we are to exercise our autonomy efficaciously in the world. And the categorical imperative and the principle of instrumental reason, as the laws of autonomy and efficacy, are the solution to that problem. They are therefore the principles by which, with the aid of the virtues, we constitute our agency.

Christine M. Korsgaard
January, 2008

Part 1

The Principles of Practical Reason

1

The Normativity of Instrumental Reason

1. The Problem

Most philosophers think it is both uncontroversial and unproblematic that practical reason requires us to take the means to our ends. If doing a certain action is necessary for or even just promotes a person's aims, the person obviously has at least a prima facie reason to do it. Just as obviously, this reason is what we nowadays call an "internal" reason, one that is capable of motivating the person to whom it applies. So those who hold that practical reasons *must* be internal point to the instrumental principle as a clear case of a source of reasons that pass that test.[1] But philosophers have, for the most part, been silent on the question of the normative foundation of this requirement. The interesting question, almost everyone agrees, is whether practical reason requires anything *more* of us than this.

In fact, in the philosophical tradition, three kinds of principles have been proposed as requirements of practical reason. First, there is the instrumental principle itself. Kant, one of the few philosophers who does discuss its foundation, identifies the instrumental principle as a kind of hypothetical imperative, a technical (*technisch*) imperative. But the instrumental principle is nowadays widely taken to extend to ways of realizing ends that are not in the technical sense "means," for instance to what is sometimes called "constitutive" reasoning. Say that my end is outdoor exercise; here is an

---

[1] See, e.g., Bernard Williams in "Internal and External Reasons," in Williams, *Moral Luck*, essay 8, pp. 101–13. For a thorough discussion of the varieties of internalism, see Robert Audi, "Moral Judgment and Reasons for Action," in *Ethics and Practical Reason*. Audi's focus, however, is on the internalism of moral judgments, while I am talking about the internalism of reasons or reason judgments more generally. In recent years, the literature on internalism has become increasingly intricate, and the *point* of settling the question whether a given type of consideration is "internal" or not has become somewhat obscure. In my own view, practical reasons *must* be internal in the sense given in the text, and therefore the point of settling the question whether moral considerations or judgments are internal is that they cannot be regarded as *reasons* unless they are. As I will argue in section 3, however, showing that a consideration is internal, although necessary, is not sufficient to show that it is a reason.

opportunity to go hiking, which is outdoor exercise; therefore I have reason to take this opportunity, not strictly speaking as a means to my end, but as a way of realizing it. This is a helpful suggestion, but it should be handled with care. Taken to extremes, it makes it seem as if any case in which your action is guided by the application of a name or a concept to a particular is an instance of instrumental reasoning. Compare, for example: I need a hammer; *this* is a hammer; therefore I shall take *this*, not as a means to my end but as a way of realizing it. In this way the instrumental principle may be extended to cover *any* case of action that is self-conscious, in the sense that the agent is guided by a conception of what she is doing.[2] Now I do think that this is a natural way to extend the instrumental principle, and later I will suggest that this fact throws light on its foundation. But there is also a danger that such extensions will conceal important differences among the distinctive forms of reasoning by which human beings can be motivated.[3]

Second, there is what I will call the principle of prudence, which is sometimes identified with self-interest.[4] This principle concerns the ways in which we harmonize the pursuit of our various ends. Its correct formulation or extension is a matter of controversy. Some philosophers think it requires us to maximize the sum total of our satisfactions or pleasures over the course of our whole lives; others, that it requires us merely to give some weight, possibly

---

[2] Kant also called the technical imperative an imperative of skill, so one might put the point I am making here this way: the instrumental principle is now seen as requiring us to exercise not merely skill, but also judgment, in the pursuit of our ends. But any self-conscious action must be guided by judgment. Some of Aristotle's examples of practical syllogisms are explicitly like the example in the text. Consider for example: "I want to drink, says appetite; this is drink, says sense or imagination or thought: straightaway I drink" (MA 701a33–34). Or consider the notorious "dry food" syllogism of *Nicomachean Ethics* 7, in which Aristotle toys with the idea that incontinence occurs in a man who believes that "Dry food is good for any man" when he reasons that "I am a man" and "such and such food is dry," but then fails to exercise the knowledge that "this food is such and such" (NE 7 1147a1–10). In these cases, there is no question of using technical means, but simply of the application of a principle to a case or a concept to a particular. This fact throws light on what Aristotle meant when he said that practical reasoning is not about ends but about what contributes to them (NE 3 1112b12): in particular, it suggests that this remark is not meant to imply *any* limitation in the scope of practical reasoning. See also my "From Duty and for the Sake of the Noble: Kant and Aristotle on Morally Good Action," Essay 6 in this volume.

[3] This is a difficulty, I think, in the strategy Williams adopts in "Internal and External Reasons," in *Moral Luck.* His argument seems to show that only natural extensions of the instrumental principle can meet the internalism requirement, but he is prepared to extend the instrumental principle so far that this turns out to be no limitation at all. See my "Skepticism about Practical Reason," CKE essay 11. Interestingly, however, the view I defend in this essay also tends to break down the distinctions among the different principles of practical reason. See note 60.

[4] As others have noticed, we use the term "prudence," confusingly, to refer both to attention to self-interested reasons and to attention to one's future reasons, whether or not they are self-interested (see Nagel, in *The Possibility of Altruism,* p. 36). Since I am not taking a stand on the formulation of the principle of prudence here, I don't bother to sort through this issue in the text. For further discussion, see my "The Myth of Egoism," Essay 2 in this volume.

discounted, to the ends and reasons we will have in the future as well as the ones we have now. What Derek Parfit calls "present aim" theory requires only that we try to satisfy our "present" desires, projects, and aims to as great an extent as possible.⁵ The common element in all of these formulations is that they serve to remind us that we characteristically have more than one aim, and that rationality requires us to take this into account when we deliberate. We should deliberate not only about how to realize the aim that occupies us right now, but also about how doing so will affect the possibility of realizing our other aims. The principle of prudence is often understood as a requirement that we should deliberate in light of what is best for us on the whole, or of what I will call our "overall good," where that is conceived as a special sort of higher-order *end* to which more particular ends serve, in an extended sense, as means. Partly because he has something like this in mind, Kant supposes that the principle of prudence is also a hypothetical imperative.⁶

Finally, of course, many philosophers have claimed that moral principles, which Kant identifies as categorical imperatives, represent requirements of practical reason. If all of these claims are true, we exhibit practical irrationality in failing to take the means to our ends; in pursuing local satisfactions at the expense of our overall good; and in acting immorally.

In the *Groundwork*, Kant asks "how are all these imperatives possible?" What he wants to know, he explains, is "how the necessitation of the will, which the imperative expresses in the problem, can be thought" (G 4:417). In other words, Kant seeks an explanation of the normative force of all *three* kinds of imperatives. But this approach has not usually been followed in the Anglo-American tradition. Empiricist moral philosophers, as well as the social scientists who have followed in their footsteps, have characteristically assumed that hypothetical imperatives do not require any philosophical justification, while categorical imperatives are mysterious and apparently external constraints on our conduct. Moral requirements, they think, must therefore be given a foundation in one of two ways. Either we must show that they are based on the supposedly uncontroversial hypothetical imperatives—say, by showing that moral conduct is in our interest and so is required by the principle of prudence—or we must give them some sort of ontological

⁵ Parfit, *Reasons and Persons*, esp. chapter 6, section 45.
⁶ Kant's other (and I think better) reason for regarding the imperative of prudence as hypothetical is that it holds only conditionally—it may be overridden when duty demands that we do something contrary to our interest. As some of the things I will say later suggest, I think that there are problems about understanding the principle of prudence as a hypothetical imperative and that Kant's account of this principle is in need of revision. Unfortunately I cannot give full treatment to the complex question of the status of prudence here. For further discussion, see my "The Myth of Egoism," Essay 2 in this volume.

foundation, by positing the existence of certain normative facts or entities to which moral requirements somehow refer.[7] The first option is the empiricist's own preferred method; while the second, moral realist option, represents the road taken by the dogmatic rationalists of the eighteenth century, as well as by many contemporary philosophers. Some philosophers with sympathies to the rationalist tradition—most notably Butler in the eighteenth century and Nagel in the twentieth—have pointed out that prudence, no less than morality, needs a normative foundation, and have proposed to throw light on the foundation of morality by investigating that of prudence. Parallel accounts of these two forms of normativity, they suggest, may be constructed.[8] But the instrumental principle has received very little attention from anyone.

One of the things I wish to do in this essay is to offer a diagnosis of this situation. Part of the problem is that empiricist philosophers and their social scientific followers have obscured the difference between the instrumental principle and the principle of prudence by making the handy but unwarranted assumption that a person's overall good is what he "really" wants. Prudent action is then just a matter of taking the means to your *true* end; and the instrumental principle is the only non-moral imperative we need. I will say more about this in section 2. More importantly, both empiricists and rationalists have supposed that the instrumental principle itself either needs no justification or has an essentially trivial one. Specifically, they have thought that the "necessitation of the will" to which Kant refers can be conceived either as a form of causal necessity or as a response to logical necessity. Empiricists who conceive it as a form of causal necessity suppose that the instrumental principle is either obviously normative or does not need to be normative because we are reliably motivated to take the means to our ends. Instrumental thoughts cause motives. Rationalists who conceive it as a response to logical necessity suppose that conformity to the instrumental principle is normative because "whoever wills the end also wills the means" is an analytic or logical truth, to which a rational agent as such conforms his will.

Behind these two accounts of instrumental reason lie two implicitly held conceptions of what it means for a person to be practically rational in general. On an empiricist view, to be practically rational is to be caused to act in a certain way—specifically, to have motives which are caused by the recognition of certain truths which are made relevant to action by one's

---

[7] As suggested for instance by John Mackie, in *Ethics: Inventing Right and Wrong.*

[8] Butler, *Fifteen Sermons Preached at the Rolls Chapel*, especially Sermons 1–3; and Nagel, *The Possibility of Altruism.* A parallel between the two problems is also suggested by Sidgwick in *The Methods of Ethics*, pp. 418–19, and, following him, by Parfit in *Reasons and Persons*, pp. 307 ff.

pre-existing motives.[9] On a rationalist view, by contrast, to be rational is to deliberately conform one's will to certain rational truths, or truths about reasons, which exist independently of the will. In this essay, I will argue that neither of these general conceptions of practical rationality yields an adequate account of instrumental rationality. A practical reason must function both as a motive and as a guide, or a requirement. I will show that the empiricist account explains how instrumental reasons can motivate us, but at the price of making it impossible to see how they could function as requirements or guides. The rationalist account, on the other hand, allows instrumental reasons to function as guides, but at the price of making it impossible for us to see any special reason why we should be motivated to follow these guides.[10]

Kant is usually thought of as a rationalist, but the Kantian conception of practical rationality represents a third and distinct alternative. According to the Kantian conception, to be rational *just is* to be autonomous. That is: to be governed by reason, and to govern yourself, are one and the same thing. The principles of practical reason are *constitutive* of autonomous action: they do not represent external *restrictions* on our actions, whose power to motivate us is therefore inexplicable, but instead *describe* the procedures involved in autonomous willing. But they also function as normative or guiding principles, because in following these procedures we are guiding ourselves.

The course of my argument requires an explanation. In section 2, I argue against the empiricist view, focusing on the Humean texts that are usually taken to be its *locus classicus*. In section 3, I argue both *against* the dogmatic rationalist view, and *for* the Kantian view, through a discussion of Kant's own remarks about instrumental rationality in the second section of the *Groundwork*. This structure is dictated in part by a fact about Kant's own development.[11] At the time he wrote the *Groundwork*, Kant's views were in a transitional stage, and traces of the dogmatic rationalist view can be found in

---

[9] The clearest statement of this view is again that of Williams in "Internal and External Reasons," in *Moral Luck*. The cumbersome phrase in the text is an attempt to do justice to Williams's attempt to express this theory in a way that leaves it open what forms of practical reason there are.

[10] The rationalist may of course speculate or stipulate that insofar as we are rational we must be motivated by the (alleged) principles of reason, and in this way meet the internalism requirement, but this leaves their power to motivate us essentially inexplicable. I discuss the difficulties with this sort of stipulation in section 3. I believe that in "Skepticism about Practical Reason" (CKE essay 11), I may give the impression that I think a stipulation of this kind sufficient to meet the worries of those who complain that moral principles do not meet the internalism requirement. I don't believe that, although I now think, as I will explain later, that the real worry behind the internalism requirement is inadequately expressed by that requirement. In fact this shows up in the fact that the internalism requirement may be met by such a stipulation, but that this does not resolve the real worry.

[11] It is also partly dictated by the unavailability (at least as far as I know) of detailed discussions of the instrumental principle by the dogmatic rationalists themselves.

what he says, especially in this part of the text. By seeing what goes wrong with his early presentation of the instrumental principle, we are led to the mature Kantian view, which traces both instrumental reason and moral reason to a common normative source: the autonomy or self-government of the rational agent.[12]

My arguments for these points have another implication which I will be concerned to bring out in the course of the essay, namely, that the instrumental principle cannot stand alone. Unless there are normative principles directing us to the adoption of certain ends, there can be no requirement to take the means to our ends. The familiar view that the instrumental principle is the *only* requirement of practical reason is incoherent.

2. Hume and the Empiricist Account

It is common among empiricists to equate the question whether pure reason can be practical with the question whether we are ever motivated by belief alone. The impetus for this view comes from the so-called "belief/desire" model of rational action. When we act in accordance with hypothetical imperatives, it is alleged, motivation is provided by the combination of a belief and a desire: say, I desire to avert the toothache foreseen, I believe that a trip to the dentist will enable me to do so, so I am motivated to go to the dentist. Since categorical imperatives are by definition not based on the presupposition of an existing desire, we must in following them be motivated by belief alone: perhaps simply the belief that a certain action is right or wrong, or, in a more complicated story, a belief, say, that someone else is in need.[13] Since the idea of being motivated by belief alone seems mysterious, the suspicion arises that categorical imperatives cannot meet the internalism requirement, and they are therefore supposed to be especially problematic.

But as Nagel points out in *The Possibility of Altruism*, the specifically rational character of going to the dentist to avert an unwanted toothache depends on *how* the belief and the desire are "combined." It is certainly not enough to say that they jointly *cause* the action, or that their bare co-presence effects a motive, for a person might be conditioned so that he responds in totally crazy ways to the co-presence of certain beliefs and desires. In Nagel's own

---

[12] At the end of section 2, I will argue that even within the confines of a reconstructed Humean account, the normativity of the instrumental principle must be traced to the agent's self-government, specifically to his capacity to be motivated to shape his character in accordance with an ideal of virtue. So this is actually not just a point about how a Kantian account of reason works.

[13] I have in mind Nagel's account, in *The Possibility of Altruism*, although his view more strictly speaking is that we can be directly motivated by beliefs about other people's *reasons*.

example, a person has been conditioned so that whenever he wants a drink and believes the object before him is a pencil sharpener, he wants to put a coin into the pencil sharpener.[14] Here the co-presence of belief and desire reliably lead to a certain action, but the action is a mad one. What is the difference between this person and one who, rationally, wants to put a coin in a soda machine when she wants a drink? One may be tempted to say that a soda machine, unlike a pencil sharpener, is the source of a drink, so that the right kind of conceptual connection between the desire and the belief obtains. But so far that is only to note a fact about the relationship between the belief and the desire themselves, and that says nothing about the rationality of the *person* who is influenced by them. If the belief and desire still operate on that person merely by having a certain causal efficacy when co-present, the rational action is only accidentally or externally different from the mad one. After all, a person may be conditioned to do the correct thing as well as the incorrect thing; but the correctness of what she is conditioned to do does not make *her* any more rational. So neither the joint causal efficacy of the belief and the desire, nor the existence of an appropriate conceptual connection between them, nor the bare conjunction of these two facts, enables us to judge that a person acts rationally. For the person to act rationally, she must be motivated by her own *recognition* of the appropriate conceptual connection between the belief and the desire. We may say that she *herself* must combine the belief and the desire in the right way. A person acts rationally, then, only when her action is the expression of her own mental activity, and not merely the result of the operation of beliefs and desires *in* her.[15]

As a preliminary formulation of this point, let us say that a rational agent is one who is motivated by what I will call the *rational necessity* of doing something, say, of taking the means to an end, and who acts accordingly. Such an agent is *guided* by reason, and in particular, guided by what reason presents as necessary.[16] A comparison will help to illustrate the point. If all women are mortal, and I am a woman, then it necessarily follows that I am mortal. That is logical necessity. But if I *believe* that all women are mortal, and I *believe* that I am a woman, then I *ought* to conclude that I am mortal. The necessity embodied in that use of "ought" is rational necessity. If I am guided by

[14] Nagel, *The Possibility of Altruism*, pp. 33–4.

[15] This point is related to an idea which Michael Smith emphasizes in "A Theory of Freedom and Responsibility," in *Ethics and Practical Reason*, namely, that part of what is involved in regarding and interacting with someone as a person who has, and is responsible for, his beliefs is attributing to him the capacity to recognize and respond appropriately to the norms that govern belief. See especially p. 296.

[16] I characterize this as a "preliminary formulation" since I am ultimately going to argue that a rational agent is guided by herself, that is, that being governed by reason amounts to being self-governed.

reason, then I will conclude that I am mortal.[17] But of course it is not logically necessary that I accept this conclusion, for, if it were, it would be impossible for me to fail to accept it. And it is perfectly possible for someone to fail to accept the logical implications of her own beliefs, even when those are pointed out to her. A rational believer is *guided* by reason in the determination of her beliefs. A rational agent would be *guided* by reason in the choice of her actions.[18]

But reason, in turn, is often thought to be guided by the passions; indeed, according to Hume, to be the slave of the passions. And empiricists who endorse the view that reason plays only an instrumental role in action commonly claim Hume as the founding father of their view (T 2.3.3,415). Hume's view, however, seems to have a much more radical implication than that. The rationality of an action, I have just suggested, depends upon the agent's being motivated by her own recognition of the rational necessity of doing the action. But Hume repeatedly asserts that there is only one coherent sense to be given to the idea of necessity (T 1.3.14,171; T 2.3.1,400). All necessity is causal necessity, in Hume's somewhat special sense: the necessity with which observers draw the conclusion that the effect will follow from the cause (T 1.3.14,171). Accordingly, it looks as if all Hume can say is that the person is in fact caused to act by the recognition that an action will promote her end. And all that in turn means is that observers who know what the person's ends are may predict that certain conduct will follow. The person herself, the one whose behavior is in this way predicted, is not *guided* by any dictate of reason. This suggests that Hume's view is that there is no such thing as practical reason at all.[19]

[17] I don't of course mean to imply that a rational agent in fact actively entertains all of the logical consequences of her beliefs, since not all such consequences are presented as necessary, or presented at all.

[18] Kant holds that a moral agent's actions are not merely in accordance with duty but done *from* it (G 4:397). One way to put the point of this paragraph is to say that a rational agent must act not merely in accordance with reason but *from* it. The rational agent has a conception of her actions as rational or at least as required, called for. The debate between the rationalists and the empiricists about rationality could then be constructed as proceeding in the way their debate about the relative merits of acting in accordance with duty and acting from it actually did. For an account of that debate, see my "Kant's Analysis of Obligation: The Argument of *Groundwork I*" (CKE essay 2). For more on the idea that a rational agent acts not merely in accordance with reason but from it, see my "Acting for a Reason," Essay 7 in this volume.

[19] Some readers may be tempted to think that Hume's special notion of causality is at fault here: rationality must be something "inside" of the rational agent; causal judgments, as Hume understands them, are in the eye of the beholder, and therefore rationality cannot be reduced to a certain way of being caused, on Hume's conception. But (one might think) this doesn't show that rationality cannot be a certain way of being caused on some other, more objective, conception of causality. Now I don't think that this is right. The main argument of this part of the essay, as the reader will see, does not depend in any way on Hume's special notion of causality. But something close to it is right: namely, that causal judgments are essentially third-personal, and rational ones are essentially first-personal. (For more on this point, see SN 1.2.2, pp. 16–18.) This is what prevents the empiricist reduction of

And in fact there is another problem with supposing that Hume could have believed in instrumental reason. The instrumental principle, because it tells us only to take the means to our ends, cannot by itself give us a reason to *do* anything. It can operate only in conjunction with some view about how our ends are determined, about what they are. It is routinely assumed, by empiricists who see themselves as followers of Hume, that, absent any other contenders, our ends will be determined by what we desire. But if you hold that the instrumental principle is the *only* principle of practical rationality, you cannot also hold that desiring something is a *reason* for pursuing it. The principle, "take as your end that which you desire," is neither the instrumental principle itself nor an application of it. If the instrumental principle is the only principle of practical reason, then to say that something is your end is not to say that you have a reason to pursue it, but at most to say that you are *going* to pursue it (perhaps inspired by desire). And this shows that the instrumental principle will be formulated in different ways, depending on whether our theory of practical reason includes principles which determine ends or not. If we allow reason a role in determining ends, then the instrumental principle will be formulated this way: "if you have a *reason* to pursue an end then you have a reason to take the means to that end." But if we do not allow reason a role in determining ends, then the instrumental principle has to go like this: "if you are *going* to pursue an end, then you have a reason to take the means to that end." Now that first formulation—if you have a *reason* to pursue an end then you have a reason to take the means to that end—derives a reason from a reason, something normative from something normative. But the second formulation—if you are *going* to pursue an end then you have a reason to take the means to that end—derives, or attempts to derive, a reason from a fact. Now if Hume believed in instrumental reason, he would have to accept the second formulation, since it is perfectly clear that he thinks that reason does not play a role in the determination of ends. He would have to believe that the instrumental principle instructs us to derive a reason from what we are *going* to do. But Hume, after all, is famous for arguing that you cannot derive an *Ought* from an *Is*. And in the argument that follows, I will show why he is right. This seems to me to be grounds for doubting that Hume himself could have believed in instrumental reason.

rationality to a form of causality. So what matters here is not, so to speak, where the cause operates, but the point of view from which we make the judgment that it operates.

It's worth noticing that a parallel argument could be constructed for theoretical reason, suggesting that Hume doesn't believe in that either. I don't take this to be a problem for my account, for I don't think that Hume believes in rational belief any more than he does in rational action. His view is that beliefs are sentiments that are caused in us by perceptions and habits. Reason doesn't really enter into it.

Let's take as a point of comparison Hume's attitude towards the other (supposedly) hypothetical imperative, the principle of prudence. Hume clearly denies that prudence is a rational requirement. In a very famous passage, he says:

'Tis not contrary to reason for me to prefer the destruction of the whole world to the scratching of my finger. 'Tis not contrary to reason for me to chuse my total ruin, to prevent the least uneasiness of an *Indian* or person wholly unknown to me. 'Tis as little contrary to reason to prefer even *my own acknowledg'd lesser good* to my greater, and have a more ardent affection for the former than the latter. (T 2.3.3,416, second emphasis mine)

But Hume does not claim that we in fact live for the moment, like the grasshopper in the fable, and never take the future into account. He offers us an alternative explanation of what is going on when we take our future interests into account. Three passages are relevant.

First of all, there is a discussion in Book 1, in the section entitled: "Of the Influence of Belief." Flatly contradicting the belief/desire model of action, Hume argues here that beliefs operate on us in the same way that present impressions do. Hume offers this argument as evidence for his view that what distinguishes a belief from a mere idea is the fact that it is forceful and vivacious in nearly the same way that an impression is. When you are convinced, by causal reasoning, that a certain painful effect will occur, you recoil from the causes of that effect in much the same way that you would recoil from the effect itself, from present pain. You draw back from putting your hand *into* the flame with the same automatic character with which you would draw your hand *out of* the flame if it were already in. And if the painful effect would be caused by an action you propose to yourself, you recoil in just this way from performing the action. This is how the future consequences of our actions motivate us.[20] Hume describes this as a kind of middle way which nature has taken in the construction of animals. He points out that if we could be motivated only by present impressions, we would always be getting into trouble, and foresight could not help us to avoid it. On the other hand, if we were motivated indiscriminately by all of our ideas, we would never enjoy a moment's peace and tranquility. The bare idea of fear would fill us with fear. Hume says:

Nature has, therefore, chosen a medium, and has neither bestow'd on every idea of good and evil the power of actuating the will, nor yet has entirely excluded this

---

[20] In *The Possibility of Altruism*, Nagel appeals to exactly this sort of belief—a belief about future desires/pleasures/reasons—to show how odd the belief/desire model is. His point is that it would be bizarre to think that we needed a special desire to give motivational or normative force to a belief about a reason we will have later. Although for different reasons, Hume would agree.

influence. Tho' an idle fiction has no efficacy, yet we find by experience, that the ideas of those objects, which we believe either are or will be existent, produce in a lesser degree the same effect with those impressions, which are immediately present to the senses and perception. (T 1.3.10,119)

What is most notable about this passage is what Hume does *not* say. He does not say that it is rational to be motivated by a belief, because you think that the object of a belief exists and therefore really is apt to affect you, while the object of a mere idea need not exist, and so there is no reason to think that it will affect you.[21] He merely says that we are in fact so constructed.

This thought is picked up later in the introduction to the discussion of the direct passions. Hume says:

The mind by an *original instinct* tends to unite itself with the good, and to avoid the evil, tho' they be conceived merely in idea, and be consider'd as to exist in any future period of time. (T 2.3.9,438; my emphasis)

An "original instinct" in Hume's terminology, is a psychological tendency that admits of no further explanation. In both passages, then, Hume asserts that our tendency to act prudently is not the result of our rational nature but rather of the original instincts which nature has implanted in us.

The third passage is in the section "On the Influencing Motives of the Will." Here we learn that the most general form of this tendency to desire the good—"the general appetite to good, and aversion to evil, consider'd merely as such"—is a calm passion, that is, one we know more from its effects than from its emotional turbulence (T 2.3.3,417). When we are under the influence of this calm passion we do prudent things, say, we pursue our overall good at the expense of present pleasure. Hume thinks that we tend to confuse the operation of the calm passions with the operations of reason because those are also calm. This is why we imagine that prudent conduct is a form of rational conduct: when we act under the influence of the general desire for good, our minds are calculating and cool. Nevertheless, when we are not under the influence of this calm passion, and pursue present pleasure at the expense of our overall good, there is no irrationality in the case.

From all of this it is clear that Hume thinks that it is a not requirement of reason that we should have concern for our future, but that it is natural to have such a concern. By the *original* arrangements of human nature, we

---

[21] This makes Hume sound perverse, but in fact, given his account of belief, it is a tautology. If you thought that the thing were going to affect you then you would believe in its existence; that is, that's more or less what believing it amounts to. Even apart from Hume's theory, this doesn't seem completely crazy. One plausible, if rather idealistic (in the philosophical sense) account of what is meant by claiming that something exists is that it could conceivably affect you.

have the capacity to be motivated, at least sometimes, by our beliefs about what will happen in the future. Of course a *rational* requirement of prudence, if it existed, would demand much more than this. A rational requirement of prudence would not demand merely that we give some weight, some of the time, to considerations of our overall good. It would demand that we *do* what conduces to our overall good.[22] By contrast, the calm passion that Hume calls "the general appetite to good" is just one desire among others, which occasionally takes precedence.

But why does Hume believe this? A moment ago I quoted the famous passage in which Hume rejects the rational requirement of prudence. It continues this way:

'Tis not contrary to reason to prefer even my own acknowledg'd lesser good to my greater, and have a more ardent affection for the former than the latter. A trivial good may, from certain circumstances, produce a desire superior to what arises from the greatest and most valuable enjoyment; nor is there anything more extraordinary in this, than in mechanics to see one pound weight raise up a hundred by the advantage of its situation. (T 2.3.3,416)

Hume here appeals to the fact that a desire for present pleasure may get the better of prudence, having been rendered stronger by "the advantage of its situation." But how is that fact supposed to show us that prudence is not rationally required? We might take this passage to be an argument, based on the internalism requirement. Hume could be thinking that since prudence sometimes fails to motivate us, the principle of prudence fails to meet the internalism requirement, and so cannot count as a rational principle.[23] As I have argued elsewhere, however, such an argument would have to be based on a *misunderstanding* of the internalism requirement.[24] The internalism requirement can only specify that practical reasons must motivate us *insofar as* we are susceptible to the influence of reason. The requirement cannot be that a consideration must *in fact* motivate a person in order to *count* as a reason,

---

[22] Unless, perhaps, a sacrifice of one's personal interests is required by some yet more stringent principle of reason, such as a moral principle. Hume, however, does not think that this possibility is likely to arise. See 2E 9, 278–84.

[23] Later Hume will argue that moral considerations cannot be based on reason, because reason does not motivate and moral considerations do (T 3.1.1,457). This suggests that he accepts internalism about moral considerations. Of course, it also suggests that he thinks reason cannot motivate us, generally speaking, and that may make the interpretative proposal in the text look implausible: if Hume doesn't think reason motivates, why should he suppose that considerations of prudence must motivate in order to be reasons? The answer, I think, is that Hume is an internalist about requirements, and the argument quoted above is supposed to show that reason cannot make prudence a requirement, and, more generally, that reason does not yield requirements. As we'll see later, Hume does think prudence is a requirement of virtue.

[24] "Skepticism about Practical Reason" (CKE essay 11), pp. 318–21.

for, in that case, we could never judge that a person has acted irrationally; if the person were not moved by the consideration, we would have to say that it was not a reason for him. In any case, whether we do judge that an instance of imprudent conduct is irrational *depends* upon our views about whether prudence is a rational requirement, and not the reverse.

To see this, consider the case of Howard. Howard, who is in his thirties, needs medical treatment: specifically, he must have a course of injections, now, if he is going to live past fifty. But Howard declines to have this treatment, because he has a horror of injections. Let me just stipulate that, were it not for his horror of injections, Howard would have the treatment. It's not that he really secretly wants to die young anyway, or anything fancy like that. Howard's horror of injections is really what is motivating him. Notice that there are three different ways in which we may explain his conduct.

First, we may suppose that Howard *is* governed by what Hume calls the general appetite to good (or by prudence), but that he is miscalculating. He thinks that having a course of injections will be so dreadful that it is worth dying young to avoid it, even though he believes that if he had the treatments, a long and happy life would await him at the other end. While it might be interesting to know how someone could make this particular mistake, the possibility of mistake is not in general very interesting. In any case, I want to leave this interpretation aside, so let's again stipulate that he has not miscalculated or made a mistake. He sees that, if he were governed by considerations of prudence, he would have the injections: he agrees that a long and happy life is a greater good than avoiding the injections. But he still declines to have them: he chooses "his own acknowledg'd lesser good."

What we say next depends on whether or not we think that the principle of prudence is a rational requirement. If we think that it is, we will regard Howard's dread of the injections as something that interferes with his rationality, as a source of weakness of the will. But if we reject the idea that prudence is rationally required, we may say simply that, because Howard so dreads the needle, avoiding the injections is what he wants most. His decision to decline the needed medical treatment is then not irrational. Absent a principle determining which ends we should prefer, such as the principle of prudence, a person will follow his stronger desire and will not be irrational for doing so. The point is not that it is *rational* for him to follow his stronger desire because it is stronger. The point is that he is rational in the only remaining sense—he is (apparently) following the instrumental principle. Refusing to take the injections is the means to his end, in the sense that it is the means to the end he is *going* to pursue: namely, a life free from injections.

So what we say about this case depends on our attitude about the principle of prudence. If we suppose prudence is a rational requirement, we will say: fear prevents Howard from pursuing the end he *ought* to prefer, his overall good, and therefore he is acting irrationally. But if we reject the claim that prudence is a rational requirement, we will say: fear determines what Howard's preferred end is, but there is no irrationality in the case, for reason has nothing to say about which ends we should prefer.

Does Hume think that the instrumental principle, unlike the principle of prudence, is a rational requirement? If he does, then as the argument above shows, there should be cases in which Hume would be prepared to identify someone's conduct as "instrumentally irrational," that is, cases in which, without miscalculating or making a mistake, people fail or decline to take the means to their own "acknowledg'd" ends. Now Hume does not discuss this kind of case, but he does explicitly allow that actions can be irrational in two *derivative* ways: we act "irrationally" when our passions are provoked by non-existent objects, or when we act on the basis of false causal judgments (T 2.3.3,416). Both of these are cases of mistake; the actions that result are not, strictly speaking, irrational. And after discussing them, Hume asserts:

The moment we perceive the falsehood of any supposition, or the insufficiency of any means our passions yield to our reason without any opposition. (T 2.3.3,416)

This suggests that Hume thinks no one is ever guilty of violating the instrumental principle. Making a mistake, after all, is not a way of being irrational, and Hume thinks we do take the means to our ends as soon as mistakes are out of the way. But this is worrisome. How can there be rational action, in any sense, if there is no irrational action? How can there be an imperative that no one ever actually violates?

The problem is exacerbated when we see that Hume's view is not just that people don't *in fact* ever violate the instrumental principle. He is actually committed to the view that people *cannot* violate it. To see this, we need only consider why Hume might be led to deny that people are ever instrumentally irrational. Offhand, that denial doesn't seem very plausible. People fail to take the means to what they *say* are their ends all the time. And this does not happen only when those ends are demanded by abstract or distant considerations of what will conduce to the person's overall good. It happens in the case of more local ends that are expressly and directly wanted or chosen for their own sakes. You want to ride on this immense roller coaster but you are prevented by terror. Every night of the carnival you go and look at it, get in line for a ticket, and then lose your nerve and shuffle meekly away. You don't think riding the roller coaster is essential to your overall good. Maybe you even think it's risky and a little foolish. But you've made up your mind to do it. And all you have to do is buy a ticket and get on—only you can't bring yourself to. You want to see the movie but you are too idle to go downtown; you want to go out with him but you are too shy to call and ask him for a date; you want to work but depression holds you in its smothering embrace.

If we believe that the instrumental principle is a rational requirement, we will say that these people's terror, idleness, shyness, or depression is making them irrational and weak-willed, and so that they are failing to do what is necessary to promote their own ends. We will see these things as forces that block their susceptibility to the influence of reason. Now in the case of prudence, the other option was to reject the principle and say that Howard simply prefers to avoid the injections at any cost, and that he is not irrational for doing so. In this case, what is the other option? Could we *reject* the instrumental principle and say that the people in these examples simply *prefer* to indulge their terror, idleness, shyness, or depression, and that they are not irrational for doing so?

Well, notice that if we do say that, then it turns out that these people are *not* after all violating the instrumental principle, at least as Hume would have to formulate it. They are taking the means to the ends they are *going* to pursue, so we would not have rejected the instrumental principle after all. Now one thing that this means is that Hume cannot talk about the instrumental principle in the same way he talks about the principle of prudence. That is, if he *did* want to deny that the instrumental principle is a rational requirement, he could not do it by dramatically announcing: "It is not contrary to reason to refuse to take the means to my end . . ." because according to Hume *that cannot happen*. Whatever you do is the means to the end that you are *going* to pursue. But how then can we claim that the instrumental principle is a principle of reason? Hume's view seems to exclude the possibility that we could be *guided* by the instrumental principle. For how can you be guided by a principle when anything you do counts as following it? In fact, this argument shows that Hume's famous dictum is correct: you cannot derive an *ought* from an *is*. In this case, we cannot derive the *requirement* of taking the means from *facts* about which end an agent is actually going to pursue.[25]

---

[25] Readers of earlier drafts of this essay have alerted me to the importance of making it clear what I am saying about Hume at this point. My primary target in this part of the essay is actually empiricists who endorse the view that the instrumental principle is the only principle of practical reason and who claim Hume for the founding father of their view. I am arguing that Hume could not have held such a view. I do not mean, however, to suggest that Hume himself tried to hold this view and failed: I do not believe that he thought the instrumental principle was a principle of reason. In note 39 below, however, I argue that Hume's arguments for the normativity of virtue may depend on the normativity

Now it is clear enough where the problem here is coming from. The problem is coming from the fact that Hume identifies a person's *end* as what he *wants most*, and the criterion of what the person wants most appears to be what he actually *does*. The person's ends are taken to be revealed in his conduct. If we don't make a distinction between what a person's end is and what he actually pursues, it will be impossible to find a case in which he violates the instrumental principle. So the problem would be solved if we could make a distinction between a person's ends and what he actually pursues. Two ways suggest themselves: we could make a distinction between actual desire and rational desire, and say that a person's ends are not merely what he wants, but what he has reason to want. Or, we could make a more psychological distinction between what a person thinks he wants or locally wants and what he "really wants." After all, it does seem odd to say of the people in my examples that what they "really want" are ends which are shaped by their terror, idleness, shyness or depression. We know that these people would wish these conditions away if only they could. So perhaps it is plausible to say that these people do not do what they really want to do, and that therefore they are irrational.

But in order to distinguish rational desire from actual desire, it looks as if we need to have some rational principles determining which ends are worthy of preference or pursuit. So the first option takes us beyond instrumental rationality. The instrumental principle then tells us to promote those ends we have reason to want. But really the second option—the claim that these people are irrational because they do not promote the ends that they "really want"—also takes us beyond instrumental rationality, although this may not be immediately obvious. If we are going to appeal to "real" desires as a basis for making claims about whether people are acting rationally or not, we will have to argue that a person *ought* to pursue what he *really* wants rather than what he is in fact *going* to pursue. That is, we will have to accord these "real" desires some normative force. It must be something like a requirement of reason that you should do what you "really want," even when you are tempted not to. And then, again, we will have gone beyond instrumental rationality after all.

Let me now pay off a promissory note. According to a theory very fashionable in the social scientific and economic literature, sometimes called the

of prudence, and I think that a parallel and related point can be made about the normativity of the instrumental principle. Of course some interpreters also deny that Hume is trying to establish the normativity of virtue, but this is not the line that I have taken. For my interpretation of Hume's account of the normativity of morality, see SN 2.2.1–2.2.7, pp. 51–66. I thank Annette Baier and Barbara Herman for prodding me to be clearer on this point.

self-interest or economic theory of rationality, it is rational for each person to pursue his overall good: to act on some variant of the principle of prudence. Many people who believe the self-interest theory of rationality *think* that they also believe the theory that all practical reasons are instrumental. This combination of ideas is incoherent. The instrumental principle says nothing about our ends, so it is completely unequipped to say either that we ought to desire our overall good or that we ought to prefer it to more immediate or local satisfactions. The self-interest theory of rationality, because it is committed to the principle of prudence, *has to* go beyond the instrumental theory. Now how could the purveyors of this theory make such an obvious error? I believe that the answer lies in what I have just said. People who hold this theory *assume* that what a person "really wants" is her overall good, and therefore that her ends, her real ends, just *are* the things that are consistent with or part of her overall good. The standard move is to treat the possibility that someone might desire something inconsistent with her overall good as if it were an uninteresting little piece of theoretical untidiness like the possibility that she might miscalculate or make a mistake. We all know that we cannot even start a discussion of rationality until we have applied *a little* spit and polish to people's desires. (You know the sort of thing I mean: "we won't say that his desire to eat the apple provides a reason for him to do so, if it is based on his ignorance that it is made of wax . . ." etc.) Self-interest theorists treat harmonizing someone's local ends with her overall good as if it were just a part of this preliminary cleaning-up process. Following Hume (and with just as little plausibility), they might say "The moment we perceive that an end is inconsistent with our overall good our passions yield to our reason without any opposition."[26] The fans of morality could just as well stipulate that what we "really want" are things consistent with love and respect for everybody, and then they too could claim that we don't need to go beyond instrumental rationality. Nothing is gained by such devices.[27]

But Hume, unlike his would-be followers, does not build consistency with one's overall good into his notion of an end. As we have seen, he thinks we neither ought-to-want nor really-want only those ends which are consistent with our overall good. And that apparently means that he must accept the

[26] As Plato points out in the *Protagoras*, one idea that drives this position is the idea that the objects of desire are commensurable. If the choice is between getting $5 or 5 units of pleasure now, and $12 or 12 units of pleasure next week, it is *a little* more plausible to say that passion will conform *automatically* to the dictate of prudence—although only a little. But if the choice is between six weeks of passion with a charming scapegrace now, and a lifetime of marriage to a man of sweet reason, the claim that passion will yield *automatically* to prudence seems absurd. Economists, of course, do tend to assume commensurability.

[27] For further discussion, see my "The Myth of Egoism," Essay 2 in this volume.

claim that local desires determine our ends, and with it, the implication that we cannot violate the instrumental principle. If we cannot violate it, then it cannot guide us, and that means that it is not a normative principle. This suggests that for Hume the desire to take the means to our ends is just a calm passion, one we have by the original constitution of our nature. Hume might say of it just what he said of the principle of prudence, that we mistake it for reason because when we are under its influence our minds are calculating and cool.

One way to rescue the normativity of the instrumental principle is open to Hume. We might argue that the principle that distinguishes "my end" from "whatever I actually pursue" does not have to be a principle of reason. It only has to be some *normative* principle, since it has to pick out something I ought to pursue even if I don't.[28] Perhaps virtue itself picks out the ends we ought to pursue, and then the instrumental principle requires us to take the means to those. It is instructive here, that although Hume denies that prudence is a rational requirement, he certainly does think it is a virtue. He says:

What we call strength of mind, implies the prevalence of the calm passions above the violent; tho' we may easily observe, there is no man so constantly possess'd of this virtue, as never on any occasion to yield to the sollicitations of passion and desire. (T 2.3.3, 418)[29]

The parallel claim, about the instrumental principle, would be that resoluteness in the pursuit of our ends is itself a virtue, and that this accounts for the normativity of the instrumental principle. We can be guided by it insofar as we can be motivated to pursue an ideal of virtue.[30] But it would have to be

[28] I owe this suggestion to Erin Kelly; I would also like to thank Charlotte Brown and Andrews Reath for discussions of this point.

[29] But there is a deep incoherence here. In Hume's moral theory, prudence is supposed to be a virtue because we approve of it from the general point of view. From this point of view, we approve of those qualities that are useful or agreeable to an agent himself or his associates. Hume identifies prudence as one of the virtues that is supposed to be good (because useful) for the agent who has it. But if an agent himself has no reason to prefer his greater good to the satisfaction of his local desires, then I do not see why we should think it is good for him to prefer it, and therefore why we should count it as a virtue. The real trouble, I think, is that Hume uses the word "good" to describe the sum of satisfactions or pleasures over the course of a person's whole life without explaining either what entitles him to that usage or what follows from it. If the word "good" is supposed to import normativity, it may seem like a raw contradiction to say an agent has no reason to prefer his greater good. Or to make the same point in reverse, if we have no reason to care about future pleasures and satisfactions, then there is no content to the idea that adding them up makes a "greater good."

[30] Notice that if this reconstruction works, it traces normativity to self-government, and in that sense, anticipates the view I will argue for in section 3. But there are problems about the extent to which Hume can give a satisfactory explanation of this kind of motivation. These problems are explored in Charlotte Brown, "Is Hume an Internalist?," and "From Spectator to Agent: Hume's Theory of Obligation."

resoluteness in the pursuit of *virtuous* ends, for, otherwise, there would be no way to distinguish cases of resoluteness from any other actions. We would not say, except as a kind of joke, that Howard exhibits the virtue of resoluteness in steadfastly rejecting the medical treatment that he needs, or that my other exemplar displays it in slinking timidly away from the roller coaster she longs to ride. If the theory we are now constructing on Hume's behalf works, we will call somebody "resolute" only when he pursues ends of which we approve. The normativity of taking the means can then be derived from the normativity that our moral approval attaches to the end.[31]

But if Hume took this option, it would begin to become unclear why it should matter whether we use the words "reason" and "rational" to signify that normativity or whether we use "virtue" and "virtuous" or some other words. We will have rescued the instrumental requirement for Hume, but only at the cost of showing that the word "virtue" simply does the work in his account of action that the word "reason" does in his supposed opponent's accounts. Hume will have been engaging in what he supposedly despises, a verbal dispute. And he would still have to grant the central point of this argument, which is that a *normative* principle of instrumental action cannot exist unless there are also normative principles directing the adoption of ends.

Earlier, I suggested that the instrumental principle cannot function as a requirement in Hume's theory because he has no resources for distinguishing a person's ends from what she actually pursues. Another way to put the same point, which in the end comes to the same thing, is to say that Hume has no resources for distinguishing the activity of the person *herself* from the operation of beliefs, desires, and other forces *in her*. Unless Hume endorses the kind of reconstruction I have just described, his model does not allow us

---

[31] In ordinary discourse we move freely between characterizing ends as real and characterizing them in normative terms, for our practices of psychological attribution are themselves normatively loaded in a rather deep way. Suppose a graduate student comes to your office and says, in despair: "I'm going to give it up and leave graduate school, I am getting nowhere, it is all hopeless and I'd better just bag it and go to law school." You might reply "You don't *really want* to do that." You're only partly talking about psychic reality—you are also guiding, giving a pep talk, *trying to create* psychic reality, and you and your student *both* know that. You mean something like: "Don't give up: you are still capable of being what you think it's best for you to be." Or suppose a man asks "what do I really want?" and someone replies "to kill your father and make love to your mother." At least outside of the psychoanalytic context, this answer is a kind of category mistake; the man is not asking about the actual condition of his id. It is important, I think, to recognize how pervasive this normative use of psychological language is. "You can do it!" we cheer from the sidelines of one another's lives. "You're a reasonable person" I begin my argument, looking steadily into my opponent's eyes. In one sense, this sort of thing may seem to be, to use Bernard Williams's term, bluff. But if it is, then we ought to have a lot of respect for bluff. It plays an essential role in our efforts to hold ourselves and each other together, to stay on track of our projects and relationships in the face of the buffeting winds of local temptation and desire. See Williams, "Internal and External Reasons," in *Moral Luck*, p. 111.

to see a person as guided by normative principles in her actions and choices because it leaves no room for the *person* to act and choose at all. Desire, fear, indolence, and whim shape the Humean agent's ends, and, through them, her actions. When her passions change, her ends change, and when her ends change, so do her actions. We can explain everything that she does without any reference to *her* at all. To say that reason is the slave of the passions, and to say that a person is the slave of her passions, turn out to be one and the same thing.

3. Kant and the Rationalist Account

I have suggested that the instrumental principle can be rescued only if we take "my end" to be something other than "what I actually, just now, desire." One possibility is to distinguish desire from volition, and to say that your end is what you *will*, not merely what you want.[32] This distinction is at the heart of Kant's moral psychology. In Kant's view, an inclination is a kind of attraction to something, which is grounded in our sensuous nature, and in the face of which we are passive.[33] By themselves, inclinations have no normative force; they are not reasons. But they do serve as "incentives"—which means that we are predisposed to treat them as reasons, and so to adopt maxims of acting on them. Of course Kant thinks that they are not the only incentives, for reason also generates an incentive of its own, respect for the moral law, which inclines us to act morally. Volition consists in adopting a maxim of acting on some incentive or other. When we decide to act on an inclination—to do a desired action or seek a desired end—then its object becomes an object of volition. The essential point here is that the adoption of an end is conceived as the person's own free act. Inclination proposes, but it is the person herself who disposes. Given all this, it is not surprising to find Kant's version of the instrumental principle formulated in terms of the will, not in terms of desire. In general or schematic form, the instrumental principle tells us that if we *will* an end, then we ought to will the means to that end.[34] And Kant's argument

---

[32] This possibility wasn't canvassed in section 2 because it is not open to Hume or other empiricists. Hume thinks the will is merely the impression that accompanies voluntary action (T 3.1.1, 399); other empiricists think it is merely the last desire that emerges from deliberation. Either way, volition does not provide a distinctive account of what it means to be an end.

[33] There are of course objections to this view, which I have discussed in section 3 of the Reply in SN, pp. 238–42.

[34] Kant talks about both "the" categorical imperative and categorical imperatives plural; but he does not talk about "the" hypothetical imperative. I do not think that anything important turns on this fact: in this, as in much else in this part of the essay, I am in agreement with Thomas Hill, Jr, in his paper "The Hypothetical Imperative," essay 1 in *Dignity and Practical Reason*. Yet there's a

for the instrumental principle depends essentially on the fact that it is formulated that way. He says:

> How an imperative of skill is possible requires no special discussion. Whoever wills the end, also wills (insofar as reason has decisive influence on his actions) the indispensably necessary means to it that are within his power. This proposition, is, as regards the volition, analytic; for in the volition of an object as my effect, my causality as acting cause, that is, the use of means, is already thought, and the imperative extracts the concept of actions necessary to this end merely from the concept of a volition of this end. (G 4:417)

Kant then adds that we do need some synthetic propositions—some causal laws—to arrive at these imperatives, but not for grounding the act of the will, only for determining what the means to the end are.

In other words, the imperative derives the concept of willing the means from the concept of willing the end, with the aid of some synthetic proposition telling us what the means are. So we begin with some willed end, say, health, and a causal (and so synthetic) proposition, say, that exercise is a cause of health. From the combination of these we derive the necessity of a will to exercise. What makes the derivation possible is an "analytic proposition," namely, that whoever wills the end wills the means to that end, insofar as reason has decisive influence on his actions. This proposition is analytic because to will an end, rather than just to wish for it or desire it, is to be committed to causing that end actually to exist.[35] "In the volition of an object," Kant explains, "my causality as acting cause" is "already thought." And to cause an end is of course to take the means to it. It follows that if someone

---

possible issue here, for we can imagine someone interpreting the asymmetry along these lines: "Kant thinks that although we can violate particular hypothetical imperatives, we could not in general violate "the" hypothetical imperative and still count as beings with rational wills, and, that being so, "the" hypothetical imperative isn't really an imperative. We can, however, violate the categorical imperative in general and still count as beings with rational wills, so it really is an imperative."

According to this view, the hypothetical imperative is merely descriptive of a rational will, while the categorical imperative is normative for but not descriptive of it, and so in effect represents a restriction on the will. It will emerge in due course that I think this view is wrong, both in fact, and as an interpretation of Kant's more considered position; but also that I think Kant had some tendency to fall into it in the *Groundwork*. As I will explain later, I think that both requirements, strictly speaking, represent procedures for constructing maxims rather than restrictions applied to them, and as such they are both constitutive and normative for the rational will. See note 60 for more on this topic.

[35] I am using "wish" here in an ordinary sense, to refer to a sort of idle desire. In *The Metaphysical Principles of Virtue*, Kant uses the term *Wunsch* (MM 6:213), translated by both Mary Gregor and James Ellington (in his translation in *Ethical Philosophy*) as "wish," to describe the state in which an end is rationally endorsed, as a morally good end, but in which the agent sees no way to pursue it. In that sense of "wish," a wish does involve a commitment to taking the means, should they arise. There Kant says that willing includes both "choice"—an immediate determination to try and bring the object about—and "wish." See note 47.

wills to be healthy, then insofar as reason has decisive control over his actions, he wills to exercise.

Now the reconstruction I just gave is vague, for I have not said exactly *how* the analytic proposition makes it possible to combine willing the end with knowledge of the means so as to arrive at the necessity of willing the means. And it turns out that there is a problem about how this is supposed to work. The problem is revealed by two glitches that infect the argument as it stands. First, the claim that whoever wills the end wills "the indispensably necessary means to it that are within his power" seems to leave something out: the person in question must *know* that these are the means. It is not true that if someone wills to be healthy, then he necessarily wills to exercise. He must also *know* that exercise is a cause of health. This point is more important than it looks, because it suggests that the agent *himself* must combine willing the end with knowing the means to arrive at the necessity of willing the means. And this recalls a point I made earlier, namely, that the rationality of action depends on the way in which the person's own mental activity is involved in its production, not just on its accidental conformity to some external standard.

So the agent himself must combine willing the end and knowing the means to arrive at the necessity of willing the means. And the analytic proposition is supposed to make this possible for him somehow. But at this point we run into the second glitch in the argument. There is a recurring caveat: the analytic proposition is that whoever wills the end wills the means *insofar as reason has decisive influence on his actions*. This caveat, as I will explain below, turns out to give rise to a problem in Kant's argument. Before explaining that, it will be helpful to consider why Kant adds the caveat.

In one sense, I think the answer is clear. At the beginning of the discussion, Kant says that imperatives are expressed by an *ought* because they are addressed to wills that are not necessarily determined by the objective laws of reason. After identifying the good with the practically necessary, Kant says, "They [imperatives] say that that to do or to omit something would be good, but they say it to a will that does not always do something just because it is represented to it that would be good to do that thing" (G 4:413). In other words, imperatives are addressed to beings who may follow them or not. And this is true of the instrumental principle as well as of the others.

Now if this is right, it must be possible for a rational being (one who is subject to the instrumental principle) to disobey, resist, or fail to follow that principle. It must be possible for someone to will an end, and yet to fail to will the means to that end. And this means, once again, that there will be different ways to explain what happens when someone *apparently* fails to take the means to her end, or to what she says is her end.

Suppose someone claims that she wills an end: she asserts that all things considered, she has decided to pursue this end. And yet, when a means to this end is at hand she always fails to take it, even when it is expressly pointed out to her that it would promote or realize the end she has chosen. Timid Prudence says she has resolved to lead a more adventurous life, but when the opportunity for adventure knocks, Prudence always says "tomorrow." How are we to explain her conduct? One possible explanation of course is that she does not really will to lead a more adventurous life. When she says that she does, she is self-deceived or she is lying to the rest of us. We finally say to Prudence in disgust, "You really mean to live on the safe side of the street, and you had better just admit it." Notice that in this case we imply that she is guilty of insincerity rather than of instrumental irrationality. If she doesn't really will to have an adventurous life, it is not irrational of her to let these opportunities go by, although it is insincere for her to pretend she has resolved upon adventure.

A second possible explanation appeals to the fact that the instrumental principle is hypothetical, and says that *if* you will an end you must be prepared to take the means. The hypothetical character of the principle implies that you can actually conform to it in either of two ways: you may take the means, or you may cease to will the end. It matters here that willing, unlike desiring, is an act, one we can decide to refrain from, or to cease to do. Sometimes, when we see what taking the means to an end will involve, we cease to will the end, deciding that all things considered it is not worth the trouble or the price. There is no irrationality in this, and it may be what happens to Prudence. Perhaps she believes that the means to adventure which are pointed out to her will be so painful or terrifying that she decides that, all things considered, an adventurous life is not worth it after all. So she gives the idea up. Prudence says: "Well, I had resolved on leading a more adventurous life, but if I take any of the ways open to me right now, I am likely to end up in jail. I'd like to have more adventure, but it isn't really worth going to jail for." Again she is not guilty of any irrationality.

Both of those explanations say that Prudence doesn't really will to have adventures after all. This being so, she has not violated the instrumental principle, which only instructs her to take the means to those ends which she does will. The third explanation is that she does violate the instrument-al principle, and fails to take the means to her end, because something is interfering with her susceptibility to reason. This might happen, for instance, because she has been rendered inert by depression, or paralyzed by ter-ror, or because the means are painful and, although she judges the end to be worth the pain, she is simply unable to face it. Now we can say that she is violating the instrumental principle, and is guilty of irrational willing.[36]

Although we may not be sure which of these explanations is the best, the third one must be possible if the instrumental principle is a rational requirement. And it is worth noticing that there are cases where this third explanation seems to be the best in any case. Consider a standard scene of horror in Western or Civil War movies. The doctor must saw off Tex's leg in order to save his life, and there is no anesthetic or even any whiskey left in the house. Tex screams "No, no, don't"; he tries to escape from the men holding him down; he tries to push the doctor away. Yet if the doctor asks "Tex, don't you want to live?" Tex will of course say "yes." It would be stupid to say that because Tex rejects the means he is being insincere and doesn't really want to live, or that as the saw approaches he reconsiders his situation and makes a decision that all things considered, living isn't worth it. The right thing to say is that fear is making Tex irrational. After all, the judgment that someone is irrational doesn't have to be a criticism. The government of reason, like any other, requires certain background conditions in order to maintain its authority. Faced with the prospect of having his leg sawed off, Tex's sensible nature is quite understandably in revolt.

Kant, unlike the followers of Hume, recognizes that we cannot be guided by an imperative unless we can also fail to be guided by it. The caveat is necessary, then, because it must be logically possible for someone to fail to follow the instrumental principle, that is, to will an end but fail to will the means. The proposition is supposed to be analytic, so if we don't put the caveat in, failure to take the means to one's end will be logically impossible. But that means that without the caveat, the proposition can't be true after all.

But this in turn gives rise to the glitch I mentioned earlier, for it creates a problem about *how* the analytic proposition is supposed to make it possible for the agent to combine willing the end with knowing the means to *arrive at* a rational requirement of willing the means. On the model suggested by Kant's account, the agent arrives at the requirement by plugging himself in, so to speak, to a syllogism, of which the analytic proposition is the first premise:

Whoever wills the end wills the means.
I will the end.
∴ Therefore I will the means.

---

[36] Peter Railton also emphasizes the necessity of allowing for this kind of case in "On the Hypothetical and Non-Hypothetical in Reasoning about Belief and Action," in *Ethics and Practical Reason*, pp. 72–3.

The trouble with this suggestion is obvious. As we have just seen, the principle "whoever wills the end wills the means" isn't true. This shows up in the fact that the syllogism puts the modal operator in the wrong place: its conclusion is not that I must will the means, but rather that it must be the case that I will the means, which is false. The only proposition which Kant can claim is an analytic truth is the one with the caveat in it: the proposition that "whoever wills the end wills the means insofar as reason has decisive influence over his actions." So it looks as if the first premise of the syllogism must include the caveat. Then it goes like this:

Whoever wills the end wills the means insofar as he is rational.
I will the end.
∴ Therefore I will the means insofar as I am rational.
∴ Therefore I *ought* to will the means.

(Recall that imperatives are expressed by an *ought*, according to Kant, because they are addressed to wills that do not necessarily do what reason demands: that's how this last step is made.)

But we cannot in any non-trivial way invoke this second syllogism to explain *why* the agent finds it rationally necessary to take the means to his end, for this syllogism's first premise trivially incorporates the claim that taking the means to one's ends is rationally required.

I believe that there is an historical explanation for what has gone wrong here. At the time he wrote the *Groundwork*, Kant apparently identified our capacity to resist the dictates of reason with the imperfection of the human will, for he asserts rather confusingly that a perfectly good will, although it would "stand under" the laws of reason, would not be necessitated to follow them and so would not be addressed in imperative form and in an *ought*. The reason for this is supposed to be that human beings are subject to incentives of inclination as well as those generated by reason itself, while a perfectly good will is moved only by the incentives generated by reason. Kant says: "Hence no imperatives hold for the *divine* will and in general for a holy will; the *ought* is out of place here, because volition is of itself necessarily in accord with the law" (G 4:414). This idea is picked up again in the third section of the *Groundwork*, when Kant claims that if we had only an intelligible existence (and so were perfectly rational) the moral law would be a "would" for us rather than an "ought" (G 4:454).[37] The structure of argument suggested by

---

[37] This remark gives rise to serious problems, for since our actions spring from our intelligible nature, it seems to make the existence of immoral actions a mystery. I take these problems up in "Morality as Freedom," CKE essay 6. For a somewhat different resolution of the problem presented

these remarks is this: God *does* so-and-so (or, a perfectly rational being does so-and-so) and therefore I *ought* to do so-and-so. This structure of argument is indeed found in the writings of dogmatic rationalists such as Leibniz and Clarke.[38] And it seems to be the model evoked in the second syllogism above: a perfectly rational being *would* take the means to his ends, therefore I *ought* to take the means to my ends. The model suggests that the normativity of the *ought* expresses a demand that we should emulate more perfect rational beings (possibly including our own noumenal selves) whose own conduct is not guided by normative principles at all, but instead describable in a set of logical truths. And this in turn suggests that rationality is a matter of conforming the will to standards of reason that exist independently of the will, as a set of truths about what there is reason to do. That is, it implies an essentially realist theory of reasons, and, as I am about to argue, a realist theory cannot provide a coherent account of rationality.[39]

According to dogmatic rationalism, or realism more generally, there are facts, which exist independently of the person's mind, about what there is reason to do; rationality consists in conforming one's conduct to those reasons. According to *moral* realism, facts about the rightness or wrongness of actions

directly by the passage at hand—the seeming implication that the laws of reason are not normative for purely rational beings—see note 28 of "Creating the Kingdom of Ends: Reciprocity and Responsibility in Personal Relations," CKE essay 7, especially pp. 218–19. Despite what I say here, that note suggests that there are ways of reading almost all of Kant's remarks that makes them come out true on what I believe is his more considered view.

[38] See, for instance, the selections from Samuel Clarke's *A Discourse Concerning the Unchangeable Obligations of Natural Religion, and the Truth and Certainty of the Christian Revelation*, The Boyle Lectures, 1705, in D. D. Raphael, ed., *British Moralists 1650–1800*, Volume 1, especially p. 199, Raphael paragraph 231.

[39] In his later ethical works, in particular in the *Critique of Practical Reason* and *Religion Within the Limits of Reason Alone*, Kant rejects the claim that susceptibility to sensuous incentives is what makes the will imperfect. In the *Religion*, he denies the claim that sensibility is a source of evil (REL 6:34–35). In the *Critique of Practical Reason*, he acknowledges the possibility of noumenal evil (see C2 5:96–100). He does not explicitly give up the view that the will's imperfection is what makes us subject to an *ought*, but it seems to me that he should have, for imperfection is a red herring here. Even a perfectly rational will cannot be conceived as *guided* by reason unless it is conceived as capable of resisting reason. It may be true, as Kant insists, that a divine will is not subject to temptation and so just would do what reason requires, but it is not true, as he seems to infer, that no *ought* applies to the divine will. There are a number of places where Kant suggests that we should only use "ought" or "duty" when the agent is necessitated *and* that this can only happen when the agent might want to resist the claim, some of them in the later writings. For example, in the *Metaphysical Principles of Virtue*, Kant says that we cannot have a duty to pursue our own happiness because we inevitably want it anyway (MM 6:386). Obviously, one of the central ideas of this essay is that we can be subject to normative principles only if we can resist them, because without that possibility they cannot function as guides. But I do not agree with Kant that the absence of any specific temptation to resist them removes the possibility of resistance in the sense needed for normativity. It is not imperfection that places us under rational norms, but rather freedom, which brings with it the needed possibility of resistance to, as well as of compliance with, those norms.

support those reasons; according to what we might call *instrumental* realism, facts about the instrumentality of actions to our ends support those reasons. The difficulty with this account in a way exists right on its surface, for the account invites the question why it is necessary to act in accordance with those reasons, and so seems to leave us in need of a reason to be rational. I have an end, and out there in the universe is a law saying what I must do if I have an end (take the means), but the reason why I must obey this law has not yet been given. To put the point less tendentiously, we must still explain why the person finds it *necessary* to act on those normative facts, or what it is about *her* that makes them normative *for her*. We must explain how these reasons get a grip on the agent. The dogmatic rationalist's inability to do that is illustrated by the impossibility of forming a syllogism that shows, in any illuminating way, how the agent manages to *arrive at* the rational necessity of taking the means to her ends.

Now the *moral* realist may be tempted to try to overcome this problem by appeal to the extended version of the instrumental principle which I mentioned earlier, the one that sees the application of a concept as a limiting case of the discovery of a means. We would first have to assume (or produce an argument to show) that doing what is right is a necessary end for a rational agent. (This parallels the social scientific strategy, which we looked at in section 2, of assuming that pursuit of the overall good is a necessary end for a rational agent.) With such an argument in hand, it might seem that we could connect the alleged normative facts about the right to the person's practical reason by way of the extended version of the instrumental principle. Consider: my end is to do what is right, in these circumstances *this* is the right action, therefore I shall do *this*. The extended instrumental principle in this way is supposed to lend *its* normative or motivational character to the independent facts about the rightness of certain actions.

But there are two problems with this strategy. The first and more obvious problem is that all the philosophical work has been transferred to the (missing, or anyway unspecified) argument that is supposed to show that doing what is right is a necessary end for a rational agent. (Just as, in the social scientific case, all the work is really done by the missing argument that shows that we what we "really want" must be consistent with our overall good.) The second problem concerns the instrumental principle itself. If it is to provide the needed connection between the rational agent and the independent facts about reasons, it cannot in turn be based on independent facts itself. Suppose it is just a fact, independently of a person's own will, that an action's tendency to promote one of her ends constitutes a reason for doing it. Why must she care about *that* fact? We cannot now appeal to the instrumental principle itself to explain how that fact gets a grip on the agent, for that is the principle we are trying to ground. You can see this by considering how the argument would have to go: doing whatever promotes your own ends is a necessary end for a rational being; this action promotes one of your ends; therefore it promotes your end of doing what promotes your ends; and therefore you have reason to do it. The circularity, or infinite regress, is obvious.[40] The instrumental principle cannot be an evaluative truth that we apply in practice, because it is essentially the *principle of application* itself: that is, it is the principle in accordance with which we are operating *when* we apply truths in practice. So if we are to use the extended instrumental principle to make the connection between the rational agent and the external facts about reasons, we cannot give the instrumental principle a realist foundation. But if we cannot give a realist account of the instrumental principle, it seems unlikely that we will end up giving realist accounts of the other principles of practical reason.

Another way to understand the argument I have just given goes like this: moral realism (or for that matter, realism about reasons of prudence) may be criticized on the grounds that it fails to meet the internalism requirement. The moral realist I am imagining tries to overcome that problem by tapping into the supposedly incontrovertible internalism of instrumental reason. The problem is that, on a realist interpretation, astonishingly enough, the instrumental principle *itself* fails to meet the internalism requirement. For all we can see, an agent may be indifferent to the fact that an action's instrumentality to her end constitutes a reason for her to act.

Now while that way of understanding the argument has some advantages, I have come to think that there is a problem with thinking of these issues in terms of the internalism requirement. The internalism requirement is concerned only with whether a consideration that purports to be a reason is capable of motivating the person to whom it applies. And I think the real question is not only whether the consideration can motivate the person, but whether it can do so while also functioning as a requirement or a guide. This, after all, is what is wrong with the empiricist account treated in section 2: the empiricist *can* explain how we can be motivated by instrumental thoughts, but at the price of not being able to explain how we could see such thoughts as embodying a requirement or a guide. The dogmatic rationalist account does show how the instrumental principle can guide us. But it does not show why we must be motivated to follow that guide. The theory I just examined tries to patch together an empiricist account of instrumental reason with a rationalist

---

[40] Peter Railton makes the same point in "On the Hypothetical and Non-Hypothetical in Reasoning about Belief and Action," in *Ethics and Practical Reason*, pp. 76–7.

account of morality and prudence, in order to patch together the motivational force of the one with the guiding force of the other.[41] But it ends up with neither, and that is revealed in the fact that the first of the two problems with the proposed strategy still stands: the patchwork account makes no progress towards showing *why* a rational agent must care about doing what is right.

There is one way in which the realist strategy still might seem to work. We could simply *define* a rational agent as one who responds in the appropriate way to reasons, whatever they are, and we could then give realist accounts of all practical reasons, including instrumental ones. There is a set of normative facts, about which reasons there are, and a rational agent is *by definition* someone whose actions are motivated by these reasons. But this proposal falls prey to a problem we looked at before. If all we mean is that the person is reliably caused to act in accordance with reasons, we fail to capture what is rational about the person. His actions may be rationally appropriate, but not because he sees that they are so: it seems to be a sort of accident that his motivational wiring follows the pathways of reason. On the other hand, if what we mean when we say that the person's actions are motivated by reasons is that the person is caused to act by his *recognition* of certain considerations *as* reasons, then we must say *what it is* that he recognizes.[42] And the argument I have just given shows that what it is that he recognizes cannot be that "whoever wills the end wills the means" is an analytic proposition. Because, as I have just argued, it is not. We seem to be back where we started, with Kant's argument, interpreted in a dogmatic rationalist way, having achieved nothing.

The point here is that we need a reciprocal account of rationality—as some sort of human function or capacity—and of reasons. We need an account that shows what those two things have to do with each other. The dogmatic rationalist's strategy is to first identify reasons—by asserting them to be parts of reality—and then to define rationality in terms of reasons: a rational being is by definition one who responds to reasons in the right way. This strategy necessarily leads to a purely definitional account of rationality, and can tell us nothing substantive about what function or power of the human mind rationality is. The alternative and more truly Kantian strategy is to first give an account of rationality—as we will see, as the autonomy of the human

---

[41] Leaving aside the argument in the text, I am inclined to treat such eclectic proposals as prima facie objectionable. But not everyone would agree that we should expect to give parallel accounts of the normativity of all of the principles of practical reason. To take one example, in *A Theory of Justice*, Rawls suggests that the principles of justice are chosen or (in Rawls's later terms) constructed, while the principles of goodness are not (section 68). In Rawls's later work he avoids or anyway can avoid taking a position on this; constructivism is adopted only for political purposes and we do not need to say anything about general theories of rationality or the good.

[42] For further discussion, see my "Acting for a Reason," Essay 7 in this volume.

mind—and then to define reasons in terms of rationality, say, as that which can be autonomously willed, or as those considerations which accord with the principles of autonomous willing.

In other words, the dogmatic rationalist is unable to explain how reasons get a grip on the agent, because he supposes that reasons exist independently of the rational will, and as a result he misconceives the relationship between rational principles and the will. The dogmatic rationalist pictures that relationship this way: the person is willing something, so to speak *anyway*, and, inspired by an ambition to be rational, consults the principles of practical reason to see what restrictions they impose on his willing. When we translate this picture into Kantian terms it looks like this: I make a maxim, and *then* I see whether it meets the three standards of reason by determining first whether my action is a means to my end, then whether the pursuit of my end is consistent with my overall good, and finally whether my maxim is moral, that is, universalizable. The model, as I said earlier, seems to invite the question: but suppose I don't care about being rational? What then? And in Kant's philosophy this question should be impossible to ask. Rationality, as Kant conceives it, is the human plight that gives rise to the necessity of making free choices—not one of the options that we might choose or reject.[43]

One of the benefits of focusing on the instrumental principle is that it reveals how odd the dogmatic rationalist conception of reason's relation to the will is. The idea that you could make a maxim and *then* apply the instrumental principle to it makes no sense. A maxim that does not already at least aspire to conform to the instrumental principle is no maxim at all. So the instrumental principle does not come in as a restriction that is applied *to* the maxim. Instead, the act of making a maxim—the basic act of will—conforms to the instrumental principle by its very nature. To will an end just is to will to cause or realize the end, hence to will to take the means to the end. This is the sense in which the principle is analytic. The instrumental principle is *constitutive* of an act of the will. If you do not follow it, you are not willing the end at all.

Now this sounds like one of the views I have already rejected, so care must be taken here. The act of will of which conformity to the instrumental principle is *constitutive* in the way I have just described is not the act of will third-personally conceived. If we took "willing an end" to be equivalent to "actually pursuing or trying to pursue the means to that end" then we would get the paradox I have been insisting on all along. No violation of the instrumental principle would be possible, and it therefore could not function as a requirement or guide. If willing an end just amounted to actually attempting to realize

---

[43] See SN 3.2.1–3.2.3, pp. 92–8, for more on this point.

the end, then there would be, so to speak, not enough distance between willing the end and willing the means for the one to *require* the other.[44] The dogmatic rationalist view, in which one conforms to a principle independent of the mind, achieves that distance, and so allows the principle to function as a guide. But as we have seen it gives rise to a new problem. Essentially, dogmatic rationalism conceives willing an end as being in a peculiar mental state or performing a mental act which somehow logically necessitates you to be in another mental state or perform another mental act, namely, willing the means. But we've just seen that this does not work either, for no mental state or act can logically necessitate you to be in *another* mental state or perform another mental act.[45] So willing the end is neither *the same as* being actually disposed to take the means nor as being in a particular mental state or performing a mental act that is *distinct from* willing the means. What then can it be?[46]

The answer is that willing an end just is *committing* yourself to realizing the end. Willing an end, in other words, is an essentially first-personal and normative act.[47] To will an end is to give oneself a law, hence, to govern oneself. That law is not the instrumental principle; it is some law of the form: realize this end. That of course is equivalent to "Take the means to this end." So willing an end is equivalent to committing yourself, first personally, to taking the means to that end.[48] In willing an end, just as Kant says, your causality—the use of means—is already thought. What is constitutive of

---

[44] In other words, the rationalist who takes "trying to get" as a criterion of volition runs into exactly the same problem as the empiricist who takes "trying to get" as a criterion of the strongest desire. The problem might seem even more likely to arise for the rationalist, for "trying to get" is a more tempting criterion for volition than for the strongest desire. But if we make it our criterion of volition we can give no account of rationality.

[45] This is just another way of saying that the analytic principle is false without the caveat.

[46] A large part of the inspiration for this essay came from an occasion when Warren Quinn pressed me very hard on this point, and I am grateful to him for making me see the difficulty. Peter Railton takes on what is essentially the same problem that I am examining here in his "On the Hypothetical and Non-Hypothetical in Reasoning about Belief and Action," in *Ethics and Practical Reason*. If we say that willing the means is *constitutive* of willing the end then irrationality is impossible, while if we say that willing the means is not constitutive of willing the end then there is room for a skeptic to ask why he must do it. Thus there seems to be no possibility of a identifying a prescription which we must, but do not inevitably, follow. Obviously something has gone wrong.

[47] One of the advantages of this account is that it makes it possible to explain how "wish" (*Wunsch*), as a species of rational willing, in the sense described in note 35 above, is possible. If willing were just the third-personal or objective act of *trying to get*, we could not make sense of this idea.

[48] Willing an end is in this respect like making a promise, and, accordingly, the contortions Hume undergoes when he tries to discover what act of the mind "making a promise" is are relevant here (T 3.2.5,516–517). Hume ends by deciding that there is no such act, and this is not surprising, given that only third-personal options are available to him. Nietzsche's characterization of a promise as requiring a "memory of the will" is, by contrast, right on target. (See Walter Kaufmann and R. J. Hollingdale, trans., *On the Genealogy of Morals* in *On the Genealogy of Morals and Ecce Homo*, p. 58.)

willing the end is not the outward act of actually taking the means but rather the inward, volitional act of prescribing the end along with the means it requires to yourself.

Let me make the same point in another way. In my discussion of Hume, I contrasted two formulations of the instrumental principle. The first was "if you *have a reason to pursue* an end, then you have a reason to take the means to that end" and the second was "if you are *going* to pursue an end, then you have a reason to take the means to that end." I argued that the second of those two formulations is defective because it attempts to derive an *Ought* from an *Is* (a reason from what you are *going* to do) and any imperative that attempts to do that cannot be followed because it cannot be violated. What about Kant's own formula? If it is to be like my first formulation, the one that works, then we get this result: for the instrumental principle to provide you with a reason, you must think that the fact that you will an end *is a reason* for the end. It's not exactly that there has to be a *further* reason; it's just that you must take the act of your own will to be normative for you.[49] And of course this cannot mean merely that you are *going* to pursue the end. It means that your willing the end gives it a normative status for you, that your willing the end in a sense makes it good. The instrumental principle can only be normative if we take ourselves to be capable of giving laws to ourselves—or, in Kant's own phrase, if we take our own wills to be *legislative*.

For this, of course, is almost already the third formulation of the categorical imperative, which Kant associates with "the concept of every rational being as one who must regard himself as giving universal law through all the maxims of his will" (G 4:433).[50] The only difference is that the conception of oneself as a lawmaker required for the instrumental principle does not yet (or not obviously) involve universalizing over every rational agent.

Then what does it mean to say I take the act of my own will to be normative? Who makes a law for whom? The answer in the case of the instrumental

[49] This is the basis of my account of Kant's argument for the Formula of Humanity in SN 3.4.7–3.5.0, pp. 120–5; and in my "Kant's Formula of Humanity," CKE essay 4. The argument begins from our commitment to the conception of our own ends as good, which is traced to the conception of ourselves as ends-in-ourselves, which is in turn traced to the view of our own wills as legislative.

[50] It's worth noticing that here and elsewhere, Kant doesn't formulate the categorical imperative as a standard that is to be applied to our maxims, but rather as a way of regarding one's maxims or even of constructing them. But of course Kant does sometimes speak, in the *Groundwork*, as if the categorical imperative were a test we applied to our maxims after formulating them. On my reading, what this test shows is whether we are actually succeeding in performing an act of free will. Obviously, this requires more argument, but it is implied by Kant's view that the moral law *just is* the law of a free will. For an explication of this point, see my "Morality as Freedom," CKE essay 6, especially pp. 162–7; and SN 3.2.3, pp. 97–8.

principle is that I make a law *for me*.[51] And this is a law that I am capable of obeying or disobeying. At this moment, now, I decide to work; at the next moment, at any moment, I will certainly want to stop. If I am to work I must *will* it—I must resolve to stay on its track. Timidity, idleness, and depression will exert their claims in turn, will attempt to control or overrule my will, to divert me from my work. Am I to let these forces determine my actions? At each moment I must say to them: "I am not you; my will is this work." Desire and temptation will also take their turns. "I am not a shameful thing like terror," desire will say, "follow me and your life will be sweet." But if I give in to each claim as it appears *I* will do nothing and I will not have a life. For to will an end is not just to cause it, or even to allow an impulse in me to operate as its cause, but, so to speak, to consciously pick up the reins, and make *myself* the cause of the end. And if I am to constitute *myself* as the cause of an end, then I must be able to distinguish between *my* causing the end and some desire or impulse that is "in me" causing my body to act. I must be able to see *myself* as something that is distinct from any of my particular, first-order, impulses and motives. So the reason that I must conform to the instrumental principle is that if I don't conform to it, if I *always* allow myself to be derailed by timidity, idleness, or depression, then I never really *will* an end. The *desire* to pursue the end and the desires that draw me away from it each hold sway in their turn, but *my will* is never active.[52] The distinction

---

[51] This remark may arouse Wittgensteinian worries, associated with the private language argument, about whether I can make a law (just) for me. As I understand it, Wittgenstein's argument does not show that I cannot make a language which only I in fact understand, but rather that I cannot make a language that only I can understand. Any language I make for myself must be in principle teachable to others. The parallel point here would be that I cannot bind myself to a hypothetical imperative which no one else could be bound by, and this does have ethical implications, for it means that I cannot make something my end whose value cannot be communicated to others. This provides one route to one of the conclusions of this essay, namely, that hypothetical imperatives cannot exist unless there are also principles of reason determining our ends, since it means that nothing can be my end unless I can explain the reasons why I value it to others, and to do this I must have some reasons for valuing it. I have explored these points, albeit tentatively, in Lecture 4 of *The Sources of Normativity* and in "The Reasons We Can Share: An Attack on the Distinction Between Agent-Relative and Agent-Neutral Values," CKE essay 10. I am grateful to Tamar Schapiro for alerting me to the possible relevance of this issue here.

[52] A story: Jeremy settles down at his desk one evening to study for an examination. Finding himself a little too restless to concentrate, he decides to take a walk in the fresh air. His walk takes him past a nearby bookstore, where the sight of an enticing title draws him in to look at a book. Before he finds it, however, he meets his friend Neil, who invites him to join some of the other kids at the bar next door for a beer. Jeremy decides he can afford to have just one, and goes with Neil to the bar. When he arrives there, however, he finds that the noise gives him a headache, and he decides to return home without having a beer. He is now, however, in too much pain to study. So Jeremy doesn't study for his examination, hardly gets a walk, doesn't buy a book, and doesn't drink a beer. If your reply is that Jeremy is a distractible adolescent, and following desire is not always like this, Kant's reply in turn will be that it is only an *accident* when it is not.

between my will and the operation of the desires and impulses in me does not exist, and that means that I, considered as an agent, do not exist. Conformity to the instrumental principle is thus constitutive of having a will, in a sense it is even what gives you a will.[53]

Now I need to clarify these remarks in one important way. In the above argument I appealed to the possibility of being tempted away from the end on another, temporally later occasion. But the argument does not really require the possibility of a temporally later occasion. It only requires that there be two parts of me, one that is my governing self, my will, and one that must be governed, and is capable of resisting my will. The possibility of resistance exists even now, on this occasion. The possibility of self-government essentially involves the possibility of its failure; and the principles of reason are therefore ineluctably normative.[54]

It is worth pointing out that an exactly parallel argument could be made about believing. We are neither inevitably inclined nor logically necessitated to believe the logical implications of our beliefs. The rational necessity of believing the logical implications of our beliefs cannot be explained by our plugging ourselves into a syllogism, like this: "No one who believes X also believes ∼X. I believe X, therefore I do not believe ∼X." The first premise of such a syllogism is false, and if we add the caveat—that no one who is rational believes both of these things—then the syllogism cannot provide a non-trivial explanation of why it is irrational to believe a contradiction. The rational necessity of believing the implications of our beliefs can only be explained if we regard believing itself as a normative act. To believe something is not to be in a certain mental state, but to make a certain commitment. It is, we might say, to be committed to constructing one's view of the world in one way rather than another.

And trying to persuade someone who actually doubted the instrumental principle that she should act on it would be like trying to persuade someone

---

[53] This is not the place to spell this thought out, but I also take the view I have put forward here to be essentially the same as the view that Plato advances in the *Republic*: namely, that the normativity of the principles of practical reason springs from, or reflects that fact that, the soul that does not follow them ultimately disintegrates. See also SN 3.3.1, pp. 100–2. If one of the central arguments of this essay is also correct—that there can be no instrumental norms unless there are also unconditional norms—then this lends support to Plato's claim that a completely unjust soul would also be incapable of "achieving anything as a unit" (R 1.351e–352a). David Velleman's remark that "unless we can commit ourselves today in a way that will generate reasons for us to act tomorrow, we shall have to regard our day-old selves as either beyond the control of today's decisions or as passive instruments of them" makes a similar point to the one I am making in the text—that without the power of commitment implicit in conformity to the instrumental principle, the autonomous self shatters into a sequence of time slices (see "On Deciding How to Decide," in *Ethics and Practical Reason*, p. 46).

[54] The last two paragraphs are lifted almost verbatim from section 1 of my Reply in SN, pp. 219–33; see especially pp. 230–1.

who actually doubted the principle of non-contradiction that he should believe it. It would be *exactly* like that. When Aristotle said that trying to persuade someone of the principle of non-contradiction is like trying to argue with a vegetable, he was not just being abusive (M 4.4 1006a15). A person who denies the principle of non-contradiction asserts that anything may follow from anything, and that therefore he is committed to nothing. And if he commits himself to nothing there is nothing he believes, and so no point from which to start the argument. This is why Aristotle says that if you can just get him to assert something, you have already won the argument. A person who rejects the principle of non-contradiction does not reject a particular restriction on his beliefs. Since he commits himself to nothing, he rejects the very project of having beliefs.[55] And parallel points can be made about someone who denies the instrumental principle. This is why it matters that, as I pointed out at the beginning, the instrumental principle can naturally be extended so that it seems to be the principle of self-conscious action quite generally. A rejection of the instrumental principle is a rejection of self-conscious action itself.[56]

On reflection, it looks as if no other solution is possible. We are trying to justify a norm, a principle, which claims to govern a certain activity. Why must we conform to the instrumental principle? Here we come to an important distinction, between norms that are constitutive of, and so internal to, the activities that they claim to govern, and norms that are external to those activities. If I say "bake a cake, and make it taste good" and you ask *why* you should make it taste good, we may think that you don't know what baking cakes is all about. But if I say "bake a cake, and make it ten feet high" and you ask *why* you should make it ten feet high, your question is perfectly in order. External norms give rise to further questions, and space for skeptical doubt. But if we can identify something as an internal norm, the question why you should conform to the norm answers itself. And some norms, unlike the norm of making cakes taste good, come not from the desired product of the activity, but from the nature of the activity itself. "Put one foot in front of the other" is a norm of walking, and "a sentence must contain both a subject and a verb"

---

[55] Peter Railton makes a parallel point—that someone who rejects the requirement that his beliefs be true is rejecting the project of having beliefs—in his "On the Hypothetical and Non-Hypothetical in Reasoning about Belief and Action," in *Ethics and Practical Reason*, pp. 56–9.

[56] Recent work in the philosophy of mind and action has been hampered by the presupposition that "belief" and "desire" are analogous states, the one demanding that the mind match the world, and the other demanding that the world match the mind. As the view in the text suggests, I think that the analog of belief is volition or choice; desire is more properly construed as the analog of perception. Of course, the view advanced in the text—that belief and choice must be understood as first-personal commitments if we are to make sense of rationality—has important implications for the philosophy of mind.

is a norm of linguistic action.[57] And yet, you can try to walk, fail to put one foot in front of another, and trip; and, as all of us who grade student papers know, you can try to take linguistic action, and yet founder for want of a verb. Although these norms are constitutive, they are still norms, and not *mere* descriptions of the activities in question. They are, as it were, instructions for performing the activities in question. And so there's no room to ask why you should follow them: if you don't put one foot in front of the other you will not be walking and you will get nowhere; if you don't have both a subject and a verb you will not be speaking and you will say nothing. The instrumental principle is, in this way, a constitutive norm of willing, of deliberate action. If you are going to act at all, then you must conform to it.[58] And, being human, you have no choice but to act.

Although of course I cannot give the argument for it here, it is important now to recall that, on Kant's view, the moral law *just is* the law of an autonomous will. To say that moral laws are the laws of autonomy is not to say that our autonomy somehow requires us to *restrict* ourselves in accordance with them, but rather to say that they are constitutive of autonomous action. Kant thinks that insofar as we are autonomous, we just *do* will our maxims as universal laws. What I have argued in this essay is that this is also true of the principle of instrumental reason.[59] Kant therefore has a *unified* account of practical rationality: to be guided by reason just is to be autonomous, to give laws to oneself.[60]

Now let me go back to my other point. I claimed before that what my argument showed was that hypothetical imperatives cannot exist without

---

[57] I owe the linguistic example to Barbara Herman.

[58] I also discuss the idea of constitutive norms in SN, section 2 of the Reply, pp. 234–7, and in "Self-Constitution in the Ethics of Plato and Kant", Essay 3 in this volume.

[59] If, contrary to the argument of this essay, the instrumental principle were the only norm constitutive of rational action, then rational action would essentially be production, and action that was good qua action would be action that achieved its end. Aristotle explicitly rejects that view in Book 6 of the *Nicomachean Ethics*, and this is part of his reason for thinking that actions are subject to special standards—ethical standards—that mere productions as such are not. For a discussion of the similarity between Aristotle and Kant on this point, see my "From Duty and for the Sake of the Noble: Kant and Aristotle on Morally Good Action," Essay 6 in this volume.

[60] This remark will naturally evoke the question what then becomes of Kant's claim that the moral law is synthetic, while the instrumental principle is analytic. In fact, on my reading, it may seem unclear what distinction is marked by those terms. In one way, I make it sound as if both the moral principle and the instrumental principle are analytic, for both are, if Kant's arguments succeed, constitutive of rational agency. In another way, I make it sound as if both the moral principle and the instrumental principle are synthetic, for both depend on the freedom inherent in the deliberative standpoint, and this parallels the way that synthetic principles of the understanding depend on the spacio-temporal structure of intuition. Choices are presented to us *in* freedom, just as objects are presented to us *in* space and time. On the other hand, Kant's more mundane point still holds: the necessity of taking the means is analytically derivable from our commitment to the end, while our commitment to the end is not in that way analytically derivable from anything. On my reading, however, this difference throws little important light on the source of their normativity. I am not certain what to say on this point, but

categorical ones, or anyway without principles which direct us to the pursuit of certain ends, or anyway without *something* which gives normative status to our ends. Does this account support that claim? The long answer to that question is another essay, but the short answer will do for now. If I am to will an end, to be and to remain committed to it even in the face of desires that would distract and weaknesses that would dissuade me, it looks as if I must have something to *say to myself* about why I am doing that—something better, moreover, than the fact that this is what I wanted yesterday. It looks as if the end is one that has to be *good*, in some sense that goes beyond the locally desirable. I have to be able to make sense to myself of effort and deprivation and frustration, and it is hard to see how the reflection that this *is* what I wanted yesterday can do that by itself, especially when I want something else today. I do not have an argument that shows that this is *impossible*. I suppose that through some heroic existentialist act, one might just take one's will at a certain moment to be normative, and commit oneself forever to the end selected at that moment, without thinking that the end is in any way good, and perhaps for no other reason than that some such commitment is essential if one is to have a *will* at all. But it is hard to see how a self-conscious being who must talk to herself about her actions could live with that solution. To that extent, the normative force of the instrumental principle does seem to depend on our having a way to say to ourselves of some ends that there are reasons for them, that they are good.[61] However that may be, though, even

I am inclined to think that my argument shows the distinction to be less important than Kant thought. I am indebted here to a discussion with Sidney Morgenbesser.

I also want to thank Sidney Morgenbesser, Joseph Raz, and Michael Thompson for pointing out a related and in a way more radical implication of the argument here, which is that it tends to break down the distinction between the different principles of practical reason described at the outset of this essay. If the argument of this essay is correct, moral or unconditional principles and the instrumental principle are both expressions of the basic requirement of giving oneself a law, and bring out different implications of that requirement. This lends support to Onora O'Neill's claim, in "Reason and Politics in the Kantian Enterprise," that the categorical imperative is the supreme principle of reason in general (see O'Neill, *Constructions of Reason*, essay 1). But it also raises issues about the distinguishability of different kinds of practical rationality and irrationality. I am inclined to think that the right thing to say about this parallels what I take to be the right thing to say about Aristotle's theory of the unity of the virtues. There is really only one virtue, but there are many different vices, different ways to fall away from virtue, and when we assign someone a particular virtue, what we really mean is that she does not have the corresponding vice. In a similar way, there is only one principle of practical reason, the categorical imperative viewed as the law of autonomy, but there are different ways to fall away from autonomy, and the different principles of practical reason really instruct us not to fall away from our autonomy in these different ways.

61 In his "On the Hypothetical and Non-hypothetical in Reasoning about Belief and Action," in *Ethics and Practical Reason*, pp. 62 ff, Peter Railton distinguishes between "High Brow" accounts of practical reasoning, according to which rational agents necessarily aim at the good, and "Low Brow" accounts, like Hume's, according to which rational agents may aim simply at the satisfaction of their

the heroic existentialist is committed to the view that an act of his own will is the source of a reason—and *that* reason cannot possibly be derived from the instrumental principle. So the conclusion in any case follows—the view that all practical reason is instrumental is incoherent, for the instrumental principle cannot stand alone.

4. Epilogue

I won't attempt to sum up the long and complex argument of this essay. But by way of conclusion, it may be useful to say something about where, if my argument is correct, it leaves us.[62] What do I suppose I've shown, and if I'm right, what is both still necessary and still possible in the theory of practical reason?

First, as I've just said, I think the argument shows that the instrumental principle cannot stand alone. Unless something attaches normativity to our ends, there can be no requirement to take the means to them. Of course, even if our ends lack such normativity, so long as they continue to be the ends we have in view, or the ones we effectively want most, we may certainly be inspired by instrumental thoughts to take the means to them: that is, instrumental thoughts may *cause* us to *want* to take those means. This is how it is with intelligent but non-rational animals, and, if Hume were right, this is how it would be with us. Indeed, this kind of instrumental *intelligence* seems pretty clearly to be a prerequisite for instrumental *rationality*, and, to that extent, this *is* how it is with us. But no account of a *requirement* of taking the means to our ends can be derived from the mere fact that we possess this kind of intelligence. If there is a principle of practical reason which *requires* us to take the means to our ends, then those ends must be, not merely ones that we happen to have in view, but ones that we have some reason to keep in view. There must be unconditional reasons for having certain ends, and, it seems, unconditional principles from which those reasons are derived. So now two

desires or ends. Because I have argued that the instrumental principle cannot stand alone, my argument favors High Brow views. The case of the heroic existentialist, however, shows that the sense in which it does so is rather thin. The heroic existentialist's ends are not merely the objects of his desires, but rather of his will, so he is not merely given them by nature: he has endorsed them, and to that extent he does see them as things he has reason to pursue. But since he has not endorsed them for any further reason, it would be a bit of a stretch to say that he thinks they are good. The claim in the text—that the heroic existentialist's position is hard to live with—shows why I think that my argument also gives rise at least to pressure towards a more substantively High Brow view. I say a little more about this in the Epilogue below.

[62] I have been pressed on this point by quite a few people who read or heard drafts of this essay, but I would particularly like to thank Allan Gibbard.

further questions arise: have I done anything towards showing whether there are any such principles, or what they would have to be like?

In one sense, the answer to the first question, whether I have shown that there are unconditional principles, is no. The conclusion of this essay is hypothetical: the argument shows that *if* there are any instrumental requirements, then there must be unconditional requirements as well. Conversely, if there are unconditional requirements to adopt certain ends, then there are also requirements to take the means to those ends, since a commitment to taking the means is what makes a difference between willing an end and merely wishing for it or wanting it or thinking that it would be nice if it were realized. But these arguments show only that unconditional and conditional requirements are mutually dependent. Complete practical normative skepticism is still an option, although its price is high—a point I will come back to.[63]

The answer to the second question—"does this argument show us anything substantive about the unconditional principles of practical reason, about what they would have to be like?"—is also no. At least I have shown nothing so far about the *content* of those principles. As far as the argument of this essay goes, they could be principles of prudence, or moral principles, or something else. In fact, as the possibility of the "heroic existentialist" I described at the end of section 3 shows, the reason to pursue the end which is needed to support the reason to take the means can be as thin and insubstantial as the agent's arbitrary will, his raw and unmotivated decision that he will take a certain end to be normative for himself, for no other reason than that he wills it so.

Yet even my heroic existentialist is autonomous, and this leads me to the more positive side of the argument: for I think that the argument of section 3 establishes not only that instrumental principles depend on unconditional ones, but also that particular instrumental requirements must be self-given laws, grounded in our autonomy. This raises the further question whether the unconditional reasons on which hypothetical reasons depend must also be, according to my argument, grounded in autonomy, or whether we could give, say, a dogmatic rationalist account of the unconditional reasons for having certain ends.[64] I believe that the argument does show that unconditional reasons, as well as hypothetical ones, must be grounded in autonomy. This is because the arguments of section 3, both those against dogmatic rationalism, and those in favor of the view that the principles of practical reason are constitutive norms of autonomy, are not specific to the principle of instrumental reason. They are concerned with the question how

---

[63] See also SN 4.4.1–4.4.2, pp. 160–4.
[64] Here again I would especially like to thank Allan Gibbard.

we can account for the normativity of practical reasons generally. The point of focusing on the instrumental principle is really just that this conclusion is, in its case, more unexpected and striking.

But if the argument shows that our unconditional principles must be laws of autonomy, then it brings us back home to the old Hegelian question: can any substantive requirements be derived from the mere fact of our autonomy? How much determinate content do the constitutive norms of autonomy have? And does this content coincide with, or include, morality? For this is the real question behind the familiar worry whether Kant's Formula of Universal Law has content. As I see it, then, only three positions are possible: either (i) the Kantian argument that autonomy commits us to certain substantive principles can be made to work; or (ii) we are left in the position of the heroic existentialist, who must ultimately define his will through acts of unconditional commitment that have no further ground; or (iii) complete practical normative skepticism is in order.

My own view is that the Kantian argument can be made to succeed, but that of course is another story—if I am right, it is *the* other story, where practical reason is concerned.[65] But it's worth saying something here about what's left to choose between existentialism and complete practical normative skepticism, if the Kantian project does not work out. And this brings us back to the question of the price of complete practical normative skepticism.

The argument of this essay makes a strong connection between having a will, and being bound by the principles of practical reason—or, at least, by the principle of instrumental reason. Conformity to the principle of instrumental reason—prescribing to oneself in accordance with this principle—is constitutive of having a will. And having a will, I believe, is constitutive of being a person. As I have argued in both section 2 and section 3, a person who does not conform to the instrumental principle becomes a mere location for the play of desires and impulses, the field of their battle for dominance over the body through which they seek satisfaction.[66] The price of complete practical normative skepticism, then, is nothing short of the loss of personal identity. The existentialist, however arbitrarily, does preserve his will and so his identity. It's important to see that the practical form in which I'm putting these claims—the skeptic *loses* his identity; the existentialist *preserves* his will—is

[65] The question whether there are substantive, constitutive norms of autonomy, and whether those coincide with moral norms, is a complex question that may be divided into a number of different parts, responsive to different ways in which the claim can be challenged. For an account of these different challenges, and of my own attempts to respond to them, see SN, section 1 of the Reply, pp. 220–2.

[66] See section 2, pp. 45–6 and section 3, pp. 58–60. This is part of the reason why Plato thinks that the soul completely ungoverned by reason ultimately becomes "tyrannical." See note 53 above and *Republic*, Book 9.

not a mistake or a literary conceit. With realism denied, the question becomes a practical one. It is not the question whether we really have such wills as are constituted by these principles, but whether we are to conduct ourselves so as to have such wills, by acting in accordance with these principles. The final answer, then, to the question—what gives the instrumental principle its normativity?—is this: conformity to the instrumental principle is an essential part of what makes you a person. There is no position from which you can reject the government of instrumental reason: for if you reject it, there is no you.[67]

5. Afterword, 2008

This complicated essay has particular resonance for me, because it set the agenda for much of the work I have done since. The moment it struck me to add footnote 53, in which I note the similarity between my view that the instrumental principle unifies and constitutes the will and Plato's view that justice unifies and constitutes the soul was the moment when I conceived the idea for my book *Self-Constitution: Agency, Identity, and Integrity*. But the purpose of this afterword is to notice the way in which I didn't quite come to the end of my thought in this essay—or rather, I did, but somehow I only managed to mention it as an afterthought in footnote 60. One of the conclusions I draw in this essay is that the instrumental principle cannot stand alone—there is no normative instrumental principle unless there are normative principles

[67] This essay leaves me with many debts. Final revisions were made while I was a Fellow at the University Center for Human Values in Princeton, for whose support I am deeply grateful. I discussed the essay or parts of the essay with audiences at the Twenty-First Annual Meeting of the Hume Society, with commentary by Charlotte Brown; the St Andrews conference on Ethics and Practical Reason, with commentary by Ralph Wedgwood; at the Central Division Meetings of the American Philosophical Association, with commentary by Allan Gibbard; to the Fellows Seminar at the Center for Human Values in Princeton, with commentary by Michael Thompson; to the Philosophy Departments at Bowling Green University, the University of California at Irvine, the University of California at Los Angeles, the University of Michigan, and the University of Reading; to the Columbia Legal Theory Workshop; and to the New York University Colloquium in Law, Philosophy, and Political Theory. I am grateful to all of these audiences, and my commentators especially. I also received generous and extremely helpful written comments from Annette Baier, Kurt Baier, Alyssa Bernstein, Barbara Herman, Brad Hooker, Peter Hylton, Arthur Kuflik, Andrews Reath, Tamar Schapiro, Allen Wood and the editors of *Ethics and Practical Reason*, in which it first appeared, Garrett Cullity and Berys Gaut. I also received excellent written comments in addition to their presented commentaries from Charlotte Brown and Allan Gibbard. I would also like to thank John Broome, Erin Kelly, Edward McClennan, Sidney Morgenbesser, John Rawls, Joseph Raz, and Michael Robins for useful remarks made in discussion, and Barbara Herman for extensive discussion in addition to her written comments. I thank all of these people for their incisive criticisms, many of which I have not been able to answer, and for their interest and support. Finally, I would like to reiterate my gratitude to the late Warren Quinn for pressing me to clarify Kant's account of the hypothetical imperative.

directing us to adopt certain ends. That, I now believe, is not the proper way to describe the conclusion. In fact, there are two things wrong with the way I described my conclusion in this essay. First, the instrumental principle is not a principle of practical reason that is separable from the categorical imperative: rather, it picks out an *aspect* of the categorical imperative: the fact that the laws of our will must be practical laws, laws that constitute us as agents by rendering us efficacious. Second, the categorical imperative is not a principle of practical reason that tells us to have certain ends, and that is separable from the principle that tells us to take the means to those ends. Practical principles govern the will, and a principle that governs the will must tell us to *do* something—even if it is just, indeterminately, to do whatever we can (legitimately) do in the pursuit of certain ends. It cannot tell us simply to *have* certain ends. To describe the categorical imperative as a principle governing ends is to fail to take the full force of Kant's view, in the *Critique of Practical Reason*, that to be a good in the normative sense—an "object of practical reason" as he calls it—is to be "an effect possible through freedom" (C2 5:57). So let me here state the conclusion of my argument properly. There is only one principle of practical reason, and it is the categorical imperative.

2

The Myth of Egoism

> Man does not pursue happiness. Only the Englishman does that.
>
> Nietzsche, *Twilight of the Idols*[1]

Introduction

Many philosophers believe there is a principle of practical reason that directs the rational agent to maximize the satisfaction of his own desires and interests. I will call this "the egoistic principle," and the person who believes in it an "egoist." Some philosophers believe that conformity to the egoistic principle is equivalent to the pursuit of happiness, or—if these are different—to the pursuit of the individual's own good. In the social sciences, especially economics, it is widely believed that some form of the egoistic principle is both normative and descriptive: that is, that it tells us not only how we should act, but also how, at least in clear-headed moments, we do act. Philosophers who endorse this view sometimes take the egoistic principle to be *definitive* of practical rationality, and therefore suppose that the way to show that we have "reason to be moral" is to show that conformity to moral requirements will somehow maximize the satisfaction of our own desires and interests.

This is not, of course, how the rationality of morality has been understood in either the Kantian or the rationalist tradition. Both Kant and Sidgwick, for instance, claimed that the moral principle is a principle of reason in its own right.[2] But they also accepted the idea that something like the egoistic principle

---

[1] Friedrich Nietzsche, *The Twilight of the Idols*, Maxims and Arrows, number 12. I found the quotation in *Twilight of the Idols and The Anti-Christ*, translated by R. J. Hollingdale, p. 23, though Hollingdale uses "strive after" rather than "pursue."

[2] Sidgwick is a utilitarian about the content of the moral principle, but his account of its normative foundation is rationalistic. See Henry Sidgwick, *The Methods of Ethics*, especially Book 3, chapter 13. Eighteenth-century rationalists, such as Clarke and Price, think that moral principles are rational principles, and tend to see the principle of rational self-interest as a branch of duty. For them the rival of morality is not rational self-interest but passion, vice, and corruption. But twentieth-century ethical rationalists like Ross and Prichard seem to hold the view that duty and interest are different forms of reason.

is a normative rational principle.[3] For Sidgwick, the egoistic principle is a rival to the moral principle of utility. Kant's various remarks about the nature of happiness are not entirely consistent, but at one point he defines it as "the sum of satisfaction of all inclinations" (G 4:399).[4] Kant thinks that the rationality of pursuing one's own happiness is represented by the imperative of prudence, which he sometimes appears to believe governs the conduct both of wicked people all the time and of good people once the demands of morality are satisfied.[5] But both those who think that the egoistic principle is definitive of rationality and those who think there is a separate rational principle of morality commonly believe that the egoistic principle has an advantage over the moral one. The egoistic principle, they suppose, more obviously meets the requirement of internalism—that is, the requirement that practical reasons must be capable of motivating us—since the egoistic principle essentially tells us to do what we want most. Even Kant believed that imperatives of prudence are hypothetical imperatives whose normativity can be established just as easily, and on essentially the same grounds, as that of instrumental principles. Contemporary egoists go one step further, and suppose that egoism is an expression of the instrumental principle itself. Egoism sees itself as a naturalistic view, which requires no extravagant assumptions about the metaphysics of the good or the possibility of pure practical reason.

[3] I say "something like the principle of egoism" because Sidgwick thinks of egoism as a principle of maximizing one's own pleasure or "agreeable consciousness" rather than of maximizing the satisfaction of one's desires. See Henry Sidgwick, *The Methods of Ethics*.

[4] Kant's remarks on happiness are not easy to reconcile with one another. Elsewhere in the *Groundwork* Kant says that happiness is "an ideal of the imagination" or "an indeterminate concept" because I cannot be sure which elements I should include in it in order to achieve "a maximum of well-being in my present condition and in every future condition" (G 4:418). In these passages Kant portrays the agent as wondering which ends to will as the elements of happiness—whether to will health, wealth, or knowledge, say. What seems to make these elements candidates for inclusion in the happy life is not that they are the objects of the agent's own inclinations but that they are the sorts of things that usually bring about, or constitute, "well-being." Sometimes these remarks are interpreted hedonistically—happiness is not the satisfaction of inclination but pleasure, to which the satisfaction of inclination is related causally. This is in part because Kant makes other remarks that seem to call for a hedonistic interpretation, most notably the parallel remarks in the *Critique of Practical Reason* (C2 5:23–26). In another passage, Kant defines happiness as an ideal in which "all inclinations unite in one sum" (G 4:399), suggesting that happiness is not just a maximum of satisfaction but rather an ideal of having *everything* one wants. And it is arguable (although I will not argue it here) that the argument of the Dialectic of the *Critique of Practical Reason* makes best sense if happiness is understood as success in attaining one's willed ends. These are all different ideas.

[5] That is, Kant thinks this if we suppose that the principle of self-love, which according to Kant governs the evil will, dictates something like the maximization of a person's satisfaction. Kant does sometimes seem to think of the principle of self-love that way, in particular in the opening sections of the *Critique of Practical Reason*. But at other times, in particular in the first section of the *Groundwork*, he seems to think of it more as a "wanton" principle, the principle of (unreflectively) following the desire of the moment. I have argued that this is how it should be understood in "From Duty and for the Sake of the Noble: Kant and Aristotle on Morally Good Action," Essay 6 in this volume.

In this essay I will present some reasons for doubting these familiar views. In section 1, I will examine some possible views about the normative foundations of the egoistic principle. I will argue that the view that egoism is a form of instrumentalism is based on a pair of false assumptions about the nature of practical rationality. When we abandon these assumptions, it becomes clear that the idea of a maximum of satisfaction is a substantive conception of the good. Egoism, I will argue, is essentially a rationalistic position: its normativity is grounded in a non-natural conception of the good, and its psychology requires the possibility of motivation by pure practical reason. In section 2, I will take a closer look at the content of this conception of the good. I will ask what exactly we must mean by a "maximum of satisfaction" if that idea is to ground a principle which is at once both plausibly rational and distinctively egoistic. I will argue that the relevant conception of the good is one recognizably grounded in the psychological assumptions of classical eighteenth-century British empiricism. Egoism therefore requires a familiar empiricist conception of the good, whose normativity can be defended only on rationalist grounds. It does not therefore follow that it is an incoherent position. It does however follow that it cannot be defended on any of the grounds that egoists usually offer in its favor.

1. Normative Foundations for the Egoistic Principle

1.1 *Instrumental Egoism*

Not everyone believes that any argument needs to be made for the normativity of the egoistic principle. Characteristically, philosophers and social scientists who believe that the egoistic principle is definitive of practical rationality also consider themselves to be instrumentalists about practical reason. That is, they endorse the view that the only principle of practical reason is the principle that directs us to take the means to our ends. For shorthand, I am going to call this position "instrumental egoism" and the person who believes it an "instrumental egoist." Instrumental egoists usually also believe that the instrumental principle itself is either obviously normative or does not need to be normative, since we are in fact motivated to act in accordance with it. Elsewhere I have argued, as against that last view, that the instrumental principle is normative and that an account of its normative force is therefore required.[6]

However that may be, the view that egoism is a form of instrumentalism is incoherent on its surface. The instrumental principle tells us only that we must take the means to our ends; it says nothing whatever about what our

---

[6] In "The Normativity of Instrumental Reason," Essay 1 in this volume.

ends should be. It therefore does not say either that we ought to pursue a maximum of satisfaction, or that we ought to prefer that maximum to the satisfaction of particular desires in cases of conflict. Since egoism requires us both to pursue a specific end and to prefer that end to all others, it has to go beyond the theory that all practical reasons are instrumental.

But instrumental egoists deny that the egoistic principle requires you to pursue a specific end. Happiness in the egoist's sense is supposedly not a specific end: it is just the maximum realization of the ends you already have. And more generally, all that the principles of rational choice do is apply some formal structure to the ends, whatever they might be, that are fed into its formulas. It is neutral about the good—or so its defenders claim.

I think that there is a mistake here like the one that John Stuart Mill makes in his proof of the principle of utility. Mill says that the only thing that "proves" that anything is desirable and therefore good is that it is desired. Each person desires his own happiness, so the sum of everyone's happiness is desirable and therefore good.[7] But, we may object, at least for all we know, no one desires the sum of everyone's happiness, so if only desire makes for desirability, what makes the sum desirable? Mill wants to mean that each *part* of it is desired, by the person whose happiness it is.[8] But of course a maximum does not include its parts in *that* way: maximizing happiness is not like adding one acre of ground to another that adjoins it. Conflicts are possible, and if the calculation turns out so, I may have to sacrifice my happiness in order to maximize the total, and then where is my part? In the same way, if my happiness consists in the maximum satisfaction of my desires, it is unlikely to include the satisfaction of each of my desires. And just as the individual person whose happiness is sacrificed for the sake of overall utility seems to have some right to protest, so also the individual desire whose satisfaction is sacrificed for the sake of overall happiness seems to have some right to protest. There are moments when the question "why should I be prudent?" is as much in need of an answer as its more famous cousin.

Why then does the instrumental egoist suppose that it is possible to believe both in instrumentalism and in egoism? How can he even imagine that these

---

[7] John Stuart Mill, *Utilitarianism* (1861; Indianapolis: Hackett Publishing Company, 1979), chapter 4, especially p. 34.

[8] Mill actually says this is what he meant in a letter to Henry Jones: "As to the sentence you quote from my *Utilitarianism*, when I said that the general happiness is a good to the aggregate of all persons I did not mean that every human being's happiness is a good to every other human being; though I think, in a good state of society & education it would be so. I merely meant in this particular sentence to argue that since A's happiness is a good, B's a good, C's a good, &c, the sum of all these goods must be a good." *The Later Letters of John Stuart Mill*, ed. Francis E. Mineka and Dwight N. Lindley, Volume 3, p. 1414. I owe the reference to Charlotte Brown and Jerome Schneewind.

two positions are compatible? The instrumental egoist has to believe both that people do in fact desire maximum satisfaction and also that no real conflict can possibly arise between a person's desire for this maximum and her desires for particular things. One way to reach that conclusion is to suppose that satisfaction itself is the *only* thing which people want for its own sake, and that all desired objects are wanted as mere means to satisfaction. That is the view famously attacked as incoherent by Bishop Butler, on the grounds that an object cannot give us satisfaction unless we want it for its own sake.[9] I propose to set it aside here, not merely on the good Bishop's authority, but also because it so *obviously* involves a substantive, and controversial, conception of the good. I believe that the more common assumption behind instrumental egoism is that what a person *really* wants, deep down, just *are* the things that are consistent with or part of her happiness. According to this view, once you have understood that something would be detrimental to your happiness, you will cease to desire it. Our desires, when we are clearheaded, accord with prudence.

With that idea in mind, the instrumental egoist treats the possibility that someone might desire something inconsistent with her happiness as if it were exactly on a par with the possibility that she might miscalculate or simply make a factual error. Suppose someone mistakes white vinegar for vodka. "You do not *really want* to drink *that*," we say to her; and she does not; we are absolutely right. The instrumental egoist must suppose that it is true in *just that way* that the addict does not *really want* the heroin, or that the angry person does nor *really want* to break the window, or that the adulterer does not *really want* to have the affair that will destroy his marriage. In these cases, the instrumental egoist must say, the person's mind is so clouded by addiction, rage, or lust that he is unable to identify what he really wants.

But considered as a psychological hypothesis, the idea that human beings "really" have all and only these domesticated desires seems not only false but hilarious. As Bishop Butler wrote in his *Sermons*:

Men daily, hourly sacrifice the greatest known interest to fancy, inquisitiveness, love, or hatred, or any vagrant inclination.[10]

Someone who says the addict does not "really want" the heroin must be using "want" in some specialized sense, for in one familiar sense he very obviously does want it.

[9] Joseph Butler, *Fifteen Sermons Preached at the Rolls Chapel*, reprinted in *Five Sermons Preached at the Rolls Chapel and A Dissertation Upon the Nature of Virtue*, Sermon 4 (originally Sermon 11), especially pp. 47–9.
[10] Joseph Butler, in the Preface to the *Fifteen Sermons Preached at the Rolls Chapel*, reprinted in *Five Sermons Preached at the Rolls Chapel and A Dissertation Upon the Nature of Virtue*, p. 21.

In my view, if we are tempted to think that the addict does not really want the heroin, that temptation must be *based on* our belief that it is irrational for him to want it, together with a certain conception of rationality. It is the hallmark of a rational agent, one may suppose, that his desires are directed and reshaped by his rational deliberations. So if the addict were thinking rationally, he would not want the heroin. But even if that is right, we cannot allow the egoist to posit that this reshaping has happened before the deliberation ever *starts*: that is, that his "real" desires somehow *already* accord with the results of his deliberations.

This is the first of the two false assumptions about practical rationality that I mentioned at the outset of this essay: the view that practical reasoning really just serves to uncover our "real" desires. On this assumption, what we call "practical reason" is actually a form of theoretical reasoning about our psychology. This view is not one to which people openly subscribe, but rather an unconscious assumption which shows up in the way they argue, and we will see it at work again later on.[11] But practical deliberation is not aimed at psychological knowledge: its conclusions are not just *reminders* of what we already want, deep down. It is rather a way of determining what is good for us, what we ought to want.

In any case, the belief that it is irrational for someone to want heroin cannot be *based* on the instrumental principle, since is a belief about what his ends should be. So if the instrumental egoist asserts that the addict does not "really want" the heroin, there must be a substantive view about what it is rational to want hiding under the cover of that word "really." This is what enables the instrumental egoist to imagine that the only really *practical* reasoning going on here is instrumental.

This is even clearer when the egoist reverts to the use of that dangerous word "interests." Until now I have been talking about desires and interests as if these ideas were interchangeable, but in fact this is correct only if we take the word "interest" in a rather peculiar sense. When we say that someone "has a desire" for something, we are naturally understood as talking about an item in his natural psychology, an urge, or an attraction, or a disposition to find the object pleasurable, or something of that sort.[12] We may then see the principle

---

[11] The assumption that practical reasoning reveals our "real" desires to us is an expression of romantic metaphysics in the most literal sense, and it is tempting to speculate that its influence on Anglo-American philosophy springs from Hegel. The distinction that Aristotle and Kant make between theoretical and practical reason is elided by the assumption. But it may also be an expression of the empiricist view, found for example in Hume, that "reason" just is "the discovery of truth and falsehood" (T 3.1.1,458).

[12] The word "desire" is a source of confusion in philosophy because of the many ways it is used. The idea voiced in the text—that "desire" refers to an item in one's natural psychology—might

of maximizing satisfaction as a principle of naturalistic construction, which applies a maximizing formula to certain items regarded as naturally or prima facie good, with the individual's happiness or overall good coming out as the result of the exercise. Let me call that result "the maximum compossible set" of the objects of desire. The items from which the set is constructed must have some sort of prima facie normative *weight*—given by how strongly you desire them, for example—so that we can perform a maximizing operation. But they do not yet have what we might call a normative *ranking*—that is, we have not yet decided which of them you ought to pursue in preference to which. It is the point of the maximizing operation to *assign* them a normative ranking. It is important not to get confused about this: the prima facie weights do not settle the question of the normative ranking, since, for instance, a very strong desire may have to be suppressed (given a low or negative ranking) for the sake of maximizing the total. Now when we say that someone "has an interest" in something, we may not be referring to a natural psychological item, or at least not to one not yet normatively ranked, for the phrase "has an interest" is also used in a way that already implies a normative ranking. In this sense, when we say that someone "has an interest" in something, we imply *that reason favors his pursuing it over other options*. If we suppose that reason favors the satisfaction of those desires whose objects fit together into the maximum compossible set, then *those* are the desires in whose satisfaction you "have an interest," and the idea of maximizing the satisfaction of your *interests* just says the same thing twice over. This is why the word "interest" is dangerous. The normative use of the word "interest" gives the formulation "maximizing the satisfaction of one's interests" an agreeably rational ring, but in fact the egoist cannot mean "interest" in this normative sense without reducing his principle to an empty tautology.

Some rational choice theorists like to use the word "preference" (maximize the satisfaction of one's preferences) but in my view this is even more misleading, for "preference" carries the idea of a comparative ranking on its *surface*. Of course it may not be a comparative *normative* ranking, but if that is not what it refers to then it must refer to a comparative natural ranking, perhaps one based on the comparative strength of desire. So why not say so? If the idea of egoism is that we can generate the notion of a person's good or of his happiness simply by performing a maximizing operation on some naturally existing items, it is really better to keep this clearly before our minds

---

be disputed, or anyway deemed misleading, by philosophers who think desire is a response to the perception of reasons. The instrumental egoist, however, needs to understand the idea of desire naturalistically, since he thinks there are only instrumental reasons.

by calling those items "desires." But if we stick to "desire" and keep in view that we are talking about some natural psychological items, then the claim that a person's "real desires" are directed to all and only those things that are consistent with his happiness seems patently false.

At this juncture it may be useful to review the points I have just made. Instrumental egoism is inconsistent on its surface. I have suggested that what enables people even to imagine that it might be right is that they make an implicit assumption—the assumption that people "really want" the things that make them happy, that is, that accord with their maximal satisfaction. Reasoning about how to get what you ("really") want and reasoning about how to promote your maximal satisfaction therefore coincide. This assumption, I have argued, is in turn based on a false view of the role of practical reason—the view that practical deliberation "uncovers" our real desires—together, of course, with certain background assumptions about what those real desires must be.

But there is a second and even more serious problem with the assumption behind instrumental egoism. If it were true that we really desired all and only those things that are consistent with our happiness, egoistically understood, then we would automatically conform to the dictates of the egoistic principle, not because it is rational to do so, but because we would naturally want to. If someone did act against his own best interests, this would not be because he failed to conform his will to the egoistic principle, but rather because he was making some mistake in his calculations, and did not understand where his interests really lay. But if this were so, what need would there be for an egoistic principle of *practical* reason?

The point I am making turns on the distinction between making a mistake and true practical irrationality—that is, violating a principle of practical reason. When a person's action is based on a mistake, the person does the wrong thing, objectively speaking, but that does not show that the person is truly irrational. A person who adds a little dry vermouth and some olives to a glass of white vinegar, believing it to be a glass of vodka, is not doing anything irrational, for by her own lights the action makes perfectly good sense. There is nothing amiss with her motivation, nothing, if I may put it this way, wrong with her will: it is only her factual judgment that needs correcting. According to the assumption behind instrumental egoism, a person who desires to take heroin must suppose that it is consistent with his happiness to take it; otherwise he could not even imagine that he really desires it. But that means he *is* conforming to the egoistic principle, by his own lights. His problem therefore is not true practical irrationality, but simply mistaken judgment. The mistake may have its source in his addiction—it may somehow be caused by the addiction—but what the addiction causes is not practical irrationality; it is bad theoretical judgment. But if people cannot ever be guilty of violating the egoistic principle by their own lights, then it is not a rational principle. It is simply a description of the inevitable effect that a certain kind of judgment has on the human will: prove to us that something is contrary to our happiness and we will forthwith cease to desire it.

This is the second of the two false assumptions about practical rationality that stand behind instrumental egoism: the view that rational principles are *essentially* descriptions of the *effects* that certain judgments have on the will. This assumption is also behind the commonly held view, mentioned earlier, that the instrumental principle is either already normative or does not need to be normative, because people actually are motivated to take the means to their ends. According to this view, if someone fails to take the means to an end, we are entitled to conclude either that he does not really want the end after all, or that he is making a mistake about how to promote it. But prove to him that the action will promote his end, and he will forthwith be motivated to do it. So no one ever violates the requirement of instrumental reason by his *own* lights. The principle of instrumental reason turns out to be essentially a description of the *effect* that means/end judgments have on the human will.[13]

The trouble with this conception of rationality is that it cannot support the normative use of "ought." For according to this view, if I say to you "you really ought to see a dentist about that tooth" all that I mean—*all*—is that if you came to understand that a visit to the dentist is essential to the achievement of an end requisite for your happiness, you would in fact be motivated to go. The rational judgment is not really a recommendation, but rather a sort of hypothetical prediction. And it is *not* that I predict you would be motivated to go if you understood that going would promote your happiness because you would then see that you have a *reason* to go. It is not *that*, for on this view the claim that you have a reason to go *just amounts to* the claim that if you made the judgment you would in fact be motivated to go. So it turns out that what looks like the normative "ought" is really just a version of the "ought" of

---

13 The two false assumptions may be thought related: it is because the instrumental egoist supposes that the conclusion of practical reasoning uncovers your real desire that he supposes it will cause a motive in you. But I am not certain of this. Consider the theoretical analogues of the two false assumptions. The analog of the first assumption would seem to be the view that logical reasoning is actually a sort of empirical reasoning that uncovers our "real" beliefs—or, alternatively, a Platonic view that makes all a priori reasoning a matter of recollection. The analog of the second false assumption is that logical reasoning is a matter of the (merely causal) effect of certain conjunctions of judgments on the mind. The first assumption seems to me to be more commonly made about practical reasoning than about theoretical reasoning, and made as a way of making all reasoning seem theoretical. But as I will suggest later, I think the second assumption is commonly made about both kinds of reasoning. This makes me think the two errors may have separate sources.

expectation. On this view, saying of someone on the brink of toothache that he ought to go to the dentist is exactly like saying of someone who is late that he ought to be home by now. Given human nature, we would have predicted that the person on the brink of toothache would be motivated to go to the dentist; just as given the distance, we would have predicted that the person who left the office an hour ago would be home about now. If these predictions turn out false we know that something has gone wrong. But what has gone wrong can no more properly be described as a failure of practical reason in the first case than in the second.

The inadequacy of the view is clear from this fact: there may be many principles that accurately describe the way human beings are characteristically motivated. And this conception of rationality leaves us with no way of distinguishing which ones are principles of reason and which ones are not. We *can* reliably predict that people will be motivated to take the means to their ends. But suppose that we also could reliably predict that when criticized people will cry and stamp their feet. We would not be tempted to think that it follows that such behavior is rationally required of us.

1.2 *The Imperative of Prudence*

We might at first think that a better account of the normativity of the egoistic principle is available in the *Groundwork of the Metaphysics of Morals*. Kant recognized both that the imperative of prudence, as he called it, is not the same as the instrumental principle and that it stands in need of a normative foundation. In the second section of the *Groundwork*, Kant proposes that there are three kinds of practical imperatives. First, there are rules of skill or technical imperatives—that is, instrumental principles. Second, there are counsels of prudence or pragmatic imperatives, which direct us to pursue our own happiness, identified, as I mentioned earlier, with "the sum of satisfaction of all inclinations" (G 4:399). And finally, of course, there are commands of morality, or categorical imperatives (G 4:416).

Kant appears to leave room for the normativity of prudence, for in the *Groundwork* at least he seems to believe that we do not inevitably follow imperatives of prudence by our own lights. One of the four examples he uses in the first section of the *Groundwork* to explicate the difference between acting from duty and acting from inclination concerns a man who is tempted to imprudence; when prudence fails to govern him, morality steps in. Kant says:

To assure one's happiness is a duty (at least indirectly); for, want of satisfaction with one's condition . . . could easily become a great *temptation to transgression of duty*. But in addition, all people have already . . . the strongest and deepest inclination to happiness because it is just in this idea that all inclinations unite in one sum. However, the precept of happiness is often so constituted that it greatly infringes upon some inclinations, and yet one can form no determinate and sure concept of the sum of satisfaction of all inclinations under the name of happiness. Hence it is not to be wondered at that a single inclination, determinate both as to what it promises and as to the time in which it can be satisfied, can often outweigh a fluctuating idea, and that a man—for example one suffering from the gout—can choose to enjoy what he likes and put up with what he can since, according to his calculations, on this occasion at least he has not sacrificed the enjoyment of the present moment to the perhaps groundless expectation of a happiness that is supposed to lie in health. But even in this case, when the general inclination to happiness did not determine his will . . . there is still left over here . . . a law, namely to promote his happiness not from inclination but from duty; and it is then that his conduct first has properly moral worth. (G 4:399)

Unfortunately—but interestingly—the example is muddled. Kant portrays the man as falling into doubt about whether the imperative of prudence that forbids the unhealthy treat is well-founded or not, being based on "the perhaps groundless expectation of a happiness that is supposed to lie in health." Obviously, if there were *good reason* to doubt whether forgoing the unhealthy treat is a means to happiness, then the man's resistance to the imperative that forbids the unhealthy treat would to that extent be *rational*. And in that case the indirect duty to pursue one's happiness would no more forbid the unhealthy treat than the imperative of prudence does. It seems likely that what Kant is really thinking is that the man has a tendency to rationalization. "Oh, how does anyone know that health really leads to happiness anyway?" he says to himself, licking his lips at the thought of the treat. And then the thought of his duty stiffens his resolve. Even then it is not clear how exactly the example is supposed to work, since the rationalization works against the thought of duty in the same way it works against the thought of prudence. But at all events the case does show that Kant thought one could resist the normative force of prudence when that force "infringes upon some inclinations." And indeed this is necessary to his account, for Kant recognizes that a principle cannot be normative unless it is possible to violate it. Imperatives are addressed to creatures who can violate them and so they are normative:

All imperatives are expressed by an *ought* and indicate by this the relation of an objective law of reason to a will that by its subjective constitution is not necessarily determined by it . . . They say that to do or omit something would be good, but they say it to a will that does not always do something just because it is represented to it that it would be good to do that thing. (G 4:413)

How then is the normativity of prudence to be established?

Rules of skill, or principles of instrumental reason, are hypothetical imperatives, taking the form "if you will this, then you must also will that." According to Kant, their normative force is based on the principle that "whoever wills the end also wills (insofar as reason has decisive influence on his actions) the indispensably necessary means to it that are within his power" (G 4:417). This principle, Kant claims, is analytic, because "in the volition of an object as my effect, my causality as acting cause, that is, the use of means, is already thought" (G 4:417). To will something is not merely to desire it, but to set yourself to bring it about—that is, to cause it—and so willing something essentially involves determining yourself to use the means to it.

Imperatives of prudence, Kant claims, are also hypothetical imperatives, arising from the fact that we necessarily will happiness. He says:

There is, however, *one* end that can be presupposed as actual in the case of all rational beings . . . and therefore one purpose that they not merely *could* have but that we can safely presuppose they all actually *do have* by a natural necessity, and that purpose is *happiness*. (G 4:415)

And therefore:

If only it were as easy to give a determinate concept of happiness, imperatives of prudence would agree entirely with those of skill and would be just as analytic. For it could be said, here just as there: who wills the end also wills (necessarily in conformity with reason) the sole means to it that are within his control. (G 4:417–418)

We run into problems, however, when we try to make out what Kant could possibly mean when he claims that we "have" the end of happiness by a natural necessity. He could mean either that we necessarily *will* happiness, or that we necessarily *desire* it, but there are difficulties either way. On the one hand, if he means that we necessarily *will* happiness—that is, we necessarily choose it, when no moral obligation prevents us—the claim seems to be contrary to his own views about our essential freedom of the choice of ends. In the *Metaphysics of Morals* Kant says:

An end is the object of the choice (of a rational being), through the representation of which choice is determined to bring this object about.—Now, I can indeed be constrained by others to perform *actions* that are directed as means to an end, but I can never be constrained by others *to have an end*; only I can *make* something my end. (MM 6:381)

Here Kant argues that adopting an end is an internal action to which we cannot be compelled; hence it must be a free act. Although his contrast here is between freedom and constraint by other people, the claim that "only I can make something my end" seems equally to exclude ends determined by nature. More generally, Kant's argument for the moral law starts from the definition of a free will as one that is not determined by any law outside itself, and involves the premise that we must regard ourselves, insofar as we are rational, as having free wills. We choose maxims for ourselves autonomously, and our ends are chosen as part of our maxims. The idea that we necessarily will happiness seems inconsistent with all of this.[14]

On the other hand, if all Kant means is that we cannot help but *desire* happiness, it is puzzling that he singles out a special sort of imperative to guide our pursuit of this desired end. For in the first place, there are many things, most notably the satisfaction of our physical needs, which we cannot help but desire, but Kant does not single out special imperatives for them. In the second place, and more importantly, mere desires for ends do not support hypothetical imperatives, which are based on the principle that whoever *wills* an end wills the means, and therefore cannot be derived from mere desires. Desiring an end does not analytically involve the thought of "my causality as acting cause," in the way that willing an end does. And in the third place, the mere *desire* for happiness would be only one desire among others, which would have to compete for our attention with other, more particular, desires and ends. In fact, even if Kant did have an argument to show that we necessarily *will* happiness as an end, it would not automatically follow that we should always rationally prefer it to more particular ends; nor does Kant give any argument at all to that effect. Happiness would at most be established as one end among others. And if there were a principle of practical reason, an imperative, directing us both to *have* happiness as an end and to *prefer* happiness to every other end, that principle would seem to lie somewhere in between Kant's two categories of hypothetical and categorical imperatives. Unlike a hypothetical imperative, it would command us to pursue a certain end no matter what else we happened to want; but unlike a categorical one,

---

14 In "Korsgaard on Choosing Non-Moral Ends," Hannah Ginsborg argues that Kant's view is that we are free to act against our happiness only when the moral law demands it. There are certainly passages in his works that can be taken to support that view. But I do not see how it can be squared with the claim that we "act under the idea of freedom." Admittedly, the foundational argument in the *Critique of Practical Reason* is often thought to be different from, and to represent a rejection of, the foundational argument of the *Groundwork*, and in the second *Critique* Kant does not appeal to the thesis that we act under the idea of freedom. In fact he argues there that our freedom is revealed to us only by the experience of moral obligation: we know we are free to act against even our strongest desire, since we know that we can do what we ought (C2 5:29–31). Morality is the *ratio cognoscendi* of freedom, although freedom is the *ratio essendi* of morality (C2 5:4 n.). But the freedom thus revealed must be general. For even here Kant argues that freedom is the *ratio essendi* of morality—the moral law applies to us because we have free will, not the reverse. For more on these arguments, see my "Morality as Freedom," CKE essay 6 and "Motivation, Metaphysics, and the Value of the Self: A Reply to Ginsborg, Guyer, and Schneewind."

it would hold only conditionally, since our pursuit of this end would have to give way to moral considerations.[15]

Of course Kant might after all mean that we always do pursue happiness, by our own lights, at least when not forbidden by duty. Later he seems to come around to this view, for in *the Metaphysics of Morals*, after arguing that "what everyone wants unavoidably, of his own accord, does not come under the concept of duty" (MM 6:386), Kant says:

Since it is unavoidable for human nature to wish for and seek happiness, that is, satisfaction with one's state, so long as one is assured of its lasting, this is not an end that is also a duty. (MM 6:387)[16]

But if we cannot have a duty to pursue our own happiness because we inevitably do pursue it, then neither can there be an imperative of prudence, for the same reason. So this leaves us back where we were.

1.3 *A Kantian Conception of Rationality*

Perhaps it will seem that in making this argument I am rejecting the very idea of a theory of rationality that is at once both normative and descriptive. For I am insisting that if we necessarily do conform to a certain principle, then it cannot be normative. But the lesson need only be that that correlation must be understood in a different way. We can suppose that rational principles are descriptive of rational procedures or activities, and of human beings insofar as we engage in those procedures or activities. This is a view most naturally associated with Kant. Kant's account of the imperative of prudence in the *Groundwork* does not yet, in my view, express his mature conception of rationality.[17]

Kant views reason as the *active* aspect or dimension of the human mind, that is, as its power of self-determination. The principles of reason describe the active contribution of the mind to belief and to action. They are procedures we follow in determining our beliefs and actions, insofar as we are rational. A comparison may help to show why this makes them both normative and descriptive. The principles of English grammar are both normative and

---

[15] This discussion is largely lifted from my "Motivation, Metaphysics, and the Value of the Self: A Reply to Ginsborg, Guyer, and Schneewind."

[16] It is unclear whether Kant means to imply that the duty to pursue happiness can only be an indirect one (not an end in itself, but only a means to the avoidance of temptation) or whether he has changed his mind about the duty to pursue one's own happiness altogether. But either way he now seems to think we do inevitably pursue happiness.

[17] I make a similar argument—that Kant's account of instrumental imperatives in the *Groundwork* does not represent his mature view—in "The Normativity of Instrumental Reason," Essay 1 in this volume.

descriptive because they describe procedures we follow in constructing our sentences insofar as we are speaking English.[18] To speak English is essentially to be guided by those principles; we may say that being guided by those principles is constitutive of speaking English. In the same way, the most general function of the mind is to think, and to think is essentially to be guided by the principles of logic. According to Kant, the mind is also faced with the more specific task of constructing a unified conception of the world from the phenomena, and to do this is to be guided by the principles of the understanding. And the mind is faced with the task of choice or volition, of the determination of our actions; and to will is to be guided by the principles of practical reason.

The important thing to emphasize about this conception of rationality is that rational principles describe activities: they tell us what the rational mind as such *does* with certain items that are given to it, rather than merely describing the effect which those items will have on the mind. The principles of logic and the canons of evidence describe what the thinker as such *does* with the incoming evidence: arriving at a belief through reasoning is an active process, a process by which the mind determines itself to a conclusion. Rational principles may be seen as *directions* in the most literal way. Given P and *if P then Q* infer Q: modus ponens is a direction for thinking. We can predict with some confidence that the rational mind when confronted with this argument will believe Q, but it is certainly not inevitable. And if the mind does believe Q when faced with the argument, that is an *effect* of its rationality, not the *essence* of its rationality. Inferring Q from P and *if P then Q* is no more the same as merely being caused to believe it than jumping off a cliff is the same as merely being caused to fall off of it, for the aspect of self-determination is missing. What makes your beliefs logical is not that *they* conform to the rules of logic, for you could believe P, Q, and *If P then Q*, and never notice any connection between them. Nor is it that believing the premises causes you to believe the conclusion, for this too could happen without your notice. What makes your belief logical is that you *put* the two premises together in the way required by modus ponens, and so *cause yourself* to believe it. In the same way, the principles of practical reason describe what the *will* as such does with certain items, say beliefs and desires, that are given to it. Volition, the determination of our actions, is an active process, a process by which we cause ourselves to act. It is not just something that happens in us or to us. The instrumental principle, for instance, on this view, is an *instruction* for willing: if you are to *will* the end, rather than merely wishing for it or wanting it, and these are the means, then you must determine yourself to take these.

[18] I owe the example to Barbara Herman.

Now it may seem as if there is something paradoxical about this conception of rationality. The principles of practical reason govern action. Yet I am claiming that reasoning *itself* must be seen as a kind of action, in order to capture the element of self-determination that is essential to volition. If reasoning must be seen as a kind of action, what captures the element of self-determination that is essential to reasoning itself? Do we need some deeper sort of rational activity that in turn captures that? A regress obviously threatens. We are here confronting one of the deepest problems of philosophy, the problem of identifying the exact nature of the self-determination that distinguishes actions and activities from mere events. This problem rests behind the persistent philosophical temptation to try to reduce both action and reason, as forms of self-determination, to special forms of causation. One expression of that temptation is what I have identified as the second false assumption about rationality, the view that the principles of reason merely describe the effects that certain judgments have on the will or the mind.

Kant offers us a way to block the regress. To explain it, it will be helpful to distinguish between a weaker and a stronger version of the Kantian conception of rationality. According to both versions, the principles of reason are principles of rational activity, principles that describe the mind's active contribution to thinking or volition. The stronger version adds a further thought, namely, the thought that we can derive the *content* of the principles of reason from this very conception of what they are. The principles of reason, on this view, are not just principles that direct us to do this or that, but principles whose content captures the very essence of activity or self-determination. Consider once more the way I formulated the instrumental principle a moment ago: if you are to *will* the end, rather than merely wishing for it or wanting it, then you must determine yourself to take the means. Seen this way, the instrumental principle is intended to capture something about the very essence of volition, in particular what makes volition different from mere desire. You are not *willing* the end at all unless you determine yourself to cause the end to come about, that is, to use the means. The categorical imperative, in its universal law formulation, wears this thought on its face, for what it tells us to do is to give ourselves a law—that is to say, what it tells us to do is to determine ourselves. The Kantian arguments for these principles are meant to establish that you succeed in exercising the self-determination that is the essence of volition only to the extent that you follow these principles.[19]

---

[19] I say "to the extent" because it is important to this account that self-determination can be partial and therefore defective. Something must count as trying to determine yourself and failing, for example willing the end but failing to will the means. Otherwise it will be impossible to violate practical

Now let me return to a point I made earlier. I argued that if we support instrumental egoism with the view that people do not "really want" things that are inconsistent with their happiness, we must say that people who pursue ends which are in fact inconsistent with their happiness are guilty of mistake, of bad theoretical judgment. But I also said that the mistake might be caused by the agent's condition—by addiction or rage or lust, for instance. Whereas the instrumental egoist regards these conditions as causes of confusion, making people unable to see what they really want, the Kantian will say that they are, directly, causes of true practical irrationality—or to put the same point another way, conditions that undermine our power of self-determination. We do not have to suppose, as the instrumental egoist does, that the addict's condition makes it impossible for him to *understand* that there is good reason for him not to take heroin. We can say that his addiction makes it impossible, or maybe just hard, for him to guide himself in accordance with that reason. Or rather, if we do imagine that he says to himself, at least at the very moment when he takes the stuff, that it is consistent with his happiness—for I am inclined to think that something like that does happen—we can see that as *rationalization*. That is, if he says to himself that just now, this time, just once, it really is good for him, or anyway not bad, to take the drug, we can see that as an attempt to conceal his failure of self-determination or self-control from himself, rather than seeing it as a mistake that causes behavior which is not actually irrational by his own lights. So the order of what happens is different. The instrumental egoist says that the addiction causes an error of judgment which in turn leads to conduct which only looks practically irrational from the outside, but which is not really so by the addict's own lights. The Kantian says instead that the addiction causes genuinely, inwardly, practically irrational conduct—causes a defect in the will—which the agent then scrambles to *rationalize* by the invocation of the mistaken belief.

Apart from the fact that this second way of seeing the situation is consistent with the possibility of practical reason, while the first way is not, the second way seems to me to be getting things the right way around. In fact there is room here for an interesting account of what rationalization is and why it

---

imperatives: you will either determine yourself successfully or not at all. To see the importance of this, consider the comparison to language again. If you violate the rules of English, there is a sense in which we might say "You are not speaking English." But in another sense, if you were not speaking English, the rules of English would not apply to you and so you would have done nothing amiss. If not speaking English at all were the only alternative to speaking English perfectly, the rules of English would not be normative, since the moment they failed to be followed they would also fail to apply. But of course that is not how it is: you can certainly violate a rule of English and still be, recognizably, trying to speak English. What matters is that your efforts at speaking are generally guided, even if unsuccessfully, by the rules. This is what makes normativity possible.

is so pervasive. Because we are self-conscious, we are faced with the task of self-determination, both of our beliefs and of our actions. It is a task that requires a degree of vigilance and self-command that is often beyond our powers. The need to maintain the fiction that we are always in control, both in our own eyes and in those of others, is a deep human drive. Think of the difficulty older people have in admitting they have dozed off for a moment. Or the temptation to make an awkward physical movement look as if it were some sort of deliberate step. Or the temptation, in the heat of argument, to defend a thesis just because it has somehow fallen out of your mouth, and someone else has objected to it. Get a person to do some odd action under the influence of post-hypnotic suggestion, and then ask him why he did it. He will not say "I do not know." He will make up a plausible story and tell himself as well as you that that is what he had in mind. The use of rationalization to conceal our failures of self-determination in thought and action from ourselves is all of a piece with these things, an attempt to maintain the appearance of perfect self-command.

1.4 *Implications of the Kantian Conception for Egoism*

In this essay I am not going to argue for the stronger version of the Kantian conception of rationality, the version that derives the content of rational principles from the very idea of self-determination. But I cannot resist mentioning one ramification of that view for rational egoism. I hope that you can at least see how someone might be tempted to think that the categorical and hypothetical imperatives are principles that capture the very essence of self-determination. But it is not even remotely plausible to suppose that *the egoistic principle* captures the very essence of self-determination. That is, it is not plausible to think that you only succeed in exercising self-determination if you aim to maximize the satisfaction of your desires; or that you are not really willing at all unless *what you will* is maximum satisfaction. If we accept the stronger version of the Kantian conception, then the egoistic principle simply seems to be *the wrong sort of thing* to be a principle of practical reason. To put the point in somewhat more old-fashioned Kantian terms, the egoistic principle is concerned with the *content* of the will, not with the very *form* of willing.

But as I said, I do not propose to argue for the stronger version of the Kantian conception here. I do mean to argue, however, that in order to get the normative "ought" we need to see the principles of reason, as Kant does, as principles that describe mental activities, and not just the effects of judgments on the will. But even this weaker version has important implications for the way we conceive of rational egoism. For if we accept it, there are certain elements of Kantian moral psychology that we must accept along with it.

In Kantian moral psychology, the mind determines itself by operating in accordance with a rational principle on certain items that are given to it. The rational principle is descriptive of the mind's activity, of what it does with the items given to it. In the case of practical principles, some of these items have a prima facie motivational force: they present a possible action to the will as eligible. Kant calls such a motivational item an "incentive." Desires, in Kant's view, function as incentives. So every willed action involves both an incentive and a principle: something presented to the will, on which it then acts. If a desire directly caused a person to act, there would be no contribution from the agent's own activity or self-determination, and so it would not be a case of volition. Suppose that an agent experiences a desire, and acts on it. To the extent that the agent determines himself, he *takes* the desire to be a reason to act; and that is not the same as its causing him to act. We may represent this fact—the contribution of his own activity—by saying that it is his *principle* to do what he wants. The principle describes his activity. If we want to reserve that troublesome word "motive" for what actually produces the outward act, then it is not quite right to say his desire is a motive. His desire is an incentive. His motive is, speaking very roughly, that he takes the desire to be a reason.

This has two implications. The first is that rational egoism is not the same as the thesis that only desires are motives. In fact it is inconsistent with that thesis. If desires produced human actions directly, without the intervention of principles, we would not be practically rational in any sense, egoistic or otherwise.[20] The second implication is less obvious. It is that rational egoism is not the same as the thesis that only desires are incentives. It is also inconsistent with that thesis.

I can most easily bring out the reason for this by means of a comparison. As an internalist, Kant supposed that the moral law applies to us only if respect for law can serve as an incentive for the will. The reason is simple. Suppose that your principle is to act only on a maxim that can serve as universal law. Suppose also that, with some ordinary desire serving as the incentive, you formulate a maxim that turns out to be incompatible with that principle. Wanting to spend the day at the beach, you are tempted to break your promise

---

[20] Actually, something stronger is true: there would be no actions. A movement caused by a desire or a passion is not an action. Blushing, trembling, and salivating are not actions. This is not to say that one must employ rational principles in order to act; the other animals act. But in their case instincts play the role of principles: they determine what the animal does with the sensory and desiderative inputs that assail it. See my "Motivation, Metaphysics, and the Value of the Self: A Reply to Ginsborg, Guyer, and Schneewind," especially pp. 49–54.

to help your neighbor paint his house on the first sunny day. You test your maxim, it is rejected, and you therefore do help your neighbor to paint his house as you had promised. If rational action always involves both an incentive and a principle, what is your incentive for doing that? What presents "keeping your promise" to your mind as an eligible action? According to Kant, it is respect for law, the moral law's operation as its own incentive. In other words, the thought that you are required to keep a promise can itself serve as the incentive for keeping it. This is what Kant means by being motivated by pure practical reason—that the thoughts generated by the rational principle can serve as incentives for the will.

In a similar way, if there is an egoistic principle of practical reason, it must be capable of generating an incentive of its own, an incentive for doing those things which we must do if we are to maximize our satisfactions, and which we do not otherwise want to do. Suppose for instance you are tempted not to go to the dentist, since you are afraid of the drill. Let us suppose that the egoistic principle says that you must go, since your desire to avoid the toothache ahead gets a higher normative ranking than your desire to avoid the drill now. It is no use insisting that the incentive you act on when you conform to the egoistic principle is your desire to avoid the toothache ahead, for if that were a sufficient incentive to get you to go to the dentist, you would not have been tempted to violate the egoistic principle in the first place. To suppose that your desire to avoid the toothache ahead is, *after all*, strong enough to overcome your fear of the drill is to revert to a version of the first assumption about rationality I criticized. It is to suppose that the role of practical deliberation is to uncover the psychological facts, to show you that you already, deep down, prefer to brave the dentist than to face the toothache later. We have seen that that assumption is not warranted. Your incentive must rather be provided by the thought that it is better for you overall if you go to the dentist. So *rational* egoism is not compatible with the view that only desires can serve as incentives. Only completely wanton action is compatible with that. Rational egoism requires the possibility that we can be motivated by pure practical reason, in exactly the same way that morality does. It is only *what* it tells us to do that is different.

1.5 *The Realist Egoist*

We have seen that the egoistic principle cannot be reduced to the instrumental principle. If it is a rational principle at all, it must be a principle in its own right. If it is to be a normative principle, associated with a normative ought, the egoistic principle must describe a rational activity. So in order to determine whether the egoistic principle is a normative principle, we need a way to identify rational activities. The stronger version of the Kantian conception, which tries to derive the content of rational principles from the very idea of self-determination, gives us one way of doing that, but we have seen that it is not a promising route for the egoist to take. The remaining option seems to be a form of realism. Just as realists think that following the principles of logic and the canons of evidence is guiding yourself in matters of belief by the aim of achieving the True, so they may think that following the principles of practical reason is guiding yourself in matters of action by the aim of achieving the Good. A person's happiness is *her own good*, so of course it is normative for her. Or perhaps it is just plain *good*, and so normative for us all.

Now it is important to see that by itself, this sort of move does not get us to rational egoism. Suppose that we say that a person's happiness is good for her (or just good, it does not matter for this argument), meaning that maximum satisfaction is good for her. It seems natural to give one of two explanations of what makes happiness in this sense good. The first is that the satisfaction of each of her desires is a good thing for her, so that by maximizing her satisfactions she is maximizing good things. The second is that her happiness is good because she in fact desires it, and so good for her for the same reason that each of the objects of her particular desires is good for her. In whichever of these ways we establish the goodness of happiness, we get the result that each of the person's particular desires has the same kind of normative claim on her that her happiness does. So if the aim of maximizing satisfaction comes into conflict with the aim of satisfying one of her desires, she now has a normative reason to do each of these things, and she needs some further reason to prefer the maximum satisfaction to the particular satisfaction. The problem of why she should be prudent, which before seemed to be a problem about *whether* there is a normative principle of prudence, has simply reappeared in the guise of a conflict among a plurality of normative principles.

Now perhaps you will agree that this problem does arise for someone who claims that happiness is good because we desire it, and therefore places happiness exactly on a footing with the other objects of desire. But you may be tempted to think it does not arise for someone who claims that happiness is good because the satisfaction of each of her desires is a good thing, and therefore that happiness is a maximum of good things. For it is obvious that a maximum of good things is better than any one good thing, on the principle that more is better. But recall that we are not claiming that satisfaction is the only thing you want for its own sake, so we are not talking here about getting more of the only thing you want. You also want the particular objects of your desires. So the trouble with this argument is that it does not explain the authority of the egoistic principle, but rather simply asserts it. The imprudent person is not denying that he will get more satisfaction if he acts prudently—he is asking why he therefore has a reason to do so, especially since he may have to give up something else he wants.[21]

There is one final move available to the realist egoist, though. Earlier I claimed that behind instrumental egoism stands a certain psychological thesis, namely, the thesis that people only *really want* what is consistent with their happiness. The realist egoist can transform this thesis into a view about what is *really good*. He can say that only the maximum compossible set of the objects of a person's desires, and the various objects that are parts of that set, are really good. So only those desires whose satisfaction is consistent with happiness have normative standing, and others do not. By turning that thesis into a thesis about the good, rather than a thesis about real desires, the realist egoist escapes the problems I mentioned earlier. He avoids the charge of domesticating human psychology, since he is no longer making a psychological claim. And he also avoids the charge of emptying the principles of practical reason of their normative content, by making us incapable of disobeying them. He is not claiming we can be *motivated* only by the good, for we have non-normative desires that also move us.

But he avoids these charges at the cost of giving up the view that the egoistic principle is a principle of naturalistic construction, and embracing in its place a pure form of dogmatism. For now the good is not constructed out of items regarded as naturally or prima facie good. The realist egoist can no longer explain the goodness of happiness in terms of the goodness of satisfying desires, in either of the ways I mentioned above. For now he has embraced the view that not every satisfaction is good, and more generally that not everything a person desires is good. This form of egoism is a top-down version, which tells us that it is prima facie rational to be motivated by our desires only *because* the maximum compossible set of their objects is the Good.

On this view, the good for a person *just is* the maximum compossible set of his desires. This is not because the maximum compossible set is necessarily *what he wants most*, for we have dropped the assumption that an agent always *actually* prefers his happiness to any particular desired end, in order to secure

---

[21] To see this, recall the comparison to Mill. The argument for the principle of utility depends on the idea that each person's happiness is a good and therefore the utilitarian must grant that each person's happiness is the source of a normative claim. Again what we get in the first instance is a plurality of normative principles, one for each person's happiness, and one—assuming that adding makes sense—for the total. Someone who challenges the principle of utility when his own happiness is to be sacrificed is not denying that there will be more total happiness if we follow the principle of utility. He is asking why he therefore has a reason to give up his own happiness, which the utilitarian must agree is also a good.

the normativity of the egoistic principle. Nor is it because it includes *most of what he wants*—for we have dropped the assumption that an agent's wanting something is in itself the source of a normative claim, in order to avoid generating a plurality of normative claims that will conflict with that of the egoistic principle itself. The claim that the maximum compossible set of one's desires is the good is therefore a dogmatic claim. The answer to the question why you should be prudent is simply that prudence is the pursuit of the maximum compossible set and that *just is* your good. This position appears to be logically unassailable, but that is no reason to pass out cigars. All dogmatic positions are logically unassailable.

So egoism is a dogmatic rationalist view, which derives the normativity of its principle from a substantive conception of the good. Let us now look more closely at this conception.

2. The Content of the Egoistic Principle

2.1 *Balancing and Particularity*

I want to begin this part of the essay by saying something about the intuitive ideas that the egoistic principle is meant to capture. By way of approach to one of these ideas, notice that there is widespread agreement that reason requires us to take the means to our ends. But many people believe that this by itself does not capture the demands of instrumental reason. Surely we should take the most efficient means, and there are problems about how those are to be specified; and of course there are the notorious problems about how to handle risk when we are pursuing ends under uncertainty. Many people think of solving these problems as part of working out the correct formulation of the instrumental principle.

Actually, however, these problems are generated by the same very basic idea that also seems to stand behind the egoistic principle. To formulate this idea, I will use the word "project" as a neutral term for anything that gives you a reason, whether it is a goal you are pursuing, a principle you live by, a cause you adhere to, your standing concern for the welfare of a friend, or whatever. I will speak of "promoting projects" and ask you to remember that promoting a project need not always involve pursuing a goal. The basic idea I have in mind is that you have more than one project and rationality requires you to take into account the impact which promoting one project will have on the others. Considerations of efficiency and caution spring from this idea in a generalized form: if you have reason to minimize your expenditure of time and resources, it is for the sake of your other projects, not for the sake of the project you are promoting right now.

I am going to call this basic idea the requirement of balancing—meaning that whenever we make a choice, we are required to balance the reasons stemming from the project we are now pursuing against the reasons stemming from our other projects.[22] The idea that there is a requirement of balancing is an important element in egoism, but there is nothing inherently egoistic about it. The belief in egoism also seems to import another idea, which is that the overall good you are pursuing or constructing when you engage in this balancing is particularly your own. I am going to call that idea the idea of particularity. The familiar ambiguity in the term "prudence" picks up both the ideas of balancing and particularity: people are described as prudent when they remember to attend to interests they will have in the future as well as the ones they have now, and also when they seem to be especially attentive to their own good.[23]

There is room for disagreement about how exactly the egoistic principle captures the idea of particularity—about what it is that makes egoism *egoistic*. What makes the successful pursuit of a project a part of my own good? Is it just that the project is mine, or is there some subset of my projects whose success constitutes "my own good"? Or is it rather something about the *way* the egoist proposes to meet the requirement of balancing, which is by maximizing his own satisfaction? On the first of these options, the idea of particularity is supposed to be captured by the kind of items that go into the egoistic calculation—they are mine, my desires, my projects, my personal concerns. The egoist reasons from egoistic materials. On the second, the idea

---

[22] Is the principle of balancing, taken by itself, a principle of reason? Let me first back up. In both *The Sources of Normativity* and "The Normativity of Instrumental Reason" (Essay 1 in this volume), I argue that the principle of instrumental reason is normative on the grounds that it is a constitutive principle of willing. I mean this in a strong sense of constitutive: there is a sense in which acting on the principle of instrumental reason *gives* you a will, that is, an agency that is unified and distinct from the particular incentives over which it has authority. More precisely, it makes you such an agency. The general idea is that if you were swayed from the pursuit of an end *whenever* you experienced an incentive (say, difficulty, boredom, temptation) that made you reluctant to take the means to that end, you could not be said to have a will to pursue the end—or, taking the point generally, to have a will at all. Since you would be moved by any incentive or impulse that came along, you would not be distinct from your impulses, and so would be a sort of disunified heap of impulses. (In *The Sources of Normativity* and "Self-Constitution in the Ethics of Plato and Kant" (essay 3 in this volume), I make a similar argument about the principle of universalization.) The principle of balancing also seems necessary to secure the unity of your will, at a sort of next level up from the instrumental principle: we might say that without it, you are a mere heap of projects, each wholly engrossing you, and so in effect being you, at the moment of its ascendancy. This is vague and I am not perfectly happy with it, but it may be taken to indicate that unlike the egoistic principle, the principle of balancing *is* the right sort of thing to be a rational principle. For the relevant arguments, see SN, section 1 of the Reply, especially pp. 225–33; "The Normativity of Instrumental Reason," Essay 1 in this volume, especially pp. 58–60; and "Self-Constitution in the Ethics of Plato and Kant," Essay 3 in this volume.

[23] My attention was drawn to this by Thomas Nagel, in *The Possibility of Altruism*, p. 36.

of particularity is supposed to be captured by the structure or form of egoistic deliberation: it is because *satisfaction* is the basis for assigning weights to the items in the egoistic calculation that egoism counts as a pursuit of the agent's own good. The egoist reasons about a general range of materials, but reasons in a specifically egoistic way. In what follows, I will examine each of these possibilities in turn.

2.2 *Reasoning from Egoistic Materials*

First, are the materials that go into egoistic reasoning somehow inherently egoistic? For instance, is the egoist pursuing his own good because the incentives on which the egoistic principle operates are his desires? The trouble with this thought is that the word "desire" either refers to a particular kind of incentive, or it does not. If the word "desire" refers to anything that can serve as an incentive for the will, or perhaps we should say any incentive except those generated by the egoistic principle itself, then all of one's incentives are trivially "desires," and nothing is added to the idea of balancing. On the other hand, if "desire" refers to some particular kind of incentive, say those that are associated with appetite or pleasure, then we are owed an explanation of why the egoistic principle commands us to promote projects grounded in this particular kind of incentive in preference to or at the expense of other projects. Whatever that explanation might be, it will not refer to the fact that the other incentives are not *your own*, but rather to the fact that the other incentives are not *desires*. There is no obvious sense in which a principle like that is either rational or egoistic.

A more tempting option is that it is not the bare fact that something is a desire but its content that is relevant. In his essay "Egoism and Altruism" Bernard Williams proposes that we can isolate a category of egoistic desire by means of a device intended to isolate the content of a desire. The device is to represent the desire in this way:

I want that (. . .)

where what we put in the parentheses is a description of the desired state of affairs. Then we can say that a desire is egoistic if the self appears somewhere in that description:

I want that (. . . I . . .)

Williams calls such a desire an I-desire.[24]

---

[24] Bernard Williams, "Egoism and Altruism," in *Problems of the Self*. My discussion throughout this essay owes much to Williams. Williams borrows the device of the I-desire from Anthony Kenny, who uses it in *Action, Emotion, and Will*.

But actually this device does not seem to capture the intuitive idea of egoism. In fact, what it seems to capture is rather the idea of narcissism. For instance, someone in the grip of a pathological case of remorse or masochism might want that he should suffer. Or someone might want to be the author of some good thing of which he himself may never get the benefit, like someone who wants to be the one who discovers a cure for cancer. And then there are the desires we would most naturally formulate not in terms of "I" but in terms of "my own," like the godfather's desire that his own family should remain in power or the patriot's desire that his own country should be free. Or suppose an artist wants his own paintings to make the world a more beautiful place. Are these desires egoistic? They contain a self-reference, but they certainly do not all concern things that you want *for yourself* in any intuitive sense. Or course we could say that a desire is only egoistic if the person wants something good for himself but then we cannot use these desires to *define* the notion of a person's good.

Nevertheless, let us suppose that the device does pick out a category of egoistic desire. Now we must be careful to avoid a confusion. Psychological egoism, in one of its many forms, is the view that human beings have only egoistic desires. Those who believe it usually also believe that all human projects are grounded in desire. If these things were true, you would always pursue things you wanted for yourself, and the requirement of balancing would require you to pursue your own overall good. But this would not be because it is rational to pursue your own good as such. The only rational element in this picture is the requirement of balancing, which is not essentially egoistic; the egoism here is psychological. If the requirement of balancing has only egoistic materials to work on, it commands the pursuit of your own good by default, and not because a focus on your own good is rational.

So if the question of *rational* egoism is even going to come up, we must suppose that human beings have both egoistic and non-egoistic projects. Suppose you want things both for yourself and for others, and perhaps have some impersonal desires for states of the world in general. According to this view, it is a requirement of reason that you should prefer those things you want for yourself to the things you want for others or impersonally, no matter how badly you want those other things. Why would this be rational? Do not be tempted by the thought that your I-desires are favored by reason *because* they are the ones directed to your own good. The claim here is not that you first form some conception of the good, and then form egoistic desires by applying it to your own case. If that is the way it is, the good is not a maximum of satisfaction, but something else altogether, which desire merely aims at. This version of egoism is rather the view that your good is *constituted* by the maximum compossible set of the objects of your I-desires, *whatever* those happen to be, and even if they include things like wanting yourself to suffer.

That is not very plausible. But in any case it is not the route that most egoists take. Social scientific egoists, in particular, have insisted that they can be neutral about what sorts of elements may go into the maximum compossible set. If this is right, then what is egoistic about egoism must be the form of balancing that it directs us to do. It must be that it is the pursuit of satisfaction.

2.3 *The Pursuit of Satisfaction*

The view that we are to maximize the satisfaction of our desires is ambiguous, because the idea of "satisfaction" is ambiguous. "Satisfaction" may refer either to an objective or a subjective state. Objective satisfaction is achieved when the state of affairs that you desire is in fact realized. For instance, you want your painting to hang in the Metropolitan Museum of Art, and it does. Obviously, you could achieve the satisfaction of your desire in the objective sense without knowing anything about it: you may never know that your dream of artistic fame has been realized. Subjective satisfaction by contrast is a sort of pleasurable consciousness that objective satisfaction obtains. You know that your picture has been hung in the museum, say, and you feel good about it; you reflect on the fact with pleasure. Although subjective satisfaction is pleasurable, it is important to distinguish it from pleasure in general; and in particular from pleasure that is caused by the satisfaction of a desire by any route whatever.[25] Egoism is not supposed to be the same thing as hedonism. Subjective satisfaction is a specific kind of pleasure, pleasure taken in the knowledge or belief that a desire has been satisfied.

Now someone who deliberates with the aim of achieving the maximum sense of subjective satisfaction over the whole course of his life seems to be in a recognizable sense egoistic. His conduct is governed by the pursuit of something that will be experienced as a good by himself. But there is a problem about saying that he is rational. Subjective satisfaction is the pleased perception of objective satisfaction and so is conceptually dependent upon objective satisfaction. And so, one would think, its importance must be dependent on the importance of objective satisfaction as well. There would be something upside down about thinking it mattered that you should achieve subjective satisfaction independently of thinking that it mattered that you should achieve objective satisfaction. You can see the problem by imagining a case in which they pull apart. John Rawls used to tell the following story in his classes.

[25] See note 26.

A man is going away to fight in a war, in which he may possibly die. The night before he leaves, the devil comes and offers him a choice. Either while he is away, his family will thrive and flourish, but he will get word that they are suffering and miserable; or while he is away his family will suffer and be miserable, but he will get word they are thriving and happy. He must choose now, and of course he will be made to forget that his conversation with the devil and the choice it resulted in ever took place.

The problem is obvious. The man loves his family and wants them to be thriving and happy, and this clearly dictates the first choice, where his family thrives but he believes they do not. But the goal of achieving subjective satisfaction seems to favor the second choice, where he gets to enjoy the satisfaction of believing they thrive when actually they do not. So here we have *rationality* dictating the choice of a pleasing delusion over a state of affairs which the man by hypothesis genuinely cares about. He must care about it, or he could not get the subjective satisfaction: that was Butler's point. The pursuit of subjective satisfaction in preference to objective satisfaction can lead to madness, in the literal sense of madness: you can lose your grip on *reality*.

So suppose instead that we take the claim that we should maximize our satisfaction to be a claim about objective satisfaction. Now we run into a new problem. The idea of *maximizing* objective satisfaction makes no obvious sense. Even supposing that we had some clear way of individuating and so counting our desires, nobody thinks that maximizing objective satisfaction is rational if that means maximizing the raw number of satisfied desires, for everyone thinks that our desires differ greatly in their importance and centrality to our lives. Maximizing satisfaction must have something to do with giving priority to the things that matter more to us. So we need some way of assigning prima facie weights or measures of some kind to our desires or more generally to our projects before we know how to maximize satisfaction. And these weights or measures must be based either on reason or on our psychology.

Suppose first that the weights are grounded in reason: we ask how strong a reason, relatively speaking, is provided by each of our projects. There are two things we might mean by this. First, we may be asking how important the project is to our happiness, how much of a contribution it makes. As I have already suggested, when I talked about the dangerous word "interest," the egoist cannot use this measure going in to his calculations, for it is precisely this measure that is supposed to emerge from his calculations. Finding out how to maximize satisfaction is supposed to *tell* him which projects he must give priority to if he is to be happy. Second, we may be asking how strong a reason the project provides by some other rational measure, some measure that may derive in part from rational considerations or convictions other than those springing from the egoistic principle itself. For instance, one may hold the view that reasons deriving from morality or, say, friendship are weightier than reasons deriving from personal comfort. Roughly speaking, the measure of a project's importance is given by how good a reason there is to promote it. Provided we have a theory of practical reason rich enough to assign such measures, this is certainly an intelligible procedure. But it is not egoistic, for this is simply the procedure of determining what we have most reason to do. In other words, this is simply the requirement of balancing, taken all by itself, and in its most starkly formal sense. Furthermore, and importantly, if we are going to allow the initial measures to reflect rational considerations, we must leave it open whether it will turn out that balancing will take a maximizing form or not. For perhaps some reasons are unconditional and some are not, or perhaps some are by their nature lexically prior to others. If these things are so, balancing requires us to take them into account. Balancing is a matter of maximizing only if we start with items that vary only in a raw commensurable weight.

So if we are to get a distinctively egoistic principle, and not just the requirement of balancing, it seems as if the initial weights we assign to our projects must be based on something psychological, something about our own attitudes towards them. An initial temptation is to turn back to the idea of subjective satisfaction, which may seem like the relevant sort of quantum. Although we can agree that it is objective satisfaction that matters, the test of how much it matters is subjective: that is, it is how much subjective satisfaction we would experience if we knew that the desire were objectively satisfied. But the problem of the conceptual dependence of subjective satisfaction upon objective satisfaction again arises. Surely the degree of our subjective satisfaction should depend on how important the objective state of affairs is to us, and not the reverse. Subjective satisfaction cannot serve as an independent measure.

This means that the measure must be provided by some subjectively identifiable or anyway psychological quantum other than the degree of satisfaction. In other words, it has to be something roughly along the lines of intensity of desire. In this case egoism is normally misdescribed, for conformity to the egoistic principle will really lead to a maximum of *satisfaction* only on the hypothesis that the degree of subjective satisfaction exactly corresponds to the intensity of the desire which gets satisfied. This was indeed the assumption of the British empiricists who originally brought us this theory. "Every affection," Hume declares, "when gratified by success, gives a satisfaction proportioned to its force and violence" (2E 9,281–282).[26] We need not linger over the question

---

[26] Hume, following Butler (that is, following the argument mentioned in note 9 above), is arguing that satisfying the passion of benevolence makes at least as much of a contribution to your own

whether that is true, because it is inessential to the theory. The essential idea is that egoism is egoistic because the measure of a desired object's prima facie weight is how badly you want it. It is as if adding up all the intensities of your particular desires produces, in the case of the maximum compossible set, a single desire for the set as a whole with such a high degree of intensity that it *transmutes* into normative force.

However that may be, the use of intensity of desire as the measure means that the egoist cannot have the neutrality he often claims about the kinds of items that go into the calculation. In fact a dilemma faces the egoist here. On the one hand, we may allow the items that go into the calculation to get their initial weights from any source, including normative sources such as personal commitments or the other principles of reason. The gives us the desired neutrality, but in that case what is supposed to be the egoistic principle is really just the requirement of balancing, and the form that that requirement takes will not necessarily be a maximizing one. Or we may insist that the items going into the calculation are items of a quite particular kind, psychological items with a measurable intensity or some other introspectively accessible psychic magnitude that reflects our personal attitudes. Then we get egoism, but we do not get the desired neutrality. To this extent, the egoistic principle cannot after all be detached from its origins: it is a child of introspective psychology, grounded in the British empiricist theory of happiness or the good.

Conclusion

Let me now sum up my conclusions. Egoism is not consistent with instrumentalism or with the view that human beings are motivated only by desires.

---

happiness as satisfying a less altruistic desire. Like Butler, Hume goes on to throw certain pleasures into the calculation along with that proportional satisfaction—the immediate feeling of benevolence, which he says is "sweet, smooth, tender, and agreeable" (2E 9,282), the pleasing consciousness that we have done well, and so forth. The argument is hedonistic, and satisfaction is thrown as one of the relevant pleasures; and yet it follows from the argument that we could not get the satisfaction if we acted for the sake of the satisfaction *rather than* for the sake of helping the other. If this argument were intended to motivate an agent, authentic benevolence and the desire for one's own satisfaction and pleasure would have to be combined somehow in the agent's motivation. With a theory of volition such as the Kantian account described in this essay, we might explain how this combination is possible. The benevolent person *desires* the other's good for its own sake, but he *chooses* to act on that desire rather than some other desire because of its special advantages. But Hume and Butler do not have a theory of volition, so their accounts leave it unclear how we could be moved at one and the same moment by the desire for another's good and the desire for our own. I do not consider this to be a problem for Hume, since in his case I think the argument is not intended to motivate; its aim is rather to establish congruence between the moral and the self-interested points of view. (See Charlotte Brown's essay "Hume Against the Selfish Schools and the Monkish Virtues," and my own account in SN 2.2.4–2.2.7, pp. 60–6.) But it may be a problem for Butler.

Like any substantive theory of what it is rational to do, egoism requires the possibility of motivation by pure practical reason. The egoistic principle differs from the categorical imperative by having a different content, not by the kind of motivation it involves. The egoistic principle tells us that we must treat a certain conception of the good as having normative authority over our conduct. This conception of the good is not philosophically neutral, nor is it merely the result of imposing a little order on the natural prima facie goods that it starts from. In fact, if the arguments of both parts of this essay are correct, egoism must be based on a rational intuition that happiness as it was conceived by the British empiricists is the Good, and is therefore the source of a normative principle. I therefore think that Nietzsche was right in the *Twilight of the Idols* when he dismissed rational egoism as a myth. Man does not pursue happiness, at least as happiness must be conceived by the rational egoist. Only the Englishman does that.[27, 28]

[27] The argument of this essay may leave the reader with a pair of related worries. First, one may wonder why, if the idea of rational egoism is as confused as I have claimed, the temptation to believe in the egoistic principle is so strong and so perennial. Second, and more importantly, one may wonder where the argument leaves the idea of happiness or the individual human good, and the rationality of pursuing that good. I have not discussed hedonism much in this essay, but like many of my readers I do not find it plausible, at least in its modern, Benthamite form. But if we reject both hedonism and the desire-satisfaction model, it may seem as if we are left with only a kind of "external realist" conception of the individual's good or happiness. On such a conception, the good is something defined independently of the individual's natural desires and capacities for interest and enjoyment. This seems absurd, since most of us believe that a person's good or happiness must be something *necessarily* capable of motivating, interesting, or pleasing him. And of course there is a connection between these two worries, for the unpalatability of external realism about happiness or a person's good has something to do with the perennial temptation to believe in egoism. To do justice to these questions would require another essay, and it is a topic I hope to take up on some future occasion. For now I will only indicate where I think the answer lies. The ancient Greeks, especially Aristotle, offer a conception of the human good which is psychologically grounded, but which cannot be identified with either the desire-satisfaction model or Benthamite hedonism. The rough idea is that happiness rests in the excellent activity of our healthy faculties, an activity that we necessarily experience as pleasurable, although not because it is the cause of a pleasant sensation. I believe some version of this conception can be shown to be much more plausible than its modern, less sophisticated, alternatives. See Aristotle's *Nicomachean Ethics* and the discussion of pleasure and pain in SN 4.3.1–4.3.10, pp. 145–53.

[28] This essay was written to be the Lindley Lecture at the University of Kansas, and was also delivered as the Patterson Lecture at Duke University, and at a conference on Practical Reason at Loyola Marymount University. I am grateful to the audiences on those occasions. I also thank audiences at the University of California at Berkeley, the University of Wisconsin at Madison, Washington University in St Louis, the University of Iowa and Georgetown University.

3

Self-Constitution in the Ethics
of Plato and Kant

1. Introduction

One of the most famous sections of Hume's *Treatise* begins with these words:

Nothing is more usual in philosophy, and even in common life, than to talk of the combat of passion and reason, to give the preference to reason, and to assert that men are only so far virtuous as they conform themselves to its dictates. Every rational creature, 'tis said, is oblig'd to regulate his actions by reason; and if any other motive or principle challenge the direction of his conduct, he ought to oppose it, 'till it be entirely subdu'd, or at least brought to a conformity with that superior principle. (T 2.3.3,413)

As Hume understands these claims, reason and passion are two forces in the soul, each a source of motives to act, and virtue consists in the person going along with reason. Why should the person do that? Hume tells us that in philosophy:

The eternity, invariableness, and divine origin of [reason] have been display'd to the best advantage: the blindness, unconstancy, and deceitfulness of [passion] have been as strongly insisted on. (T 2.3.3,413)

Hume proposes to "shew the fallacy of all this philosophy," but in his demonstration he does not exactly deny what I will call "the Combat Model." He simply argues that reason is not a force, and therefore that there is no combat.

I think that there are a few questions Hume should have asked first, for the Combat Model makes very little sense. From the third-person perspective, we do sometimes explain a person's actions as the result of one motive being "stronger" than another, for instance when the person has conflicting passions. But is the difference between reason and passion then pretty much the same as the difference between one passion and another? And are a person's actions merely the result of the play, or rather the combat, of these forces within her? How then would actions be different from blushes or twitches or even biological processes?

Now we may try to solve this last problem by bringing the person, the agent, back into the picture—action is different from other physical movements because the person *chooses* to follow either reason or passion. But this makes the Combat Model even more perplexing. For what is the essence of this person, in whom reason and passion are both forces, *neither* of them identified with the person herself, and between which she is to choose? And if the person identifies neither with reason nor passion, then how—on what principle—can she possibly choose between them? The philosophers Hume describes here seem to be imagining that the person chooses between reason and passion by assessing their merits—reason is divine and reliable, passion blind and misleading. But surely that presupposes that the person *already* identifies with reason, which is what assesses merits. But how then could the person choose passion over reason? The Combat Model gives us no clear picture of the *person* who chooses between reason and passion.

The tradition supplies us with another model of the interaction of reason and passion in the soul, which makes better sense, because it assigns to them functional and structural differences.[1] I call it the Constitutional Model, because its clearest appearance is in Plato's *Republic*, where the human soul is compared to the constitution of a polis or city-state. I believe that the Constitutional Model has important implications for moral philosophy, and my project in this essay is to spell these implications out. Specifically, the Constitutional Model implies a certain view about what an *action* is, which in turn has implications about what makes an action good or bad. These implications are a little difficult to articulate clearly in advance of the argument, but the main idea is this: what distinguishes action from mere behavior and other physical movements is that it is *authored*—it is in a quite special way attributable to the *person* who does it, by which I mean, the *whole* person. The Constitutional Model tells us that what makes an action yours in this way is that it springs from and is in accordance with your constitution. But it also provides a standard for good action, a standard that tells us which actions are most truly a person's own, and therefore which actions are most

---

[1] One might think that Hume is also presenting a constitutional model, since his own argument suggests that the function of passion is to determine our ends and the function of reason is to discover means to ends. Elsewhere, however, I have argued that Hume does not really believe in a principle of instrumental *practical reason*, which instructs us to take the means to our ends, and which would be needed to integrate the two functions (the determination of the end and the identification of the means) into *a single system which produces actions*. Because of that, Hume is unable to work up a *person* out of these meager resources. What I've just said will become clearer as this essay proceeds, for it is actually, in a sense, a short version of the whole argument of this essay. For the argument that Hume does not believe in a principle of instrumental practical reason, see my "The Normativity of Instrumental Reason," Essay 1 in this volume, especially pp. 32–46.

truly *actions*. Now this is the hard part to say in advance of the argument: The actions which are most truly a person's own are precisely those actions which most fully unify her and therefore most fully constitute her as their author. They are those actions that both issue from, and give her, the kind of volitional unity that she must have if we are to attribute the action to her as a whole person. What makes an action bad, by contrast, is that it springs in part not from the person but from something at work *in* or *on* the person, something that threatens her volitional unity. I sum these claims up by saying that according to the Constitutional Model, action is self-constitution.

2. Plato

In Book 1 of the *Republic*, Socrates and his friends discuss the question what justice is. The discussion is interrupted by Thrasymachus, who asserts that the best life is the unjust life, the life lived by the strong, who impose the laws of justice on the weak, but ignore those laws themselves. The more completely unjust you are, Thrasymachus says, the better you will live, for pickpockets and thieves, who commit small injustices, get punished, while tyrants, who enslave whole cities and steal their treasuries, lead a glorious life, and are the envy of everyone (R 336b–339d). Socrates, distracted by these claims, drops the discussion of what justice is, and takes up the question whether the just or the unjust life is best.

Socrates proceeds to construct three arguments designed to show that the just life is the best. The one that is central to my own argument goes like this (R 351b–352c): Socrates asks Thrasymachus whether a band of robbers and thieves with a common unjust purpose would be able to achieve that purpose if they were unjust to each other. Thrasymachus agrees that they could not do that. Justice, as Socrates says, is what brings a sense of common purpose to a group, while injustice causes hatred and civil war, and makes the group "incapable of achieving anything as a unit" (R 352a). Thrasymachus is then induced to agree that justice and injustice have the same effect wherever they occur, and therefore, the same effect within the individual human soul as they have in a group. Injustice, therefore, makes an individual "incapable of achieving anything, because he is in a state of civil war and not of one mind." The more complete this condition is the worse it is, for according to Socrates "those who are all bad and completely unjust are completely incapable of accomplishing anything" (R 352c).[2]

---

[2] The other two arguments are the "outdoing" argument used to establish that justice is a form of virtue and knowledge (R 349a–350d) and the function argument used to establish that the just person is happiest (R 352d–354a).

Now there's nothing obviously wrong with this argument, except of course that it flies in the teeth of the fact that we seem to see unjust people all around us, doing and accomplishing things right and left. So what is Socrates talking about? The argument leaves Socrates's audience puzzled and dissatisfied. So Plato's brothers, Glaucon and Adeimantus, demand that Socrates return to the abandoned question, what justice is, and what effect it has in the soul. It is this demand that sets Plato off on his attempt to identify justice in a larger and more visible object, the ideal city, and his famous comparison between the constitution of the city and the constitution of the soul.

It will help to review the main elements of that comparison. Plato identifies three classes in the city. First there are the rulers, who make the laws and policies for the city, and handle its relations with other cities. Second, there are the auxiliaries, a kind of combination soldier and police force, who enforce the laws within the city and also defend it from external enemies, following the orders of the rulers. The rulers are drawn from the ranks of these auxiliaries, and the two groups together are called the guardians. And finally there are the farmers, craftspeople, merchants, and so forth, who provide for the city's needs.

The virtues of the ideal city are then identified with certain properties of and relations between these parts. The wisdom of the city rests in the wisdom of its rulers (R 428b–429a). We aren't told much about this at first, except that the rulers of the ideal city, unlike Thrasymachus's rulers, rule with a view to the good of the city as a whole, and not with a view to their own good. The courage of the city rests in the courage of its auxiliaries, which is identified with their capacity to preserve certain beliefs, instilled in them by the rulers, about what is to be feared, in the face of temptation, pleasure, pain, and fear itself (R 429a–430c). The city's *sophrosyne*—its moderation or temperance—rests in the agreement of all the classes in the city about who should rule and be ruled (R 430e–432b). And its justice rests in the fact that each class in the city does its own work, and no one tries to meddle in the work of anyone else (R 433a ff.).

Plato then undertakes to find the same three parts in the human soul. The Constitutional Model, like the Combat Model, starts off from the experience of inner conflict. Socrates puts it forth as a principle that if we find in the soul opposite attitudes or reactions to a single thing at the same time, we must suppose that the soul has parts (R 436b–c). For example, the soul of a thirsty person is impelled by its thirst towards drinking. So if the soul at the very same time draws back from drinking, it must be with a different part. And this is an experience people actually have: there are thirsty people who decide not to drink. This happens when they judge that the drink will be bad for them. As Socrates says:

Isn't there something in their soul, bidding them to drink, and something different, forbidding them to do so, that overrules the thing that bids? . . . Doesn't that which forbids in such cases come into play as a result of rational calculation? (R 439c–d)

So reason and appetite must be two different parts of the soul.

In fact, however, Socrates's emphasis on conflict is slightly misleading, for, even if there is no conflict, two parts of the soul may be discerned. Suppose instead that the drink has nothing wrong with it, and the person who is thirsty does drink. In this kind of case, Socrates says,

the soul of someone who has an appetite for a thing wants what he has an appetite for and takes to himself what it is his will to have, and . . . insofar as he wishes something to be given to him, his soul, since it desires this to come about, nods assent to it as if in answer to a question. (R 437c)

The soul does not act directly from appetite, but from something that endorses the appetite and says yes to it. Even when conflict is absent, then, we can see that there are two parts of the soul.

Socrates next argues that there is a third part, *thymos* or spirit, which is distinct from both reason and appetite, although it is the natural ally of reason (R 439e–441c). That it is distinct from appetite shows up in the fact that anger and indignation, which are manifestations of spirit, are often directed against the appetites themselves. This is illustrated by the story of Leontius, who was disgusted at himself for wanting to look at some corpses, and berated his own eyes for their evil appetites (R 439e–440a). Socrates claims that spirit always fights on reason's side in a case of conflict between reason and appetite. Yet it is distinct from reason, for it is present in small children and animals, who don't have reason; and, furthermore, it sometimes needs to be controlled by reason (R 440e–441c).

By these arguments Socrates establishes that the soul has the same three parts as the city. Reason corresponds to the rulers and its function is to direct things, for the good of the whole person. Spirit corresponds to the auxiliaries and its function is to carry out the orders of reason. The appetites correspond to the rest of the citizens, and their business is to supply the person with whatever he needs.

Now if the soul has parts the question is going to arise what makes them one, what unifies them into a single soul. And part of the answer is that the parts of the soul must be unified—they *need* to be unified, like the people in a city—in order to act. Specifically, we can see the three parts of the soul as corresponding to three parts of a deliberative action. Deliberative action begins from the fact we have certain appetites and desires. We are conscious of these, and they invite us to do certain actions or seek certain ends. Since we are rational, however, we do not act on our appetites and desires automatically, but instead decide whether to satisfy them or not. As Socrates put it in a passage we looked at a moment ago, it is as if what appetite does is put a request to reason, and reason says yes or no. And then finally there is carrying the decision out—actually doing what we have decided to do. For of course we don't always do what we have decided to do, but are sometimes distracted by pleasure or pain or fear from the course we have set for ourselves. So we can identify three parts of a deliberative action corresponding to Plato's three parts of the soul, namely:

Appetite makes a proposal.
Reason decides whether to act on it or not.
Spirit carries reason's decision out.

This line of thought supports Plato's analogy between the city and the soul. For a city also engages in deliberative actions: it is not just a place to live, but rather a kind of agent that performs actions and so has a life and a history. And we can see the same three parts in a political decision. The people of the city make a proposal: they say that there is something that they need. They ask for schools, or better health care, or more police protection. The rulers then decide whether to act on the proposal or not. They say either "yes" or "no" to the people. And then the auxiliaries carry the ruler's decisions out.

In fact, the main purpose of a literal political constitution is precisely to lay out the city's mode of deliberative action, the procedures by which its collective decisions are to be made and carried out. A constitution defines a set of roles and offices that together constitute a procedure for deliberative action, saying who shall perform each step and how it shall be done. It lays out the proper ways of making proposals (say, by petition, or the introduction of bills, or whatever), of deciding whether to act on these proposals (the legislative function), and of carrying out the resulting decisions (the executive function). And in each case it says who is allowed to carry out the procedures it has specified. The constitution in this way makes it possible for the citizens to function as a single collective agent.

And this explains Socrates's puzzling definition of justice. Justice, he says, is "doing one's own work and not meddling with what isn't one's own" (R 433a–b). When Socrates first introduces this principle into the discussion (R 369e ff.), he's talking about the specialization of labor, and that's what the principle sounds like it's about.[3] But if we think of the constitution as laying out the procedures for deliberative action, and the roles and offices that constitute those procedures, we can see what Socrates's point is. For usurping the office of another in the constitutional procedures for collective action is *precisely* what we mean by injustice, or at least it is one thing we mean. For instance, if the constitution says that the president cannot make war without the agreement of the congress, and yet he does, he has usurped congress's role in this decision, and that's unjust. If the constitution says that each citizen gets to cast one vote in the election, and through some fraud you manage to vote more than once, you are diminishing the voice of others in the election, and that's unjust. So injustice, in one of its most familiar senses, is usurping the role of another in the deliberative procedures that define collective action. It is meddling with somebody else's work.

I said in one sense, for this is very much what is sometimes called a *procedural* conception of justice, as opposed to a *substantive* one. This distinction represents an important tension in our concept of justice, and a standing cause of confusion about the source of its normativity. On the one hand, the idea of justice essentially involves the idea of following certain procedures. In the state, as I have been saying, these are the procedures which the constitution lays out for collective deliberative action: for making laws, waging wars, trying cases, collecting taxes, distributing services, and all of the various things that a state does. According to the procedural conception of justice, an action of the state is just if and only if it is the outcome of actually following these procedures. That is a *law* which has been passed in form by a duly constituted legislature; this law is *constitutional* if (say) the supreme court says that it is; a person is *innocent* of a certain crime when he has been deemed so by a jury; someone is *the president* if he meets the legal qualifications and has been duly voted in, and so forth. These are all normative judgments—the terms *law, constitutional, innocent,* and *president* all imply the existence of certain reasons for action—and their normativity *derives from* the carrying out of the procedures that have established them.

On the other hand, however, there are certainly cases in which we have some independent idea of what outcome the procedures ought to generate. These independent ideas serve as the criteria for our more substantive judgments—in some cases, of what is just; in other cases, simply of what is right or best. And these substantive judgments can come in conflict with the actual outcomes of carrying out the procedures. Perhaps the law is unconstitutional, though the

---

[3] Socrates not only openly acknowledges this oddity later on, but actually suggests that the principle of the specialization of labor is "beneficial" because it is "a sort of image of justice" (R 443c).

legislature has passed it; perhaps the defendant is guilty, though the jury has set him free; perhaps the candidate elected is not the best person for the job, or even the best of those who ran, or perhaps due to the accidents of voter turnout he does not really represent the majority will. As this last example shows, the distinction between the procedurally just and the substantively just, right, or best, is a rough and ready one, and relative to the case under consideration. Who should be elected? The best person for the job, the best of those who actually run, the one preferred by the majority of the citizens, the one preferred by the majority of the registered voters, or the one elected by the majority of those who actually turn out on election day . . .? As we go down the list, the answer to the question becomes increasingly procedural; the answer above it is, relatively, more substantive. We may try to design our procedures to secure the substantively right, best, or just outcome. But—and here is the important point—according to the procedural conception of justice, the normativity of these procedures nevertheless does not spring from the efficiency, goodness, *or even the substantive justice* of the outcomes they produce. The reverse is true: it is the procedures themselves—or rather the actual carrying out of the procedures—that confers normativity on those outcomes. The person who gets elected holds the office, no matter how far he is from being the best person for the job. The jury's acquittal stands, though we later discover new evidence that after all the defendant was guilty.

Now if the normativity of the outcomes springs from the carrying out of the procedures, where, we may ask, does the normativity of the procedures themselves come from? And here we run into the cause of confusion I mentioned at the outset, for there is a standing temptation to believe that the procedures themselves must derive their normativity from the good quality of their outcomes. That cannot be right, as I've just been saying, for if the normativity of our procedures came from the substantive quality of their outcomes, we'd be prepared to set those procedures aside when we knew that their outcomes were going to be poor ones. And as I've just been saying, we don't do that. Where constitutional procedures are in place, substantive rightness, goodness, bestness, or even justice is neither necessary nor sufficient for the normative standing of their outcomes.

Perhaps we may now be tempted to say that what makes the procedures normative is the *usual* quality of their outcomes, the fact that they get it right most of the time. After all, even if we stand by the outcomes of our procedures though in this or that case they are bad, we would certainly change those procedures if their outcomes were bad *too often*. But this cannot be the whole answer, both because it isn't always true—think of the jury system—but also because, as act utilitarians have been telling us for years, it is irrational to follow a procedure merely because it usually gets a good outcome, when you know that this time it will get a bad one. So perhaps we should say that the normativity of the procedures comes from the usual quality of their outcomes *combined* with the fact that we must have some such procedures, and we must stand by their results. But why must we have such procedures? Because without them collective action is impossible. And now we've come around to Plato's view. In order to act together—to make laws and policies, apply them, enforce them—in a way that represents, not some of us tyrannizing over others, but all of us acting as a unit, we must have a constitution that defines the procedures for collective deliberative action, and we must stand by their results.[4]

According to Plato, the normative force of the constitution *consists* in the fact that it makes it possible for the city to function as a single unified agent. For a city without justice, according to Plato, above all lacks unity—it is not one city, he says, but many (R 422d–423c; see also R 462a–e). When justice breaks down, the city falls into civil war, as the rulers, the soldiers, and the people all struggle for control. The deliberative procedures that unify the city into a single agent break down, and the city *as such* cannot act. The individual citizens and classes in it may still perform various actions, but the city cannot act as a unit.

And this applies to justice and injustice within the individual person as well. Socrates says:

One who is just does not allow any part of himself to do the work of another part or allow the various classes within him to meddle with each other. He regulates well what is really his own and rules himself. He puts himself in order, is his own friend, and harmonizes the three parts of himself like three limiting notes in a musical scale—high, low, and middle. He binds together those parts and any others there may be in between, and from having been many things he becomes entirely one, moderate and harmonious. Only then does he act. (R 443d–e)

But if justice is what makes it possible for a person to function as a single unified agent, then injustice makes it impossible. Civil war breaks out between appetite, spirit, and reason, each trying to usurp the roles and offices of the others. The deliberative procedures that unify the soul into a single agent break down, and the person *as such* cannot act. So Socrates's argument from Book 1 turns out to be true. Desires and impulses may operate within the unjust person, as individual citizens may operate within the unjust state. But the

---

[4] I have also discussed these points in "Taking the Law into Our Own Hands: Kant on the Right to Revolution," Essay 8 in this volume, pp. 246–7. The discussion here is in large part lifted from that discussion.

unjust *person* is "completely incapable of accomplishing anything" (R 352c) because the unjust *person* cannot act at all.

3. Kant

Now let's turn to Kant. The best way to see that Kant is thinking in terms of the Constitutional Model is to consider the argument he uses to establish that the categorical imperative is the law of a free will (G 4:446–448). Kant argues that insofar as you are a rational being, you must act under the idea of freedom. And a free will is one that is not determined by any alien cause—by any law outside of itself. It is not, in Kant's language, "heteronomous." But Kant claims that the free will must be determined by some law or other—I will take up the argument for that in section 7—and so it must be "autonomous." That is, it must act on a law that it gives to itself. And Kant says that this means that the categorical imperative *just is* the law of a free will.

To see why, we need only consider how a free will must deliberate. So here is the free will, completely self-governing, with nothing outside of it giving it any laws. And along comes an inclination, and presents the free will with a proposal. Now inclinations, according to Kant, are grounded in what he calls "incentives," which are the features of the objects of those inclinations that make them seem attractive and eligible.[5] Suppose that the incentive is that the object is pleasant. Then inclination says: end-E would be a very pleasant thing to bring about. So how about end-E? Doesn't that seem like an end to-be-produced? Now what the will chooses is, strictly speaking, actions, so before the proposal is complete, we need to make it a proposal for action. Instrumental reasoning determines that you could produce end-E by doing act-A. So the proposal is: that you should do act-A in order to produce this very pleasant end-E.

Now if your will were heteronomous, and pleasure were a law to you, this is all you would need to know, and you would straightaway do act-A in order to produce that pleasant end-E. But since you are autonomous, pleasure is not a law to you: nothing is a law to you except what you make a law for yourself. You therefore ask yourself a different question. The proposal is that you should do act-A in order to achieve pleasant end-E. Since nothing is a law to you except what you make a law for yourself, you ask yourself whether you could take *that* to be your law. Your question is whether you can will the maxim of doing act-A in order to produce end-E as a law. Your question,

[5] For a more complete account of these ideas and Kant's moral psychology generally see the first section of my "Motivation, Metaphysics, and the Value of the Self: A Reply to Ginsborg, Guyer, and Schneewind."

in other words, is whether your maxim passes the categorical imperative test. The categorical imperative is therefore the law of a free will.

Inclination presents the proposal; reason decides whether to act on it or not, and the decision takes the form of a *legislative act*. This is clearly the Constitutional Model.

4. Standards for Action

The main point of resemblance between the theories of Plato and Kant shows up, however, in their treatment of bad action. On the Combat Model, what happens when a person acts badly? The answer must be that the person is overcome by passion. But on the Combat Model we could just as well say that when a person acts well, she is overcome by reason, for the two forces seem to be on a footing. According to the Constitutional Model, on the other hand, a person acts well when she acts in accordance with her constitution. If reason overrules passion, she should act in accordance with reason, not because she identifies with reason, but because she identifies with her constitution, and it says that reason should rule.[6] So what happens when a person acts badly? Here we run into what looks, at first, like a difficulty for the Constitutional Model. It turns out to be the source of its deepest insights.

The difficulty is, of course, that according to the account of Plato I just gave, an unjust *person* cannot act at all, because an unjust person is not unified by constitutional rule. When a city is in a state of civil war, it does not act, although the various factions within it may do various things. The analogy suggests that when a soul is in a state of civil war, and the various forces within it are fighting for control, what looks to the outside world like *the person's actions* are really just the manifestations of forces at work *within* the person. So it looks at first as if *nothing exactly counts as a bad action*.

And there's an *exact* analogy to this difficulty in Kantian ethics. For a well-known problem in the *Groundwork* is that Kant appears to say that only autonomous action, that is, action governed by the categorical imperative, is really free action, while bad or heteronomous "action" is behavior *caused* by the work of desires and inclinations in us (G 4:453–55). But if this were so, then it would be hard to see how we could be held responsible for bad

---

[6] Julia Annas and others have pointed out to me that there is some tension between this idea and certain passages in the latter books of the *Republic* which strongly suggest that Plato's view is that we should identify with reason—most notably the passage at 588b–e in which Plato compares the three parts of the soul to a many-headed beast (appetite), a lion (spirit), and a human being (reason). I agree, but I think that the tension is within the text of the *Republic* itself, that it is part of a general tension between the conceptions of the soul in the earlier and later books.

or heteronomous action, or why we should even regard it as something we *do*. It seems more like something that happens in us or to us. This problem arises because of the argument by which Kant establishes the authority of the categorical imperative, the argument we just looked at. For that argument seems to show that action is *essentially* autonomous. Action must take place under the idea of freedom; and a free will must be autonomous. So it looks at first as if *nothing exactly counts as a bad action*.

It's important to observe that the *structure* of the problem in these two theories is exactly the same. Kant first identifies action with autonomous action, claiming that it is essential to action that it should be autonomous. He then identifies autonomous action with action governed by the categorical imperative, universalizable action. In exactly the same way, Plato first identifies action with action that emerges from constitutional procedure, claiming that it is essential to action that it should emerge from constitutional procedure. He then identifies action that emerges from constitutional procedure with just action. In other words, each argument first identifies an essential metaphysical property of action—autonomy in Kant's argument and constitutionality in Plato's—and then in turn identifies this metaphysical property with a normative property: universalizability in Kant's argument and justice in Plato's. And this is how the case for the normative requirement is made.

Furthermore, in both arguments the identification of the metaphysical property is an attempt to capture a specific feature of action, an important thing that distinguishes an action from a mere event, namely, that an action is *attributable* to the person who does it. The metaphysical property Plato and Kant are looking for is the one that makes it true that the action is not just something that happens in or to the person but rather is something that he as a person *does*. It is the property that makes the *person* the author of the action. Plato's explicit use of the Constitutional Model makes it clear that he is trying to identify this property. For we certainly do distinguish the actions we attribute to a city as such from the actions we would attribute only to some of the individuals in it. And the basis of this distinction is whether the action was the outcome of following constitutional procedures or not. If a Spartan attacks an Athenian, for instance, we do not conclude that *Sparta* is making war on Athens unless the attack was made by a soldier acting under the direction of the rulers: that is, unless it issues from Sparta's constitutional procedures. By the analogy, we will only attribute an action to a person, rather than to something in him, if it was directed by his reason, his ruling part. In a similar way, Kant thinks that what makes an action attributable to the person is that it springs from the person's autonomy or self-government. The exercise of the person's autonomy is what makes the action *his*, and so what makes it an action.

And so we get the problem. It is the essential nature of action that it has a certain metaphysical property. But in order to have that metaphysical property it must have a certain normative property. This explains why the action must meet the normative standard: *it just isn't action* if it doesn't. But it also seems as if it explains it rather too well, for it seems to imply that only good action really is action, and that there is nothing left for bad action to be.

Now rather than finding in this a reason for rejecting these arguments, I think we should see it as our main reason for embracing them. For what we have just observed is that, according to Plato and Kant, the moral standards we apply to actions are what I have elsewhere called "internal standards"—standards that a thing must meet in virtue of what it is.[7] An internal standard is one that arises from the nature of the object to which it applies, from the functional or teleological norms that make it the object that it is. Say that a house, for instance, is a habitable shelter. Then a good house is a house that has the features that enable it to serve as a habitable shelter—the corners are properly sealed, the roof is waterproof and tight, the rooms are tall enough to stand up in, and things like that. These internal standards are what make something *a good house*.

We need to distinguish here between something's being a good or bad *house* and it's being a house that happens to be a good or bad *thing* because of some external standard. The large mansion that blocks the whole neighborhood's view of the lake may be a *bad thing* for the neighborhood, but it is not therefore a *bad house*. A house that does not successfully shelter, on the other hand, is a bad house. Let me give this kind of badness a special name. An entity that does not meet its internal standards is *defective*.

The distinction between internal and external standards is important, because internal standards meet challenges to their normativity with perfect ease. Suppose you are going to build a house. Why shouldn't you build a house that blocks the whole neighborhood's view of the lake? Perhaps because it will displease the neighbors. Now *there* is a consideration that you may simply set aside, if you are selfish or tough enough to brave the neighbors' displeasure. But because it does not make sense to ask why a house should serve as a habitable shelter, it also does not make sense to ask why the corners should be sealed and the roof should be waterproof and tight. For if you fall too far short of the internal standard for houses, what you produce will simply not be a house. And this means that there's a sense in which even the most venal

---

[7] Or, sometimes, constitutive standards. I discuss the conception of an internal or constitutive standard in "The Normativity of Instrumental Reason," Essay 1 in this volume. See especially pp. 61–2. There I argue that the hypothetical imperative is an internal standard for acts of the will.

and shoddy builder must try to build a good house, for the simple reason that there is no other way to try to build a house. Building a good house and building a house are not different activities: for both are activities in which we must be guided by the functional or teleological norms implicit in the idea of a house. Obviously, it doesn't follow that every house is a good house. It does, however, follow that building bad houses is not a different activity from building good ones. *It is the same activity, badly done.*

Just actions in Plato, universalizable actions in Kant, are actions that are good *as* actions, the way a house that shelters successfully is good as a house. And if this is right, we should get the same conclusions. If justice and universalizability are internal standards, then they are not extraneous considerations whose normativity may be doubted. An agent cannot simply set aside the question whether his action is universalizable or just, for if he falls too far short of the internal standards for actions, what he produces will simply not be an action. In effect this means that even the most venal and shoddy agent must try to perform a good action, for the simple reason that there is no other way to try to perform an action. Performing a good action and performing an action are not different activities: for both are activities in which we must be guided by the functional or teleological norms implicit in the idea of an action. Obviously, it doesn't follow that every action is a good action. It does, however, follow that performing bad actions is not a different activity from performing good ones. *It is the same activity, badly done.*

5. Defective Action

So if we could make these claims plausible, or even intelligible, we would have an important result here: an answer to the question why our actions must meet moral standards. Unjust or non-universalizable actions would be *defective*: they would be bad *as actions*. But how can actions be defective, and still *be* actions? The Constitutional Model again provides us with the resources for an answer. For we all know that the action of a city may be formally or procedurally constitutional and yet not substantively just. Indeed, nothing is more familiar: a law duly legislated by the congress and even upheld by the supreme court may for all that be unjust. So it's not as if there's no territory at all between a perfectly just city and the complete disintegration of a civil war. A city may be governed, and yet be governed by the wrong law. And so may a soul. This, according to Plato and Kant, explains how bad action is possible.

In Kant's work this emerges most clearly in the first part of *Religion within the Limits of Reason Alone*. There we learn that a bad person is not after all one who is pushed about, or caused to act, by desires and inclinations. Instead, a bad person is one who is governed by what Kant calls the principle of self-love, by a principle which subordinates moral considerations to those arising from inclination (REL 6:36). The person who acts on the principle of self-love *chooses* to act as inclination prompts (REL 6:32–39). Let me try to make it clear why Kant thinks that an action based on the principle of self-love is *defective*, rather than merely externally bad.

Imagine a person I'll call Harriet, who is, in any formal sense you like, an autonomous person. She has a human mind, is self-conscious, with the normal allotment of the powers of reflection. She is not a slave or an indentured servant, and we will place her—unlike the original after whom I am modeling her—in an advanced modern constitutional democracy, with the full rights of free citizenship and all her human rights legally guaranteed to her. In every formal legal and psychological sense, what Harriet does is *up to her*. Yet whenever she has to make any of the important decisions and choices of her life, the way that Harriet does that is to ask Emma what she should do, and then that's what she does.[8]

This is autonomous action and yet it is *defective* as autonomous action. Harriet is self-governed and yet she is not, for she allows herself to be governed by Emma. Harriet is heteronomous, not in the sense that her actions are caused by Emma rather than chosen by herself, but in the sense that she allows herself to be governed in her choices by a law outside of herself. It even helps my case here that Harriet does this because she is afraid to think for herself. For, as I have argued elsewhere, this is how Kant envisions the operation of the principle of self-love.[9] Kant does not envision the person who acts from self-love as actively reflecting on what he has reason to do and arriving at the conclusion that he ought to do what he wants. Instead, Kant envisions him as one who simply follows the lead of desire, without sufficient reflection. He's heteronomous, and gets his law from nature, not in the sense that it causes his actions, but in the sense that he allows himself to be governed by its suggestions—just as Harriet allows herself to be governed by Emma's.

The analogous doctrine in Plato is much more elaborate, and this is to Plato's credit. For what Kant says here is incomplete and confusing. Minimally, it seems, Kant ought to have distinguished between a wanton principle of self-love—the principle of acting on the desire of the moment—and a prudent principle of self-love, which seeks, say, the greatest satisfaction of desires over

---

[8] The model for my Harriet is the persuadable Harriet Smith in Jane Austen's novel *Emma*.
[9] See my "From Duty and for the Sake of the Noble: Kant and Aristotle on Morally Good Action," Essay 6 in this volume, especially pp. 181–5.

time.[10] Both of these characters *are* found in Plato, and others besides. In Books 8 and 9 of the *Republic*, Plato in fact distinguishes five different ways that the soul may be governed, comparing them to five different kinds of constitutions possible for a city: the good way, which is monarchy or aristocracy; and four bad ones, growing increasingly worse: timocracy, oligarchy, democracy, and, worst of all, tyranny. In the three middle cases, what makes the constitution bad is that the unity of the person who lives under it depends upon contingent circumstances.

Nearest to the aristocratic soul is the timocratic person, who, like the city he is named for, is ruled by considerations of honor. Such a person loves the outward form, the beauty, of goodness, almost as if it were goodness itself. This person goes wrong, and becomes divided against himself, in a certain kind of case—namely, the kind of case in which the right thing is something which seems dishonorable. Suppose, for instance, the timocratic person is fighting for the good of the city, but we reach a point where really surrender is the better course. The timocratic person may be so fixed on the honorableness, the beauty, the glamour if you will, of this kind of action, of fighting-for-the-good-of-the-city, that he may be unable to give up, even though it is really for the good of the city that he should do so.[11]

Next comes the oligarchic person, who appears to be ruled by prudence: he is cautious, non-luxurious, and concerned with long-term enrichment. In describing him Plato employs a distinction between necessary desires, whose satisfaction is beneficial or essential to survival, and unnecessary or luxurious desires, which are harmful and should not be indulged. The oligarchic person is attentive to the necessary desires and to money, while he represses his unnecessary desires. But he represses them because they are unprofitable, rather than because it is bad to indulge them. The result of this forceful repression, according to Socrates, is that "someone like that wouldn't be

---

10 If I am right in saying that Kant sees self-love as operating unreflectively, this might seem to favor a wanton principle of self-love. Sometimes, however, it is clear that Kant has a prudent principle of self-love in mind—see for instance C2 5:35–36. While I think that the wanton principle does square better with Kant's arguments, I also think it should be possible to make the second *Critique* passages consistent with the view that those who act from self-love are unreflective. We just need to argue that there is a difference between being *reflective* and being *calculating*.

11 Although space constraints don't allow me to spell out the idea in sufficient detail here, I am tempted to say that the problem with the timocratic person is that he is unable to deal with the contingencies that call for the application of what I have elsewhere called, following John Rawls, "non-ideal theory" (see my "The Right to Lie: Kant on Dealing with Evil," CKE essay 5, especially pp. 147–54). That is, he acts well, except in those moments when true goodness calls for concession, compromise, a less strict rule, or even—though this is rare—actions that are formally wrong. See my "Taking the Law into Our Own Hands: Kant on the Right to Revolution," Essay 8 in this volume, for a discussion of this kind of case.

entirely free from internal civil war and wouldn't be one but in some way two." This kind of prudence rules despotically over the appetitive part, like the rich ruling over a discontented working class. Should some outside force—perhaps simply a sufficient temptation—strengthen and enliven his unnecessary desires, the oligarchic person may quite literally lose control of himself. If generally the oligarchic person manages to hang together, it is because he has the sort of imitation virtue which Socrates makes fun of in the *Phaedo*, the virtue of those who are able to master some of their pleasures and fears because they are in turn mastered by others.[12] Socrates has in mind here such arguments as that you should be temperate because that way you will get more pleasure on the whole. Generally, Plato seems to think that honor and prudence are principles of choice sufficiently like true virtue to hold a soul together through most kinds of stress, although in the oligarchic person the fault lines are increasingly visible.[13]

Next in line is the democratic person, in whom the unnecessary desires are not repressed, and who as a result is a wanton. Socrates says that the democratic person:

puts his pleasures on an equal footing . . . always surrendering rule over himself to whichever desire comes along, as if it were chosen by lot. And when that is satisfied, he surrenders the rule to another, not disdaining any but satisfying them all equally. (R 561b)

Democracy is a degenerate case of self-government, for such a person governs himself only in a minimal or formal sense, just as choosing by lot is different only in a minimal or formal sense from not choosing at all. The coherence of the democratic person's life is completely dependent on the accidental coherence of his desires. To see the problem, consider a story:

Jeremy, a college student, settles down at his desk one evening to study for an examination. Finding himself a little too restless to concentrate, he decides to take a walk in the fresh air. His walk takes him past a nearby bookstore, where the sight of an enticing title draws him in to look at the book. Before he finds it, however, he meets his friend Neil, who invites him to join some of the other kids at the bar next door for a beer. Jeremy decides he can afford to have just one, and goes with Neil to the bar.

---

[12] See Plato, *Phaedo* 68d–69c.

[13] A number of people have argued that the problem described here would not arise for the rational egoist in the more ordinary modern sense, the person who seeks to maximize the satisfaction of his own interests. Indeed this is suggested by my own remarks about how imitation virtue can help hold the oligarch together, for modern egoism is much like Plato's imitation virtue. If correct, this objection would suggest that you can constitute yourself through the egoistic principle. A full response to this objection requires a full treatment of the claim that there is a coherently formulable principle of rational egoism. See my "The Myth of Egoism," Essay 2 in this volume.

While waiting for his beer, however, he finds that the noise gives him a headache, and he decides to return home without ever having the beer. He is now, however, in too much pain to study. So Jeremy doesn't study for his examination, hardly gets a walk, doesn't buy a book, and doesn't drink a beer.[14]

Of course democratic life doesn't have to be like this; it's only an accident that each of Jeremy's impulses leads him to an action that completely undercuts the satisfaction of the last one. But that's just the trouble, for it's also only an accident if this does *not* happen. The democratic person has no resources for shaping his desires to prevent this, and so he is at the mercy of accident. Like Jeremy, he may be almost completely *incapable of effective action.*

It is from the chaos resulting from this kind of life that the tyrannical soul emerges. This kind of soul is once again unified, but not under the government of reason looking to the good of the whole. According to Plato, the tyrannical soul is governed by some erotic desire (R 572d–573a), which subordinates the entire soul to its purposes, leaving the person an absolute slave to a single dominating obsession (R 571a–580a).[15]

In Plato's story, as in Kant's, bad action is action governed by a principle of choice which is not reason's own: a principle of honor (timocracy), prudence (oligarchy), wantonness (democracy), or obsession (tyranny). It is action, because it is chosen in accordance with the exercise of a principle by which the agent rules himself and under whose rule he is—in a sense—unified. Yet it is defective, because it is not reason's own principle, and the unity that it produces is, at least in the three middle cases, contingent and unstable. And Plato can say with Kant that the person who governs himself in one of these ways isn't after all completely self-governed. For he is propped up, so to speak, by the fact that the circumstances that would create civil war in his soul don't happen to occur.

6. Good Action and the Unity of the Platonic Soul

Now we are almost ready to talk about what makes action good. But first I want to take up a possible objection. I've just said that in the conditions of

---

[14] I have lifted this example from footnote 52 of my "The Normativity of Instrumental Reason," essay 1 in this volume.

[15] The problem with tyranny is not the same as that with timocracy, oligarchy, and democracy—it is not that the unity it produces in the soul is contingent. Plato envisions tyranny as a kind of madness (see R 573c ff.). As I imagine the tyrant, his relation to his obsession is like a psychotic's relation to his delusion: he is able, and prepared, to organize everything else around it, but at the expense of a loss of his grip on reality, on the world. But that is only a sketch, and a fuller treatment of this principle, and of the question why a person cannot successful integrate himself under its governance, is required for the completeness of the argument of this essay.

timocracy, oligarchy, and democracy, your unity and so your self-government are propped by external circumstances, by the absence of the conditions under which you would fall apart. But what, you might ask, is so bad about that? The defect in these characters is like a geological fault line, a potential for disintegration that does not necessarily show up, and so long as it doesn't, these people have constitutional procedures and so they can act. So why not just go ahead and be, say, oligarchical? You'll hold together most of the time, you'll be able to perform actions, and you'll save all that money besides.

There is yet another way to ask this same question, which is to ask whether Glaucon's challenge is not too extreme. Glaucon wants Socrates to tell him what justice and injustice do to the soul. So he sets up the following challenge: take on the one hand a person who has a completely unjust soul, and give him all of the outward benefits of justice, that is, all the benefits that come from people believing you are just. And take on the other hand a person who has a completely just soul, and give him all of the outward disadvantages of injustice, all the disadvantages that come from people believing you are unjust (R 360d–361e). In particular, the just person who is believed to be unjust will be—and I'm quoting now—"whipped, stretched on a rack, chained, [and] blinded with fire" (R 361e). Socrates is supposed to show that it is better to be just than unjust *even then*. But isn't that too much to ask?

In the context of the argument of the *Republic*, it is not. For the question of the *Republic* is asked as a *practical* question: it is the question whether the just life is more worthy of *choice* than the unjust life. And if you choose to be a just person, and to live a just life, you are thereby choosing to do the just thing even if it means you will be whipped, stretched on the rack, chained, and blinded with fire. You can't make a conditional commitment to justice, a commitment to be just unless the going gets rough. Your justice rests in the nature of your commitments, and a commitment like that would not *be* a commitment to justice. So when deciding whether to be a just person, you've got to be convinced in advance that it'll be worth it even if things do turn out this way.

Suppose—for it's plausible enough—there's a person who lives a just life, is decent and upstanding, always does his share, never takes an unfair advantage, sticks to his word—all of that—but then, one day, he is put on the rack, and under stress of torture does something unjust. Say he divulges a military secret, or the whereabouts of a fugitive unjustly pursued. Am I saying that this shows that he was never really committed to justice, because his commitment must have been conditional? *Of course not.* What the case shows is that the range of things people can *be* is wider than the range of things they can choose, so to speak, *in advance* to be. This person was committed to keeping his secrets on the rack, but he failed, that's all—and very understandably too. But the fact that you can be a just person who in these circumstances will fail does not show that you can decide in advance to be a just person who in these circumstances will fail: that is, it doesn't show that you can make a conditional commitment to justice. For suppose you surprise yourself and you do hold out and you keep the secret even when they put you on the rack. Did you then fail to *keep* your conditional commitment?

So Glaucon's challenge is a fair one. But Plato more than meets it. For he doesn't merely prove that the just life is the one most worthy of choice. He proves the just life is the only one you can choose. Let me try to explain why.

Consider Plato's account of the principle of just or aristocratic action. Plato says of the aristocratic soul that:

when he does anything, whether acquiring wealth, taking care of his body, engaging in politics, or in private contracts—in all of these, he believes that the action is just and fine that preserves this inner harmony and helps achieve it, and calls it so, and regards as wisdom the knowledge that oversees such actions. And he believes that the action that destroys this harmony is unjust, and calls it so, and regards the belief that oversees it as ignorance. (R 443e–444a)

In other words, the principle of justice directs us to perform those actions that establish and maintain our volitional unity. Now we have already seen that according to Plato volitional unity is essential if you are to act as a person, as a single unified agent. So reason's own principle *just is* the principle of acting in a way that constitutes you into a single unified agent. Deliberative action is self-constitution.

In fact, deliberative action by its very nature imposes constitutional order on the soul. When you deliberate about what to do and then do it, what you are doing is organizing your appetite, reason, and spirit, into the unified system that yields an action that can be attributed to you as a person. Deliberative action pulls the parts of the soul together into a unified system. Whatever else you are doing when you choose a deliberative action, you are also unifying yourself into a person. This means that Plato's principle of justice, reason's own principle, is the *formal* principle of deliberative action. It is as if Glaucon asked: what condition could this be, that enables the just person to stick to his principles even on the rack? And it is as if Plato replied: don't look for some *further* condition which has that as an *effect*. Justice is not some other or further condition that enables us to maintain our unity as agents. It is that very condition itself—the condition of being able to maintain our unity as agents.

To see that this is formal, consider the following comparison. One might ask Kant: what principle could this be, that enables the free person to be autonomous, to rule herself? And Kant would reply: don't look for some *further* principle that has that as an *effect*. The categorical imperative is not some other or further principle that enables us to rule ourselves. It is that very principle itself, the principle of giving laws to ourselves.

On the one hand, this account of the aristocratic soul shows us why the demands of Platonic justice are so high. On certain occasions, the people with the other constitutions fall apart. For the truly just person, the aristocratic soul, there are no such occasions. She is entirely self-governed, so that all of her actions, in every circumstance of her life, are really and fully her own: never merely the manifestations of forces at work in her or on her, but always the expression of her own choice. She is completely self-possessed: not necessarily happy on the rack—but *herself* on the rack, herself even there.

And yet at the same time, Plato's argument shows that this aristocratic constitution is the only one you can choose. For you can't, in the moment of deliberative action, choose to be something less than a single unified agent. And that means you can't exactly choose to act on any principle other than the principle of justice. Timocratic, oligarchic, and democratic souls disintegrate under certain conditions, so deciding to be one would be like making a conditional commitment to your own unity, to your own personhood. And that's not possible. For consider what happens when the conditions that cause disintegration in these constitutions actually occur. If you don't fall apart, have you failed to keep your commitment, like the conditionally just person who holds out on the rack after all? But if you do fall apart, *who is it* that has kept the commitment? If you fall apart, there is no person left. You can be a timocratic, oligarchic, or democratic person, in the same way that you can be a just person who fails on the rack. But you cannot decide in advance that this is what you will be.

Of course this doesn't mean that everyone chooses the just life. What it means is that choosing an unjust life is not a different activity from choosing a just one. It is the same activity—the activity of self-constitution—badly done.

7. Good Action and the Unity of the Kantian Will

It remains to show that this is also Kant's view; and for that we need to revisit the argument by which Kant establishes that action must be in accordance with the categorical imperative, and fill in its missing step. Kant argues that insofar as you are a rational being, you must act under the idea of freedom—and this means that you do not think of yourself, or experience yourself, as being impelled into action, but rather as deciding what to do. You take *yourself*, rather

than the incentive on which you choose to act, to be the *cause* of your action.[16]
And Kant thinks that in order for this to be so, you must act on a universal law.
You cannot regard yourself as the *cause* of your action—you cannot regard
the action as the product of your will—unless you will universally.

To see why, let us consider what happens if we try to deny it.[17] If our reasons
did not have to be universal then they could be completely particular—it
would be possible to have a reason that applies only to the case before you,
and has no implications for any other case. Willing to act on a reason of this
kind would be what I will call "particularistic willing." If particularistic willing
is impossible, then it follows that willing must be universal—that is, a maxim,
in order to be willed at all, must be willed as a universal law.

Now there are two things to notice here. First of all, the question is not
whether we can will a new maxim for each new occasion. We may very well
do that, for every occasion may have relevant differences from the one we last
encountered. Any difference in the situation that is actually relevant to the
decision properly belongs in our maxim, and this means that our maxim may
be quite specific to the situation at hand. The argument here is not supposed
to show that reasons are general. It is supposed to show us that reasons are
universal, and universality is quite compatible—indeed it requires—a high
degree of specificity.

The second point is that it will be enough for the argument if the principle
that is willed be willed, as I will call it, as provisionally universal. To explain
what I mean by that I will use a pair of contrasts. There are three different ways
in which we can take our principles to range over a variety of cases, and it is
important to keep them distinct. We treat a principle as *general* when we think
it applies to a wide range of similar cases. We treat a principle as universal,
or, as I will sometimes say, *absolutely universal*, when we think it applies to
absolutely every case of a certain sort, but all the cases must be exactly of that
sort. We treat a principle as *provisionally universal* when we think it applies
to every case of a certain sort, unless there is some good reason why not.
The difference between regarding a principle as universal, and regarding it as
provisionally universal, is marginal. Treating a principle as only provisionally
universal amounts to making a mental acknowledgment, to the effect that you

[16] To put it somewhat more strictly, you take yourself to be the cause of your intelligible movements,
since it is only really an *action* if you are, or to the extent that you are, the cause. I think that there
are important philosophical questions, yet to be worked out, about exactly how this point should
be phrased, but for now I leave the more familiar formulation in the text. I am indebted to Sophia
Reibetanz and Tamar Schapiro for discussions of these points.

[17] The argument that follows made its first appearance in section 1 of the Reply in SN pp. 225–33.
Another version is found in my book *Self-Constitution: Agency, Identity, and Integrity*. This essay is in
fact a very short version of the argument of that book.

might not have thought of everything needed to make the principle universal, and therefore might not have specified it completely. Treating principles as general, and treating them as provisionally universal, are superficially similar, because in both cases we admit that there might be exceptions. But in fact they are deeply and essentially different, and this shows up in what happens when we encounter the exceptions. If we think of a principle as merely general, and we encounter an exception, nothing happens. The principle was only general, and we expected there to be some exceptions. But if a principle was provisionally universal, and we encounter an exceptional case, we must now go back and revise it, bringing it a little closer to the absolute universality to which provisional universality essentially aspires.

The rough causal principles with which we operate in everyday life (I am not talking now about quantum physics) are provisionally universal, and we signal this sometimes by using the phrase "all else equal." The principle that striking a match causes a flame holds all else equal, where the things that have to be equal are that there is no gust of wind or splash of water or oddity in the chemical composition of the atmosphere that would interfere with the usual connection. There are background conditions for the operation of these laws, and without listing and possibly without knowing them all, we mention that they must be in place when we say "all else equal." Although there are certainly exceptions, natural law is not merely general, for whenever an exception occurs, we look for an explanation. Something must have made this case different: one of its background conditions was not met.

To see how it works in the practical case, consider a standard puzzle case for Kant's universalizability criterion. It may seem as if wanting to be a doctor is an adequate reason for becoming a doctor, for there's nothing wrong with being a doctor—in fact, really, it's rather admirable—and if you ask yourself if it could be a law that everyone who wants to be a doctor should become one, it seems, superficially, fine. But then the objector comes along and says, but look, suppose *everyone* actually wanted to be a doctor and nobody wanted to be anything else. The whole economic system would go to pieces, and then you couldn't be a doctor, so your maxim would have contradicted itself! So does this show that it is wrong to be a doctor simply because you want to?

What it shows is that the mere desire to enter a certain profession is only a provisionally universal reason for doing so. There's a background condition for the rightness of being a doctor because you want to, which is that society has some need for people to enter this profession. In effect the case does show that it's wrong to be a doctor merely because you want to—the maxim needs revision, for it is not absolutely universal unless it mentions as part of your reason for becoming a doctor that there is a social need. Someone who decides to become a doctor in the full light of reflection also takes that into account.

That case is easy, but there's no general reason to suppose we can think of everything in advance. When we adopt a maxim as a universal law, we know that there might be cases, cases we haven't thought of, which would show us that it is not universal after all. In that sense we can allow for exceptions. But so long as the commitment to revise in the face of exceptions is in place, the maxim is not merely general. It is provisionally universal.

So particularistic willing is neither a matter of willing a new maxim for each occasion, nor is it a matter of willing a maxim that you might have to change on another occasion. Both of those are compatible with regarding reasons as universal. Instead, particularistic willing would be a matter of willing a maxim for exactly this occasion without taking it to have any other implications of any kind for any other occasion. You will a maxim thinking that you can use it just this once and then so to speak discard it; you don't even need a reason to change your mind.

Now I'm going to argue that that sort of willing is impossible. The first step is this: to conceive of yourself as the cause of your actions is to identify with the principle of choice on which you act. A rational will is a self-conscious causality, and a self-conscious causality is aware of itself as a cause. To be aware of yourself as a cause is to identify yourself with something in the scenario that gives rise to the action, and this must be the principle of choice. For instance, suppose you experience a conflict of desire: you have a desire to do both A and B, and they are incompatible. You have some principle that favors A over B, so you exercise this principle, and you choose to do A. In this kind of case, you do not regard yourself as a mere passive spectator to the battle between A and B. You regard the choice as yours, as the product of your own activity, because you regard the principle of choice as expressive, or representative, of yourself. You must do so, for the only alternative to identifying with the principle of choice is regarding the principle of choice as some third thing in you, another force on a par with the incentives to do A and to do B, which happened to throw in its weight in favor of A, in a battle at which you were, after all, a mere passive spectator. But then you are not the cause of the action. Self-conscious or rational agency, then, requires identification with the principle of choice on which you act.

The second step is to see that particularistic willing makes it impossible for you to distinguish yourself, your principle of choice, from the various incentives on which you act. According to Kant, you must always act on some incentive or other, for every action, even action from duty, involves a decision on a proposal: something must suggest the action to you. And in order to will particularistically, you must in each case wholly identify with the incentive of your action. That incentive would be, for the moment, your law, the law that defines your agency or your will.

It's important to see that if you had a particularistic will you would not identify with the incentive as representative of any sort of type, since if you took it as a representative of a type you would be taking it as universal. For instance, you couldn't say that you decided to act on the inclination of the moment, *because you were so inclined.* Someone who takes "I shall do the things I am inclined to do, whatever they might be" as his maxim has adopted a universal principle, not a particular one: he has the principle of treating his inclinations *as such* as reasons. A truly particularistic will must embrace the incentive in its full particularity: it, in no way that is further describable, is the law of such a will. So someone who engages in particularistic willing does not even have a democratic soul. There is only the tyranny of the moment: the complete domination of the agent by something inside him.

Particularistic willing eradicates the distinction between a person and the incentives on which he acts. But then there is nothing left here that is the *person*, the agent, that is his will as distinct from the play of incentives within him. He is not one person, but a series, a mere conglomeration, of unrelated impulses. There is no difference between someone who has a particularistic will and someone who has no will at all. Particularistic willing lacks a subject, a person who is the cause of these actions. So particularistic willing isn't willing at all.

If a particularistic will is impossible, then when you will a maxim you must take it to be universal. If you do not, you are not operating as a self-conscious cause, and then you are not willing. To put the point in familiar Kantian terms, we can only attach the "I will" to our choices if we will our maxims as universal laws.[18] The categorical imperative is an internal standard for actions, because conformity to it is constitutive of an exercise of the will, of an action of a person as opposed to an action of something within him.

And this argument also shows that Kant's view is the same as Plato's. For if particularistic willing is what breaks us down, universal willing is what holds us together. For Kant, as for Plato, deliberative action by its very nature imposes unity on the will. It is only when you ask whether your maxim can be a universal law that you exercise the self-conscious causality, the autonomy, that yields an action that can be attributed to you as a whole person. So whatever else you are doing when you choose a deliberative action, you are also unifying yourself into a person. For Kant, as for Plato, action is self-constitution.

---

[18] I owe this formulation of my point to Govert den Hartogh.

8. Conclusion

I will conclude by reviewing the course of the argument and saying what I take it to have established. I started by criticizing the Combat Model for failing to identify the person who is the author of her actions. I hope that by now it is clear why it fails in that way. The Combat Model is not a picture of the human soul. It is a picture of the human soul in ruins, torn apart by civil war and therefore unable to act. According to the Constitutional Model, an action is yours when it is chosen in accordance with your constitution. Your constitution is what gives you the kind of volitional unity you need to be the author of your actions. And it is the person who acts in accordance with the best constitution, the most unified constitution, who is most truly the author of her actions. For Kant as for Plato, integrity is the metaphysical essence of morality.

The argument of this essay does not, by itself, get us all the way to the necessity of acting morally. The aim of the argument has been to establish that the Platonic principle of justice and Kant's categorical imperative are formal standards of deliberative action. Both Kant and Plato believed that a certain content, the content of ordinary morality, could be derived from these formal principles. Plato's conviction appears at one of the most notorious moments of the *Republic*, when Socrates proposes to Glaucon that they can dispel any doubts they might have about their definition of justice "by appealing to ordinary cases" (R 442d–e). Accordingly, he asks Glaucon whether the just person as Socrates has described him would embezzle deposits, rob temples, steal, betray his friends or his city, violate his oaths or his other agreements, commit adultery, be disrespectful to his parents or neglect the gods, to all of which Glaucon says, with a complaisance startling to the reader, no, he would not, the just person Socrates has described him would not do these kinds of things. We are not told exactly why he is so sure. Kant, of course, does try to show us how content can be derived from his formal principle, and to that extent his version of the argument is superior to Plato's, although the success of his efforts is the subject of an old and famous debate. I think Kant's case can be made, but I haven't been trying to do that here.[19] Both Plato and Kant's arguments move (1) from the metaphysical property of action that makes it authored and so makes it action—autonomy in Kant's case, constitutionality in Plato's—to (2) a formal normative requirement that actions must meet

---

[19] In lecture 3 of *The Sources of Normativity* I give an argument that aims to move from the formal version of the categorical imperative to moral requirements by way of Kant's Formula of Humanity. See especially SN 3.3.7–3.4.10, pp. 112–25.

if they are to have that property—universalizability in Kant's case, justice in Plato's—and then through (3) the derivation of content from the formal requirement to arrive at ordinary moral requirements. It is the first two steps that have been my subject here.

At least in the formal sense, then, Platonic justice and Kant's categorical imperative are internal standard for actions, because it is only insofar as your actions issue from your whole person, rather than something in you, that they can be actions. It doesn't exactly follow that we ought to choose actions justly and in accordance with the categorical imperative, for in a sense we cannot possibly choose in any other way. Choosing bad actions is not a different activity from choosing good ones. It is the same activity—the activity of self-constitution—badly done.[20]

[20] I have discussed this essay or the longer unpublished manuscript from which it is drawn with audiences at the inaugural meeting of the Society for Ethics, the University of Amsterdam, the University of Constance, the Humboldt University of Berlin, the University of Pittsburgh, the University of Virginia, the University of Salzburg, the University of Toronto, York University of Toronto, and the University of Zurich. I am grateful to all of these audiences for their interest, insightful comments and challenging questions. I would like to thank Charlotte Brown, Barbara Herman, Govert den Hartogh, Anton Leist, Richard Moran, Amélie Rorty, and Theo van Willigenburg for reading and commenting on the manuscript.

Part 2
Moral Virtue and Moral Psychology

4

Aristotle's Function Argument

1. Introduction

The purpose of the *Nicomachean Ethics* is to discover the human good, that at which we ought to aim in life and action. Aristotle tells us that everyone calls this good *eudaimonia* (happiness, flourishing, well-being), but that people disagree about what it consists in (NE 1.4 1059a15ff.). In 1.7, Aristotle suggests that we might arrive at a clearer conception of happiness if we could first ascertain the *ergon* (function) of a human being (NE 1.7 1097b24). The justification of this line of inquiry is that "for all things that have a function or activity, the good and the 'well' is thought to reside in the function" (NE 1.7 1097b26–27). The compact argument that follows establishes that the human function is "an active life of the element that has a rational principle" (NE 1.7 1098a3–4). The human good therefore is the activity of the rational part of the soul performed well, which is to say, in accordance with virtue (NE 1.7 1098a15–17).

Aristotle's argument, which I will present in more detail in the next section, is a descendant of one offered by Plato at the end of the first book of the *Republic* (R 352d–354b). Here Socrates is trying to establish that the just life is happiest and best, and he argues as follows. First of all, each thing has a function, which is what one can do only or best with that thing (R 352e). Furthermore, everything that has a function has a virtue, which enables it to perform its function well (R 352b–c). The function of the soul is "taking care of things, ruling, deliberating, and the like," since these are activities you could not perform with anything except your soul. A few lines later Socrates also proposes that "living" is a function of the soul (R 353d). Since the soul only performs its function well if it has the virtue associated with its function, a good soul rules, takes care of things, and in general "lives" well, while a bad soul does all this badly (R 353e). Since earlier arguments have supposedly established that justice is the virtue of the soul, Socrotes concludes that the just soul lives well, and therefore is blessed and happy, while an unjust one lives badly and so is wretched.

Both versions of the argument seem to depend on a connection between being a good person and having a good or happy life, and their aim is to connect both of these in turn to rationality. Aristotle's version of the argument in particular has provoked a great deal of criticism, some of which I describe in the next section. In this essay, I offer an account of what Aristotle means by "function" and what the human function is, drawing on Aristotle's metaphysical and psychological writings. I then reconstruct Aristotle's argument in terms of the results. My purpose is to defend the function argument, and to show that when it is properly understood, it is possible to answer many of the objections that have been raised to it. For reasons I will explain below, I think it is essential to make good sense of the function argument, because the theoretical structure of the *Nicomachean Ethics* collapses without it. Part of the defense is conditional, and shows only that if one held Aristotle's metaphysical beliefs, the function argument would seem as natural and obvious as it clearly seemed to him. But part of it is intended to be unconditional, and to show that, given certain assumptions about reason and virtue, which, if not obvious, are certainly not crazy, the function argument is a good way to approach the question how to live well.

2. The Function Argument and its Critics

Aristotle opens his version of the argument with these words:

Presumably, however, to say that happiness is the chief good seems a platitude, and a clearer account of what it is is still desired. This might perhaps be given, if we could first ascertain the function of man. For just as for a flute player, a sculptor, or any artist, and, in general, for all things that have a function or activity, the good and the "well" is thought to reside in the function, so it would seem to be for man, if he has a function. Have the carpenter, then, and the tanner certain functions or activities, and has man none? Is he naturally functionless? Or as eye, hand, foot, and in general each of the parts evidently has a function, may one lay it down that man similarly has a function apart from all these? (NE 1.7 1097b22–33)

After quoting this remark, W. F. R. Hardie comments "the obvious answer is that one may not, unless one is prepared to say that a man is an instrument designed for some use."[1] Only in light of controversial religious or metaphysical assumptions can we view human beings as having a function, or being designed for a purpose.

We can read the passage quoted in either of two ways. We can read it as an expression of astonishment: "What! All these other things have a function, and a human being has none?" Or we can read it as an argument: bodily parts have functions, but that only makes sense if there is a function of the whole

---

[1] W. F. R. Hardie, *Aristotle's Ethical Theory*, p. 23.

relative to which the parts have a function; the various trades and professions have functions, but that only makes sense if there is some general function of human life to which they make a contribution. Either way, the argument seems to depend on a teleological conception of the world that we no longer accept: in the first case, the simple assignment of a purpose to everything; in the second, a form of reasoning from relative to absolute purposes that may be illegitimate.[2]

Even supposing that human beings do have a function, it is unclear why the good *for* a human being should reside in the good performance of the human function. Granted that a human being who performs the human function well is (in some sense) a good human being, we can still ask whether it is good for a human being to be a good human being.[3] We can ask whether it will make the person happy, in a recognizable sense having something to do with pleasure, or with the quality of the person's experiences, or at least with some condition welcome from the person's own point of view. Certainly, not all of the standard Greek examples of function will support an inference from being a good X in the sense of being good at one's function to achieving the good for an X. Aristotle himself uses the example of a horse, and says that the virtue of the horse "makes a horse both good in itself and good at running and at carrying its rider and at awaiting the attack of enemy" (NE 2.6 1106a19). But it is not obvious that a horse achieves its own good in being "a good horse" if what that means is a horse good for human military purposes. Might not a skittish unmanageable horse win for itself a fine free horse-life away from the dangers of warfare? One of Plato's examples is a pruning knife (R 353a), but it would be absurd to infer that a good pruning knife achieves the good for a pruning knife. An even more serious problem is posed by the fact that in the *Republic*, when Adeimantus complains that the guardians in the ideal state will not be very happy, Socrates replies that he is aiming at the happiness of the whole, not of any one part (R 419–421c). The ideal state is explicitly formed on the principle of each part performing its function, yet here Socrates admits (at least temporarily) that the guardians, in performing their function, may not get what is best for themselves.

Aristotle proceeds:

What then can this [the function] be? Life seems to be common even to plants, but we are seeking what is peculiar to man. Let us exclude, therefore, the life of nutrition

---

[2] These criticisms are mentioned and discussed, though not endorsed, by Martha Nussbaum in *Aristotle's De Motu Animalium*, pp. 100 ff.

[3] See Peter Glassen, "A Fallacy in Aristotle's Argument about the Good." For a discussion of Glassen's criticism, see Kathleen V. Wilkes, "The Good Man and the Good for Man in Aristotle's Ethics," in *Essays on Aristotle's Ethics*, pp. 341–57.

and growth. Next there would be a life of perception, but *it* also seems to be common even to the horse, the ox, and every animal. There remains, then, an active life of the element that has a rational principle. (NE 1.7 1097b3–1098a4)

This move gives rise to further objections. Why should the human function be one of these three things—the life of nutrition and growth, the life of perception, and the life of reason? And of these, why should it be the one that is "peculiar" to us? If dolphins or Martians also reasoned, would it be any the less our function to reason?[4] And aren't other things "peculiar" to us? Bernard Williams comments:

If one approached without preconception the question of finding characteristics which differentiate men from other animals, one could as well, on these principles, end up with a morality which exhorted man to spend as much time as possible in making fire; or developing peculiarly human physical characteristics; or having sexual intercourse without regard to season; or despoiling the environment and upsetting the balance of nature; or killing things for fun.[5]

And Robert Nozick asks:

If man turned out to be unique only in having a sense of humor, would it follow that he should concentrate his energies on inventing and telling jokes?[6]

Even if we suppose that for some reason the human function must be one of the three kinds of life among which Aristotle makes his selection, why only one? Thomas Nagel points out that it may be more plausible to argue that human flourishing involves the well-functioning of all of our essential capacities, and not just one.[7]

Finally, even if we do manage to isolate a unique and characteristic human capacity that seems to be a plausible candidate for the human function, won't it turn out to be a capacity that can be used either for good or for evil? Why should the good performance of the human function make one a *morally* good human being? Bernard Williams says:

For if it is a mark of a man to employ intelligence and tools in modifying his environment, it is equally a mark of him to employ intelligence and tools in destroying others. If it is a mark of a man to have a conceptualized and fully conscious awareness of himself as one among others, aware that others have feelings like himself, this is a preconception not only of benevolence but . . . of cruelty as well.[8]

---

[4] I draw these examples from Robert Nozick in *Philosophical Explanation*, p. 516; and Terence H. Irwin, "The Metaphysical and Psychological Basis of Aristotle's Ethics," in *Essays on Aristotle's Ethics*, p. 49.

[5] Williams, *Morality: An Introduction to Ethics*, p. 64.

[6] Nozick, *Philosophical Explanations*, p. 516.

[7] Nagel, "Aristotle on Eudaimonia," in *Essays on Aristotle's Ethics*, pp. 7–14.

[8] Williams, *Morality: An Introduction to Ethics*, p. 64.

In this way nearly every premise and presupposition of the function argument has been criticized. The idea that human beings even *have* a function is supposed to be based on a dubious teleological principle or an illegitimate piece of teleological reasoning. The inference that the good performance of this function, supposing that it did make you a good human being, would therefore be good *for you*, has been deemed a "fallacy."[9] The assumption that the good performance of the function *would* make you a good human being is called into question by the thought that any human capacity can be used—and used, in a non-moral sense, excellently—either for good or for evil. Even if these problems were resolved, Aristotle's method of selecting the function—by choosing the kind of life that is unique to human beings—raises a whole new set of problems, since his critics cannot see either why it should be one of these or why it should be the one that is unique.

For all of these reasons, even sympathetic readers sometimes dismiss the function argument as a piece of antique metaphysics, or as an unfortunate contrivance for supporting the philosopher's characteristic prejudice in favor of rationality. Some of the critics seem to think of the function argument merely as a preliminary argument in favor of the contemplative life that Aristotle will champion in Book 10, and therefore perhaps as something we may simply lay aside. On this reading, the function argument is simply "reason is the unique human capacity, therefore human happiness consists in thinking and doing science and philosophy." This makes the bulk of the *Nicomachean Ethics*, Books 2–9, appear as a kind of digression.[10]

In fact, however, the function argument cannot be set aside without a serious loss to Aristotle's theory of the moral virtues. Both Plato and Aristotle recognize a conceptual connection between *ergon*, function, and *arete*, virtue (R 353 b–c; NE 2.6 1106a14ff.; NE 6.2 1139a18). A virtue is not merely an admirable or socially useful quality: it is quite specifically a quality that makes you good at performing your function.[11] An important part of Aristotle's task in the *Nicomachean Ethics* is therefore to show that the characteristics that we commonly think of as the moral virtues really are *virtues* in this technical sense—qualities that make us good at rational activity. So Aristotle needs the conclusion of the function argument not only to support his views about

---

[9] Peter Glassen, "A Fallacy in Aristotle's Argument about the Good."

[10] The text does not bear this reading in any case, since after Aristotle identifies the function as the active life of the part that has a rational principle, he adds that one part "has" such a principle in the sense of being obedient to it and another in the sense of possessing it and exercising thought. It is of course practical reason, not theoretical reason, to which the moral virtues are in some sense "obedient."

[11] Sarah Broadie also points this out in her discussion of the function argument in *Ethics with Aristotle*, p. 37.

what sort of life is best, but also in order to give us a theoretical basis for the claim that certain qualities are virtues. The key to Aristotle's theory of the virtues rests in the connection Aristotle establishes between moral virtue and practical rationality, in the claim that *phronesis* or practical wisdom cannot be achieved without moral virtue. To understand why that is so is to understand what moral virtue really is and why it matters. If we set aside the function argument and with it the technical connection between function and virtue, Aristotle's careful descriptions of the virtues are merely that—descriptions of widely admired qualities and nothing more.

One may object, of course, that the descriptions are obviously something more: they are aimed at showing us that the virtues all fit a certain pattern, namely, that they involve having responses that rest in a certain kind of mean between two extremes. After all, in 2.6 Aristotle proposes what is generally acknowledged to be a kind of definition of virtue: it is a state "concerned with choice, lying in a mean relative to us, this being determined by reason and in the way in which the man of practical wisdom would determine it" (NE 2.6 1106b35ff.). Aristotle's aim is to show that all of the moral virtues can be understood in this way. But it is essential to observe that that same section, 2.6, opens with an announcement of the technical connection between function and virtue:

We must, however, not only describe it [virtue] as a state, but also say what sort of state it is. We may remark, then, that every virtue both brings into good condition the thing of which it is the virtue and makes the function of that thing be done well. (NE 2.6 1106a14ff.)

Aristotle's descriptions of the virtues are therefore not merely intended to show us that virtue is in a mean, but to show us how having qualities that are in a mean makes us good at rational activity.

If we set aside the function argument, then, we set aside the key to Aristotle's theory of the virtues. And that means that if we set aside the function argument, we will not know how to read the *Nicomachean Ethics*, since we will not know how to look for the facts about the virtues that Aristotle is trying to make us see.

3. Form, Matter, and Function

Those who object to the function argument on the grounds of its alleged dependence on an illicit teleological principle or method of reasoning are usually interpreting function as being more or less equivalent to "purpose." A number of Aristotle's defenders have pointed out that function or *ergon* has a wider range of meanings than just "purpose." It can be used to mean work or workings or product or characteristic activity.[12] In fact *energeia*, activity, and *ergon*, function, are etymologically linked (M 9.8 1050a21–22).

And the notion of an activity—an *energeia*—is central to Aristotle's metaphysics, because of its connection to the important metaphysical notion of form. In *Metaphysics* 7–9, in the course of an investigation into the idea of *ousia*, substance, Aristotle explores the distinction between form and matter. The distinction serves to explain how things (substances) can come to be and pass away (M 7.7 1032a20ff.). A thing comes to be, as the kind of thing that it is, when a certain form is imposed on matter. But Aristotle raises questions about how we are to understand the ideas of form and matter, and which of the two is more essential to a substance. The form, Aristotle argues, is what gives us the real essence of the thing, for it is in terms of the form that we can explain the properties and activities of the thing. As the argument proceeds, the fairly simple notion of form as the shape of a thing and matter as what is thus shaped gives way to a notion of form as the functional construction of a thing and matter as the material or the parts which get so constructed. The thing is what it is when its parts are arranged in a way that makes it capable of the activities that are essential to or characteristic of it—capable of performing its function. In later stages of the argument, which I will not be taking up in this essay, the notion of form as the functional construction of a thing in turn gives way first to the more complex notion of form as the actuality of which matter is the potentiality, and finally to the notion of form as the activity itself. Aristotle does not give up the simpler accounts, but rather reinterprets them in light of the more complex ones. In this way he establishes a tight link between a thing's form, its function, and the characteristic activities that make it what it is. It is in terms of this link that the function argument of the *Nicomachean Ethics* must be understood.

Aristotle's central examples of things that can be understood in terms of form/matter distinction are material substances. His favorite cases are plants and animals (M 7.8 1034a3). The elements—earth, air, fire, and water—are also material substances (M 7.2 1028b9ff.; M 8.1 1042a7ff.). So are the other sorts of things, characterized by mass nouns, which are most immediately composed of them: iron, bronze, wood, and flesh, for instance (M 7.9 1034b8ff.). These are often mentioned as matter, since they are matter relative to other substances, but they are also substances in their own right and as such must have a form and a matter of their own. The parts of animals and plants are also sometimes

---

[12] See especially Terence H. Irwin, "The Metaphysical and Psychological Basis of Aristotle's Ethics," in *Essays on Aristotle's Ethics*, pp. 35–53; Martha Nussbaum, in *Aristotle's De Motu Animalium*, pp. 100 ff.

classed as substances, although in the end Aristotle rejects that view. A related and important problem case is the things into which a substance dissolves when it loses its form: a corpse or skeleton, for example, or the bricks and timbers of a fallen house. These turn out to have a kind of privative form (M 7.7 1033b7ff.). And finally there are artifacts: a hammer, a house, and so forth.[13]

In identifying what is form and what matter in each of these cases, we must keep in mind certain constraints on the notion of form, which emerge in the course of the argument. The form of a thing is its essence. To know a thing is to know its essence or form (M 7.7 1032a). Demonstrations, which yield scientific knowledge, start from a statement of the essence (M 7.6 1031b6; 7.9 1034a31ff.).[14] So the form must be something in terms of which we can explain the properties and activities of the thing (M 7.17 1041a9ff.). To be a craftsman is to have the form of your product in your mind, and to work from it (M 7.7 1032b1–20; 7.9 1034a24). And two things that are of the same species have the same form (M 7.12 1038a16ff.; 7.13 1038b21–22).

Considering these constraints and Aristotle's own examples, we can generate some cases of the form/matter distinction. Aristotle often introduces the form/matter distinction by identifying form with shape. He mentions a bronze cube, of which the bronze is the matter and the form is the "characteristic angle"; a bronze statue, of which the bronze is the matter and the shape is the plan of its form; and a brazen sphere made out of brass and the sphere (M 5.25 1023b19ff., 7.3 1029a2, 7.8 1033b8ff.). He also mentions stone and wood as materials out of which various things are made (M 7.11 1036a30ff.), and such things are often made by shaping.

For most things, however, shape in this sense—contour—has little explanatory value. This is evidently true of things characterized by mass nouns, such as the bronze, stone, and wood that are identified as matter in the above cases. These are also, as I said earlier, substances in their own right, and as such have a form. Aristotle says these are characterized by the "ratio" or, as one might put it, the recipe. For instance, when criticizing the Pythagorean view that forms are numbers, Aristotle remarks that "the substance of flesh or bone is number

---

[13] Aristotle applies the distinction in other kinds of cases as well. For instance, he says that mathematical objects, such as the circle or the plane, also have a form and a matter: these cases lead him to make a distinction between two sorts of matter, perceptible and intelligible (M 7.10 1036a7ff.; M 7.11 1037a1ff.; M 8.6 1045a34). Intelligible matter seems to be a kind of bare extension. Aristotle also says that since any change must be explained in terms of the three basic principles of form, matter, and privation, we must posit a form and a matter even for qualitative or "accidental"—as opposed to substantial—change (M 7.4 1030a23; PHY 1.6–9). In such cases, the matter is the concrete material substance, already a form-in-a-matter, and the form is that of the quality itself. For instance, in the case of tanning, the *human being* is the matter or substrate of the change, and the form is the form of the dark color acquired (not the form of the human being, who of course remains a human being).

[14] This is also clear from *Posterior Analytics* 2.

only in this way, 'three parts of fire and two of earth' "(M 14.5 1092b17ff.). He says of "the things formed by mixture, such as honey-water" that they are characterized by "the mode of composition of their matter" (M 8.2 1042b15ff.). And we would similarly give the form of bronze as copper plus tin in a certain ratio, and so on.

In the case of plants and animals neither contour nor recipe can be the form. The contour may be the same in a statue and the person it depicts, yet these are different kinds of substance, and animate beings are certainly not mere mixtures. Aristotle sometimes describes the parts of a living thing as its matter: flesh, bone, and so forth (M 7.10 1035a15ff.). In this case it is tempting to identify the form as the structural arrangement: it is when the flesh, bone, and organs are put together in a certain way that they become a human being or a tiger or a sparrow. A similar point could be made about a more complicated artifact, say a machine, which actually is created in this fashion: it is made, say, of coils, wheels, cogs, springs, nuts, bolts, and so forth; when these are organized in a certain way, it becomes a clock or a vacuum cleaner or a drill.

A problem with the idea of identifying structural arrangement with form, however, is that things with quite different structural arrangements are of the same species, and so, according to Aristotle's theory, should have the same form. For example, a native American's teepee, a Victorian house, and a medieval castle are all houses, even leaving aside the further range of nests, burrows, and so forth, and yet they have little structural similarity. An abacus and an electronic calculator are both calculators, although they do not work the same way. It is perhaps possible to treat some of these cases as involving different species of a single genus. But it is not possible to treat different kinds of human beings as different species of a single genus, yet a giant and a pygmy, a woman and a man, an adult and a child exhibit obvious structural differences. These kinds of cases, together with the connection Aristotle makes between the form of a thing and its characteristic activity, suggest the idea that the form is the *function* of a thing (M 7.10 1035b17).

A functional account of form is also suggested by the idea that to know a thing is to know its form. After all, you might get a quite complete notion of the structural arrangement of a thing, say by taking it apart or dissecting it, without any idea what it does or what it is for. In that case you could hardly be said to know what the thing is. The person who knows what a thing *does* knows more about what it is than the person who has minutely examined its structural arrangements but has no idea what it does.

But appeal to what a thing does, by itself, does not seem to explain its properties and activities. It seems only to gesture at where the explanation might lie. I think it is helpful here to distinguish two possible senses of "function." In many cases it is quite natural to identify a thing's function with its purpose, with what it is for or simply what it does. Some of the examples mentioned earlier suggest that Plato and Aristotle do identify a thing's function with its purpose, and in the *Metaphysics* Aristotle occasionally says things that identify a thing's form with its final cause. For instance, in one place, he gives an example of a definition, which is supposed to be a statement of a thing's essence and so of its form, which is straightforwardly purposive: a house is "a covering for bodies and chattels" (M 8.2 1043a15). Similarly, in *On the Soul*, Aristotle argues that the soul is the form of the body, and illustrates this by remarking that if the eye were an animal, sight would have been its soul (OS 2.1 412b19). And sight is the function of the eye.

There is, however, another way of understanding the idea of function, which in a way subsumes the concept of structural arrangement, and which is a more appropriate candidate for form. Function can refer to the way a thing functions or *how* it works, to its function-*ing*. If we use "function" in this sense—"how a thing does what it does"—it will diverge from "purpose," which is simply "what it does." Consider, for example, a complicated machine. Such a thing might have many purposes, but in the sense I am discussing now it has only one function—one way of functioning. For instance, a computer serves a great variety of purposes, things as different as word processing, solving mathematical problems, writing music and playing chess. But to describe its function, in this second sense, is to describe what we might call its functional construction, the mechanisms that enable it to do all these things. Superficially, we might say that its function is the electronic storage and retrieval of information according to a program, or some such thing. But in the strict sense, only someone who actually understands how computers work can tell you what their function is. Or, to take another example, you could say of a radio that among its purposes is to broadcast music and live entertainment, provide a medium for advertisement, keep people up to date on the news and serve as an early warning system in an emergency. These are all "what it does." But if we wanted to talk about "how it does what it does" we would have to talk about transmitting electromagnetic waves of certain frequencies and rendering them audible, and about the mechanisms that make this possible. The various things the device does are its purposes; the second thing, *how* it does all this, is its form or function.

Of course the two notions are closely related. The notion of purpose is embedded in the notion of function, the "what it does" in the "how it does what it does." And there will be cases in which the two are virtually identical. Think for example of a very simple device like a fork or a shelf; in these cases to say what the thing does and to say how it does what it does is pretty much the same thing. (What is the function of a shelf? To put things on. How does it work? Well, you put things on it.) Another, very different sort of case where function and purpose coincide is where the function itself is the thing's purpose or end. This is how Aristotle thinks of the functions of those things that he regards as "natural purposes," especially plants and animals whose "final cause" or purpose is essentially to preserve their specific form of functioning, through their own survival and reproduction.

The main argument for taking function in this second sense to be the correct notion of form comes from the role of form as the object of knowledge and the locus of craft. As I noted earlier, the person who minutely observes the structural arrangements of a thing but does not know what it does could not be said to know or understand the thing. But neither can purpose by itself be the object of knowledge in any very strong sense of "knowledge." All of us know, for example, what the heart is for, and to this extent we know what it is, but this does not make us all cardiologists. But someone who knows what the heart is for, and its structural arrangements, *and* how those arrangements enable it to do what it does can truly be said to understand it. Or take an artifact. Aristotle says that the art of building is the form of a house. But knowing the purpose of a house does not make one an architect. The architect knows both the structure and the purpose, and how the structure makes the purpose possible: she understands the construction of the house functionally. She knows, for instance, not just that the bricks and timbers are arranged thus and so; and that the house must withstand the winter storms; but how this arrangement of bricks and timbers enables the house to withstand the winter storms. So, function in the sense of "how a thing does what it does," of structure as tending to purpose, is from the point of view of knowledge the best candidate for form. This account also allows for varying structures in the same kind of object, since various structural arrangements could tend to the same end, and the expert would know how each does so. The accomplished architect knows how the construction of both teepees and castles enables them to withstand the winter storms.

In Aristotle's text, the notions of shape, recipe, purpose, and functional construction all seem to be candidates for form. Different ones work better in different cases. The bronze sphere and cube do not exactly have any purpose, so the shape seems to suit them. Recipe suits things whose contours are not so much of the essence as the ratio of their mixture. The form of a simple tool is virtually identical to its purpose. More complex things seem to be best characterized by their functional construction. As it turns out, there are other candidates as well. In *Metaphysics* 8, Aristotle undertakes to show that items from almost any of the categories can serve as the form of a thing.

But evidently there are many differences; for instance, some things are characterized by the mode of composition of their matter, e.g. the things formed by mixture, such as honey-water; and others by being bound together, e.g. a bundle; and others by being glued together, e.g. a book; and others by being nailed together, e.g. a casket; and others in more than one of these ways; and others by position, e.g. threshold and lintel (for these differ by being placed in a certain way); and others by time, e.g. dinner and breakfast; and others by place, e.g. the winds; and others by the affections proper to sensible things. (M 8.2 1042b)

These accounts differ, but without too much strain all of them can be understood in terms of functional construction. In each case the matter is organized or constructed (or simply placed, or mixed) in a certain way; this organization or construction enables the thing to do what it does; to understand how the construction makes the thing capable of doing whatever it does is to have knowledge of the thing, and this knowledge is a grasp of its form. Usually the construction is an internal one, but as the cases of the lintel and the winds show, this need not be so. But in each case the form of a thing can be understood as its functional construction, and so as how it does what it does.

4. The Human Function

With that in view, let us return to the objections to the function argument. First of all, does the claim that a human being has a function amount to, or imply, the claim that a human being has a purpose? And if so does it depend upon an unacceptable teleological metaphysics?

Arguably, anything that does anything has a function in the sense of a "how it does what it does." It doesn't matter how or why the thing came into existence, or whether it was made for a purpose. Suppose, for instance, I construct a little mechanical device which, when set on a table, hops around in a circle. Perhaps it has no purpose—that is, perhaps there is no reason anyone would want something that does this, I don't want it, I was not trying to make something that did this, but something else, or I was just fiddling around, and I made this thing by accident, and it is not even good for a toy, since it is not especially amusing. Nevertheless, there is something that this device does and a mechanically-minded person could tell you how it does it: she could tell you, in this sense, what its function is. And this would be the person who understands it, and so knows best what it is.

Of course, there are limits to the intelligibility of assigning functions to things without purposes. If what the thing does is not a purpose, we may not know exactly when to say that the thing has broken down. Perhaps my device sometimes misses a step. Has it malfunctioned? Is it clumsily tripping or happily skipping? There is nothing to say. But according to Aristotle, a living thing does have a definite purpose, in the sense of a "what it does." That purpose is to keep its own form, its own manner of functioning, in existence. It does this in two ways: first, through the continuous self-rebuilding activities of nutrition, which maintain its form in a spacio-temporally continuous stream of matter, and, second, through reproduction, by which it imposes its form on individually distinct entities. This is not a controversial metaphysical thesis about what living things are for, but rather a definition of "living." If a thing has a form that is self-maintaining in these basic ways, then it counts as "living." So far as this goes, there is nothing objectionable about Aristotle's teleology. The appropriateness of teleological explanations need not have anything to do with claims about how or why the object whose parts and activities we seek to explain came into existence. Teleological explanations may be appropriate to an object simply because it has a self-maintaining form. We seek such explanations when we ask what contribution its arrangements or parts make to its self-maintenance. That is why Aristotle says that teleological or final cause explanations in nature tell us that something is better "not without qualification, but with reference to the substance in each case" (PHY 2.198b). Suppose a lion pursues an antelope, catches it, and eats it. We can give a teleological explanation of why the lion gives chase, kills, and eats—that is, of how these activities contribute to a lion's self-maintenance, and are better for the lion. And similarly we can give a teleological explanation of why the antelope attempts to escape. We cannot give a teleological explanation of why the lion succeeds in this case, nor could we if she failed. Aristotle's is not the complete teleology of Leibnizian optimism, or at least we need not understand it in that way. Anything capable of maintaining itself has a way that it does that. Consequently, any living thing has a function.

So when Aristotle says that the function of a human being is the activity of the rational part of the soul, he does not mean simply that reasoning is the purpose of a human being. Nor does he mean merely that it is *a* characteristic activity of human beings, if we understand that to mean only that it is an activity which, as it happens, picks out the species uniquely. He means rather that rational activity is *how we human beings do what we do*, and in particular, how we lead our specific form of life.

This brings us to the list from which Aristotle selects our function—the list of the three kinds of life. I have already suggested that the "purpose" of an animate being is to maintain itself—to live—and its function is how it lives. But there is not just one kind of thing that lives and maintains itself. Quite differently constructed things live, all of the different kinds of plants and animals. Each of these has its own form, which is to say its own specific manner of maintaining itself. But though in one sense each species of living thing has its own manner of living, living things can be divided into larger groups which "live" in different senses. In *On the Soul*, Aristotle asserts that there are three forms of life, corresponding to what he sometimes calls three "parts" of the soul (OS 2.2). At the bottom is a life of basic self-maintenance, a vegetative life of nutrition and reproduction, common to all plants and animals. Animals are distinguished from plants in being alive in a further sense, given by a complex of powers related to the possibility of perception and action (or at least self-guided locomotion)—perception, sensation, locomotion, appetite, and imagination. The third form of life is that distinctive of human beings—the life of reason, and in particular, as I will argue, the life of rational choice.

Each "part" of the soul, and each corresponding form of life, supervenes on the one below it. The addition of each new part of the soul changes the *sense* in which the thing is said to be alive or to have a life, *both* by influencing the way the "lower" functions are carried out and by adding new kinds of activities. Because it has the complex of powers that make perception and action possible, an animal *lives* or *has a life* in a sense that a plant does not. An animal is conscious; it *does* things; it pursues what it desires and flees what it fears; in some cases it builds a home and raises a family; if it is a "higher" animal it may even know how to love and to play. But these are not just powers added, so to speak, on top of the animal's nutritive and reproductive life: they also change the way the animal carries out the tasks of nutrition and reproduction. The animal's capacity for perception and action determines the way it gets its food and ensures the existence of its offspring. But these capacities also lead the animal to engage in activities not possible for a plant, like love and play. These things make the "life" of an animal a different sort of thing from the "life" of a plant.

And a human being in turn *lives*, or *has a life*, in a sense in which a non-human animal does not. For a non-human animal's life is mapped out for it by its instincts; and any two members of a given species basically live the same sort of life (unless the differences are biologically fixed, as by age and gender, or by kinds as among bees). A human being has a life in a different sense from this, for a human being has, and is capable of choosing, what we sometimes call a "way of life" or, following John Rawls, a "conception of the good."[15] Where her way of life is not completely fixed by some sort of cultural regulation—and the *Eudemian Ethics* quite explicitly addresses itself to those who get to choose (EE 1.2 1214b6)—a human being decides such things as

---

[15] John Rawls, *Political Liberalism*, p. 19.

how to earn her living, how to spend her afternoons, who to have for friends and how to treat them, which fields of knowledge, arts, causes, sports, and other activities she will pursue, and, in general, how she will live and what she will live for. And again, we find a double result. The power of choice changes the way we carry out the activities we share with the other animals, such as housebuilding, childrearing, hunting or collecting food, playing, and sexual activity. Human beings approach these activities creatively and develop various ways of going about them among which we then choose. But we also do things the other animals don't do at all, like tell jokes and paint pictures and engage in scientific research and philosophy. So rational choice introduces a whole new sense of *life*, a new sense in which a person can be said to "have a life." And—importantly—it is life in this sense that we primarily have in mind when we say of someone that he lived well or badly—whether he was *eudaimon* or not. So this is the sense of "life" relevant to the function argument. Reason is the function of a human being, because it is *how we do what we do*, which is to lead a specifically human form of life.

We are now in a position to see not only why it makes sense to speak of human beings as having a function, but also why that function turns out to be rational activity. It is because *eudaimonia* is goodness of *life* that Aristotle's candidates for the human function are the three functional complexes of the soul associated with the three senses of "life" (M 9.8 1050b1). And it is because *eudaimonia* is not something that the other animals achieve or fail to achieve that Aristotle looks for that sense of "life" which distinguishes us from the other animals (NE 1.9 1099b33ff.; EE 2.7 1217a25ff.). Aristotle looks for what is unique or peculiar to us not because he values uniqueness for its own sake but because he already supposes that this particular kind of "goodness of life" is distinctive of human beings. If there were other beings capable of rational choice, this would not undermine Aristotle's argument, for they too would lead the kind of life that can be *eudaimon* or not. And in response to Nagel's question—why only one of the three kinds of life should be identified as our function—I think Aristotle could say that reason is the function relevant to *eudaimonia* because of the way that it transforms our manner of performing those activities and tasks that we share with plants and the other animals.

5. Performing Our Function Well

At this point it is important to make explicit something that has been implicit in the argument all along. The function argument depends on the fact that terms such as "reason," "rational," and their Greek equivalents admit of either a descriptive or a normative use. When we use these terms descriptively, we use them to refer to a certain kind of activity, an activity that can be performed well, badly, or not at all. Plato, for example, characterizes the function of the soul as ruling or deliberating, things that can be done well or badly. The important point about the descriptive sense is that one counts as acting "rationally" though the reason is bad. In the descriptive sense, for example, a person who turns the hose on her neighbor because his clothes are on fire and a person who turns the hose on her neighbor because she thinks he is possessed by the devil are both acting rationally, though one of the reasons is good and the other presumably bad. But the person who turns the hose on her neighbor when she is startled into turning around suddenly does not do this rationally: she has not arrived at any deliberative conclusion in favor of hosing down her neighbor. When we use the terms normatively, however, we describe someone as being rational or reasonable only when she is reasoning *well*. It is because there are these two uses that we can say "That's a terrible reason" (descriptive sense) and "That's no reason at all" (normative sense) and mean essentially the same thing. When Plato and Aristotle identify rational activity as the function of the soul or the human function, it is clear that they are using reason in the descriptive sense. This is because their claim is that we need to discover the human function because our good will lie in performing it *well*—in accordance with the relevant virtues. The argument is not "rational activity is the function of a human being, so spend your life engaged in rational activity." Rather, it is "rational activity is how a human life is conducted, how a human being does what he or she characteristically does, so a *good* life depends on performing rational activities *well*."

But once that is clear, some readers may feel that there is something askew about the function argument as I have presented it. Aristotle began by saying that we were looking for the function because when something has a function, its good "resides" in its function. The conclusion we expect is that *eudaimonia* or happiness *consists in* performing your function well. The argument as I have presented it, however, may seem at best to suggest that *eudaimonia* or happiness *results from* performing your function well. While it is almost uncontroversial to claim that insofar as your happiness is within your own power, it depends on the quality of your choices, it would be not merely controversial but false to say that happiness consists in deliberating and making choices, even good ones. Most of us do not spend the happiest moments of our life trying to figure out what to do. So, it may be thought, Aristotle must identify happiness not with rational activity but with its results.

And when we look at the argument more carefully, that at first seems right. Plato's version of the argument identifies *deliberation* as the function of the *soul*. Aristotle's version seeks the function not of the soul, but of *the human being*, and identifies it as "an active life of the element that has a rational principle," "activity of the soul in accordance with, or not without, a rational principle," and "activity or actions of the soul implying a rational principle" (NE 1.7 1098a5–15). We need not identify the activity that involves a rational principle, and is supposedly constitutive of happiness, as deliberation itself. Nor, given that his three candidates for the main constituents of the happy life are hedonistic pursuits, politics, and contemplation, does Aristotle seem to have that in mind. So we may conclude that Aristotle must mean that our other activities—engaging in politics, science, philosophy, athletics and crafts, consorting with our lovers and friends, eating and drinking and carousing, performing noble actions, or whatever it might be—count as "activities of soul implying a rational principle" insofar as they *result* from choice. But while this defense is available, it may seem to concede, rather than evade, the difficulty—or rather to make it worse. For if this is right, it looks as if happiness isn't the activity of reasoning, but rather something that reasoning *gets* you. But in that case the whole argument threatens to become absurdly circular. For if all we mean by performing our function well is performing actions that result from good deliberation, and *if what we mean by good deliberation is successful deliberation about how to achieve happiness*, then of course happiness will consist in performing our function well. But if that is what the function argument amounts to, its claim to connect rationality to happiness is rather trivial, and its claim to connect rationality to moral virtue is probably void.

To see how Aristotle can avoid this criticism, we must take a closer look at his accounts of deliberation and choice. Earlier I pointed out that Aristotle is using "rational activity" in the descriptive sense. In fact, Aristotle needs the three options associated with the descriptive sense (acting for a good reason, acting for a bad reason, and not acting for a reason at all) in order to distinguish his four character types—good, bad, continent, and incontinent. For the bad person is distinguished from the good person by the fact that the bad person acts on a bad reason, while both are distinguished from the incontinent person by the fact that the incontinent person is not acting rationally at all. To put the same point another way, the bad person does what he does by choice (*prohairesis*), while the incontinent person, according to Aristotle, does not act from choice (NE 3.2 1111b14–15; NE 7.3 1146b22–24).

Now the claim that the incontinent person does not act from choice presents the reader with a puzzle. For choice is the outcome of deliberation, and deliberation, as Aristotle describes it in Book 3, *appears* to be essentially instrumental deliberation about how to achieve some wished-for end.[16] But Aristotle certainly does not mean to deny that incontinent people sometimes engage in instrumental deliberation about how to satisfy their unruly passions. For in a section devoted to excellence in deliberation, Aristotle tells us that the incontinent person, who does not act from choice, may also deliberate, and in one sense (but not the sense needed for practical wisdom) deliberate correctly. "For the incontinent man and the bad man will reach as a result of his calculation what he sets himself to do, so that he will have deliberated correctly, but he will have got for himself a very great evil" (NE 6.9 1142b17ff.). So all four of Aristotle's character types can deliberate correctly in the sense of deliberating about how to achieve a certain end. But if the incontinent person's action is the outcome of deliberation, then why doesn't it count as chosen? Certainly, the incontinent person's action does not seem *inadvertent*, like that of my earlier exemplar who hoses down her neighbor by accident. If you ask him why he does what he does, he can give you an answer: say, he is going to the refrigerator in order to get another beer.

It is of course possible to solve this problem simply by stipulating that the outcome of deliberation only *counts* as a choice if the agent believes that the end pursued is a good one. But this has the disadvantage of making the difference between deliberative choice and the kind of deliberation that leads to the incontinent person's action external to the deliberation itself. And that seems to leave Aristotle open to a charge of obfuscation: when he says that the incontinent person does not choose, he makes it sound as if that person does something (descriptively) different, whereas in fact he does the same thing, only with a different belief about the normative status of his end. But there are grounds in Aristotle's text for conceiving of deliberative choice in a way that distinguishes it more clearly from what the incontinent person does. And it is this sense of deliberative choice, I believe, that gives us the "rational activity" that is relevant to the function argument.

In a number of passages in the *Ethics*, Aristotle tells us that the good person acts on the right principle—the *orthos logos*—specifying that this means that the good person does the right act at the right time in the right way *and for the right aim* (NE 2.9 1109a25–30).[17] Elsewhere I have argued that Aristotle sees a

---

[16] Enlarging the concept of instrumental reasoning to include deliberation about the constituents of the end will not by itself solve the problem I am working on here. Or, rather, it will solve the problem, but only given the view of the constituents of the end that I am about to advance in the text: that the constituents of the end, or of the good, are noble actions and activities, considered as including their aims.

[17] See also NE 2.6 1106b20–24, NE 3.7 1115b15–21, and NE 6.5 1126b5ff. In these passages it is the feeling, not the action, which conforms to the right rule, although in the first Aristotle says the point also applies to the action.

principle of this kind as a description of an action that the agent chooses for its own sake. To introduce a bit of technical terminology, I am distinguishing between an "act" and an "action," where the action includes both the act and the end or aim for the sake of which the act is done. For example, giving a donation is an act, and giving a donation in order to help a friend in need is an action. Including both the act and the end in the description of the chosen action enables us to harmonize what might otherwise seem to be incompatible things that Aristotle says about virtuous motivation.[18] Aristotle tells us that a virtuous person does a good action for its own sake (NE 6.5 1140b6ff; 6.12 1144a16) and for the sake of the noble (for instance, at NE 3.8 1116b30; 1117a7–10; NE 3.12 1119b15). But it also seems clear that such an agent acts for the sake of certain particular ends: the courageous person fights in order to defend his city, the liberal person gives in order to help someone out, the ready-witted person wants to entertain his audience, and so on. The key to harmonizing these accounts rests in the idea that the object of choice is an action, that is, an act-for-the-sake-of-a-certain-end, where that whole thing is chosen for its own sake and because it is noble (NE 4.1 1120a23ff.). The courageous person, for example, wishes to defend his city, and so he considers performing a certain action: "fighting (at a certain time and place, in a certain way) for the sake of defending my city." He decides that this would indeed be a noble action, and chooses it—for its own sake—as such. The end is not simply given to him, by his appetite or even by his rational desire or wish (*boulesis*); rather, it is part of what he chooses, when he chooses to pursue it in a certain way here and now. He adopts both the end and the act together, as standing in the right relation to each other (NE 4.2 4–6).

A rational principle or *logos*, therefore, represents the agent's conception of *what is worth doing for the sake of what*, and especially, of what *in his particular circumstances* is worth doing for the sake of what. It is not merely a view about which ends to pursue and how to pursue them, although of course it is that, but also a view that the end is one that, here and now, in one's circumstances, makes the act in question, and so the whole action, worth doing. The deliberation that issues in a choice is not merely instrumental because this must be its conclusion: that the entire action is a thing worth doing for its own sake.

The incontinent person's action does not count as *chosen* because he does not take it to be worth doing for its own sake; he just wants very badly to do it,

---

[18] See "From Duty and for the Sake of the Noble: Kant and Aristotle on Morally Good Action," Essay 6 in this volume, especially pp. 187–96.

or is hurried into it by anger.[19] In fact, Aristotle tells us that the incontinence of anger is less disgraceful than that of appetite because it at least *seems* to the angry person as if avenging oneself for an insult is an action worth doing. But the person who is incontinent from appetite is under no such delusion—he just wants the object or end.

> For reason or imagination informs us that we have been insulted or slighted, and anger, reasoning as it were that anything like this must be fought against, boils up straightway; while appetite, if reason or perception merely says that an object is pleasant, springs to the enjoyment of it. Therefore anger obeys reason in a sense, but appetite does not. (NE 7.6 1149a30–1149b1)[20]

If the person who is incontinent from appetite does engage in deliberation about how to achieve his end, we may say that he *follows* the course mapped out for him by deliberation. But he does not act *on* its conclusion in the same sense as the intemperate person does. He does not adopt its conclusion as his *logos* or principle, and he therefore does not adopt the end as his good, for he does not believe that going to the refrigerator in order to get another beer to drink is a thing worth doing for its own sake—as the intemperate person certainly does.

Deliberation, then, if it is to issue in an action that is chosen, is not merely about how to achieve a certain end, but about what, in the circumstances, is worth doing for the sake of what. Such deliberation issues in rational principles, which direct us to do certain acts for the sake of certain ends, and when we make choices—act in accordance with these principles—we are choosing both the means and the end. The specifically human function is a life of activity in accordance with such principles: a life, as we might put it now, in which your actions are shaped and directed by your values. Furthermore, a principle of this kind is not external to the action performed in accordance with it, the way an end is external to the means. Rather, it is a description of the action itself.[21] So the relation of deliberative choice to action is not merely the relation of a process to a result external to that process. A human being's activities and actions are an *embodiment* of his deliberative choices. The specifically human function is activity that represents the person's conception of what in his particular circumstances is worth doing, a kind of contextualized realization of his conception of the good. Nor is Aristotle claiming that doing

---

[19] That remark of course is not intended as an explanation of what happens in the case of incontinence—it is just a description of the phenomenon that needs explaining.

[20] I take it that Aristotle is following up on Plato's idea that *thumos* (anger, spirit) is the natural ally of reason. *Thumos* responds to the *appearance* of nobility.

[21] I discuss this idea at greater length in "Acting for a Reason," Essay 7 in this volume.

things that are worth doing for their own sakes will *get* you happiness as a kind of result or external end, although he does think that worthwhile activities are, under normal circumstances, inherently pleasant. Rather, he is claming that doing things worth doing for their own sakes, at least in sufficiently fortunate circumstances, *is* happiness. Happiness therefore does after all "reside" in the performance of our function.

Recall now Bernard Williams's criticism—that any human capacity may be used either for good or for evil. That does not seem to be true of the human capacity to act in accordance with our views about what is worth doing for the sake of what. This capacity may indeed be exercised badly, as the bad person exercises it. But one cannot *undertake* to use one's capacity for deciding which actions are worth doing for an evil end, the way one can undertake to use one's capacity for instrumental reasoning or one's knowledge of medicine for an evil end. Since the end is included in the idea of an action that is worth doing for its own sake, you cannot choose such an action for an evil end. Or at least, the claim that you could deliberately use the capacity to choose what is worth doing for its own sake for an evil end is paradoxical in the same way as the claim that one can choose evil for its own sake, and perhaps even more so. For to deliberately use this capacity to do evil, you would have to decide to do something that was ignoble and worthless, even *given* its aim. That is, you would have to decide that it was worth doing, *for its own sake*, something that you had already decided was either not worth doing or even worth avoiding for its own sake.

I think it is also true that, at least schematically, this conception of the human function explains why Aristotle found it so natural to connect the good performance of the human function with being both happy and good. Certainly, if we do not start from the view that being virtuous and being happy must be quite different things, it is natural to suppose that the person who knows *what in his particular circumstances is worth doing* will be both, to the extent that his circumstances allow. And the claim that you would need the moral virtues in order to exercise this capacity has a prima facie plausibility. For while anyone might know that, say, the defense of one's city is an end worth pursuing, someone who fears the wrong things or fears the right things too much will not be a good judge of which particular risks are worth taking for the sake of this end, and so of which actions are worth doing.

But a final verdict on this last point must await a more detailed study of the process of deciding what is worth doing for the sake of what, and how exactly the moral virtues enter into that process. For recall that it is only the expert who really understands an object's function in the sense of *how* the object does what it does. Earlier I said that an architect, for example, must understand the functional construction of a house. That is, she must understand not merely that the bricks and timbers are arranged thus and so; and that the house must withstand the winter storms; but *how* this very arrangement of bricks and timbers enables the house to withstand the winter storms. The expert on the human function must understand our functional construction in a similar way. In particular, she must know *how* reason and the non-rational desires and appetites work together to inform an agent's view of which actions are worth doing. That is why, once they have offered their respective versions of the function argument, both Plato and Aristotle proceed to take up the study of the constitution of the soul, and of how the parts of the soul work together to produce human actions and choices (NE 1.13; *Republic* Books 2–4). To make good on the function argument, Aristotle must show us that the qualities that we ordinarily regard as moral virtues are virtues in the technical sense, properties that make us good at our function. And to do that, he must show us *how* having these qualities contributes to our capacity to make good choices. That is the task of the *Nicomachean Ethics*.[22, 23]

[22] I examine Aristotle's answer to this question in "Aristotle on Function and Virtue," Essay 5 in this volume.

[23] This essay is a somewhat distant descendant of a paper I began to write in the 1980s and never finished. That paper was intended as a companion piece to my "Aristotle on Function and Virtue" (Essay 5), which follows. In it I aspired to trace the connection between the function argument of the *Ethics* and the later and more complex notions of form and matter as actuality and potentiality and of form as activity in *Metaphysics* 8 and 9, as well as giving part of the defense of the argument presented here. But I became convinced that little short of a book could do that, or could do it convincingly. I owe thanks to Myles Burnyeat, Richard Kraut, and Ian Mueller for extensive comments on that early version. I have had invaluable help giving shape to this version from Charlotte Brown.

5

Aristotle on Function and Virtue

1. The Relation of Function and Virtue

In 1.7 of the *Nicomachean Ethics*, Aristotle suggests that we might be able to determine what *eudaimonia* is "if we could first ascertain the *ergon* (function) of man" (NE 1.7 1097b24). Aristotle reasons that if anything has a function, its good lies in performing that function well. So if human beings have a function, the human good, *eudaimonia*, will be the good performance of that function. Examining the various activities or forms of life that are characteristic of living things, Aristotle decides on "an active life of the element that has a rational principle" as the uniquely human function (NE 1.7 1098a4). *Eudaimonia* is therefore "an activity or actions of the soul implying a rational principle" performed well, which is to say "in accordance with the appropriate *arete* (virtue)" (NE 1.7 1098a14–15).

The function argument has been attacked at many points. Some critics see it as an instance of an illicit style of teleological reasoning: they cannot see why our good should be thought to lie in the good performance of our function, or indeed why we should be thought to have a function at all. Some have argued against the selection of rational activity as the human function. Others have claimed that Aristotle has confused the question of what will make us morally good with the question of what will enable us to achieve the natural good, *eudaimonia*. Perhaps "virtuous" rational activity will make us morally good but not make us happy. Or, conversely, perhaps we will be happy if we are good at rational activity, but that will not make us morally good. Reason, some critics suggest, is a power that can be used either for good or for evil; and a rational activity, excellently performed, might for all that be an evil one.[1]

---

[1] W. F. R. Hardie, in *Aristotle's Ethical Theory*, finds a difficulty in saying that a human being has a function at all because a human being is not designed for a purpose (pp. 23–25). Many readers point out that there are plenty of things other than reason that seem to be unique to human beings; Bernard Williams, in *Morality: An Introduction to Ethics*, suggests making fire, having sexual intercourse without regard to season, despoiling the environment and upsetting the balance of nature, and killing things for fun; Robert Nozick, in *Philosophical Explanations*, proposes telling jokes. The objection to connecting

The defender of the function argument can proceed in two ways. The more direct method is to focus on the argument itself, filling in the necessary background from Aristotle's metaphysical and psychological works, and reconstructing the argument in a way that provides for replies to some of these objections.[2] Some good answers to the worries about whether we have a function and why it should be rational activity can be found in this way. The indirect method is to investigate the role of the function argument within the general structure of the argument of Aristotle's ethics. Such an investigation is the project of this essay.

Readers sometimes suppose that, after its appearance in Book 1 of the *Nicomachean Ethics*, the function argument is set aside, not to reappear until Book 10, when Aristotle again takes up the question of *eudaimonia*. It is also thought that Aristotle intends to use the function argument directly in defense of the contemplative life—as if the argument went simply: reason is the function of a human being, and therefore a human being will be happy—and good—if he spends his time reasoning. If this were Aristotle's argument, the third set of objections, about the connection between happiness, moral goodness, and well-performed rational activity—would certainly be in order. But this is not what happens in Aristotle's ethics, and such a portrayal obscures a fundamental feature of his theory.

The Greek philosophers generally seem to have believed that a virtue or excellence is a quality that enables a thing to perform its function well. Both Plato and Aristotle make a conceptual connection between *ergon* and *arete*. An *arete* is not merely one of a thing's good points; it is specifically a quality that makes a thing good at performing its function. In the chapter in which he undertakes to define moral virtue, Aristotle begins by reminding us of this:

We may remark, then, that every virtue both brings into good condition the thing of which it is the virtue and makes the function of that thing be done well; . . . if this is true in every case, the virtue of man also will be the state which makes a man good and which makes him perform his own function well. (NE 2.6 1106a15–23)

Again, when he initiates the discussion of intellectual virtue in Book 6, Aristotle reminds us that "The virtue of a thing is relative to its proper function"

---

the good for a human being and the goodness of a human being is made by Peter Glassen in "A Fallacy in Aristotle's Argument about the Good." The point about rational activities possibly being evil is made by Williams who, in *Morality*, argues that any attempt to base an account of the good on the unique characteristics of humanity will founder over "the moral ambiguity of distinctive human characteristics" (p. 64).

2 See, for instance, T. H. Irwin's "The Metaphysical and Psychological Basis of Aristotle's Ethics," and Kathleen V. Wilkes, "The Good Man and the Good for Man in Aristotle's Ethics," both in *Essays on Aristotle's Ethics*; and my own "Aristotle's Function Argument," Essay 4 in this volume.

(NE 6.2 1139a17). Since rational activity has been identified as the function of a human being, this means that the virtues, both moral and intellectual, should be qualities that make us good at rational activity. This inference is confirmed by the usage of Plato, who introduces the function argument in *Republic* 1 specifically in order to show that justice, which he takes to be the virtue of the soul, will make a person happy because it will make him good at the deliberative functions (R 352d–354a).

If this is right, the function argument, rather than being set aside between Books 1 and 10, should be regarded as the basis of Aristotle's theory of the virtues. This means that in order to understand Aristotle's account of the virtues, we must find an answer to this question: how do the virtues make us good at rational activity? What contribution to the well-functioning of rational activity do they make?

In *On the Soul*, Aristotle groups the various functions that characterize living beings into three sets, which are in a sense three "parts" of the soul. Nutrition and reproduction are grouped together as a vegetative soul that is common to all living things, and in virtue of which plants are said to be alive. Non-rational appetite (*epithumia*), emotion, pleasure, pain, sense perception, imagination and the power of local motion are grouped together as an animal soul, common to human beings and all other animals.[3] I will, for shorthand, call this the appetitive part of the soul, and I will use the term "passion" to refer to its motivational forces—appetites and emotions. It is to this part of the soul that moral virtues pertain. The third part, possessed only by human beings, is the rational part. The function argument identifies the activity of the rational part as the function of a human being. The moral virtues are included in the study of ethics because they are relevant to practically rational activity.

Some caveats are, however, in order here. First, Aristotle does not think that all desire (*orexis*) belongs to the non-rational part of the soul.[4] "Wish" (*boulesis*) is a rational desire, a desire for something conceived as a good. "Choice" (*prohairesis*), with which moral virtue is concerned, is "desiderative thought or intellectual desire" (NE 6.2 1139b4). Although Aristotle describes moral virtues as the excellences of an irrational part of the soul (NE 1.13), it is a part of the soul which "in a sense shares in" the rational principle.

---

[3] Actually, not all pleasure can pertain to the appetitive part of the soul, for contemplation is a pleasure; in fact one that, according to *Metaphysics* 12.7, God enjoys. Terry Penner pointed this out to me.

[4] It is a misfortune that some translators render *orexis*, the general faculty of "wanting," by "desire" and *epithumia*, non-rational wanting aimed at the pleasant, by "appetite," while others do just the reverse.

What this sense is is the subject of this investigation: precisely what is in question in the case of the moral virtues is the relationship between rational and nonrational motives and desires. Furthermore, this relationship is to be thought of not so much, I believe, in terms of causal interaction among parts that remain separate as in terms of various levels of possibility that become actualized. This is, in fact, what Aristotle means by saying that moral virtue is a *hexis*, something that we are "adapted by nature to receive" (NE 2.1 1103a24).[5]

A moral virtue is defined as a state of character, concerned with choice, lying in a mean, where the mean is relative to the agent and is determined by reason—in the way, Aristotle says, in which the person of practical wisdom would determine it (NE 2.6 1107a36–1107b2). As I understand this account, Aristotle means something like this. Each person is equipped with certain native responses, dispositions to act and to react in certain ways. Passions and reactions such as hope, fear, anger, desire, amusement, affection, and the self-regarding emotions are universal. Although it is human nature to experience all of these things in some form, individuals differ both in the degree of the response in a given situation and, to a lesser extent, in the objects that provoke it. The doctrine that virtue is a mean focuses more on the differences in the degree of response than on possible differences in the object, but what it suggests is that a certain degree of response to a given object and for a given person is appropriate. So, for example, a courageous person will fear what is genuinely dangerous to her and will fear it to the extent that it is dangerous. This is "concerned with choice" because it will help her choose to take those risks that are worth taking.[6] Those who lack the relevant virtues may exceed or fall short of the appropriate response—or, more unusually, may respond to inappropriate objects. A person whose response is, from childhood, appropriate or nearly so, has what Aristotle calls a natural virtue; as the person comes to understand the reasons for the appropriateness of the response, she comes to have the real virtue, the reason or principle (NE 6.13 1144b1–15). A person whose response is off must be trained, habituated. If the response is all wrong, it is hard to acquire the principle; it is for this

---

[5] This is why Aristotle says in *On the Soul* 3.9 that it is "absurd" to break up the faculty of desire (*orexis*); if the soul has parts, it will be found in all three parts. Since the faculty of desire gives rise to local movement, it cannot be broken up (for after all, the animal will move one way or another). Thus, if moral virtue realizes our potential to be rational, it in a sense must be by effecting a transformation of the faculty of desire generally. Aristotle is generally hesitant about the language of "parts" in *On the Soul*. I think that the fact that he is actually thinking in terms of levels of actualization explains why. I have been helped on this point by the comments of Jon Moline.

[6] For more on this point, see my "Aristotle's Function Argument," Essay 4 in this volume, especially pp. 146–9.

reason that Aristotle addresses his lectures to those who have been well brought up (NE 1.4 1095a1–11; NE 10.9 1179b23–30). It is possible, however, for one's intellectual knowledge of these issues to outstrip one's training or even one's capacity for training: this is what happens to the continent or incontinent person, who knows what is good but whose desires incline her the other way.

In certain cases we have no trouble making an intuitive judgment about whether a response is appropriate or not. We can say that someone who is afraid of spiders, or outraged by teasing, or amused by the humiliation of others, or too modest to speak up among her manifest equals is not responding appropriately, and will make some poor choices as a result. But we cannot leave matters at this. We need to know what makes a response appropriate. It is in any case unsatisfactory to leave matters to intuition, but especially so here, for the range of cases in which we will find ready and intuitive agreement about the appropriateness of response is not great. And this is where the function argument should throw the needed light on the theory of the moral virtues. For it follows from the function argument that the virtue is present, and so the response appropriate, when and only when the disposition is in a condition that is good for rational activity. By answering the question of what contribution a state of character makes to the good performance of rational activity, we should also have answered the question of what determines the mean.

So the function argument and the conceptual connection between function and virtue make it necessary to answer this question: how can the concept of being in a good condition for rational activity be used to set a standard for the appropriateness of response? What contributions can the appetitive part of the soul make to rational activity, and what state of this part of the soul counts as a good condition for rational activity?

The number of possible answers to this question for which some warrant can be found in the text of the *Nicomachean Ethics* is quite surprising. In the rest of this essay I work through five possible answers, saying something about the philosophical and textual merits and demerits of each. I will then sketch a view that I think combines the merits of several. The possible answers I will discuss are these:

1. *The Obedience Theory.* The appetitive part of the soul is in a good condition for rational activity when the passions give way to reason.
2. *The Harmony Theory.* The appetitive part of the soul is in a good condition for rational activity when the desires and emotions are in harmony with the dictates of reason.

3. *The Susceptibility to Argument Theory.* The appetitive part of the soul is in a good condition for rational activity when the desires and emotions are caused by rational considerations.

4. *The Health Analogy.* Moral virtues are qualities that in a general way make one good at the formulation and execution of rational plans and projects; their relation to rational activity is analogous to the relation of the physical virtues to physical activity.

5. *The Perception Theory.* The appetitive part of the soul is in a good condition for rational activity when what we perceive to be good (because it is pleasant to us) really is good: because we perceive evaluative qualities correctly we are able to make correct judgments about evaluative issues.

2. Obedience and Harmony

According to the obedience theory the appetitive part of the soul is in a good condition for rational activity when it is obedient to the dictates of reason. Reason somehow provides a stronger motive than the non-rational desires and emotions and is able to control them. What this view seems to suggest is that the passions are weak. Certainly, many people have understood the mean as a doctrine of weak or "moderate" passions, as if both the excess and the defect were strong passions and the mean were a quiet or calm state. There is some evidence for the obedience view in Aristotle's writings. The appetitive part of the soul is initially characterized as sharing in the rational principle because "it listens to and obeys it" (NE 1.13 1102b31). Aristotle asserts that "a man is said to have or not to have self-control according as his intellect has or has not the control, on the assumption that this is the man himself" (NE 9.8 1168b34–35). He characterizes the proper kind of self-love as that of someone who "gratifies the most authoritative element in himself and in all things obeys this" (NE 9.8 1168b30–31), and opposes this to the misguided self-love of those who gratify "their appetites and in general their feelings and the irrational element of the soul" (NE 9.8 1168b19–20). The good man is asserted to obey his reason whereas the bad man follows evil passions (NE 9.8 1169a1–5). The many are said to live by passion and pursue pleasures, having no conception of what is noble (NE 10.9 1179b9–15). There is even a passage where Aristotle states the associated view that the appetites of the good person are weak:

if appetites are strong and violent they even expel the power of calculation. Hence they must be moderate and few, and should in no way oppose reason—and this is what we call an obedient and chastened state. (NE 3.12 1119b9–11)

But there are obvious difficulties with this view. It is clear that weakness is not always or even usually what Aristotle has in mind by "the mean." In most cases, the "defect" is really a defect and the lack of passion is criticized. It is an important fact that Aristotle is one of the few moralists to single out the "insensible" person, who does not enjoy ordinary bodily pleasures enough, for criticism (NE 3.11 1119a6–7). It is even more significant that those who do not get angry enough are castigated as "fools" and as being "slavish" (NE 4.5 1126a4–8) and those who are unduly humble are declared to be commoner and worse than those who are vain (NE 4.3 1125a32–33). In these cases it is clear that whatever is supposed to happen it is not that the passion should be minimized to make way for the influence of reason. Another serious problem with the obedience view is this: Aristotle distinguishes four moral types of person: good, bad, continent, and incontinent. On the obedience view, the distinctions among the four types are greatly blurred. We could say that the good person has moderate passions that obey reason readily while the continent person has strong ones that must be overcome, but this formulation is full of problems. In the first place, we must then suppose that the strength of a passion is something that can be measured without reference to the strength of other motives, for according to this theory, rational motives overpower passions in *both* good and continent people. Nor is it clear why we would consider a "good" person so characterized to be better than a continent one, for on this view one might envision the good person as mild or unemotional, and the continent person as passionate but strong-willed. Most importantly, this is simply not Aristotle's way of making the distinction between goodness and continence. The difference between the good person and the continent person lies in the fact that the good person desires what is good and what he ought to desire, whereas the continent person desires what he knows is bad. The good person's soul is harmonious, and the mere "obedience" of the continent person's soul is a poor substitute for that:

in the continent man it [the appetitive part] obeys reason—and presumably in the temperate and brave man it is still more obedient; for in him it speaks, on all matters, with the same voice as reason. (NE 1.13 1102b26–28)

This brings us to the harmony theory, according to which the important thing is not that the passions be weak, but that they be directed to the same objects as rational principles. The soul of a good person is characterized by harmony among its parts. In the good person, reason and the appetitive part "speak with the same voice." Aristotle describes the good person's passions as being in accordance with the dictate of reason, whereas a bad person is not pleased as he ought to be or is not angry as he ought to be or is angry at the wrong things or afraid of the wrong things and, in general, is not in accord with reason.

Hence the appetitive element in a temperate man should harmonize with reason; for the noble is the mark at which both aim, and the temperate man craves for the things he ought as he ought, and when he ought; and this is what reason directs. (NE 3.12 1119b14–17)

In NE 9.4, we are told that the good person's

opinions are harmonious, and he desires the same things with all his soul . . . And he grieves and rejoices, more than any other, with himself. (NE 9.4 1166a12–27)

Whereas "inferior people"

are at variance with themselves, and have appetites for some things and wishes for others. (NE 9.4 1166b6–7)

And bad people

do not rejoice or grieve with themselves, for their soul is rent by faction; . . . [they] are laden with regrets. (NE 9.4 1166b18–24)

"We must take as a sign of states (of character) the pleasure or pain that supervenes upon acts" (NE 2.3 1104b4), for no one is good who does not enjoy good things and actions. Indeed, the fact that Aristotle holds the view that in a good person reason and passion coincide is illustrated strikingly when he raises a problem about the utility of practical wisdom. In order to have practical wisdom you must have all of the virtues—but if you do, those by themselves will lead you to do what is right, making the wisdom superfluous (NE 6.12 1143b18–25). He also discusses a whimsical view that the temperate person must not be continent, since he will then be held back from acting on passions that would have led him right (NE 7.2 1146a18–21). There can, I think, be no question, in the face of this, that Aristotle holds, with Plato, that the good person's soul is characterized by harmony. However, in Aristotle's theory at least this *cannot* by itself be the criterion of a good condition of the appetitive soul.

The reason for this will be clear if we focus on the difference between the incontinent person and the truly bad person. If harmony is the characteristic feature of a good soul, then a bad soul should be characterized by disharmony: in the bad person, then, reason would direct one course of action while strong appetites direct the opposite. There are a few places where Aristotle says this, particularly in the passages from NE 9.4 that I have just quoted. The trouble is that this disharmony characterizes the incontinent and the continent person as well. On the harmony view it seems as if the differences among continence, incontinence, and badness are just a matter of degree—of how often reason wins its battle against bad passions. But this is not what Aristotle says when he turns his attention to these distinctions in Book 7. There, he says that whereas the incontinent person acts on passion and contrary to her choice, the bad person, in this case, the intemperate person, acts according to her choice and as she thinks she ought. This point is made in many places in Book 7. For instance:

the man who pursues the excesses of things pleasant, or pursues to excess necessary objects, and does so by choice . . . is self-indulgent; for such a man is of necessity without regrets, and therefore incurable, since a man without regrets cannot be cured. (NE 7.7 1150a18–22)

incontinence and vice are different in kind; vice is unconscious of itself, incontinence is not. (NE 7.8 1150b35–36)

incontinence is not vice (though perhaps it is in a qualified sense); for incontinence is contrary to choice while vice is in accordance with choice. (NE 7.8 1151a6–7)

the incontinent man is apt to pursue, not on conviction, bodily pleasures that are excessive and contrary to right reason, while the self-indulgent man is convinced because he is the sort of man to pursue them. (NE 7.8 1151a11–13)

And the incontinent and the self-indulgent man are also like one another; they are different, but both pursue bodily pleasures—the latter, however, also thinking that he ought to do so, while the former does not think this. (NE 7.9 1152a4–6)

The intemperate person acts from choice, does what she thinks she ought, has no regrets, does not believe herself to be wrong, and cannot be cured. It looks as if this person, like the good person, has a harmonious soul: in any case she clearly does not necessarily *experience* conflict. The view is not peculiar to Book 7, for the "unconsciousness of itself" that characterizes vice shows up in the original discussion of the virtues.

Hence also the people at the extremes push the intermediate man each over to the other, and the brave man is called rash by the coward, cowardly by the rash man, and correspondingly in the other cases. (NE 2.8 108b24–26)

Even in NE 9.4, where Aristotle makes the strongest claims about the factional character of the bad person, he admits that the attributes of friendship to oneself

seem to belong even to the majority of men, poor creatures though they may be. Are we to say then that insofar as they are satisfied with themselves and think they are good, they share in these attributes? (NE 9.4 1166b2–4)

We must conclude that the bad person's rational wishes and rational judgments are harmonious with her evil passions, and are, accordingly, wrong. The bad person has a corrupted reason and so does not necessarily experience conflict; she may therefore in a sense have a harmonious soul. That reason can be thus corrupted, and is in fact corrupted as a result of poor habituation, is frequently affirmed by Aristotle. It is an important part of the doctrine of the mean that excess and defect destroy, while the mean preserves (NE 2.2 1104a10–1104b3). Sometimes Aristotle says merely that excess and defect destroy the virtue itself (NE 2.2 1104a10–17), but there are places where he puts forward the more explicit doctrine that excess and defect, or vice, destroy reason or the first principle (NE 6.5 1170b11–19). These two accounts of what is destroyed by vice are really the same, for it is Aristotle's view that a true virtue as opposed to a merely natural virtue implies not merely *coincidence with* but the *presence* of the reason or principle (NE 6.13 1144b26–28). It is, so to speak, the true first principle within the state of character that is destroyed by faulty habituation. The bad person's first principles or rational wishes, then, are in accord with her bad emotions and appetites. Her rational wishes are not directed to what is truly good but to a merely apparent good. If such a person—in whom reason and passion have been corrupted together—also has a harmonious soul, then harmony cannot be the criterion by which a good condition of the appetitive soul is identified.

This points up a difficulty that presses upon both the "obedience" and the "harmony" theories. According to both theories, reason by itself determines what is good, and the passions meet the standard of the "mean" by conforming to (or giving way to) the dictates of reason. But unless we have an independent standard for determining what the dictates of reason are, such a view leaves everything to be done. The fact that reason itself admits of corruption or a kind of error that is undetectable ("vice is unconscious of itself") implies that determining the mean by reason cannot be a straightforward matter. At least we cannot find the mean merely by engaging in some characteristic procedures of reason, for these can be misleading. For instance, we cannot determine the mean by referring to our rational wishes, for if we have vices, these too will be wrong. This is already implied in the definition of virtue—though the mean is set by reason, the way it is set is simply identified as "the way in which the man of practical wisdom would determine it." Just being rational in the sense that every human being is rational is not enough to put the dictate of reason that determines the mean at your disposal. You must have practical wisdom, and what gives you that is, of course, the virtues themselves. The result of this is that the idea that passion should conform to the dictates of reason is, by itself, uninformative. The correctness of the dictates of reason depends on the passions being in a good condition, and so the dictates of reason cannot be used to identify that condition.

3. Susceptibility to Argument

The susceptibility to argument theory can best be introduced by noticing another problem with the simple harmony theory. If the harmony theory is taken to mean a mere coincidence between the dictates of reason and the objects of passion, it is a little unclear why we should, or if we should, especially admire a virtuous character. This person has been fortunate in his or her upbringing or perhaps in native endowment; that is all. We can raise a Kantian question: does the harmonious character seek what is good and do what is reasonable because it is good and reasonable, or because she happens to want to? The continent character, though supposedly an inferior one, at least clearly aims at the good from a rational motive, and for the sake of its goodness.

The problem can be resolved by a sort of combination of the obedience view and the harmony view, which I am calling the susceptibility to argument view. Rather than saying that the appetitive part of the soul obeys reason by standing out of its way, we might say that the appetitive part of the soul "obeys" reason in the sense that rational considerations exert a causal influence on the appetites. Appetites for what is good are produced by the dictates of reason. A harmony between reason and passion is produced, not coincidentally and not merely as a result of a fortunate temperament or upbringing, but as the direct result of the causal influence of rational wish on the appetitive soul. This is why Aristotle says, for instance, that the good-tempered person is not led by passion, but is angry in the manner, at the things, and for the length of time that reason dictates. It is not that his anger is weak, but that it is formed according to dictates of reason, and indeed by them. Habituation, instead of producing the harmony between reason and appetite directly, and, as it were, externally, makes the appetitive soul receptive to the causal influence of reason. This view has several merits. It explains in a unified way passages supporting both the harmony and the obedience view that might otherwise seem to pull apart. It answers a common objection to the harmony theory, consisting in an uneasiness over the idea that virtue can be the result of mere habituation, if that is understood to be a sort of conditioning. Habituation now has the different role of preparing the way for rational influences, although we do not yet know how. It gives a new meaning to Aristotle's remark that the appetitive part of the soul obeys the rational part and "is in some sense persuaded by reason": this "persuasion" or obedience is causal. It makes an important kind of sense of the distinction between natural and real virtue and Aristotle's insistence that

it is not merely the state in accordance with right reason, but the state that implies the *presence* of right reason, that is virtue. (NE 6.13 1144b26–27)

One could imagine someone with *all* of the merely natural virtues, who therefore might do all the right things: that would be a *mere* harmony. In the truly virtuous person, by contrast, right reason is the *cause* of the correct appetite, and that is why its presence is implied. It is soon after the remark about the presence of right reason that Aristotle affirms the unity of the virtues (the true virtues, for the natural virtues can exist separately) and one can begin to see why he does: if the dictates of reason or practical wisdom are somehow unified or systematic, at least, and the virtuously conditioned soul forms itself after these dictates, then it will be the case that the full possession of one virtue implies that of the others. We can also explain why Aristotle says that the practically wise person above all is able to deliberate and to *act*. Suppose that all motivation leading to action must immediately come from the appetitive part of the soul. If the translation of reason into action must be mediated by appetites, the possibility of acting from reason will depend on the extent to which the appetitive part of the soul is in the "argument-susceptible" state. The other types are unable to act in the sense that their rational principles do not get expressed in action.

On this view, the practical syllogism represents not only a "logical" (in some sense) relation but also the psychological pathway by which motivation is influenced by rational considerations. The syllogism moves from a "universal" which is grasped by the rational soul, through a particular, which is in the sphere of perception (and so of the appetitive soul) to the action that is its conclusion. To say that the conclusion of a practical syllogism is an action is to say that a piece of reasoning is not practical unless it gives rise to motivation. This is a point that deserves emphasis. To use Aristotle's example from NE 3.7, a connection like that between "Dry food is good for every man" and "Dry food is good for me" must be one that is capable of generating *motivational* energy. In the incontinent person it is this that fails. Although this person has the universal, and knows in a theoretical way that the universal applies to him, this knowledge is not effective: he is not moved to action by it because it does not cause a desire. This is why the incontinent person is said not to act on choice, for a choice is the sort of desire that I have been describing—one that is caused by a deliberative process and so is a deliberate desire.[7] When Aristotle says that a virtue is a state of character concerned with choice, he means that the "passions and actions" associated with the virtues are in this way motivated by rational processes.

The appetitive part of the soul is in a good condition when it forms desires and emotions under the influence of rational deliberative processes, "as reason directs." The human potential for having desires and emotions that are "obedient" to reason is in this way realized by moral virtue. In a way, the mean simply is whatever reason directs in a given case; but it is also that condition of the disposition, whatever it is, that makes the soul receptive to rational influence. Habituation is aimed at making the appetitive soul susceptible to the *formation* of desires that are caused by the dictates of reason.

It is worth considering that it is not immediately obvious why the sort of habituation that produces susceptibility to argument is habituation to act in accordance with the dictates of reason—to act as you would *if* reason had the required influence. Someone who has practical wisdom and knows what reason directs takes your education in hand and makes you practice the actions that you would do if reason had the right influence on you. Somehow this gives reason influence. The educational view here is importantly different from that associated with the simple harmony theory. On the harmony theory, having desires coincident with the dictates of reason was already being virtuous. Now, we must regard this not as the end, but as an intermediate step in the educational process: having desires *coincident with* reason produces the susceptibility to desires *caused by* reason. The formation of desires under the influence of reason is real virtue. Habituation by itself, without this further step, would produce only natural virtue. It is only when we come to substitute rationally caused desires for rationally coincident ones that the real virtue, the one that implies the presence of right reason, is there. But we have not yet determined why having rationally coincident desires helps to bring about a susceptibility to having rationally caused desires, and, despite the fact that the view sounds natural enough, we need to know more about the psychological model that underlies it.

There is one set of passages in which Aristotle talks explicitly about susceptibility to argument, and these may be thought to provide a clue. They

---

[7] For a better account of incontinence, see my "Aristotle's Function Argument," Essay 4 in this volume, pp. 145–8.

occur in the very last section of the book, where Aristotle addresses the question how the good is to be produced. There he says things like this:

Now if arguments were in themselves enough to make men good, they would justly, as Theognis says, have won very great rewards . . . but as things are, while they seem to have power to encourage and stimulate the generous-minded among the young, and to make a character which is gently born, and a true lover of what is noble, ready to be possessed by excellence, they are not able to encourage the many to nobility and goodness. For these do not by nature obey the sense of shame, but only fear, and do not abstain from bad acts because of their baseness but through fear of punishment; living by passion they pursue their own pleasures and the means to them, and avoid the opposite pains, and have not even a conception of what is noble and truly pleasant, since they have never tasted it. What argument would remould such people? (NE 10.9 1179b4–16)

argument and teaching, we may suspect, are not powerful with all men, but the soul of the student must first have been cultivated by means of habits for noble joy and noble hatred . . . The character, then, must somehow be there already with a kinship to virtue, loving what is noble and hating what is base. (NE 10.9 1179b23–30)

This is why some think that legislators ought to stimulate men to virtue and urge them forward by the motive of the noble, on the assumption that those who have been well advanced by the formation of habits will attend to such influences . . . (NE 10.9 1190a6–8)

A good man (they think), since he lives with his mind fixed on what is noble, will submit to argument, while a bad man, whose desire is for pleasure, is corrected by pain like a beast of burden. (NE 10.9 1180a9–12)

These final passages represent the most direct statements of the view that what a good person is is in some way susceptible to argument. And they offer as a reason for, or at least a characterization of, this susceptibility something rather surprising: Aristotle seems to say that the good person is influenced by a concept, a motive, to which the bad person is insusceptible. The good person aims at the noble rather than the pleasant.

This portrayal is supported by many remarks Aristotle makes in his descriptions of the particular virtues. For example, he says that the courageous man

will face [dangers] as he ought and as reason directs, for the sake of what is noble; for this is the end of virtue. (NE 3.7 1115b12–14)

Similar considerations apply to temperance:

the appetitive element in a temperate man should harmonize with reason; for the noble is the mark at which both aim. (NE 3.12 1119b14–16) and liberality:

virtuous actions are noble and done for the sake of the noble. Therefore the liberal man will give for the sake of the noble. (NE 4.1 1120a23–24)

Whereas of the prodigal type, Aristotle says:

And all such things he will do not for the sake of the noble but to show off his wealth. (NE 4.3 1123a24–25)

According to these passages, the good are motivated by the thought of nobility (and chastened by shame), while the bad are motivated by punishment, fear, pleasure, pain, or even the impulse to show off. And Aristotle makes a connection between the susceptibility of the good person to arguments and the fact that good people think in terms of the noble. This seems to imply that the concept of the noble, like the concept of the good (as the object of rational wish), is a specifically rational concept, a concept from which "arguments" and true reasons proceed.[8] Appeal to it has no influence on the bad person, who doesn't have this concept or really understand it, and an insufficiently practical influence on the incontinent person, who appreciates the fact that the action is shameful but is not moved to refrain. If nobility and shame are rational concepts then, by contrast, we should perhaps say that pleasure and fear of pain are more "empirical" concepts: they are ascertained by perception and vivid even to the unreasoning imagination, and therefore available as motives to those who, lacking virtue, are not under rational direction.

This idea of good people working with different concepts and motives from bad people may at first seem to be a surprising one in the context of Aristotle's ethics. The doctrine that virtue is a mean, after all, seems to tell us that a morally good person is just a well-formed natural person. Virtue is not something superadded to nature that restrains or replaces it: it is just its perfected state. The idea of different concepts and motives seems to be in tension with this. This, however, is not a serious difficulty. What we must say is that the capacity to recognize and be motivated by the noble and truly good is a human potential that in the bad person is never fully realized. Vice is a sort of *defective* state.[9] A more serious problem is that the idea of different concepts and motives seems to be in tension with Aristotle's claims about the

---

[8] For a later account of how I think the motive of the noble operates, although one I think is consistent with what I say here, see "From Duty and for the Sake of the Noble: Kant and Aristotle on Morally Good Action," Essay 6 in this volume, pp. 191–4 and "Acting for a Reason," Essay 7 in this volume, pp. 216–18.

[9] For a related point about badness and the defective, see my "Self-Constitution in the Ethics of Plato and Kant," essay 3 in this volume, Sections 4–5, pp. 110–17.

unconsciousness of vice and the bad person's possible conviction of his own goodness. As Aristotle says:

For each state of character has its own ideas of the noble and the pleasant. (NE 3.4 1113a31–32)

Just as the good certainly have their pleasures, then, perhaps the wicked have their own ideas of the noble, and the difference between the two will be marked not by different concepts and kinds of motives, but by the degree of correctness with which they apply these concepts and the accuracy with which the good and the noble are pursued. Aristotle does say that good people judge well about the good and the noble. But, for that matter, good people are also declared to be the best judges of pleasure. This seems to put us back where we were: all of the normative concepts or motives are employed by both good and bad people, only the good person gets it right and the bad person does not. The bad person does not seem to use different concepts. He does not even seem less susceptible to argument than the good person, for he follows *his* deliberation, he is not incontinent, and he acts by choice. Thus it may seem, at first sight, as if susceptibility to argument and the related notion of being moved by considerations of the noble do not differentiate a good from a bad soul. It seems to be not susceptibility to arguments, but simply the accuracy of the premises, that makes the difference. Why then does Aristotle say, as he clearly does, that these things mark a difference between good and bad?

The answer, I think, must be something like this: though both good and bad people may be moved by considerations of the noble and the pleasant, the order of influence between the two concepts and the two parts of the soul is opposite. The bad person, whose reason has been corrupted by bad habits, has a rational conception of the good formed under the influence of and dominated by his pleasures. The good person, who has been made susceptible to argument, has, by contrast, pleasures that are caused by his conception of the noble and the good. The harmony between rational wish and non-rational passion may occur in both, but the causes that establish that harmony work in opposite directions. The good person's passions are produced by reason, while the bad person's concepts have been corrupted by passion. It seems plausible to say, too, that the bad person is less likely to think naturally of his actions in terms of what is noble, and to do so only because he has heard other people speak in this way. It is easy to imagine an intemperate person or a coward congratulating himself on not being taken in by a lot of high-minded nonsense, and thinking that he will get what is really good, but not very easy to imagine him thinking that he is doing what is really noble.

(Although a figure like Callicles might give us pause over this thought.)[10] Perhaps we should after all say that the potential to think in terms of and be motivated by the concept of the noble is one that is never actualized in a bad person. In this sense the bad person's soul is, after all, factional. Reason has not acquired the influence over the appetitive part of the soul that it ought to have.

4. The Health Analogy and Perception

I now turn to a somewhat different way in which the appetitive soul of the virtuous person might be in a good condition for rational activity. Suppose we take rational activity in a broad sense to include both the formulation and the *execution* of plans, projects, and enterprises. One might surely argue that the virtues are instrumental to rational activity in this sense. For a co-worker in plans, projects and enterprises, anyone would prefer someone who was courageous, temperate, even-tempered, and ready-witted to someone who was cowardly, intemperate, irascible, and frivolous, or someone who was rash, humorless, and easily victimized. Later, Hume will account for the virtues as qualities that are instrumental to happiness—that of their possessor or of other people. Couldn't we similarly take them to be instrumental to rational activity? In the *Politics*, pointing out the universally acknowledged advantages of virtue, Aristotle remarks:

For no one would maintain that he is happy who has not in him a particle of courage or temperance or justice or practical wisdom, who is afraid of every insect which flutters past him, and will commit any crime, however great, in order to gratify his lust for meat or drink, who will sacrifice his dearest friend for the sake of a half a farthing, and is as feeble and false in mind as a child or a madman. (POL 7.1 1323a28–34)

On this theory, virtues might be seen as sort of a personal primary good for rational activity—qualities you will want whatever else you want.[11] Part of what suggests this view is the comparison so often made between virtue and physical health. Following out this thought, we might compare the moral virtues to the physical virtues. Let us say that the function of the body is, speaking very generally, physical life and in particular physical activity. The physical virtues are qualities that make you physically well-functioning and capable of physical activity, as the moral and intellectual virtues make you rationally well-functioning and capable of rational activity. The physical virtues, like the

---

[10] In Plato's *Gorgias*. I owe the observation to Warner Wick.

[11] In *A Theory of Justice*, chapter 2, section 15, John Rawls uses the term "primary goods" for things it is rational to want whatever else you want.

moral ones, are called into play on specific occasions but also make you better at physical activity in a general way, at whatever you are doing. Among the physical virtues we would include strength, grace, suppleness, resistance to disease, energy, coordination, stamina, and, in general, all of those qualities that conduce to health and whose exercise constitutes healthy activity, the good of the body. The moral and intellectual virtues, by the parallel, would be those qualities that conduce to the good condition of the soul and whose exercise constitutes rational activity, the good of the soul. The mean is just whatever state of the disposition renders it most useful for rational activity; and the relativity of the mean to the individual is accounted for by the obvious fact that people in different circumstances draw upon different moral virtues to different extents.

While it seems undeniable that Aristotle conceives virtues on a health analogy and as instrumental to rational activity, certain problems beset the interpretation. One is that it fits some virtues better than others. It is easy to see how courage, temperance, and an even temper might be useful in almost any rational undertaking, but less easy to see a use for, say, magnificence, outside of the quite particular occasions that call that virtue into play. Aristotle himself follows up the *Politics* quotation above by remarking that though everyone agrees that the virtues have this sort of utility, this does not establish that one needs to have all of the virtues to a complete extent (POL 1323a 34–36). Furthermore, it is hard to see how we could get an argument for the unity of the virtues on this theory. The physical virtues, though related, are not unified. And the reason for this problem is important: the moral virtues are supposed to be unified because they require the presence of the right reason, which requires practical wisdom, which is one unified thing. The simple instrumentalist theory of the virtues has no way of accommodating such notions as the presence of the right reason, the difference between natural and real virtue, and the unity of the virtues.

The comparison of moral and physical virtue may be extended in a useful way, however. I have said that the physical virtues have a sort of general utility for physical activity, but it is also true that possession of the physical virtues has a determinate influence on choice. Healthy people exhibit a definite pattern of preference: they prefer the actions and activities that tend to exercise, preserve, and promote health. A person in good physical condition is better able than the rest of us to engage in the sorts of activities that preserve and promote health, but this person could probably also better survive the effects of an unhealthy activity (say of an enforced idleness). The utility of the physical virtues is neutral. But it is clear that persons in good health would *prefer* those activities that preserve health.

One might further say that a characteristic difference between the person who really is healthy and a person who has only a theoretical knowledge of health is that the healthy person takes *pleasure* in a way of life that is good for the body and chooses it for its own sake. The person who is not yet healthy but wishes to be so is like the continent person: she knows what is physically good and may obey her reason, but she may not yet enjoy what is good and therefore may be subject to temptation. Now these are all things that Aristotle says about the moral virtues—that they are a good condition; that you cannot be said to have them until their exercise is enjoyed and preferred for its own sake; and that the activities that exercise them are also the activities that tend to preserve and promote them. In Book 2, this last point is offered as the basis of the doctrine of the mean. Aristotle says:

it is the nature of such things to be destroyed by defect and excess, as we see in the case of strength and of health (for to gain light on things imperceptible we must use the evidence of sensible things); both excessive and defective exercise destroys the strength, and similarly drink or food which is above or below a certain amount destroys the health, while that which is proportionate both produces and increases and preserves it. So too is it, then, in the case of temperance and courage and the other virtues. (NE 2.2 1104a11–19)

strength . . . is produced by taking much food and undergoing much exertion, and it is the strong man that will be most able to do these things. So too is it with the virtues. (NE 2.2 1104a31–33)

In the account of intellectual virtue, this point is amplified in an important way, which I have already mentioned. The real virtue implies the presence of the first principle or right reason; the exercise of the virtue, in preserving the virtue, also preserves the first principle:

(This is why we call temperance by this name; we imply that it preserves one's practical wisdom. Now what it preserves is a belief of the kind we have described. For it is not any and every belief that pleasant and painful objects destroy and pervert . . . but the man who has been ruined by pleasure or pain forthwith fails to see any such principle—to see that for the sake of this or because of this he ought to choose and do whatever he chooses and does; for vice is destructive of the principle.) (NE 6.5 1170b11–19)

And this eye of the soul acquires its formed state not without the aid of virtue . . . for the inferences which deal with acts to be done are things which involve a starting-point, viz. "since the end, i.e. what is best, is of such and such a nature" . . . and this is not evident except to the good man, for wickedness perverts us and causes us to be deceived about the starting points of action. Therefore it is evident that it is impossible to be practically wise without being good. (NE 6.13 1144a29–37)

For virtue and vice respectively preserve and destroy the first principle, and in actions that for the sake of which is the first principle. . . . the incontinent man . . . is better than the self-indulgent man . . . for the best thing in him, the first principle, is preserved. (NE 7.8 1151a14–25)

This is, in fact, the most explicit sort of statement Aristotle makes about how the moral virtues contribute to the well-functioning of reason. The moral virtues preserve reason from the corruption that is possible for it; they enable us to "see" the first principle, which is the truth about what is good.

This is the view I am calling "The Perception Theory" of the moral virtues, and I understand it as follows. The state of your character determines, in particular cases, what we might call your evaluative perceptions. The way it does this is by determining what you find pleasant and painful, which is what you take to be good and bad. In his discussion of rational wish Aristotle says:

For each state of character has its own ideas of the noble and the pleasant, and perhaps the good man differs from others most by seeing the truth in each class of things, being as it were the norm and measure of them. In most things the error seems to be due to pleasure; for it appears a good when it is not. (NE 3.4 1113a31–34)

And in the Book 10 discussion of pleasure:

The same things do not seem sweet to a man in a fever and a healthy man—nor hot to a weak man and one in good condition. The same happens in other cases. But in all such matters that which appears to the good man is thought to be really so. If this is correct, as it seems to be, and excellence and the good man as such are the measure of each thing, those also will be pleasures which appear so to him, and those things pleasant which he enjoys. (NE 10.5 1176a12–19)

Now good is a rational concept—it is the object of rational wish, and it is the first principle which deals with it. But these passages make clear that its appearance, so to speak, is pleasure. This view is also found in the third book of *On the Soul*, where Aristotle says that "To feel pleasure or pain is to act with the sensitive mean towards what is good or bad as such" (OS 3.7 431a10–11). What the good person takes pleasure in is good. So part of the contribution made by the virtues to rational activity is perceptual. Without the virtues, you do not take pleasure in the right things and so you do not "see" what is good. But if you do not "see" what is good, your judgments and more general conceptions of the good are not going to be accurate. Your reason will be working, so to speak, with the wrong data.[12]

---

[12] I discuss this passage from *On the Soul* and the idea of correct evaluative perception in "From Duty and for the Sake of the Noble: Kant and Aristotle on Morally Good Action," Essay 6 in this volume, pp. 201–6.

5. Conclusion

By combining the perception theory, along with the health analogy, with the theory of susceptibility to argument, we can arrive at an understanding of what Aristotle means by moral virtue. Susceptibility to argument is the healthy condition for the human soul—the condition in which our capacity for rational activity is realized. Since moral virtues produce and maintain this condition, to have the moral virtues is to be in a healthy state. A morally virtuous person, who is in the argument-susceptible condition, naturally does and takes pleasure in doing those things that preserve the argument-susceptible condition, and is a sort of norm and measure of them. What the morally virtuous person finds pleasant, and so correctly judges to be good, is the kind of activity that keeps reason in control of the soul. What is morally good is what is good for the soul, and what is good for the soul is what realizes its full potential—the potential for rational activity.

The combination of the two theories also helps to explain why habituation to do what coincides with the dictates of reason produces the state of susceptibility to the causal influence of those dictates. It is like acquiring healthy habits. The appetitive part provides the pleasures and pains with which reason works in constructing its notions of what is best—but the rational part, in turn, exerts through the resulting ideas of the good a causal influence on the passions and dispositions, causing them to take a certain form. This is why the soul of a bad person may display a certain harmony, and why vice can become so impervious to considerations of what is really noble and good. (Think of a person raised in physical idleness trying to make a judgment about how much exercise is good.) Evaluative perception and rational evaluative concepts are formed together—each giving shape to the other. Unless the perceptions are correct from the start, neither will ever be perfect.[13]

It is important to notice the sense in which this account tells us what is morally good. In criticizing the obedience and harmony theories, I mentioned

---

[13] What I say here does not quite explain why the moral virtues must be acquired in childhood. The explanation of that fact, I believe, is the same as the explanation of the fact that the physical virtues must be acquired in childhood: the moral virtues must at some level be physical conditions, and in the process of maturation the body becomes set in its ways. When remarking on the status of the "affections of the soul" as "enmattered accounts," in *On the Soul*, Aristotle points out that anger, for example, is both "a boiling of the blood or warm substance surrounding the heart" and "the appetite for returning pain for pain" (OS 1.1 403a30–403b1), and that the physical conditions may cause us to experience the emotions even when their proper objects are not present (OS 1.1 403a18–25). A virtuous person is in a certain physical condition: she is disposed to experience the passions only under the influence of their proper objects. My views on this have been clarified by discussion with Charlotte Brown.

that those views do not really tell us what is good. According to those views what is good is just what is dictated by reason, and the appetitive part of the soul is in a good condition when it falls into line (in one of the two ways) with reason's dictates. This gives us no way of determining what reason's dictates are. This account gets around that objection, although the solution is in a certain sense schematic. What is morally good is what is good for the soul, and what is good for the soul is what maintains it in the argument-susceptible state, and so enables us to achieve our potential for rationality. This does not tell us any more about what we ought to do in a particular case than saying that what is good for the body is what maintains it in a healthy state, and enables it to realize its physical potential. What the view tells us is, rather, what condition we would have to be in in order to know what to do in a particular case. In Book 9 Aristotle tells us that "The intellect always chooses what is best for itself, and the good man obeys his intellect" (NE 9.8 1169a16–17).

The schematic character of the solution should not, however, be taken as a defect of the interpretation, for Aristotle would agree that no more than this can be theoretically conveyed. Recall the definition of a moral virtue: it is determined by a reason, but the way it is determined is identified simply as "the way in which the man of practical wisdom would determine it" (NE 2.6 1107a1–2). For Aristotle, virtue is in the realm of practice, not of theory. Although virtue is not an art (*techne*), it shares this feature with an art: any attempt to convey it theoretically will necessarily be schematic.

Virtue, then, is the perfected state of the human soul. It is the state in which a human being can perceive correctly, and be motivated by, considerations of what is noble and good, and so can engage in rational activity. The capacity to be motivated by these considerations is the argument-susceptible state, in which desires and emotions are caused by the dictates of reason. What reason dictates is just what maintains this condition; it chooses what is best for itself. The virtuous person prefers and chooses those actions that maintain this condition, and such actions are morally good. We should not be surprised to find Aristotle defining the morally good in terms of the good condition of the agent's soul, for Plato does the same in his account of justice (R 443c–444a).

One of the primary objections to the function argument is that it makes an illegitimate connection between being morally good, being good at rational activity, and achieving the human good. If Aristotle's account of the role of the moral virtues in keeping reason in control of the soul seems actually to be true of those qualities that all of us agree are moral virtues, such as courage and temperance, then some headway against this objection can be made, for a connection between being morally good and being good at rational activity has indeed been made. This in turn gives Aristotle a way of addressing the claim against the function argument, that reason can be used either for good or for evil, and so cannot define an ethically best life. This objection is based on a more or less empiricist view of practical reason: its use is the determination of means to ends, and ends can be good or bad. But if the proposed connection between virtue and function is correct, then this is not Aristotle's view. A person's practical reason is only well-functioning when she has the virtues, for only then is she able to form a correct conception of what is good for the soul. The good is the object of a rational wish, but reason can be corrupted.[14] Aristotle does not think of reason as determining the good *a priori* or independently of emotion and desire and the perception they provide; he is not a rationalist in that sense. The virtues of the appetitive part are necessary for practical wisdom. But he does not think the good is merely the object of emotion and desire either, like an empiricist, for he thinks that emotion and desire can be correct or incorrect, accordingly as they do or do not contribute to the rational functioning of the soul—that is, to reason's control over it.

Aristotle's view of the role of reason in ethics is thus different from the more familiar modern views. The difference rests in the fact that he regards reason as a potentiality that may or may not be adequately realized, and so regards reasoning as something that may or may not come out right, depending upon the condition one is in. This is what the function argument is all about: Aristotle thinks that we cannot have a good life unless our potential for true practical reasoning is actualized. The connection between function and virtue means that this potential cannot be realized without the moral virtues. The moral virtues are just those qualities that actualize our potential for rationality: they make us human beings.[15]

---

[14] I address these objections more fully (and more recently) in "Aristotle's Function Argument," Essay 4 in this volume, section 5. In that discussion, the distinction between a descriptive and prescriptive use of terms like "reason," "rational," and so on, does some of the same work as the idea of a distinction between a corrupted and an uncorrupted reason does here.

[15] I read a version of this essay at the University of Wisconsin at Madison, the University of Illinois at Chicago, and Virginia Commonwealth University. I learned a great deal from these discussions. I would especially like to thank Terry Penner, Jon Moline, and Charlotte Brown. I also received extensive and very helpful comments from Warner Wick, and a set of forceful and useful criticisms, not all of which I have been able to answer, from Alan Gewirth. I owe a great deal to them both.

6

From Duty and for the Sake of the Noble: Kant and Aristotle on Morally Good Action

Philosophers have long supposed that Aristotle and Kant disagree about many fundamental issues in moral philosophy. Aristotle tells us that an agent lacks virtue unless he enjoys the performance of virtuous actions, while in the *Groundwork* Kant seems to claim that the person who does her duty in the teeth of contrary inclination displays an especially high degree of moral worth. Aristotle argues for the virtuous life by attempting to prove that, given the human *telos*, some form of the virtuous life is the happiest that we can live. Kant scorns appeals to happiness as irrelevant to morality and bids us remember the special vocation of an autonomous being. Aristotle emphasizes the difficulty of formulating general principles of action, and the important role of judgment and perception in practical deliberation. Kant, on the other hand, provides us with a method for testing proposed maxims to see whether their actions are permissible, forbidden, or required. And finally, Aristotle has lately been categorized as a "virtue theorist" who holds that an action's value consists in its being the expression of a virtue; while Kant is supposedly a deontologist who thinks that the value of an action rests in its conformity to a rule.

   Yet behind these contrasts, apparent and real, is one undeniable similarity. Aristotle and Kant both believe that in human beings, reason can be practical. This is a view about what specifically human action is, or about how human action is different from that of the other animals. It is the view that human beings exercise *choice*, in a specific sense that I will explain in this essay, in the determination of our actions. Since moral or ethical value pertains only to human action, it seems natural to think that it is somehow related to, or supervenes on, the specific character of human action. And I think that we do find this idea in both Aristotle and Kant. Both of them believe that the moral value of an action is a function of the way in which it is chosen.

I believe that these claims about the practical employment of reason are deeper, both in fact and in Aristotle and Kant's theories, than philosophers have generally recognized. To say that human beings are rational is not just to say that we are rule-following or logical, but rather to say that we are capable of authentic mental activity, of an engagement with the world that goes beyond mere reaction. In Aristotle's account of theoretical reason, the ultimate expression of our rational nature is our participation in the active intellect that imparts form and intelligibility to the natural world. In Kant's more skeptical account, it is the mind's attempt to construct a systematic, unified, and intelligible world out of the confused mass of phenomena that are presented to it. To say that reason is also *practical* is to say that our actions, the expressions of our wills, can in a similar way be fully active, self-generated, or in Kant's special sense, spontaneous.[1] And if morality is the full expression of practical reason, then this is the distinguishing feature of the moral agent: that her actions are more truly active, more authentically her own, than those of agents who fall short of moral goodness. To have the distinctively moral attitude, then, is to have an active as opposed to a merely reactive relationship to the world around us.[2]

At the same time, both of these philosophers were aware that the human mind (unlike the divine one) is also passive or receptive with respect to the world. A central concern of both Aristotle's book *On the Soul* and Kant's *Critique of Pure Reason* is to explain the respective contributions of activity and passivity to our mental lives. And this is a central concern in the ethical writings of both philosophers as well. Aristotle and Kant of course acknowledge that passions, inclinations, and impulses, as well as reflective deliberation and choice, play an important role in the determination of action. And I believe that for both, the concern of a theory of *virtue*, in particular, is to explain how that role may be accommodated in a theory of rationally governed and so authentically self-generated conduct.

These are large claims, and obviously I cannot undertake to defend them in any adequate way here. I offer them as background to the argument I am going to make, which concerns the very first contrast that I mentioned. In the first

---

[1] Spontaneity, in Kant's sense, means having an original source in the agent's own mind or will, rather than in some external cause.

[2] It's worth noticing the comparison with Nietzsche, who also places a high value on this attitude, although of course with more ambivalence about whether it may be identified with the moral attitude. In Essay One of *The Genealogy of Morals*, Nietzsche proposes that the values "good" and "bad" were born from the spontaneous evaluative acts of the noble or master types, as an expression of the value they set on themselves, while the opposed values "evil" and "good" were the result of *reaction* against the masters on the part of the oppressed and enslaved. (See Walter Kaufmann and R. J. Hollingdale, trans., *On the Genealogy of Morals*, in *On the Genealogy of Morals and Ecce Homo*, especially sections 10–11, pp. 36–43.)

section of the *Groundwork*, Kant claims that a person who helps others with pleasure from motives of natural sympathy displays no moral worth, while a person who lacks any natural inclination to help others but nevertheless does so, from the motive of duty, does display moral worth (G 4:398). This appears to be in stark contrast with Aristotle's claim that it is the mark of a good person to take pleasure in moral action (NE 1.8 1099a16–21). In this essay I will argue that this apparent contrast does not reflect any ethical disagreement between the two philosophers at all. There is a disagreement at work here, but it is psychological rather than ethical. My argument will take the following course. In section 1, I will look at Kant's view of what gives an action moral worth, as presented in the first section of the *Groundwork*, and in the course of that explain why Kant says what he does about the naturally sympathetic person. In section 2, I will argue that Aristotle holds an essentially similar view about what gives an action moral worth. Both philosophers, I will argue, think that what gives an action moral value is the fact that it is chosen for its intrinsic rightness. Finally, in section 3, I will return to the question of the value of acting from natural inclination, and try to explain the real source of Kant and Aristotle's apparent difference on this point.

1. Acting from Duty

Section 1 of the *Groundwork* opens with a claim that Kant believes his readers will accept, namely, that the only thing in the world that has unconditional value is a good will. The good will is good "only because of its volition" (G 4:394), which means that it is in actions expressive of a good will, morally good actions, that we will see this unconditional value realized. Now the project of section 1 of the *Groundwork* is to discover the principle of the good will, for this will be the moral law. Kant's idea is this. Good-willed actions are good because of the way that they are willed, or, as I will put it, chosen. So once we know how they are chosen, we will know what makes them good. Since the moral law tells us to perform good actions, it will tell us to perform actions that have that feature—whatever it is—that makes actions good. Since you and I already know how the investigation turns out, I can perhaps try to say this more clearly. Kant thinks that what makes an action good is that its maxim qualifies to be a universal law. So what he is going to try to show is that the principle of a good will is that of choosing actions whose maxims qualify to be universal laws. That's what good people think about when they choose their actions—whether their maxims qualify to be universal laws.

Now in order to bring this out, Kant says, he is going to look at a particular class of good actions, namely, those that are done from duty. Duty is the good will operating under "certain subjective limitations and hindrances, which, however, far from concealing it and making it unrecognizable, rather bring it out by contrast and make it shine forth all the more brightly" (G 4:397). In order to discover what is distinctive about good-willed actions, what their principle is, Kant proposes to compare actions done from duty with actions done from other kinds of motives, to see what makes them essentially different. He mentions three other kinds of actions. Actions which are recognized as contrary to duty are set aside. It is worth attending to Kant's own words here; he says: "I here pass over all actions that are already recognized as contrary to duty, *even though they may be useful for this or that purpose*, for in their case the question whether they might have been done *from duty* never arises" (G 4:397; first emphasis mine). I take Kant to be saying that any value these actions may have must come from their utility. Kant also sets aside, and for the same reason, actions that are in accordance with duty but that are not chosen for their own sakes. The prudent merchant who always charges honestly because a good reputation helps his business exemplifies this category. Kant clearly takes it to be obvious, just as Aristotle does, that a morally good action must be chosen for its own sake. But being chosen for its own sake is not sufficient to make an action morally good. This point is brought out by the next three examples, in which people who act from duty are contrasted with people who do the same actions from direct or immediate inclination. It is possible to do an action for its own sake just because it is what you like to do. The naturally sympathetic person's action falls into this category. Kant says:

there are many souls so sympathetically attuned that, without any other motive of vanity or self-interest they find an inner satisfaction in spreading joy around them and can take delight in the satisfaction of others so far as it is their own work. But I assert that in such a case an action of this kind, however it may conform with duty and however amiable it may be, has nevertheless no true moral worth but is on the same footing with other inclinations. (G 4:398)

Some readers have supposed that what Kant is saying here is that the sympathetic person is really acting for the sake of his own pleasure; that is, that his real purpose is to please himself. According to this view, Kant believes in some sort of psychological hedonism about non-moral motives, and so supposes that our inclinations are all selfish.[3] Such a reading would be

---

[3] Terence Irwin, in his "Kant's Criticisms of Eudaemonism" (in *Aristotle, Kant, and the Stoics: Rethinking Happiness and Duty*), suggests that Kant has a hedonistic conception of desire and therefore of happiness, and that this is one basis for his criticism of his eudaemonist predecessors. It will be evident that I cannot agree with this. Irwin himself acknowledges that Kant's criticism of eudaemonism

inconsistent with several of the things Kant says, some of them in the passage I just quoted. Kant characterizes the sympathetic person as "amiable" and without any motive of self-interest, for instance. Most importantly, however, it flies in the teeth of the conclusion Kant draws from these examples, which is this:

That the purposes we may have for our actions, and their effects as ends and incentives of the will, can give actions no unconditional and moral worth is clear from what has gone before. (G 4:400)

What makes this clear is precisely the fact that a person who does a beneficent action from immediate inclination and a person who does one from duty have *the same purpose*—namely, to help someone. Both of these people help others for its own sake. Kant goes on to assert that what gives an action moral value, then, is not the agent's purpose, but rather the "maxim" or "principle of volition" on which it is done.[4]

---

need not depend on this thesis, however, since its essence is that action governed by considerations of one's own good is essentially heteronomous. Irwin thinks that this criticism is not decisive, since one may argue that eudaemonistic principles do not derive their authority from our inclination to achieve happiness. One may instead suppose, as Butler and Reid did, that the principle of pursuing our own good has an authority of its own, just as the categorical imperative does. I believe that this argument misses the main thrust of Kant's objection to eudaemonism, although I think that Kant himself is partly responsible for the misconception. There are two elements to Kant's notion of heteronomy: (a) the law is not the will's own law, but rather is given to it from outside, and (b) the will therefore can be bound by that law only through an inclination or an interest, which renders the imperative to follow the law hypothetical. As this way of putting the point makes clear, Kant himself argues as if, and may have thought, that these two elements are inseparable, and he therefore sometimes emphasizes the second element, which Irwin takes to be the essence of heteronomy. But I think that the real essence of heteronomy lies in the first element: the problem with the eudaemonistic principle is that it is not the will's *own* law. The possibility of the two elements of heteronomy coming apart is illustrated by a case I discuss later in this essay, the case of someone who is motivated by considerations of honor. One is not bound to considerations of honor by inclination or interest: one is honorable for its own sake, moved by a conception of how one ought to act. Yet this kind of action is still not fully autonomous, because the laws of honor are not the will's own laws. Only the categorical imperative, which *describes* the activity of a free will as such (a free will as such chooses a maxim it regards as a law), is the will's *own* law. (For a fuller account of this point see my "Morality as Freedom," CKE essay 6.)

[4] Kant evidently thinks that there are three ways to value, and therefore to choose, an action: as useful (as the prudent merchant values honesty); as good for its own sake, in the sense of being immediately desirable (as the sympathetic person values beneficence); and as morally required (as the dutiful person values beneficence). If the argument of this essay is correct, this coincides with Aristotle's view that there are three objects of choice—namely, the advantageous, the pleasant, and the noble (NE 2.3 1104b30–31).

Addition 2008: When I wrote this footnote I had failed to realize that the conception of action that I attribute to Kant and Aristotle in this essay makes the idea of choosing an action as useful unclear. If an action is an act done for the sake of an end—that is, the description of an action includes its end—then actions are done for their own sake. On this point, and why Kant himself may have failed to see it, see my "Acting for a Reason," Essay 7 in this volume, especially pp. 222–3.

To understand these claims it is necessary to understand the psychology behind them. According to Kant, our nature presents us with what he calls "incentives" (*Triebfedern*) which prompt or tempt us to act in certain ways. We might say that the incentives present certain actions along with their ends to us as eligible. We are, at least in part, passive with respect to these, although that is a remark I will qualify later. Among these incentives are our ordinary desires and inclinations. Now the incentives do not operate on us directly as causes of action. Instead, they are considerations that we take into account in deciding what to do. If you decide to act on an incentive, you "make it your maxim" to act in the way suggested by the incentive. How do you decide that? In the *Groundwork* and even more specifically in *Religion Within the Limits of Reason Alone*, Kant suggests that there are two principles of volition or choice that might govern this decision: morality or self-love (REL 6:36).[5] If you are operating under the principle of self-love, your choice is to do what will gratify you, what will satisfy your desires. Kant's point about the naturally sympathetic person is that he is acting under this principle of volition or choice. The trouble with him is not that he wants to help others only because it pleases him to do so. The trouble is that he *chooses* to help others *only* because he *wants* to. His action is chosen as a desirable one, one which he would enjoy doing.[6]

The person who acts from duty, by contrast, chooses the action because she conceives it as one that is required of her. And here we must be careful to draw the lesson from what has gone before. The point is not that her *purpose* is "to do her duty." As I said before, she chooses the action for its own sake: her purpose is to help. The point is that she chooses helping as her purpose *because* that is what she is required to do. Kant takes this to be equivalent to being moved by the thought of the maxim of the action, the principle of doing it, as a kind of law. The dutiful person takes the maxim of helping others to *express* a requirement. Rather subtly, the contrast between doing the right thing from duty and doing the right thing from immediate inclination is also supposed to show that seeing a maxim as a law is attending to something about its form

---

[5] This is a little oversimplified: In *Religion within the Limits of Reason Alone*, Kant argues that we are in general influenced by both moral incentives and incentives of self-love. Whether one has a good will depends on which of these is made the condition of the other (REL 6:36). This suggests that the moral principle will be something like: "Do your duty, and what you like if that is consistent with your duty," while the principle of self-love will be: "Do what you like, and your duty if that is consistent with your happiness." This complicates the picture in ways that I want to leave aside here, however, since these formulations presuppose a certain view of the role of natural inclination in the moral life, the basis of which I will call into question in section 3.

[6] For a rich and subtle account of Kant's views on the operation of the principle of self-love, see Allen W. Wood, "Self-Love, Self-Benevolence, and Self-Conceit," in *Aristotle, Kant, and the Stoics: Rethinking Happiness and Duty*.

rather than about its matter. The person who acts from immediate inclination and the person who acts from duty in a sense act in accordance with the same material principle, which Kant specifies as "to be beneficent where one can" (G 4:398). But the person who acts from self-love sees such action as desirable, while the person who acts from duty takes that principle to be a law. So the dutiful person's principle of volition is to act on those maxims that have the form of a law. This also makes a difference in the kind of value that these two agents accord to the action. For the person who acts from inclination, the action has an extrinsic value, a value that it inherits from his own desires. But the person who acts from duty sees the value of the action as intrinsic: lawlike form is a property that is internal to the maxim and so is in the action itself.[7]

Later in the *Groundwork* (G 4:421–423), and also in the second *Critique* (C2 5:67–70), we learn more about what this thought involves. To think about whether your maxim has the form of a law is to think about whether you could will to be part of an order of things in which everyone acted in the way specified in the maxim. So it is to think about what sort of world this would be if everyone acted as you propose to act. The dutiful person helps, then, because the vision of a world in which people do not help one another is in a certain way unacceptable to her, and she is moved by that fact. I do not mean, of course, that she is moved by some thought about the consequences of what she actually does—she does not see doing a beneficent action as a way of producing a world in which everyone helps. It is rather that, if we could not choose to live in a world in which no one helps, if we find that we *must* will that people should help, then the principle of beneficence must be a law by its very nature, a law in itself. Seen this way, it looks as if the difference between the two characters is that the dutiful person has a further thought about *helping*, or takes a more reflective stance towards it, than the naturally sympathetic person. Helping is not just something that it is nice to do, but something that one must do, because of the sort of action that it is. Since the good person chooses her actions by attending to their lawlike form, that is what the moral law instructs us to do—to choose those maxims which have lawlike form.

---

[7] I do not agree with J. B. Schneewind's view that "for Kant nothing possesses the kind of intrinsic value that G. E. Moore thought would belong to a beautiful world even were there no observers of it" (in his "Kant and Stoic Ethics," in *Aristotle, Kant and the Stoics: Rethinking Happiness and Duty*). Schneewind is right, of course, to insist that in Kant's account value is not independent of rational willing: a maxim is an act of rational willing, and it is the maxim, and the good will which is expressed in the maxim, which possess this value. For a comparison between Kant's conception of unconditional value and Moore's conception of intrinsic value, see my "Two Distinctions in Goodness" (CKE essay 9). For a more detailed account of the sense in which maxims have intrinsic value, see SN 3.3.5–3.3.6, pp. 107–12.

There is a hitch in this argument, which I will come back to in a moment. At this point I want to focus your attention on two important features of the account. First, Kant gives us what we might call a double-aspect theory of motivation. An agent's motivation to act involves two things—the incentive that presents the action along with its end as eligible, and the principle of volition that governs the agent's choice to act on that incentive. Second, moral value rests specifically in the principle of volition that is exercised in the choice of the action. Moral value supervenes on *choice*.

This has several important implications. One is that on this account the presence or absence of a natural inclination makes no difference to the moral value of the action. It is obviously possible to choose an action because you see it as intrinsically required while also thinking that it will be a pleasant thing to do. Kant chooses to discuss cases of good-willed motivation in which no inclination is present—that is, cases of action from duty—for exactly the reason he says he does, because in such cases the operation of the moral principle is especially perspicuous. Relatedly, as I said before, the problem with the naturally sympathetic person is not that he has an inclination and it is not that his inclination is covertly selfish, that his own pleasure is his real purpose. His inclination is disinterested, which is why Kant says he is amiable. The problem is that he chooses to help others only because he *has* this inclination. His principle of volition is the problem—it is the principle of doing what he likes to do.

Now in one way this makes it look as if Kant is, after all, saying that the naturally sympathetic person is covertly selfish. If a person chooses to satisfy his inclinations because it gratifies him, doesn't that after all show that he looks to himself? In sorting this issue out I think it will be useful to make a distinction that Kant doesn't make. Kant thinks that when we choose an action we employ some principle of volition. But obviously he does not mean that we always consciously recite this principle in our minds or even that we are always aware of it as we make the choice.[8] Sometimes, the principle is just implicit in the *way* we make the choice. Now this suggests that we can distinguish between more and less reflective versions of both of the characters we are considering here. The unreflective sympathetic person may simply be thinking "I want to help" or perhaps just "this person needs help" and he is moved by that thought. As Kant imagines him, it is his natural inclination to make others happy that interests him in helping, which is why Kant thinks he is implicitly or tacitly acting under the principle of self-love.

---

[8] For an account of why principles are always involved in human actions, see my "Acting for a Reason," Essay 7 in this volume, pp. 227–9.

The more reflective sympathetic person who *consciously* employs the principle of self-love entertains a further thought, but it is a thought about himself, not a thought about helping: "Doing this sort of thing makes me happy, makes me feel good, so I will." Or we might even imagine that he does a calculation of prudence, and works out that, of all the activities that he finds attractive, helping others will make him happiest: he enjoys it, it makes people like him, and it lacks some of the untoward side effects that other pleasant pursuits may have.[9] In this case, the pleasure he takes in helping may be disinterested, but the decision to pursue that pleasure is not. Similarly, a person may act from duty in a completely unreflective way, simply thinking of an action as required, without thinking much about why it is so or even without really thinking that there *is* a reason why it is so. We might think here of some ordinary conscientious person who has simply accepted the conventional or religious moral system according to which he was brought up. But of course there are more sinister entries into this category: the Nazi soldier who thinks of "duty" as carrying out the orders of his superiors comes immediately to mind. This, as I have tried to bring out, is not how Kant is thinking of the person who acts from duty. For Kant, to act from duty is not just to be moved by a blank conviction that an action is required, but rather to be moved by a more substantial thought which inherently involves an intelligent view of *why* the action is required.[10]

With this distinction in hand it is possible to make certain points. First of all, if we imagine the *reflective* versions of these two characters as I have just described them, it is not hard to accept the claim that the person who acts from duty exhibits a moral worth which the person who acts from inclination

---

[9] Butler, in Sermon 11 of his *Fifteen Sermons Preached at the Rolls Chapel* (Sermon 4 in Stephen Darwall, ed., *Joseph Butler: Five Sermons Preached at the Rolls Chapel and A Dissertation Upon the Nature of Virtue*, pp. 46–57), and, following him, Hume, in the conclusion of the *Enquiry Concerning the Principles of Morals* (2E 9, 281–2) make arguments in favor of beneficent action which take this form. To be fair, neither of them thinks that this is the way to establish the *moral* value of beneficence; it is just a way to establish the harmony of beneficence and self-interest. For further discussion, see SN 2.2.3, pp. 55–60, and Charlotte Brown, "Hume Against the Selfish Schools and the Monkish Virtues."

[10] Kant has some tendency to exaggerate the active reflectiveness of human beings, and the possibility of an unreflective version of the motive of duty may not even have occurred to him. In the *Critique of Practical Reason*, for example, after explaining how a natural law can serve as a "type" of the moral law, he says, "Everyone does, in fact, appraise actions as morally good or evil by this rule. Thus one says: If *everyone* permitted himself to deceive when he believed it to be to his advantage . . . and if you belonged to such an order of things, would you be in it with the assent of your will?" (C2 5:69). Probably the most startling instance of this optimism occurs at *Groundwork* 4:450, where Kant suggests that even "the commonest understanding" draws a rough distinction between the sensible and intelligible worlds. But optimism about human reflectiveness is not the only thing at work here. Perhaps the closest thing to an unreflective version of the motive of duty in Kant's system is the inclination to honor; and I will explain why Kant didn't see this as an unreflective version of the motive of duty below.

lacks. The agent who consciously employs the principle of self-love in his choice does seem to look to himself; in fact he seems to choose beneficence as one might choose a hobby. Second, I think it is pretty clear that many of the readers who find what Kant says here wildly counterintuitive are in fact comparing the *unreflective* versions of both of these characters. If we compare the person who helps impulsively, thinking nothing but "this person needs help" and being moved by that thought, with a person for whom duty is just blind obedience to an abstract rule, then the first of these two characters seems much more attractive than the second. The right thing to say to such readers, of course, is that this is simply not the comparison that Kant has placed before us.

But it does raise a question about the comparison that Kant *has* placed before us. I think that the comparison that Kant has placed before us is between the more attractive members of each of these two pairs. Kant means to compare the unreflective sympathetic person, who thinks simply "this person needs help," with the more reflective person who acts from duty with some comprehension of why helping is required. But it is also clear that Kant thinks that the unreflective sympathetic person is tacitly or implicitly acting on the principle of self-love. At least, this is what I am supposing Kant means when he says the action is on a level with other actions from inclination (G 4:398). So Kant's view seems to be that if you act unreflectively, the principle of self-love is your principle of volition by default. Why does Kant think this?

One answer that I think we should reject is that your tacit principle of volition is what you would say about your choice if you were invited to reflect on why you made it. According to this view, if we asked the impulsively sympathetic person why he helps, and he started to think about it, all he could say is: "I just like to; it gives me pleasure." Perhaps this *is* why he helps, but once he starts to reflect on his reasons, it will be natural for him to switch from a merely theoretical self-scrutiny to a more practical form of reflection. The question "why do you help people?" is naturally understood as a request for justification and so transmutes into the question why one should help people. So the claim is not that "it gives me pleasure, I like it" is what the unreflective sympathetic person *would* say if he started to think about why he helps. If he starts to think about why he helps, something altogether different will happen.[11] In fact Kant's argument relies upon this point, since he thinks that the pursuit of reflection—that is, enlightenment—will lead us

---

[11] I thank Arata Hamawaki and Michael Hardimon for pressing me on this point, and for useful discussion of this argument in general.

to a recognition of the categorical imperative as the law of our own autonomy and so to the good.[12]

So I think that all Kant means is this: so long as you *haven't* reflected on why you help, you are just following your inclinations where they lead. And so long as you are just following your inclinations where they lead, your choice is implicitly governed by the principle of doing what you are inclined to do, what you like. To say that the naturally sympathetic person acts from self-love is not to assign him an unconscious ulterior motive, or a secret selfish thought. It is, precisely, to record the fact that he hasn't thought, that he is allowing his choices to be governed by his natural inclinations, and so is simply following where nature leads.

Now I want to come back to the hitch I mentioned in the argument. I said earlier that the conclusion is that the good-willed person attends to the lawlike form of her maxim in making her choices, and therefore that that is what the moral law tells us to do: to respect, or attend to, lawlike form. But there are, in fact, two senses in which a maxim may have lawlike form. A maxim may be one that *can* be willed as a universal law—it qualifies to be a law. Action on such a maxim is permissible. Or the maxim may be a law in the sense that it *must* be willed, that is, it expresses a duty. The conclusion Kant is looking for in the first section of the *Groundwork* is that a good action is one whose maxim qualifies to be a law. The principle of a good will is to act on a maxim only if it *can* serve as a universal law. But Kant has chosen to focus on the more specific category of duties, actions whose maxims *must* be willed as laws. So the hitch is this: it is unclear how Kant wants us to make the step from the fact that people who act from duty choose their maxims because they see them as principles which *must* be willed as laws to the conclusion that the principle of a good will is that of acting only on maxims which *can* be willed as laws.

I do not know of a smooth way to rescue the presentation of the argument in the first section of the *Groundwork*, but it seems clear enough that these two ideas are related. One connection between them is revealed in the negative way in which the categorical imperative is here formulated—"*I ought never to act except in such a way that I could also will that my maxim should become a universal law*" (G 4:402). Using this formulation we discover that a maxim *must* be regarded as a law by discovering that the opposite maxim—the maxim of not doing the action in question—cannot be regarded as a law. That Kant has this connection in mind is clear from the fact that, in two of

---

[12] I describe this process of reflection and how it leads one to a recognition of the moral law in more detail in "Morality as Freedom," CKE essay 7, pp. 27–31.

the examples, it is the *same* person who first acts from immediate inclination and, later, when he has lost his inclination through sorrow or adversity, acts from duty.

Consider, for instance, the naturally sympathetic person. At the beginning of the story, he is a happy person, and full of spontaneous sympathy for others. He sees people living on the street and he feels sorry for them. He gives them food or money, and he likes to see the relief and gratitude in their eyes. He enjoys spreading joy around him as he goes about his own business. He's sympathetic and so their delight gives him direct pleasure. Then bad things happen to him. Maybe his wife gets cancer, or his child runs away, or his work, which once seemed promising, comes to nothing. And there is no pleasure in anything for him any more. He is absorbed in his own sorrows, and he has no sympathy for anyone else. But since he has always given to those in need before it occurs to him that he might, and now for the first time he *thinks* about it. Or maybe one day he passes by someone whom he has often helped before and the person says: "Aren't you going to help me today? You helped me last week, and I am just as hungry as I was last week." And now our hero says to himself, "After all, it is not just because it gives me pleasure that I should help. These poor people are living on the street, and they don't have enough to eat. Someone must help them! What sort of world would we live in if no one helped people who are in need?" Moved by this thought, he helps. And now for the first time his helping has moral worth.[13]

This is the kind of story Kant has in mind in the first section of the *Groundwork*. But what I have just said might lead to a misunderstanding. I do not mean to suggest that the only reason a good-willed person asks whether her maxim *can* be a law is as a way of ferreting out those maxims which *must* be laws. The categorical imperative test is not a kind of Geiger counter for discovering whether there are any duties in the neighborhood. I do not know

[13] There is an important similarity between this way of characterizing the difference between the naturally sympathetic person and the dutiful person and the way in which, according to Jennifer Whiting, Aristotle characterizes the difference between merely *agathos* (the merely good person) and the *kaloskagathos* (the noble and good person) in the *Eudemian Ethics*. The *kaloskagathos*, as Whiting characterizes him, is superior in his reflective understanding of the reasons for good actions and therefore chooses them for their own sake, rather than for the sake of external or natural goods (see her "Self-Love and Authoritative Virtue: Prolegomenon to a Kantian Reading of *Eudemian Ethics* 8.3," in *Aristotle, Kant, and the Stoics: Rethinking Happiness and Duty*). I would not say that the naturally sympathetic person chooses beneficence merely *for the sake of* the natural goods, but rather that he chooses it merely *as* a natural good. Whiting compares the *Eudemian Ethics'* *agathos* to a character in the *Nicomachean Ethics*, namely, the person who has merely natural as opposed to "authoritative" virtue; later in this essay I will compare this same character to the naturally sympathetic person.

how to fit this point into the argument of the first section of the *Groundwork*, but I believe that Kant's thought is that a reflective person asks herself whether the consideration on which she proposes to act may really be treated as a *reason* to act. To ask whether a consideration is a reason is to ask whether it may be taken as *normative*. And that, in turn, is to ask whether the maxim of acting on that consideration can be regarded as a kind of *law*. When we experience some incentive to act—say a desire or inclination—you might say that our nature makes a proposal to reason. The proposal is a maxim and it includes a purpose: do this for the sake of that, or do this for its own sake. Reason steps back and considers the proposal, that is, it considers the action as a whole, including the purpose, and determines whether it is a good thing, a thing to be done, or not. Its decision is an act of volition, performed in accordance with a principle of volition. So to *choose* an action is to be moved by the conception of the impulse to do it as a reason. And its being a reason is an intrinsic property, a property of the maxim's form. Reason says yes to the proposal if it can recognize its own form, the form of normativity or law, in the maxim. In that case, the reason for action and so the action itself, having reason's endorsement, are good.

But actions done from duty are reason's own actions in a special way. To see this, recall once again the person whose natural sympathy is blunted by sorrow, but who still helps from the motive of duty. He tests the maxim of not helping, and he finds he must reject it. He is thereby moved to help. What is the incentive in this case? Kant's answer is that it is the feeling of respect for law. The very thought that shows him his duty—the thought that one *must* help those in need—in this case operates as the incentive.

Kant thinks that we cannot say how it is possible for reason to provide an incentive, since that is identical to the question how reason can be practical. But in the second *Critique* he undertakes to describe what happens in us when we are so moved. Let me just quickly sketch this account. Human beings, according to Kant, have a natural tendency to treat our desires and inclinations as authoritative—that is, to think that the fact that we want to do something is in and of itself a reason for doing it. Kant calls this tendency "self-regard" or "self-love" and it is more or less identical with the tendency to operate under the principle of self-love as I have described it. There are two strands to this tendency—the selfishness that makes us long for the satisfaction of our inclinations, and the self-conceit that inclines us to take the bare fact that we want to do something as a justification for doing it. When the moral law commands us not to do an action to which we are inclined, it thwarts the inclination, and it humiliates our self-conceit. These feelings are painful. At the same time, however, we experience an awareness of our freedom, which is revealed by our capacity to set inclination aside. We experience freedom as a sense of independence from the neediness of inclination, a sense that is akin to pleasure in that it resembles the divine bliss. The complex mix of affect that results is the feeling of respect for law. Respect for law is not a desire to obey the moral law, or more generally a feeling that exists independently of the law and interests us in it. It is the law itself, the very thought of a requirement, operating as an incentive.[14]

When we are motivated by respect for law, the rational will provides not only the ground of choice but also the incentive to act in accordance with that ground. Since the incentive as well as the volition are reason's own productions, a person who is motivated by duty is to an especial degree active and truly spontaneous. She is not reacting to nature's proposals at all, but actively imposing on her own actions, and through them on the world, a kind of shape or form that is the dictate of her own mind. This is the fullest expression of autonomy, and it is this that gives her actions their special moral worth.

2. Acting for the Sake of the Noble

Aristotle, I will now argue, holds a similar conception of what gives actions moral value. That is, he also holds a double-aspect account of motivation; and he holds that what gives actions value is the way that they are chosen. Three aspects of his theory may be mentioned in support of these claims: first, the possibility of continence; second, his account of the role of choice (*prohairesis*) in human action; and third, his claim that a good action is done for the sake of *to kalon* or the noble.

The bare possibility of continence, of course, shows that Aristotle thinks that human agents have the power to step back from our inclinations and decide whether to act on them or not. We sometimes decide *not* to act on our inclinations; they do not simply drive us into action, or we could not do that. But one might be tempted to think that according to Aristotle such rational control only needs to be exercised by the continent, since the virtuous person's passions are in order, and can be trusted to direct her automatically to the good. But that cannot be right. At least, the difference between continence

[14] These remarks are based on the discussion in the *Critique of Practical Reason*'s chapter on "The Incentives of Pure Practical Reason," especially C2 5:71–76, with some supplementation from the discussion of how pleasure and pain are related to moral motivation at C2 5:116–118. For an interesting account of how the experience of respect for law is related to the workings of the principle of self-love, see Allen W. Wood, "Self-Love, Self-Benevolence, and Self-Conceit," in *Aristotle, Kant, and the Stoics: Rethinking Happiness and Duty*.

and virtue cannot lie in whether the *exercise* of reason is involved in the action. For Aristotle makes it clear that what makes continence and virtue both good states is the fact that both of them involve the right kind of choice.

What Aristotle says about choice is initially one of the more puzzling parts of the *Nicomachean Ethics*. Choice, he tells us, is voluntary, but it is not the same as the voluntary since the latter is a wider category. Children and animals do things that are voluntary, but they do not act from choice, and some adult actions—those done "on the spur of the moment"—are not chosen although they are voluntary (NE 3.2 1111a4–10). For an action to be voluntary it is enough that the moving principle is in the agent (NE 3.1 1101a14–17); for choice, something more is needed. After exploring various possibilities, Aristotle decides that since the object of choice is something in our own power that is desired after deliberation, choice must be the deliberate desire of something in our own power (NE 3.3 1113a10–12). An action is chosen when we have exercised rational deliberation in determining what we are to do, and we are moved by that deliberation to act.

But of course Aristotle also says, notoriously by now, that "we deliberate not about ends but about what contributes to ends" (*ta pros to telos*: NE 3.3 1112b12). If we take this to mean that rational deliberation is always instrumental, we will be led to conclude that choice pertains only to actions undertaken for instrumental reasons, or perhaps some natural extension of that category. Chosen actions, that is, would be those that we have determined are necessary and desirable because they will help us to realize ends other than those actions themselves. It would then be the intellectual ability to engage in such rational calculation—instrumental reasoning and other things that are like it—that distinguishes adult human beings from children and animals, and, as a result, chosen actions from the merely voluntary.

This view, however, sits very uneasily with certain other important claims Aristotle makes about choice. For instance, Aristotle tells us that virtue is a state of character concerned with choice (NE 2.6 1106b36); and that choice is more closely bound up with virtue and discriminates character better than actions do (NE 3.2 1111b5–6). He even says that the virtues are choices or involve choice (NE 2.5 1106a3). He also tells us that the continent person acts in accordance with his choice, while the incontinent person does not (NE 3.2 1111b14–15; see also 7.3 1146b22–24). We can hardly suppose that Aristotle is suggesting that instrumental reasoning or some natural extension of it is the surest sign of a person's character, or that he thinks that incontinent people do not engage in any calculation about how to achieve their goals. What is more, Aristotle says that an action is not virtuous unless it is chosen for its own sake (NE 2.4 1105a30–32; 6.5 1140b5–10). So whatever he means when he says that deliberation concerns what is towards the end rather than the end itself, he cannot mean that an action is never chosen for its own sake.

The interpretative crux here is of course the much-debated question just what sort of a limitation Aristotle means to be imposing on deliberation and choice when he says that they do not concern ends but only what contributes to ends. Some commentators have focused their attention, usefully, on the idea of what is "towards the end" or contributory to the end, emphasizing that this should not be taken to refer only to instrumental reasoning in the narrow sense. Constitutive reasoning should certainly be included, and perhaps we may also include those more distinctively moral forms of reasoning that tell us, say, that an action falls under a principle, conforms to the *orthos logos* or right reason, is in the mean, exemplifies a virtue, or whatever.

This is part of the answer, but it is also important to look closely at Aristotle's conception of an end. Aristotle tells us that wish (*boulesis*) relates to the end, and that wish is for the good or the apparent good (NE 3.4 1113a15). He says that choice is "near to" wish, and that we choose to get or avoid something good or bad (NE 3.2 1111b20; 1112a4). Wish, however, belongs to the rational part of the soul (OS 3.9 432b5–6). An end, therefore, is not merely a goal, something with a view to which some agent acts. To be an end, something must be conceived as good, where that conception in turn is an act of the rational part of the soul. And to be chosen, to be an object of deliberate desire, an action must be one that contributes to an end in *this* sense, one that contributes to what is conceived as good. If we then also take "what contributes to the end" in the widest possible sense, the puzzle about virtuous actions being chosen for their own sake dissolves. The deliberation that shows us an action contributes to the end may be instrumental, constitutive, or moral (that is, reasoning about what is in the mean, or in accordance with the *orthos logos*). That doesn't matter. What matters is that the deliberation shows us that the action is in some respect *good*. It is the *fact* we have engaged in rational deliberation to arrive at the idea that the action is good, and been motivated by that deliberation, not the *form* of the rational deliberation, that is definitive of choice.[15] So what Aristotle means is that distinctively human

---

[15] In his "Deliberation and Moral Development in Aristotle's Ethics," John McDowell suggests that Aristotle sometimes overstates the extent to which actions that reveal virtue "issue from actual courses of thinking" (in *Aristotle, Kant, and the Stoics: Rethinking Happiness and Duty*, p. 25). I do not really mean to disagree with that claim here: McDowell and I would agree, I think, that the important point is that the actions be conceived as in some way good, where the good is the object of reason or

actions, chosen actions, are ones which on deliberation we conceive to be good, and desire to do under that conception. That is why chosen actions are the best indicators of character—because they embody, express, or reflect the agent's conception of the good. The incontinent person, incidentally, does not act from choice even if he does engage in some sort of calculation about how to satisfy his vicious desires, because his calculations are not about what contributes to an *end* at all. Since the goal he is pursuing is not even an apparent good—he knows it is bad—it is not in Aristotle's sense an end.[16]

I take it that Aristotle and Kant, therefore, share a view about the distinctive character of human action, or at least—to add Aristotle's characteristic qualification—*adult* human action. Human action, to put it simply, is action that is governed by reason: that is, it is chosen. To say that an action is chosen is to say that it has the endorsement of the agent's reason, that it is conceived as good, and that it is by that conception that the agent is moved.

Kant, as we saw, moves from this picture of human action to a picture of moral value. A morally good action is one chosen because it is *intrinsically* good, because it has the intrinsic form of a law. Is there anything similar to this in Aristotle? If we do not assume in advance that what these two philosophers are saying must be different, one thing looks immediately similar. Aristotle insists that virtuous action must be in accordance with the *orthos logos*, the right reason or right rule. In fact he says it must not merely be in accordance with it but from it: "for it is not merely the state

thought. We might disagree somewhat about how articulate Aristotle expects his agents to be—and how articulate agents ought to be—in explaining why the action is good, and so about the extent to which they must be capable of providing something like a retrospective deliberation if asked to justify their actions. This however is a disagreement about a matter of degree. I am not certain what exactly McDowell has in mind when he criticizes those whom he supposes envisage a "straightforward" or "mechanical" application of principles; or at least I think it must be a misleading way to describe his worry (p. 21). The application of a principle by a thinking or conscious agent is always going to be perceptual rather than mechanical: perhaps there are places where the perceptual and the merely mechanical seem to run together, say for instance in the phototropic responses of plants, but this has nothing to do with the subject. The question, as I expect McDowell would agree, is surely about how much moral content perception must already have before we can begin to articulate, deliberate, and argue about the application of principles. I believe that even on the most algorithmic conception of the categorical imperative procedure the Kantian answer to that question could not be "none," because an agent who views others as *persons* and things and actions as possible *means and ends* has already taken up what is broadly speaking an ethical perspective on the world. But this is not the place to pursue this point.

[16] See also the somewhat more detailed account of choice, and why incontinent action isn't chosen, in my "Aristotle's Function Argument," Essay 4 in this volume, pp. 146–8. In the text above I say that the incontinent agent knows that his end is bad, but in "Aristotle's Function Argument," I say that the incontinent agent knows that the performance of a certain act for the sake of a certain end is not a thing worth doing for its own sake. I now believe that is the correct account.

in accordance with right reason, but the state that implies the presence of right reason, that is virtue" (NE 6.13 1144b26–27). This suggests that Aristotle thinks a good action is one whose agent sees it as the embodiment of right reason, just as Kant thinks that a morally worthy action is one whose agent sees it as an embodiment of the very form of law. I will come back to this point.

First, however, I want to consider the important argument that can be drawn from Aristotle's view that morally good actions are done "for the sake of the noble" (e.g. NE 3.7 1115b12; 3.8 1116b3; 3.9 1117b9; 3.9 1117b17; 3.11 1119b15; 4.1 1120a23; 4.2 1122b6). Aristotle tells us three different kinds of things about why good actions are done by virtuous agents. First of all, in at least some cases the actions are done for some specific purposes. For instance, Aristotle tells us that the courageous person who dies in battle lays down his life for the sake of his country or for his friends (NE 9.8 1169a17–30); in the same way, it seems natural to say that the liberal person who makes a donation wants to help somebody out; the magnificent person who puts on a play wants to give the city a treat, and so on. At the same time, Aristotle says that virtuous actions are done for their own sake; indeed, action is distinguished from mere production or "making" (*poiein*) by the fact that "good action itself is its end" (NE 6.5 1140b5–10). And finally, virtuous actions are done for the sake of the noble.

If we oversimplify Aristotle's moral psychology these will look like three competing accounts of the purpose or aim of virtuous action. If we take Aristotle to hold a double-aspect theory of motivation, however, there is no problem at all. When we say that the courageous person sacrifices himself in battle for its own sake, we need not be denying that he sacrifices himself for the sake of his country. It is the whole package—the action along with its purpose, sacrificing your life for the sake of your country—that is chosen for its own sake. As for nobility, Aristotle seems to think of it very much as Kant thinks of good will—it is the specific kind of *intrinsic* value that moral actions and those who perform them possess. This thought is supported by the account of nobility in the *Rhetoric*, where Aristotle says that the noble is "that which is both desirable for its own sake and also worthy of praise" (RHE 1.9 1366a33). The *Rhetoric* account also confirms the claim that nobility is a property that attaches to an action along with its purpose, for in it Aristotle assigns nobility particularly to actions done for certain purposes, such as to benefit others. In fact, Aristotle suggests here that he shares Kant's view that moral value is exhibited in a special way in actions from which we are sure the agent gets nothing. He says that nobility is exhibited in actions which benefit others rather than the agent, and actions whose advantages will only appear after the agent's death, since in these cases we can be sure the agent himself gets nothing out of it (RHE 1.9 1366b338–1367a5).[17]

Now I can be more specific. The view which I take Kant and Aristotle to share is this: when human beings act, we are not driven or directly caused to act by desire, passion, inclination, or instinct. Some incentive, to use Kant's language, presents a certain course of action to us as eligible—it suggests to us that we might undertake a certain action in order to realize a certain end. But reason gives us the capacity to stand back, form a view of this course of action as a whole, and make a judgment about its goodness. This isn't a judgment about whether doing this action will serve some further purpose, about whether it is useful. It is a judgment about its goodness considered as an *action*, not as a mere production. Both Aristotle and Kant would say that to value an action merely as a form of production, as consequentialists later did, is not yet to value it in its specifically ethical character as an *action* at all. As Aristotle says, "Making and acting are different . . . so that the reasoned state of capacity to act is different from the reasoned state of capacity to make (NE 6.4 1140a4–5) . . . while making has an end other than itself, action cannot; for good action itself is its end" (NE 6.5 1140b5–10). This is why *techne* and *praxis*, art and action, are different things (NE 6.4). It is with that same thought that Kant sets aside cases like that of the prudent merchant who is honest because it is useful as being wholly irrelevant to his attempt to analyze the moral value of actions. People who view actions merely as useful are not thinking of them, or valuing them, as *actions* at all. (On this view, we might say that consequentialism is not an ethical theory because it fails to address the subject, which is the goodness of action as such, not as a form of production.) So the capacity to choose is a capacity to make a reflective judgment about the value of an action as such and to

---

[17] I owe these references and some of what I say here about their implications to Terence Irwin, who discusses them in the notes to his translation of the *Nicomachean Ethics*. See especially the discussion of *to kalon* or as he renders it "the fine" at pp. 401–2. Julia Annas, in her "Aristotle and Kant on Morality and Practical Reasoning," focuses on these same passages to support her claim that Aristotle like Kant draws a distinction between moral and non-moral reasoning: "for the sake of the noble" is a distinctively moral reason (in *Aristotle, Kant, and the Stoics: Rethinking Happiness and Duty*, p. 241). While I am of course sympathetic to the comparison, I would prefer to phrase the conclusion in what is to some extent an opposite way: that both think there is only one kind of reason, although the considerations we use to identify a reason are complex. This is because I do not think that Aristotle would agree that you could ever really have a reason to do something base or ignoble, any more than Kant would agree that you could really have a reason to do something immoral. The person who fails to take nobility or obligation into account acts at best for an imperfect or incomplete reason, not for a different kind of reason. This is not merely a verbal fuss, for the question is whether we may avoid the Sidgwickean problems that arise when one acknowledges two distinct sources of normativity.

be moved by that judgment to perform or avoid the action. Importantly, this is at the same time a form of self-command, a capacity to give shape to our own characters and identities. When the agent asks whether the action is a good one she is also asking: do I wish to be a person who is so moved, a person who does *that* sort of act for *that* sort of end? To relinquish this prerogative of self-command for the sake of some mere experience or gratification is in Kant's language *heteronomous* and in Aristotle's *base*. To exercise it, especially under circumstances that make it difficult, is to act from duty and so to display that special form of moral worth that Aristotle calls nobility.

Now I want to raise some questions about how far this comparison can be pushed. To act from duty, as we have seen, is to do an action because you think its maxim has the form of a law, that it is intrinsically right or good. Aristotle, by contrast, does not tell us much about what property of an action "nobility" names. He certainly does not attempt to analyze the motive of nobility to arrive at a formulation of the moral principle, in the way Kant analyzes the motive of duty to show us what the principle of a good will is. Aristotle is famously skeptical about the possibility of articulating general principles that will guide our moral reasonings in any very exact way (NE 2.9 1109b13–26).[18] Still it does seem natural to identify an action's nobility with the fact that it is in accordance with the *orthos logos*, the right reason. Its being in accordance with the *orthos logos* is what makes it intrinsically right, and it is to this intrinsic rightness that the virtuous person responds. If this is right, a noble action, like a good-willed action, is one that embodies a principle of reason.

It is even possible to argue that nobility is a *formal* property. Elsewhere I have argued that we can appeal to Aristotle's concept of form to explain what

---

[18] Actually, there are two points to this skepticism. One point is the denial that we can formulate any reliable general rules to guide us morally: moral value belongs intrinsically to *particular* actions, and no set of general rules is sufficiently refined to pick them out. The other is the view that we must (therefore?) pick them out by means of perception. Now Kant has no reason to disagree with the first point. Kant certainly thinks that moral value belongs to particular actions, indeed that it is an intrinsic property of those actions. They do not inherit their value from any rules that are external to them. (See my "Kant's Analysis of Obligation: The Argument of *Groundwork I*," CKE essay 2, pp. 60–2 for a discussion of this important point.) The categorical imperative test is a test on *particular* maxims, and any circumstance that is really relevant to the moral value of an action may properly be included in its maxim. Kant himself may have had some tendency to exaggerate the extent to which the categorical imperative's findings could be captured in a set of general rules, but nothing in the theory requires this. Now precisely because there is such a thing as the categorical imperative test, Kantians must deny that the failure of general rules leaves us no recourse but perception. But of course perception and judgment must at some level play a role, as anyone must agree (see note 15). So even this disagreement between Kant and Aristotle has been exaggerated. On the essential point, that moral value is an intrinsic property of *particular* actions in all of their rich particularity, Aristotle and Kant are in accord.

Kant means by the form of a maxim.[19] In Aristotle's metaphysics, a thing is composed of a form and a matter. The matter is the material, the parts, from which it is made. The form of a thing is its functional arrangement. That is, it is the arrangement of the matter or of the parts that enables the thing to serve its purpose, or to do whatever it characteristically does. Now a maxim also may be seen as having parts. Since every human action is done for an end, we may say that a maxim of an action characteristically has two parts, the act and the end.[20] The form of the maxim is the arrangement of its parts. In particular, it is the functional arrangement, the arrangement that enables the maxim to do its job, which is to be a law. A maxim passes the categorical imperative test only if *everyone* with *that* purpose could do *that* action—that is, if the parts are combined so that the maxim can be universalized and so can serve as a law. Now when Aristotle specifies the *orthos logos*, he always gives us a list of what we might also think of as the parts of the action. The action that is in accordance with the *orthos logos* is done in the right way and at the right time, directed to the right objects, and so on. So we might think that its overall rightness consists in the way its parts are combined, that is, in its form. The parts are combined in a way that enables them to function, taken together, as a reason for action.[21]

---

[19] SN 3.3.5, pp. 107–8.

[20] Where the action is done for its own sake, these will not be different.

[21] Now that I have made some fairly strong claims about Aristotle and Kant sharing a view of moral value, I want to wave my hands a little over the vexed question of categorizing ethical theories. People used to categorize theories as deontological or teleological; lately, we have started opposing deontology to consequentialism, and what seems to be a new category, "virtue ethics," has come upon the scene, although it is unclear whether it is a rival theory or a rival view about what the direction of our attention should be. Certainly no one seems to have a very clear idea what deontology, consequentialism, and virtue ethics might be three theories *of*, but suppose we try saying that they are theories of what makes an action right. Consequentialism is the theory that what makes an action right is its consequences; deontology is the theory that the action's rightness is intrinsic, or consists in its conformity to a rule; and virtue ethics is the theory that what makes an action right is that it is the sort of action a good person would do. If "the action's rightness is intrinsic" means that the outward performance, the act, has intrinsic rightness, then perhaps only traditional rational intuitionists, like Clarke, Price, Ross, and Prichard, are deontologists, if anybody is. Kant and Aristotle, like Hume and Hutcheson, think that what makes an action right is that it is the sort of action a good person—for Kant an autonomous person and for Aristotle a person of practical wisdom—would choose. "Virtue ethics," however, would be a rather wild misnomer for this view in their case, since one does not have to have the virtues in order to choose well—even Aristotle admits that a continent person may choose well. On the other hand, suppose we say that deontology is the view that what makes an action right is its conformity to a rule of reason. Then Kant and Aristotle, along with rationalistic consequentialists like Sidgwick, are deontologists, as opposed to Hume and Hutcheson. On this view, in fact, Aristotle and Kant must be categorized as both deontologists and virtue theorists, since they think that the good person acts in accordance with, or even is the source of, a rule or at least a direction of reason. Since this seems unhelpful, suppose we say that the categories do not represent three views about what makes an action right, but three views about what gives an action moral worth. The resulting view about consequentialism—that consequences give an action moral worth—seems insane, and I am

Now I want to push the comparison one step further. Kant's analysis of the motive of duty turns on a comparison between two different ways in which we might choose a morally good action for its own sake—from duty or from immediate natural inclination. Does Aristotle similarly think that there is another way to value an action for its own sake, apart from valuing it for its nobility? Is there a character in Aristotle who, like Kant's naturally sympathetic person, simply enjoys doing the actions that are morally good, without quite grasping the reasons why they are morally good?

Of course there is. Aristotle says:

> For all men think that each type of character belongs to its possessors in some sense by nature; for from the very moment of birth we are just or fitted for self-control or brave or have the other moral qualities; but yet we seek something else as that which is good in the strict sense—we seek for the presence of such qualities in another way. For both children and brutes have the natural dispositions to these qualities, but without thought these are evidently hurtful. Only we seem to see this much, that, while one may be led astray by them, as a strong body which moves without sight may stumble badly because of its lack of sight, still, if a man once acquires thought, that makes a difference in action, and his state, while still like what it was, will then be virtue in the strict sense. (NE 6.13 1144b3–14)

And here we have an alternative description of the naturally sympathetic person of Kant's example. Humanity, of course, is not an Aristotelian virtue,

---

sure no one holds it. Consequentialists, if they are going to employ the notion of moral worth at all, will have to hold that it is the *intention* to produce good consequences which constitutes moral worth, and then their view will be a species of so-called "virtue ethics." (Of course, I have already suggested in the text that consequentialists might better be thought of as not employing this notion, or even, in this sense, as doing ethics.) Traditional rational intuitionists will hold that it is the intention to do what is right that gives an action moral worth, so they will be virtue ethicists too. This is no good. Perhaps, then, we should return to the earlier distinction, between deontology and teleology? Deontologists are interested in rightness and rules; teleology thinks that ethics has something to do with value or the good. Fine. If teleology is the view that the moral value of an action consists in its *promoting* the good, then Aristotle is a deontologist, since he thinks moral actions embody the *orthos logos* and so are good in themselves. If teleology is meant to include the view that moral actions are *themselves* good, then Kant is a teleologist, since he holds this view. Do you find that these efforts to categorize theories fill your mind with darkness rather than light? That of course is the point. Well, then maybe we should drop that, and oppose theories like Aristotle's and Hume's, which are primarily concerned with the virtues of character, with theories like Kant's and Sidgwick's, which are primarily concerned with the rightness of actions? I won't even bother to object to these tendentious descriptions of the "primary concerns" of these philosophers, since it is easier to ask what possible reason we could have for opposing theories if they have different primary concerns. Well, it may be replied, the issue is a methodological one: in subtle and even unconscious ways, our theories are shaped by their primary concerns. Now there is a great deal in this, and it is worth being aware it of when we study another philosopher's theories. But it is not a ground for opposing or categorizing different kinds of theories. Nor can we choose our own methodology by deciding in advance in which subtle and unconscious ways we would like our theories to be shaped. See also Barbara Herman, "Leaving Deontology Behind," in *The Practice of Moral Judgment*, pp. 208–40.

but that is not what concerns us here, and for the rest of the essay I will ignore that complication. If it were, Aristotle would say that Kant's naturally sympathetic person has a natural virtue.

3. Acting from Natural Inclination

This brings me back to the more specific question with which I began, the question of Kant and Aristotle's attitudes towards somebody like the naturally sympathetic person, and the more general question of the role of natural inclination in the moral life. Now at this point I hope you will see that as far as the case Kant actually discusses in section 1 of the *Groundwork* is concerned—the case of the *unreflective* or *unreasoning* sympathetic person—there is going to be little disagreement between Aristotle and Kant. Both think that his motivational state is both incomplete and unreliable until he reflects on the reasons why he should be beneficent, until his actions imply the presence of right reason. What he needs in order to become a good person is to *think*, and to act as a result of his thinking.[22]

In connection with this point, it is worth noticing that the inclination to which Kant compares natural sympathy is the inclination to honor. Kant says:

an action of this kind [that is, like the naturally sympathetic person's], however it may conform with duty and however amiable it might be, has nevertheless no true moral

[22] At this point it is worth mentioning one apparent difference between the two philosophers. Earlier I mentioned that Aristotle supposes that adult human actions done "on the spur of the moment" are voluntary but not chosen. This raises a question: would Aristotle say that an act of impulsive sympathy was voluntary but not chosen? If so, he would not only deny Kant's view that it was done under the tacit or implicit principle of self-love, but that it was done under any principle of volition. More generally, the point is that Kant seems to suppose that any adult human action is implicitly or tacitly done under *some* principle of volition, while Aristotle seems to think that merely voluntary action is still possible for adult human beings. Kant's view seems to be that the capacity for reflective choice, whether exercised or not, makes a difference to every action: adult human actions take place in the light, so to speak, of reflective thought, and *can* no longer be exactly like the actions of children and animals. Who is right? I believe that this question raises very complex issues about the third-person attribution of mental states and conditions (belief, choice, etc.), and whether those attributions are moral or merely factual. Aristotle's view suggests that a merely voluntary action performed "on the spur of the moment" is not a proper subject of moral judgment, since the agent is just following nature, and it is choice, not the merely voluntary, that reveals character. But there is something to be said for Kant's view, for surely if an adult human being performed *too many* actions on the spur of the moment, and failed to sufficiently *exercise* the power of choice, we would make a negative moral judgment about him (perhaps the judgment that he lacks character). This shows that we do think that once the capacity to exercise choice is present, it makes a difference to every action (or at least to actions in general), just as Kant says. But Kant's decision to attribute a principle of volition to people who perform thoughtless actions is not a guess about their actual volitional states. It is a moral choice: a decision that adult human beings are to be held responsible for thoughtless actions, because they might have thought. (For further discussion, see my "Creating the Kingdom of Ends: Reciprocity and Responsibility in Personal Relations," CKE essay 7.)

worth but is on the same footing with other inclinations, for example, the inclination to honor, which, if it fortunately lights upon what is in fact in the common interest and in conformity with duty, deserves praise and encouragement but not esteem; for the maxim lacks moral content, namely doing such actions not from inclination but *from duty*. (G 4:398)

The choice of honor as the comparison is important because elsewhere Kant calls the love of honor a "semblance" of morality; in the same place he describes those moved by the love of honor as "morally immature" (IUH 8:26). In the discussion of punishment in *The Metaphysical Principles of Justice*, Kant suggests that people who commit murder from motives of honor, such as young officers who become involved in duels, should perhaps not be subject to capital punishment. Legislation itself, Kant urges, is responsible for the fact that these people are still morally backwards, so that the incentives of honor are not yet attached to the proper principles (MPJ 6:337). In the *Anthropology* Kant calls the love of honor "the constant companion of virtue" (ANTH 7:257). Honor, as Kant conceives of it, seems to be a natural tendency to live up to certain standards of conduct, not for the sake of any gain from following them but for their own sake, and out of a kind of pride. It is not yet mature virtue, for the laws of honor do not spring from the honorable person's own will, and he is concerned with what others think of him; yet it does makes him receptive to the more mature state of autonomy. In a similar way, we might take sympathy to be a natural tendency to respond to the plight of others in ways that are prescribed by the Formula of Humanity. The sympathetic person is a *Menschenfreund*, a friend to humanity. In the *Anthropology*, Kant says that it was wise of nature to give us the predisposition to sympathy, as a "temporary substitute for reason" (ANTH 7:253). All of this suggests that sympathy and honor are Kantian natural virtues, corresponding to the real virtues of humanity and autonomy respectively and making us receptive to the development of those real virtues. If this is right, Kant and Aristotle need have no disagreement about this kind of case at all.

I don't think that this is quite right—I think there is still some disagreement—but its nature is best brought out by asking the more interesting question whether they would disagree about the case of actions which do have moral worth, about whether those must be done with pleasure or some other appropriate feelings. So I want to turn to that question.

Now a preliminary point is that we must not exaggerate the views of either philosopher if we are to get this right. Kant thinks that in order to be receptive to moral reasons we must cultivate the virtues, and cultivating the virtues is a matter of adopting certain obligatory ends, such as one's own perfection and the happiness of others. At this point I come to an issue I mentioned at the beginning of the essay—the fact that our mental lives have a passive or receptive as well as an active dimension. There is an important difference between giving an account of what sorts of reasons for action morality prescribes and giving an account of how *we* become receptive to those reasons. There are two problems of receptivity. One is how we are motivated by the dictates of reason when those dictates are presented to us, whether by the arguments of others or simply by the workings of our own minds. To some extent this is just the problem of how pure reason can be practical, which Kant takes to be insoluble; to the extent we can say anything about it, it is the problem Kant is addressing in his account of how the thought of the law gives rise to the incentive of respect. The second problem is how we come to *think* about our duties at all, how we come to *notice* which reasons we have. The negative character of the Formula of Universal Law reveals this problem in an especially acute way. Under the Formula of Universal Law you arrive at the duty of helping when you consider the maxim of not helping, but it is only under extremely unusual circumstances that you would consider the maxim of not helping. The naturally sympathetic person, whose mind becomes clouded by sorrow, is in such circumstances. As I portrayed him, he considers the issue of helping for the simple reason that he used to help, or perhaps because someone reminds him of that fact. But what if the idea of helping simply doesn't occur to you one way or another? As Kant himself says in *The Metaphysics of Morals*, "Maxims are here regarded as subjective principles which merely qualify for a giving of universal law, and the requirement that they so qualify is only a negative principle . . . How then can there be, beyond this principle, a law for the maxims of actions?" (MM 6:389) What he is asking is how there can be a law that says we must *have* certain maxims. This is the problem that Kant addresses in *The Metaphysical Principles of Virtue*. Kant argues that we have a duty to cultivate moral ends and the feelings that are naturally attendant upon having those ends so that we will notice the occasions of virtue.[23]

Sympathy is naturally associated with having the happiness of others as your end, which is required, and in *The Metaphysical Principles of Virtue*, Kant does not scruple to say that sympathetic feeling is a duty. Being sympathetic helps us to be aware of those cases when our assistance or support will be called for. And if we cultivate moral ends and the feelings that are naturally

---

[23] I do not mean in this sentence to have said what the argument is; it is actually rather subtle and I am not taking it up here.

attendant upon having such ends then in the normal course of events we will also take pleasure in successful virtuous action. If I have made your happiness my end and I do something that successfully promotes it I will of course take pleasure in that fact. It doesn't matter whether my original impetus for making your happiness my end was natural inclination or the rational acknowledgment of the value of your humanity; if it really is my end it will normally give me pleasure to promote it. This is an ordinary fact about human motivation: once you have backed a certain horse, for whatever reason, you are going to be thrilled if it wins. Since virtue requires the adoption of ends, it requires, indirectly, the development of a range of feelings, the feelings associated with having those ends. The method, not surprisingly, is habituation. Kant says:

Beneficence is a duty. If someone practices it often and succeeds in realizing his beneficent intention, he eventually comes actually to love the person he has helped. So the saying "you ought to *love* your neighbor as yourself" does not mean that you ought immediately (first) to love him and (afterwards) by means of this love do good to him. It means, rather, do good to your fellow human beings, and your beneficence will produce love of them in you (as an aptitude of the inclination to beneficence in general). (MM 6:402)

Kant both requires and expects that the virtuous person will in this way at once become receptive to the occasions of virtue and, at the same time, able to take pleasure in virtuous action. He even says:

But what is done not with pleasure but merely as compulsory service has no inner worth for one who attends to his duty in this way and such service is not loved by him; instead, he shirks, as much as possible occasions for practicing virtue. (MM 6:484)

On the other hand, even Aristotle must admit that at least in very hard cases it is only *successful* virtuous action that will necessarily bring us pleasure, and that in only a limited way. I have a specific hard case in mind. In the Book 9 account of the relation between virtue and self-love, Aristotle makes the outrageous suggestion that the person who dies in battle gets the greater good because he prefers a short and noble life to years of humdrum existence (NE 9.8 1169a22–24). In the Book 3 account Aristotle is more honest. He says:

Hence also courage involves pain, and is justly praised, for it is harder to face what is painful than to avoid what is pleasant . . . death and wounds will be painful to the brave man and against his will, but he will face them because it is noble to do so or because it is base not to do so. And the more he is possessed of virtue in its entirety and the happier he is, the more he will be pained at the thought of death; for life is best worth living for such a man, and he is knowingly losing the greatest of goods, and this is painful. But he is none the less brave, and perhaps all the more so, because he chooses noble deeds of war at that cost. It is not the case, then, with all the virtues that the exercise of them is pleasant, except insofar as it reaches its end.

After which Aristotle concludes, rather lamely:

But it is quite possible that the best soldiers may not be men of this sort but those who are less brave but have no other good. (NE 3.9 1171a33–1171b20)

And it is worth remembering that two of the cases of action from duty that Kant discusses in section 1 of the *Groundwork*, that of a person who wants to commit suicide because of the acuteness of his misery, and that of a person in the grip of some great sorrow, are tragic cases. Aristotle firmly repudiates the Stoic view that virtue is sufficient for happiness even at moments like this, although I suppose he might still want to say that there is some pleasure to be taken in the virtuous action at hand (NE 1.8 1099b1–8). But then Kant would say *that*, too—acting from respect for law does always have a pleasant dimension, although the pleasure is of a rather rarefied kind.

Aristotle and Kant might still disagree about one case. There are two characters who are beneficent from duty in the *Groundwork* examples: the one whose mind is clouded by sorrow and another, whom I haven't discussed yet, who is temperamentally cold. This person seems to be incapable of enjoying beneficent action. I suppose that Aristotle would characterize him as continent rather than virtuous, and would think that this is a less good state, and maybe, although I am not sure of this, judge that he is a less good person. Kant doesn't make the distinction between continence and virtue. But by now I hope it is clear that if he did, he would not say that continence is a *better* state, or that the cold person is a *better* person, than the virtuous person who also enjoys beneficence. What Kant says about the cold person in the *Groundwork* is only that he has a moral worth which the *unreflective* sympathetic person lacks; he does not compare him either positively or negatively to someone who helps from the motive of duty and also enjoys it. Aristotle does not, as far as I know, ever make the parallel comparison, which would be between merely natural virtue and continence. I assume he would agree with Kant, though, that continence is better than merely natural virtue, since the continent person has the first principle, and this is the important thing.[24] There remains only this difference: Kant would certainly not say that the cold person, provided he

---

[24] At least this is why Aristotle says incontinence is a better state than intemperance (NE 7.8 1151a25). Although the merely naturally virtuous person and the continent person each lack an essential element of fully realized virtue, and this might seem to put them on a footing, still, the continent person *can* perform a noble act for the sake of its nobility, and the merely naturally virtuous person cannot do this essential thing.

somehow managed to do his duty, was any less good, or was in a less morally good state, than the person who does his duty and also enjoys it.

But the reason why this one difference still remains throws light, I think, on the question why Kant doesn't characterize sympathy and honor as natural virtues, even though he comes very close. What is at work here is a difference between Kant's and Aristotle's views of what inclination is, which in turn depends on a difference in their views of what pleasure and pain are. The difference is that Aristotle thinks of pleasure and pain as something like perceptions of the reasons for actions, while Kant apparently does not believe that pleasure and pain in general play this role. Respect for law comes closest to doing this, since it is a feeling produced by the activity of reason itself, but the pleasures and pains that are associated with ordinary inclinations do not.

Let me first mention the textual evidence for these claims and then say why I think they make a difference. Aristotle tells us that passions are "feelings that are accompanied by pleasure or pain" (NE 2.5 1105b19). The accounts of pleasure in the *Nicomachean Ethics* itself are mostly concerned with the pleasures we take in activities as we do them; the question of what it means for some state of affairs to seem pleasant or painful to us in the way that is involved in passion is a little different. In *On the Soul*, Aristotle explains the relationship between pleasure and pain and passion this way:

> To perceive, then, is like bare asserting or thinking; but when the object is pleasant or painful, the soul makes a sort of affirmation or negation, and pursues or avoids the object. To feel pleasure or pain is to act with the sensitive mean towards what is good or bad as such. Both avoidance and appetite when actual are identical with this: the faculty of appetite and avoidance are not different, either from one another or from the faculty of sense perception; but their being *is* different.
>
> To the thinking soul images serve as if they were contents of perception (and when it asserts or denies them to be good or bad it avoids or pursues them). That is why the soul never thinks without an image. (OS 3.7 431a7–16)

To take pleasure in something is to perceive it *as* good or bad, that is, as a reason for pursuit or avoidance. This is why Aristotle insists, throughout the ethics, that it is so essential to get our pleasures right. Aristotle says that when we go wrong in our "wishes"—that is, our conceptions of the good—the error is due to pleasure, "for it appears a good when it is not. We therefore choose the pleasant as a good, and avoid pain as an evil" (NE 3.4 1113a35–1113b1). I don't think Aristotle means merely that we are inclined to count pleasant things among the good things. I think he means that when something is pleasant it literally *looks good* to us. Aristotle's own favorite comparison of virtue to health can be used to illustrate the point. The healthy person's appetites, which are in a mean, are a reliable guide to what is good for her, that is, to what will preserve her in health. The amount she enjoys eating and exercising are actually the amounts she needs, so that her perception of the good—of what she has reason to do—is correct. Hunger *tells* her something—that she is in need of nourishment, that she has a *reason* to eat—and if she is in good condition, hunger is right. Since the appetites and passions all involve pleasure and pain, this means that what it is to be in the grip of a passion is to see a situation as being a reason for pursuit or avoidance of a certain kind.[25] To be angry is to perceive a reason to fight, or, as Aristotle puts it: "anger, reasoning as it were that anything like this must be fought against, boils up straightaway" (NE 7.6 1149a32–33); to be scared is to perceive a certain situation as a reason to flee, and so on. And since the soul never thinks without an image, as Aristotle says in the passage above, our conceptions of good and evil *must be accompanied* by images of our circumstances as pleasant or painful in certain ways. These images provide the material with which the intellect works in conceiving the good. It is because of the way the mind works that the virtuous person must experience pleasures and pains in the right way in order to think correctly about practical matters: thinking of something as good is inseparable from imagining it, so to speak, as pleasant.

Now the merely continent person's contrary passions make it difficult for her to maintain the required images, which is why, as Aristotle says, it is the same person who is both continent and incontinent (NE 7.1 1145b10–11). Mere continence is an unstable state, for the tendency to incontinence, its inevitable partner, can bring about a battle between intellect and passion for control of the agent's perceptual imagination. This is why Aristotle says that it is not knowledge proper but perceptual knowledge that is dragged about by passion in incontinent action (NE 7.3 1147b15–17). The virtuous person's reason, by contrast, is in unchallenged control of her perceptual imagination. And this is Aristotle's solution to the problem of receptivity. In the fully virtuous person, the entire appetitive part of the soul serves as a kind of sensorium for reason.[26]

---

[25] I think this shows that McDowell is wrong in characterizing the natural virtues as "mindless behavioral propensities" that merely "correspond" with the virtues (in "Deliberation and Moral Development in Aristotle's Ethics," p. 20). But I think this conclusion is one that he should welcome as friendly to his reading of Aristotle. McDowell thinks that the result of habituation is a primitive form of practical wisdom. As I understand it, there is already a primitive form of practical wisdom built into the passions of the naturally virtuous person; the result of habituation is to refine it, and the result of intellectual training is to render it articulate. I think that this makes it clearer why habituation and intellectual training must proceed together (rather than habituation coming entirely first) and also avoids committing us to the somewhat implausible idea that habituation changes the ontological status of the passions altogether—transforming them from mere mechanical propensities into perceptions, as McDowell's view, as it stands, seems to imply.

[26] This point may be strengthened by the following consideration. What health does is preserve the form of the living body; what virtue does is preserve the form of the soul. The form of the human soul is

Kant, by contrast, denies that pleasure and pain tell us anything about anything. He says:

The capacity for having pleasure or displeasure in a representation is called *feeling* because both of them involve what is *merely subjective* in the relation of our represent-ation and contain no relation at all to an object for possible cognition of it (or even cognition of our condition). While even sensations, apart from the quality (of, e.g., red, sweet, and so forth) they have because of the nature of the subject, are still referred to an object as elements of our cognition of it, pleasure or displeasure (in what is red or sweet) expresses nothing at all in the object but simply a relation to the subject. (MM 6:211–212)

Now Kant shares Aristotle's view that inclination involves pleasure: he defines desire in the narrow sense as a determination of the faculty of desire that is caused by pleasure, and an inclination as a habitual desire (MM 6:212). But since Kant thinks that pleasure and pain are mere feeling, that they are, to put the point a little bluntly, stupid, he also thinks that inclination is stupid. The fact that you have an inclination for something does not tell you anything about that thing or even anything about your own condition. It only signals the thing's relationship to you.[27]

And this makes for an important difference between what Kant says about the naturally sympathetic person and what Aristotle would say about him if humanity were an Aristotelian virtue. We have a reason to help human beings who are in need, and Aristotle's account of inclination allows him to see our natural inclination to help as an inchoate grasp of that reason. It is the kind of perceptual starting point from which, in his methodology, we

---

that it is governed by reason: that is why reason is the human function (*ergon*). Healthy actions—those motivated by healthy appetites—tend to preserve health in the body. Virtuous actions, then, tend to preserve reason's government in the soul. This shouldn't sound wild—I mean, at least as an attribution to Aristotle—since it is the view explicitly advocated by Plato in *Republic* 4, at 443cff. I take it to be the view Aristotle is also espousing when he says "the intellect always chooses what is best for itself, and the good man obeys his intellect" (NE 9.8 1169a16–17). Of course making these claims plausible or even comprehensible is another matter. They are abstract because it seems so difficult to form a conception of how virtuous actions tend to preserve the rational form of the soul. I have discussed Aristotle's view on this question in "Aristotle on Function and Virtue" (Essay 5 in this volume); lately, it has seemed to me that Plato's attempt to explain it in Books 8 and 9 of the *Republic* may be more perspicuous. In any case, if virtue puts reason in a position to choose what is best for itself, then virtue does enable reason to be active rather than merely reactive in its relationship to the world. Choice choosing choice mimics the divine activity, the purest of all activities, thought thinking itself (*Metaphysics* 12.6–9). But I leave these extremely abstract thoughts for another occasion.

[27] The infamous passages in the second *Critique* in which Kant sounds so much like Bentham (C2 5:22–24) are actually an expression of this view. The point isn't that all we care about is our own pleasure. The point is that if our carings are just feelings, it doesn't really matter which ones we satisfy—that is, we have no *reason, intrinsic* to those carings themselves, to satisfy one rather than another.

can work up to a more conceptual grasp of the first principles or reasons involved (NE 1.2 1095a31ff., and many other places).[28] When Aristotle says that the state of the authentically virtuous person is "not the same as that of the naturally virtuous person but like it," I take him to mean that the authentically virtuous person perceives the reason for action too but perceives it in that special way in which, according to Aristotle, you perceive matters that you also understand.[29]

But Kant cannot see natural sympathy as an inchoate grasp of the fact that there is a reason to help. He thinks that an inclination signals only a certain subjective suitability between the sympathetic person and the promotion of the happiness of others, a fitness of sympathetic action to gratify this particular person. This is the real reason why Kant describes this person as acting implicitly or tacitly under the principle of self-love, rather than as having a natural virtue. For Kant, sympathy is not a proto-virtue but merely a kind of substitute for virtue which nature has given us in the meantime. And this makes it look as if the inclinations and feelings which we are required to develop in order to solve the problem of receptivity will also have to be regarded as mere tools and helps.

The question which of these conceptions of inclination is correct is an extremely difficult one. The intuitive appeal of Aristotle's conception, at least about certain cases, is obvious. Sympathy for the troubled or the needy, in particular, presents itself to us as a response to the fact that there is a reason to help them. Such sympathy is painful, not pleasant, and if we regarded it merely as a source of feeling we would take an aspirin to make it go away. We don't do that, because of what we think sympathy reveals to us—that we have a reason to relieve someone's distress.[30] Of course, as the accusation

---

[28] For more on this way of looking at Aristotle see my "Aristotle on Function and Virtue," Essay 5 in this volume, especially pp. 171–3.

[29] In *Nicomachean Ethics* 6 Aristotle seems to struggle to give a correct account of the respective relations of perception, practical wisdom, and *nous* (see, for instance, NE 6.7 1141b14–23; NE 6.8 1142a 23–30; NE 6.11 1143a 35–1143b6). I believe his view is that both practical wisdom and scientific wisdom are like perceptual states, both in the sense that you have a direct grasp of the first principles or reasons of things, and in the sense that that grasp somehow *inhabits* your actual perceptions of the particulars. To the person of practical wisdom and to the person of scientific wisdom, the world literally looks different from the way it does to those who perceive but do not yet understand. The person of scientific wisdom *sees* the essences of things unfolding in their activities; the person of practical wisdom *sees* the good, and opportunities to realize the good, in the circumstances in which she finds herself. Providing textual evidence for this view would be an immense undertaking, so for now I will just state that I think that's what he means.

[30] I defend the claim that pain is the perception of a reason at SN 4.3.4–4.3.12, pp. 147–56. In 4.3.5 I cite some other philosophers on the pains of pity in particular and it may be useful to repeat those citations here. Hutcheson says "If our sole Intention, in Compassion or Pity, was the Removal of our Pain, we should run away, shut our Eyes, divert our Thoughts from the miserable Object, to avoid

of "sentimentality" shows, we also do sometimes dismiss inclinations, pains, and pleasures as *mere* feeling. There are people—I am one—who take our natural sympathy with the other animals, our acute sense of their pain and vulnerability, to be perceptions of the reasons we have to be merciful and protective towards them. And there are other people who dismiss this as mere sentimentality, as just so much personal feeling that doesn't mean a thing. But the very fact that this is offered as a criticism, or as debunking, shows that we do not in general take our pains and pleasures to be meaningless. We take them, as Aristotle thought, to be indications of what is good or bad, and what we have reason to do.[31]

But intuition by itself cannot settle the question in Aristotle's favor. Much more work in the philosophy of mind would be needed to show how Aristotle's view could possibly be true.[32] That we are attracted to a view like Aristotle's, however, does seem to me to explain why we are uncomfortable with what Kant says about the naturally sympathetic person in the *Groundwork*. Aristotle seems to give us a superior account of what is going on in this pre-moral case, and, if he does, he may also be able to give us a superior account of how receptivity works in the case of fully realized virtue as well.

But I do not think that this marks a difference in the basic *ethical* outlooks of Aristotle and Kant. Although there is a difference in the way these two philosophers propose to solve the problem of receptivity, the problem of receptivity arises for both of them because of the deep similarity in their general conception of what ethics is all about. Human action is not like anything else: as human beings we *choose* our actions, and, because of that, it is possible for us to transcend mere reactivity in our relationship to the world. The most general and substantive question of ethics is what we should do with this power, which actions we should choose. The more specific question

the Pain of Compassion, which we seldom do: nay, we crowd about such Objects, and voluntarily expose our selves to Pain" (*An Inquiry Concerning Moral Good and Evil*, quoted in Selby-Bigge, *British Moralists*, p. 93). The point is reiterated by Thomas Nagel: "Sympathy is not, in general, just a feeling of discomfort produced by the recognition of distress in others, which in turn motivates one to relieve their distress. Rather, it is the pained awareness of their distress as *something to be relieved*" (*The Possibility of Altruism*, p. 80 n.). Wittgenstein says "How am I filled with pity *for this man*? How does it come out what the object of my pity is? (Pity, one may say, is a form of conviction that someone else is in pain)" (*Philosophical Investigations*, section 287, p. 98).

[31] Some might think that the view suggested—that there is such a thing as perceiving a reason—implies a form of realism about reasons which is inconsistent with Kant's constructivist outlook. In *The Sources of Normativity*, I present a version of Kant's view that may be characterized as constructivist, and in 4.5.5 (p. 166) I explain the sense in which it can be harmonized with a form of realism. The view of pleasure and pain sketched at 4.3.1–4.3.12, pp. 147–56, is intended to show how the thesis that pleasure and pains are perceptions of reasons fits into that view.

[32] The type of work I have in mind is exactly that Barbara Herman undertakes in her paper "Making Room for Character," in *Aristotle, Kant, and the Stoics: Rethinking Happiness and Duty*.

of *virtue*, the question to which Aristotle gave most of his attention, is the question how the receptive part of our nature needs to be configured if this kind of transcendent choice and action is to be possible. It is the question, that is, of what we have to be like, in order to choose autonomously, and for the sake of the noble.[33]

[33] This essay was originally written for the conference whose proceedings are published under the title *Aristotle, Kant, and the Stoics: Rethinking Happiness and Duty*. I am grateful to Stephen Engstrom and Jennifer Whiting for organizing one of the best conferences I have ever attended. I also read it as the Gareth Evans Memorial Lecture at Oxford, and at the Universities of California at Irvine and Michigan. I am grateful to the audiences on those occasions for discussion.

7

Acting for a Reason

1. Introduction: Reason and Reasons

The question I am going to discuss in this essay is what a practical reason is: that is, what we are referring to when we talk about "the reason for an action," and what happens when someone acts for a reason. The answer I am going to present is one that I believe is common to Aristotle and Kant, and that distinguishes them from nearly everyone else. I am also going to suggest that their answer is correct, for an important reason. As I will try to explain, the view I believe we find in Aristotle and Kant enables us to connect their account of what *reasons* are with an important feature of their account of what *Reason* is: namely, that Reason is in a particular way the *active* aspect or dimension of the mind.

More generally, when we talk about reason, we seem to have three different things in mind. In the philosophical tradition, reason refers to the active rather than the passive or receptive aspect of the mind. Reason in this sense is opposed to perception, sensation, and perhaps emotion, which are forms of, or at least involve, undergoing. The contrast is not unproblematic, for it seems clear that receptivity itself cannot be understood as wholly passive. The perceived world does not merely enter the mind, as through an open door. In sensing and responding to the world our minds interact with it, and the activity of our senses themselves makes a contribution to the character of the perceived world. Though at some level innate and automatic, this contribution may be shaped and extended by learning, changed by habituation and experience, and perhaps even consciously directed. But the mental activity that we associate with reason goes beyond that involved in even the most sophisticated receptivity. Reasoning is self-conscious, self-directing activity through which we deliberately give shape to the inputs of receptivity. This happens both in the case of theoretical reasoning, when we are constructing a scientific account of the world, and in the case of practical reasoning, where its characteristic manifestation is choice.

Reason has also traditionally been identified with either the employment of, or simply conformity to, certain principles, such as the principles of logical inference, the principles that Kant identified as principles of the understanding, mathematical principles, and the principles of practical reason. A person is called reasonable or rational when his beliefs and actions conform to the dictates of those principles, or when he is deliberately guided by them. And then finally, there are the particular considerations, counting in favor of belief or action, that we call "reasons."

The use of the English word "reason" in all of these contexts, and the way we translate equivalent terms from other languages, suggests a connection, but what exactly is it? Aristotle and Kant's conception of what practical reasons are, I believe, can help us to answer this question, by bringing out what is distinctive, and distinctively active, about acting for a reason. That, at least, is what I am going to argue.

2. Three Questions about Reasons

There are actually three, or at least three, questions about the ontology of reasons for action. The first question is what sorts of items count as reasons for action—in particular, whether reasons are provided by our mental states and attitudes, or by the facts upon which those states and attitudes are based. (I'll explain this contrast in greater detail below.) The second question is what kinds of facts about actions are relevant to reasons, and in particular whether reasons always spring from the goals achieved through action or sometimes spring from other properties of the actions, say that the action is just or kind. This question is most familiar to us from the debate between consequentialists and deontologists. The third question is how reasons for action are related to actions themselves, and in particular whether this relation is to be understood causally or in some other way.[1] Put in more familiar terms, this is the question what we mean when we say that someone is "motivated."

How do we answer these questions? Most philosophers would agree that practical reasons have at least some of the following properties. (1) They are normative, that is, they make valid claims on those who have them. (2) They are motivating, that is, other things equal, the agents who have them will

---

[1] The answers admit of a rough, though only a rough, grouping. Empiricists tend to think that reasons are provided by our mental states, especially our desires; that the relevant facts concern the desirability of the goals to be achieved through action; and that the relation between reasons and actions is causal. Rationalists tend to think that reasons are provided by the facts in virtue of which the action is good, that these facts need not be limited to the desirability of the goals that are achieved through action, but may concern intrinsic properties of the action itself; and that the action is caused not by the reason, but rather by the agent's response to the reason. To some extent, this essay follows the familiar Kantian strategy of making a case by showing how the debate between rationalists and empiricists leads to an impasse.

be inspired to act in accordance with them.² And (3) they are motivating in virtue of their normativity, that is, people are inspired to do things by the normativity of the reasons they have for doing them, by their awareness that some consideration makes a claim on them. I will call this property being "normatively motivating," and, although it is not uncontroversial, I am inclined to assume that this is what a practical reason should essentially be: a normatively motivating consideration. We answer questions about the ontology of reasons by asking whether our candidate items could possibly have the properties in question, and by keeping our eye on the connection between Reason and reasons.

The first question—whether reasons are provided by mental states or by the facts upon which those states are based—leads to a problem, which I will call the problem of the reflexive structure of reasons, and which I will describe in the next section. I will then show how Aristotle and Kant's view solves that problem, by the way that it answers the second question, about whether the value of actions rests in their consequences or elsewhere. Finally, in the last section, I will say a little about the question how reasons and actions are related, the question of motivation.

3. Mental States and Good-making Properties

Bernard Williams once wrote: "Desiring to do something is of course a reason for doing it."³ Joseph Raz disagrees. "Wants . . . are not reasons for action," he writes. "The fact that [actions] have a certain value—that performing them is a good thing to do because of the intrinsic merit of the action or of its consequences—is the paradigmatic reason for action."⁴ The debate about whether reasons are provided by mental states or by facts about the value of the actions arises in part because our ordinary practice of offering reasons seems to go both ways. Suppose I ask: "Why did Jack go to Chicago?" Sometimes we offer as the answer some mental state of Jack's. We might say "he wanted to visit his mother," for instance. The mental state might be a desire, as in the example I have just quoted, or it might be a belief. "He believed his mother needed his help." Many philosophers, of course, think that the reason is given by a belief/desire pair. For instance, he wanted to visit his mother, and believed

² These remarks are of course tautological; this is because the properties in question are essentially indefinable. These two properties I've just gestured at are sometimes referred to as normative and motivational internalism, respectively, but I prefer to avoid these terms.
³ Bernard Williams, *Ethics and the Limits of Philosophy*, p. 19.
⁴ Joseph Raz, *Engaging Reason*, p. 63. Raz actually says "options" not actions, but he means the actions among which we are choosing, so I've changed the quotation for clarity in this context.

that she was to be found in Chicago; or, he wanted to help his mother, and believed that he could help her by going to Chicago. On that showing, the answers I gave earlier are partial, offered on the assumption that the questioner can easily work out the rest for herself. When I reply "he wanted to visit his mother," for instance, I leave the questioner to conclude that he believed his mother was to be found in Chicago.

But philosophers like Raz insist that, despite the fact that we answer questions in this way, the reason is not given by Jack's mental states, but rather by certain facts that those mental states are a response to: facts about what I will call the good-making properties of the actions. An important caveat here: I do not mean by using the phrase "good-making properties" to prejudge the question whether agents always act for the sake of what they regard as good in any moral or substantial sense.[5] I am using the term "good" here to refer to whatever it is about the action that makes it seem eligible to the agent. If St Augustine is right, then the badness of an action may be one of its good-making properties in the formal sense in which I am using the term.[6] We can still ask whether what gave the young Augustine a reason to steal those famous pears is the fact that the action is bad or his desire to do something bad. The defenders of the view that good-making properties are reasons will say that it is the *fact* that the action is bad, not his desire to do the bad. After all, these philosophers urge, reasons are things that agents act *on*. The agent is confronted by the reason, and the reason makes a kind of claim on him, it calls out to him that a certain action is to be done, or at least is eligible to be done. So we should identify as reasons the kinds of items that first-person deliberators take to be reasons, the kind of items that play a role in deliberation. And—leaving Augustine and returning to the more benign Jack—unless Jack is really a very self-absorbed character, what he takes to make a claim on him are not his own mental states, but what's good about the action he proposes to do. After all, if you ask Jack why he is going to Chicago,

---

[5] In other words, I am looking for what it means to act for a reason in the descriptive sense of reason. An important feature of the terms "reason," "rational" and so forth is that they admit of either a descriptive or a normative use. In the descriptive sense, one can act "rationally" while acting for either a good reason or a bad one; rational action is opposed to non-rational action or perhaps mere movement or expression. In the normative sense, one counts as acting rationally only when the reason is good. Hence we can say either "that's a terrible reason" (descriptive sense) or "that's no reason at all" (normative sense) and mean the same thing. The point of focusing on the descriptive sense is that once we have identified which action or activity we have in mind when we talk about "acting for a reason," we may then be able to locate the normative sense by asking what counts as being *good at* this activity. As I will observe below, I think that the account of acting for a reason that I give in this essay supports the claim that acting in accordance with the categorical imperative is a way of being good at acting for a reason. See note 26.

[6] St Augustine, *Confessions*, Book 2, section 4, p. 47.

it would seem a bit odd for him to say "because I want to." He might of course say "Because I want to help my mother," but according to the defenders of good-making properties, we should not take this formulation to express the idea that his desire is his reason, for he could equally say, with exactly the same force, "Because my mother needs my help." Certainly it seems likely that when he talks to *himself* about the situation, and decides what to do, he talks to himself about his mother and her troubles, not about his own mental states. So if he does say "I am going because I want to help my mother," instead of taking that to mean that his desire is his reason, we should take it as a kind of announcement that he thinks he both has, *and is responding to*, a reason. Here he describes his response to the reason as a want, a desire. But he could equally well, or perhaps even better, say "I *need* to help my mother," or "I *have to* help my mother" where "need" or "have to" refers not merely to a psychological state (or not to a *merely psychological* state), but to a normative response—something along the lines of "I feel that I am under an obligation to help my mother."

But the view that the reasons are given by the good-making properties of the proposed actions also runs into certain objections. For there seem to be problems about saying that the (supposedly) good-making properties of action, all by themselves, can be normative or motivating. For one thing, there are the standard objections to normative realism. Objectors to realism insist that facts and natural properties by themselves (such as the fact that an action would help one's mother) are normatively inert. And for another, there are problems about explaining motivation and the sense of obligation by appeal to the good-making properties of actions alone. After all, people who are aware of the good-making properties of action sometimes fail to be motivated by them or to acknowledge that they present any sort of normative claim. For the good-making properties of actions to have normative and motivational effects, to exert a claim on the agent in light of which he acts, there must be a certain uptake: the agent must *take* them to be good-making properties and be moved accordingly. And the defender of mental states will argue that when someone fails to respond to the good-making properties in question, we can identify what we would need to *add* in order to provoke the response. To the person who is not motivated by his mother's need for help, we might add a desire to help her. To the person who finds no normative claim associated with helping his mother, we might add the belief that one ought to help one's family. And in this way we seem to come back around to the view that reason-giving force arises at least in part from the agent's mental states after all.

But the defender of good-making properties will deny this. The problem I just described, he will say, only arises from a shift in standpoint. When we talk third-personally about the fact that an agent did or did not respond to the reasons before him, we talk about his mental states, since those constitute the responses in question. But that doesn't mean that the mental states are part of the reason, or that they play any role in the agent's own deliberations. The good-making properties of the action provide the reason, and to say that the agent desires to help or feels himself obliged to help is only to say that he is responding appropriately to the good-making properties of helping. After all, if the good-making properties have no motivating or normative force on their own—if we have to *add* the mental states, in order to get the motivating or normative force—then someone who lacks the mental states in question will quite properly be unmoved by the supposedly good-making properties. But surely we *do* want to say that there is something amiss with someone who, say, finds no normatively motivating consideration in the fact that his mother needs help. The mental states are not *added*, in order to *explain* or *provide* the normative and motivational force of the reason; rather, they are simply identified third-personally as the *appropriate response* to the normative and motivational force of the reason.

A minor problem with this argument is that there appear to be two kinds of cases, running roughly along the lines of the permissible and the obligatory. There are cases in which the reason does seem to depend for its existence on a mental state, in particular a desire, and cases in which it does not. Suppose Jack's mother is not in need of help, and his only possible reason for going to Chicago would be that he would enjoy a visit with her. In that case, whether the fact that a trip to Chicago would procure his mother's company is a good-making property of going on the trip *does* depend on whether Jack desires to see his mother. And this may seem to suggest that some reasons do after all depend on mental attitudes and states. But this little difficulty may easily be finessed. The defender of the view that reasons are good-making properties may agree that one of the possible good-making properties of an action is that it satisfies the agent's desire—or perhaps more simply that it satisfies someone's desire.

But there is a deeper problem with the view that the mental states we sometimes mention when we are asked for our reasons are really just the appropriate responses to reasons that exist independently of them. For what does it mean to say that motivation or a sense of obligation is the *appropriate* response? That claim itself appears to be normative—we are not saying merely that it is the usual or natural response. So the idea seems to be that the mental states in question—desire or a sense of obligation or a belief in obligation or whatever it might be—are responses that there is reason to have. So now we seem to have reasons to be motivated and obligated by our reasons. The first layer of reasons are certain facts about the good-making properties of actions, and the second layer of reasons are facts about how it is appropriate to respond to those good-making properties. Do we then need a further layer of reasons about how it is appropriate to respond to the reasons in the second layer, and so on forever?

But the defender of good-making properties will again deny this. If someone fails to respond appropriately to the good-making properties of an action, one may argue, then he just is irrational, and that is all there is to it. That's what the normativity of the good-making properties of the action amounts to—that you are irrational if you don't respond to them in a certain way. In other words, rationality may simply be *defined* in terms of the appropriateness of certain responses. A practically rational being is *by definition* one who is motivated to perform actions by the perception or awareness of their good-making properties.[7]

But now we need to be more specific about what this means, for there are two possibilities here. One may perceive or be aware of X, but not under the description X. Does a rational agent find his reason in the good-making properties of the action themselves, or in the *fact* that those properties make the action good? Suppose it is good for a mother to protect her children from harm. Is a lioness who protects her cubs from a marauding male lion then acting for a reason, or rationally? Perhaps we do not know exactly how to think about the lioness's mental representations, but she is an agent, not a mechanism, and it seems clear that there is some sense in which she does what she does *in order to protect her cubs*.[8] That aim guides her movements, and in that sense motivates them; and given the risks to herself that she is prepared to run for the sake of her cubs, one may even be tempted to say that she acts under the influence of a normative claim. If this is all there is to rational agency, then of course it does not involve the exercise of any specifically human power which we might identify with the faculty of Reason: it is just a way we describe certain actions from outside, namely, the ones that conform to rational principles or to the particular considerations we call "reasons."

On the other hand, we may insist that there *is* something different in the human case, something that does involve the faculty of Reason. The human

---

[7] Elsewhere I have argued that this strategy cannot work, because it effectively blocks the attempt to give a descriptive account of what rationality is. See my "The Normativity of Instrumental Reason," Essay 1 in this volume, pp. 55–6. The argument of this essay is making good on that claim, even though in this essay I do not directly attack the idea of defining reason in terms of reasons.

[8] For an argument that non-human animals count as agents, see my *Self-Constitution: Agency, Identity, and Integrity*.

being is aware of the reason *as a* reason; she identifies the good-making properties of the action under the description "good" or "reason" or "right," or some such normative description. She does not act merely in accordance with a normative consideration but *on* one. So rational action is not just a matter of being motivated by certain facts about the good-making properties of actions—say, that the action will help one's mother, or that it would satisfy one's desire. Rather, it is a matter of being motivated by the awareness or belief that these facts *constitute* good-making properties of the action. To act rationally is to act from the belief that what you are doing is in some way good. But doesn't that show that the normative force belongs to a mental state after all?

To understand the answer, we must first ask what it means to believe that the facts constitute good-making properties. Recall that we are using "good" here in a minimal and formal sense. To say that the facts constitute good-making properties in this sense is just to say that they provide the agent with what the agent regards as appropriate grounds for motivation. That's all goodness in this context is—appropriate grounds for motivation. So to say that you are motivated by the awareness that the good-making properties of the action make it good is just to say that you are motivated by the awareness that you have appropriate grounds for motivation. You are motivated by the idea that your motives are good. So rational motivation in a sense takes *itself* for its object. It has an essentially reflexive structure.[9] Kant at one point actually says something like this: he says we should act on maxims that can have as their objects *themselves* as universal laws of nature (G 4:437; my emphasis). It sounds very mysterious, and as if we had run into a problem, but I don't think that we have. I think this is just a way of saying that rational action is action that is *self-consciously* motivated, action whose motivation is essentially dependent on consciousness of its own appropriateness. It is this property—*consciousness of its own appropriateness*—that the lioness's motivation lacks.[10]

---

[9] I can think of two other things that philosophers have claimed to have an essentially reflexive structure, or to take themselves for their objects. One is God, as conceived by Aristotle in *Metaphysics* 12.9, where God is identified with the divine activity of thinking on thinking—for Aristotle, the most perfect and purely active activity there can be. The other is personal identity. Some philosophers have claimed, rightly as I believe, that persons are not incidentally but essentially conscious of themselves. It's not as if you have a personal identity which you might or might not be conscious of; rather, if you are not conscious of your personal identity, then you don't have it. So the state of being a person takes itself for its object (see, for example, Robert Nozick, *Philosophical Explanations*, chapter 1, part 2, pp. 71–114). I am claiming reasons are like that, and in my view this is no accident, since, as I argue in *Self-Constitution: Agency, Identity, and Integrity*, being a person is essentially an activity, and a person is in a sense constituted by her reasons.

[10] Now at this point the defender of good-making properties may wish to argue as follows. The tangled formulation at which I have just arrived is the result of the extremely broad definition of

So to have a reason is to be motivated by the consciousness of the appropriateness of your own motivation. How is it possible to be in such a state? I will call this the problem of the reflexive structure of reasons. The problem is that you might think we have to choose between the two elements involved in the motivation. Either Jack is motivated by his mother's need for help, in which case one may complain that he is no more exercising reason than the lioness is; or Jack is motivated by the thought of his action's goodness, in which case one may complain that he is a self-absorbed jerk who really ought to be thinking about his mother instead of about how good his own actions are.

Aristotle and Kant, I am about to argue, show us the way around this: how the two elements of motivation, its content and the judgment of its goodness, may be combined. And this is no surprise, for to say that a rational agent is motivated by the appropriateness of being motivated in exactly that way is to articulate the deep root of Kant's dictum that a morally good agent acts not merely in accordance with duty but *from* it. In fact what I've just argued is that the problems usually associated with Kant's idea of acting from duty—the appearance that it somehow excludes acting from more attractive motives like a direct concern for others—is a problem that arises from the very nature of a reason for action. That is, once we understand that acting for a reason requires that one be conscious that one has a reason, we can also see that asking "Did he do it in order to help his friend, or because he thought it was his duty?" makes just as little sense as it would to ask, "Did he do it in order to help his mother, or because he thought he had a reason?" In order to explain how Aristotle and Kant solve the problem of the reflexive structure of reasons, I now turn to the second of the three questions I raised: whether the reason for

good-making property that I adopted at the outset. You will recall that I said that by good-making property I did not mean "good" in any substantial sense, but only whatever it is about the action that makes it seem eligible to the agent. If "eligible" means "appropriately motivating" then of course it follows that to be aware of the good-making properties is just to be aware of appropriate grounds for motivation. But the philosopher who proposes to define a rational agent as one who is moved by good-making properties does not mean good in this minimal or formal sense. Rather, the proposal here is that we define a rational agent as one moved by those properties that are genuinely good, in a substantial sense.

But this will not do. For we still have the problem of the lioness, and again she leaves us with two options. If protection of her cubs is genuinely good, in whatever substantial sense we have in mind, and to be rational is to be moved by the genuinely good, then on this showing she is a rational agent. Or if to avoid that, this philosopher accepts the claim that she must know that her action is genuinely good, then all that this maneuver does is add an additional clause to my definition of a rational agent. A rational agent is one who is motivated by the consciousness that her grounds for action are appropriate grounds for normative motivation *and gets it right*. This is not really a way of avoiding the issue. What I have just said amounts to an argument to the effect that we must identify a descriptive sense of reason. See also notes 5 and 7.

an action always rests in the goal that is achieved by it, or in other facts about the action.

4. The Goodness of Action

According to a number of familiar theories of goodness, the standards of goodness for a thing are given by the nature of the thing itself, especially by its functional nature. A thing is good when it has the properties that make it good at being what it is, or doing what it does. If these theories are correct, then to determine what makes an action good, we ought first to ask what an action is—what its functional nature is—and then we will know what makes it good, to what standards it is subject.

Now John Stuart Mill thought he knew the answer to both of these questions. In the opening remarks of *Utilitarianism*, he says:

All action is for the sake of some end, and rules of action, it seems natural to suppose, must take their whole character and color from the end to which they are subservient.[11]

According to Mill, action is essentially production, and therefore its function is to bring something about, to achieve some end. Whether an action is good, Mill concludes, depends on whether *what* it brings about is good, or as good as it can be.[12]

But it has not always seemed obvious to philosophers that action is essentially production. In Book 6 of the *Nicomachean Ethics*, Aristotle says:

Among the things that can be otherwise are included both things made and things done; making and acting are different . . . so that the reasoned state of capacity to act is different from the reasoned state of capacity to make. Nor are they included one in the other, for neither is acting making nor is making acting. (NE 6.4 1140a1–15)

According to Aristotle, action and production are two different things. And in the following section Aristotle remarks on one of the most important differences between them, namely that:

while making has an end other than itself, action cannot; for good action itself is its end. (NE 6. 5 1140b5–10)

---

[11] John Stuart Mill, *Utilitarianism*, p. 2.

[12] Actually, Mill is wrong about this. The theories of goodness I mention in the text seek to identify what are sometimes called "internal" or "constitutive" standards of goodness. These are standards that hold of an object in virtue of what it is. On Mill's own theory of action, the only constitutive standard of actions is effectiveness. The achievement of a good end, as opposed to whatever end is aimed at, is only an external standard for actions. Technically speaking, aiming at the good is a side constraint on action. For more on internal or constitutive standards, see "The Normativity of Instrumental Reason," Essay 1 in this volume, pp. 61–2; "Self-Constitution in the Ethics of Plato and Kant," Essay 3 in this volume, pp. 110–13; and the Introduction, pp. 7–10.

Actions, or at least good actions, Aristotle says, are chosen for their own sakes, not for the sake of something they produce.

Actually, this is one of three different things Aristotle tells us about why good actions are done by virtuous agents. First of all, in at least some cases an act is done for some specific purpose or end. For instance, Aristotle tells us that the courageous person who dies in battle lays down his life for the sake of his country or his friends (NE 9.8 1169a17–30). In the same way, it seems natural to say that the liberal person who makes a donation wants to help somebody out; the magnificent person who puts on a play wants to give the city a treat, the ready-witted man wants to amuse his audience, and so on. At the same time, as I've just mentioned, Aristotle says that virtuous actions are done for their own sakes. And finally, Aristotle also tells us that virtuous actions are done for the sake of the noble—*to kalon* (e.g. NE 3.7 1115b12; 3.8 1116b3; 3.9 1117b9; 3.9 1117b17; 3.11 1119b15; 4.1 1120a23; 4.2 1122b6).

If we suppose that the reason for an action rests in its purpose, as Mill does, these will look like three inconsistent or competing accounts of the purpose or aim of virtuous action. But when we consider Aristotle's own conception of an action we can see why there is no inconsistency here. What corresponds in Aristotle's theory to the description of an action is what he calls a *logos*—as I will render it, a principle. A good action is one that embodies the *orthos logos* or right principle: it is done at the right time, in the right way, to the right object, and—importantly for my purposes—with the right aim. To cite one of many such passages, Aristotle says:

> anyone can get angry—that is easy—or give or spend money; but to do this at the right time, with the right aim, and in the right way, that is not for everyone, nor is it easy; that is why goodness is both rare and laudable and noble. (NE 2.9 1109a25–30)

The key to understanding Aristotle's view is that the *aim* is included in the description of the action, and that it is the action as a whole, *including the aim*, which the agent chooses. Let us say that our agent is a citizen-soldier, who chooses to sacrifice his life for the sake of a victory for his polis or city. The Greeks seem to think that that is usually a good aim. Let's assume that our soldier also sacrifices himself at the right time—not before it is necessary, perhaps, or when something especially good may be achieved by it—say cutting off the enemy's access to reinforcements. And he does it in the right way, efficiently and unflinchingly, perhaps even with style, and so on. Then he has done something courageous, a good action. Why has he done it? His *purpose* or *aim* is to secure a victory for his city. But the object of his choice is the whole action—sacrificing his life in a certain way at a certain time in order to secure a victory for the city. He chooses this whole package, that is, to-do-this-act-for-the-sake-of-this-end—he chooses *that*, the whole package, as a thing worth doing for its own sake, and without any further end. "Noble" describes the kind of value that the whole package has, the value that he sees in it when he chooses it.

Now this means that Aristotle's view of the nature of action is the same as Kant's. Kant thinks that an action is described by a maxim, and the maxim of an action is also of the "to-do-this-act-for-the-sake-of-this-end" structure. Kant is not always careful in the way he formulates maxims, and that fact can obscure the present point, but on the best reading of the categorical imperative test, the maxim which it tests includes both the act done and the end for the sake of which that act is done. It *has* to include both, because the question raised by the categorical imperative test is whether there could be a universal policy of pursuing *this sort of* end by *these sorts of* means. For instance, in Kant's own *Groundwork* examples the maxims tested are something like "I will commit suicide in order to avoid the personal troubles that I see ahead" and "I will make a false promise in order to get some ready cash." What the rejection of these maxims identifies as wrong is the whole package—committing suicide in order to avoid the personal troubles that you see ahead, and making a false promise in order to get some ready cash. The question of the rightness or wrongness of, say, committing suicide in order to save someone else's life, is left open, as a separate case to be tested separately. Indeed, Kant makes this clear himself, for in the *Metaphysics of Morals* he raises the question whether a man who has been bitten by a rabid dog and commits suicide in order to avoid harming others when he goes mad from the rabies has done something wrong or not (MM 6:423–424). Committing suicide in order to avoid seriously harming others is a different action from committing suicide in order to avoid the personal troubles that you see ahead, and requires a separate test.

And "moral worth" or being done "from duty" functions in Kant's theory in the same way that nobility does in Aristotle's. It is not an alternative purpose we have in our actions, but a characterization of a specific kind of value that a certain act performed for the sake of a certain end may have. When an agent finds that she *must* will a certain maxim as a universal law, she supposes that the action it describes has this kind of value. Many of the standard criticisms of the Kantian idea of acting from duty are based on confusion about this point. The idea that acting from duty is something cold, impersonal, or even egoistic is based on the thought that the agent's *purpose* or *aim* is "in order to do my duty" *rather than* "in order to help my friend" or "in order to save my country" or whatever it might be. But that is just wrong. Sacrificing your life in order to save your country might be your duty in a certain case, but the duty will be to do that act *for that purpose*, and the whole action, both act and purpose, will be chosen as one's duty.

Let me introduce some terminology in order to express these ideas more clearly. Let's say that the basic form of a Kantian maxim is "I will do act-A in order to promote end-E." Call that entire formulation the description of an action. An action, then, involves both an act and an end, an act done for the sake of an end. In the examples we've been looking at, making a false promise and committing suicide are what I am calling "acts," or, as I will sometimes say, "act-types." Making a false promise in order to get some ready cash, committing suicide in order to avoid the personal troubles that you see ahead, and committing suicide in order to avoid harming others are what I am calling "actions."

Now a slight complication arises from the fact that *acts* in my sense are also sometimes done for their own sakes, for no *further* end, from some non-instrumental motive like anger or sympathy or the sheer pleasure of the thing.[13] In this case, doing the *act* is itself the end. To describe the whole *action*, in this kind of case, we have to put that fact into the maxim, and say that we are doing it for its own sake, for its inherent desirability, or however it might be. So for instance, if you choose to dance for the sheer joy of dancing, then *dancing* is the *act*, and *dancing for the sheer joy of dancing* is the *action*. We might contrast it to the different action of someone who dances in order to make money, or to dodge the bullets being shot at his feet. As I said before, it is the action that is strictly speaking the object of choice. And according to both Aristotle and Kant, it is the *action* that strictly speaking is, as Kant would have it, morally good, permissible, or bad; or as Aristotle would have it, noble, or at least not ignoble, or base.

The view that actions, acts-for-the-sake-of-ends, are both the objects of choice and the bearers of moral value sets Aristotle and Kant apart from many contemporary moral philosophers, less because of overt disagreement than because of unclarity about the issue. Here again, our ordinary practices of

---

[13] Kant's notorious example, from the first section of the *Groundwork*, of the sympathetic person who lacks moral worth, is like this: Kant specifies that he "has no further motive of vanity or self-interest" and does the action for its own sake (G 4:398). The agent who acts from duty also does the action for its own sake. Discussions of the argument of the first section of the *Groundwork* frequently overlook this, and suppose instead that Kant is contrasting two different purposes one may have in one's actions, one's own pleasure and duty. For further discussion, see my "From Duty and for the Sake of the Noble: Kant and Aristotle on Morally Good Action," Essay 6 in this volume, especially pp. 176–87. Kant does describe another of his *Groundwork* exemplars, the prudent merchant, as performing an action for an instrumental reason (G 4:397). If the argument of this essay is correct, Kant should not have done that: the prudent merchant in fact chooses something like "to charge my customers a fair price in order to profit from the good reputation of my business" as an action worth doing for its own sake.

offering reasons give us unclear guidance. Earlier I noticed that when we ask for the reason for an action, we sometimes cite a fact, and sometimes a mental state. But another way we often answer such questions, cutting across that debate, is to announce the agent's purpose. "Why did Jack go to Chicago?" "In order to visit his mother" is the reply. Jack's purpose is offered in answer to the question about his reason. This makes it appear as if his purpose is the reason for his choice, and as if what he chooses, in response to having that purpose, is only the act. But this appearance, I believe, is misleading.

To explicate this point I will first take a detour. One way to accommodate talk of reasons to the distinction I've just made between acts and actions would be to distinguish the reasons for acts from the reasons for actions. We could say that the act is performed for the sake of the purpose it serves, while the whole action is performed for its own sake—say, because of its nobility or lawfulness or rightness. Then we might think that confusion arises from thinking there is always "a reason" for what someone does, when in fact the phrase "the reason for what he does" is ambiguous between the reason for the act and the reason for the action.

This proposal, although tempting, is not satisfactory. One problem with it springs from the fact that reasons are supposed to be normative. If a reason for an act is its purpose, and reasons are supposed to be normative, then it follows that the purpose itself is normative for the agent. This is certainly not what either Aristotle or Kant thinks. Kant does think that there are some purposes we ought to have—our own perfection and the happiness of others, which are identified as obligatory by his contradiction in the will test. These we must stand ready to promote if an opportunity comes in our way. But he does not think that our purposes are *in general* normative for us in this way. In Kant's theory, normativity arises from autonomy—we give laws to ourselves. But we do not first choose a purpose, enact it into law, and then scramble around for some way to fulfill it, now being under a requirement to do so.[14] If it worked that way, we *would* be in violation of a self-legislated requirement every time we gave up a purpose because we were unable to find a decent and reasonable way to achieve it. But this isn't what happens. If you can't get to Paris without stealing the ticket money, stowing away on a boat, or risking your life trying to cross the Atlantic in a canoe, then you may drop

[14] In the past I have sometimes suggested that Kant could be interpreted as allowing for maxims of having purposes—for instance, in "Morality as Freedom," I imagine a maxim like this: "I will make it my end to have the things that I desire" (CKE, p. 164). I now think that is wrong, and that purposes are adopted only as parts of whole actions, for reasons given in the text. The maxims associated with the contradiction in the will test should be understood not as maxims of having purposes, but as schematic maxims of action: roughly "I will do whatever I (decently and reasonably) can to promote the happiness of others and my own perfection."

the project, and you have not thereby violated any norm.[15] What we will as laws are maxims, which describe actions, and we normally adopt a purpose as a *part* of an action.

Another problem with the proposal is that it suggests that in asking for "the reason" for what someone does, ordinary language is misleading, because there are always, so to speak, two reasons, one for the act and one for the action. But that in turn suggests a different way of looking at the situation, which does not require us to say that the idea of a reason is ambiguous, but only that we tend to misinterpret what we are doing when we offer a reason. If Aristotle and Kant are right about actions being done for their own sakes, then it seems as if every action is done for the same reason, namely because the agent thinks it's worth doing for its own sake. This obviously isn't what we are asking for when we ask for the reason why someone did something, because the answer is always the same: he thought it was worth doing. What may be worth asking for is an *explication* of the action, a complete description of it, which will show us *why* he thought it was worth doing. Now normally we already know what the act was, so the missing piece of the description of the action is the purpose or end. "Going to Chicago in order to visit one's mother" is intelligible as a worthwhile thing to do, so once we have that missing piece in place, we understand what Jack did. That the purpose by itself couldn't really be the source of the reason shows up clearly in this fact: if the purpose supplied is one that fails to make the whole action seem worthwhile, even though the purpose is indeed successfully served by the act, we will not accept the answer. Suppose Jack lives in Indianapolis, 165 miles away from Chicago. Then if I tell you that Jack went to Chicago to buy a box of paperclips, you will not accept the answer, even though one can certainly buy a box of paperclips in Chicago. You will say "that can't be the reason," not because the purpose isn't served by the action, but because going from Indianapolis to Chicago just to buy a box of paperclips is so obviously not worthwhile. Thus when we ask for the reason we are not just asking what purpose was served by the act—we are asking for a purpose that makes sense of the whole action. And as Aristotle saw, there will be cases where supplying the purpose will not be sufficient to make the action intelligible even where it is, so to speak, weighty enough to support the act. "Why did Jack go to Paris?" we ask. "He has always wanted to see the Eiffel Tower" is the reply. "No, but

[15] I now think that what I say about this in "The Normativity of Instrumental Reason," Essay 1 in this volume, on pp. 57–8, where I portray an agent as enacting ends into law prior to enacting means into law, is misleading. At the time I wrote that essay, I believed that its argument showed that hypothetical imperatives depended on categorical ones; as I say in the Afterword to that essay, I now believe it shows that, strictly speaking, there are no separate hypothetical imperatives. See note 17.

why just now?" urges the questioner, for Jack has taken off quite suddenly in the middle of the semester. And as Aristotle says, in order to be worthwhile the action must also be done at the right time and in the right way. So the practice of answering the motivational question "why?" by citing the agent's purpose does not really suggest that what we choose are acts, and our reasons are provided by our purposes. It is just that the purpose is often, though not always, the missing piece of the agent's maxim, the piece we need to have in place before we can see why the agent thought that this action as a whole was a thing worth doing.[16]

The way Kant presents the hypothetical and categorical imperatives in the *Groundwork* suggests that he himself may have fallen into the kind of confusion that I've been describing, at least about bad actions. He presents them as two different kinds of imperatives, on a footing with each other, and occasionally makes remarks suggesting that we are acting on either one *or* the other.[17] For instance, at one point, after distinguishing the two imperatives, Kant contrasts someone who avoids making a false promise because it is "in itself evil" (G 4:419) with someone who avoids making a false promise because it will damage his reputation if it comes to light.

As I have already said, what Kant's view actually implies is "in itself evil" is making a false promise in order to get some money. But the slip is understandable, although this will take a moment to explain. As I mentioned before, on the best reading of the categorical imperative test, the question whether we can universalize the maxim is a question about whether we can will the universal practice of pursuing *that* end by *that* means. Or, to put the point more carefully, you ask whether you could will to be part of an order of things in which this was the universal practice, and at the same time rationally will the maxim in question yourself. For instance, you ask whether you could will to be part of an order of things in which everyone who needed money attempted to get it by means of a false promise, and at the same time will the

---

[16] Gisela Striker reminds me that a word often translated from Greek as "reason" in the sense of "a reason" is *aition*, the why or the cause. The purpose of an action is its final cause, which appears as a part of the *logos*. Translations of this kind thus pick up the tendency to identify the reason with the purpose.

[17] I have in mind remarks that suggest that bad or heteronomous action is done on hypothetical imperatives, while good or autonomous action involves categorical imperatives. See, for instance, G 4:441, where Kant associates heteronomous accounts of morality with hypothetical imperatives. In fact, if actions are chosen for their own sakes, then every action is chosen in accordance with a law that has elements of both imperatives. The action must be chosen as something good in itself, which means it is governed by the categorical imperative. And every action must involve an act that is a means to an end, in a very broad sense of "means"—it may cause the end, constitute it, realize it or whatever it might be. The right way to think of the law governing action, I now believe, is as a practical categorical imperative, where the instrumental element enters with the thought that the law must be practical.

maxim of getting money by means of a false promise yourself. According to Kant, in such an order of things people would just laugh at promises to repay money as vain pretences, rather than lending money on the strength of them (G 4:422). Since making a false promise would then not *be* a means of getting the money you need, you could not rationally will to get money by that means. And so the maxim fails the test.

This is not the place to discuss in detail how well this test works as a guide to moral judgment.[18] What I want to point out now is that there is one sort of case in which it works almost too well. Some act-types are purely natural, in the sense that they depend only on the laws of nature for their possibility. Walking and running, slugging and stabbing, tying up and killing—these are acts-types that are made possible by the laws of nature, and accordingly, one can do them in any society. Elsewhere I have noticed the difficulty of using the universal law test to rule out maxims involving these kinds of acts.[19] But other act-types depend for their possibility not just on natural laws, but also on the existence of certain social practices or conventions. Writing a check, taking a course, running for office are act-types of this kind: you can do them only in societies with the sorts of institutions and practices that make them possible. Now where an action involves an act-type that must be sustained by practices and conventions, and at the same time violates the rules of those very practices or conventions, it is relatively easy to find the kind of contradiction that Kant looks for in the universalization test. This is because practices and conventions are unlikely to survive their universal abuse. Thus it hardly seems to matter *what* the purpose is for which you perform such an act; nearly every action involving such an act will fail the categorical imperative test. Charitably interpreted, Kant is recording this fact when he says that false promising is "in itself evil." Yet the remark is misleading at best. Even if Kant were right in thinking that any action involving the act-type "false promise" will fail the test, that would not show that the act-type is inherently evil. It would only show that members of the class of actions involving that act-type are inherently evil.

No doubt remarks like the one about false promising being "in itself evil" are part of what has led to the widespread misconception that Kant's ethical system is supposed to generate rules against act-types. But this is not just a confusion about Kant's theory. It is a familiar confusion about ethics itself. And another thing that supports this confusion is the existence of words in the language that seem to name wrong act-types, but actually name wrong

---

[18] For more extensive discussion, see my "Kant's Formula of Universal Law," CKE essay 3.
[19] "Kant's Formula of Universal Law," CKE essay 3, pp. 84–5 and 97–101.

actions, though somewhat schematically described. Aristotle himself trips over this one when he says:

> But not every action nor every passion admits of a mean; for some have names that already imply badness . . . in the case of actions, adultery, theft, murder . . . nor does goodness or badness with regard to such things depend on committing adultery with the right woman, at the right time, and in the right way, but simply to do any of them is to go wrong. (NE 2.6 1107a 9–15)

In fact, Aristotle is running together slightly different kinds of cases, but none of them shows that there are act-types that are inherently wrong. The example that best fits the point I want to make is murder. To say that murder is wrong is not to say that there is an act-type, murder, that is wrong no matter what end you have in view when you do it. Rather, "murder" is the name of a class of *actions*. A murder is a homicide committed for *some end or other* that is inadequate to justify the homicide. We don't call execution or killing in battle or killing in self-defense "murder" unless we believe that those actions are not justifiable, that punishment or war or self-defense are not ends that justify killing.

"Theft," another of Aristotle's examples, is not quite like that, or rather, it depends on how we are using the word. If by "theft" we mean "taking property that is not legally your own," we do have an act-type, but one that doesn't already imply wrongness, although it certainly gestures at a very likely reason for wrongness. It is like false promising—a violation of social practices that is *almost* sure to turn out wrong no matter what your end is. So here Aristotle may have been derailed by the same thing that derailed Kant. But of course there is a sort of colorful use of terms like "theft" in which we do use them to indicate wrongness, precisely because the case *isn't* legally one of theft. Thus if a shop charges too much for an article people desperately need, we say "that's highway robbery!" to express our disapproval. In that usage, robbery or theft, like murder, already implies wrongness, but in that usage, theft is not an act-type. It is a class of actions, roughly those that take people's property away for ends that can't justify doing that.

As for adultery, it also depends on the usage. If it means "having sexual relations with someone other than the person to whom you are married, or with a person who is married to someone else" it is like theft. It is an act-type, but again Aristotle is wrong. It *is* intelligible to ask whether perhaps at this time and in this place and with this particular person it is all right to commit adultery, just as it's intelligible to ask whether it is all right to violate society's property arrangements for some extraordinary purpose. Perhaps if your love is true and mutual and faithful, your spouse has been in a coma for the last fifteen years, the doctors say he is brain-dead but the law forbids removing life support, and divorce in these circumstances isn't legal, then adultery in this strictly legal sense isn't wrong—at least it makes sense to ask. But the word "adultery" may be used, like the word "murder," only to indicate *unjustifiable* violations of the marriage conventions. If one may say, without any misuse of language, "it isn't really adultery, for my husband and I have a very special understanding . . ." then "adultery" is like "murder", a term only used when we think the whole action is wrong.[20]

5. Motivation: The Relation Between Reasons and Actions

According to Aristotle and Kant, then, the object of choice is an action, in the technical sense I have explained—an act for the sake of an end. The reason for the action is expressed in the agent's *logos* or principle. Roughly speaking, what happens when an agent chooses an action is something like this: the agent is attracted on some occasion to promoting some end or other. The end may be suggested by the occasion, or it may be one he standardly promotes when he can. He reasons about how he might achieve this end, or what he might do in its service, and he arrives at a possible maxim or *logos*. He considers promoting a certain end by means of a certain act done in a certain way at a certain time and place. That is to say, he considers an action, and he asks himself whether it is a thing worth doing. And he determines the action to be noble or at least not base, morally worthy or at least permissible. Kant thinks he makes this determination by subjecting the maxim to a test, the categorical imperative test, and Aristotle does not, but for present purposes that is not important. Determining the action to be good, a thing worth doing for its own sake, he does the action. He is therefore motivated by the goodness of being motivated in the way he is motivated: or, to put it more intelligibly, he is motivated by his awareness that his end is one that justifies his act in his circumstances, that the parts of his maxim are related in the right way.[21]

---

[20] It is a different question whether there are categories of actions that are always regrettable because they violate the (in this case, Kantian) ideal of human relationships—that there should be no coercion or deception. In "The Right to Lie: Kant on Dealing with Evil" (CKE essay 5), I argue for a "double-level" interpretation of Kant's theory, with the Formula of Universal Law representing an absolute but minimal standard of justification, and the Formula of Humanity representing an ideal of human relations. When dealing with evil agents or certain kinds of tragic circumstances, we may have to violate our ideal standards, but we are never justified in violating the Universal Law formula. The argument of this essay takes place in the terms of the Formula of Universal Law, and so is about what can be justified given the circumstances, not about the ideal. I thank Marian Brady for pressing this question, and Tamar Schapiro for discussion of the issue.

[21] Elsewhere I have argued that Kant's notion of the form of a maxim can be understood in terms of Aristotle's sense of "form." A thing's form in Aristotle's sense is the arrangement of its parts that

Aristotle and Kant's view, therefore, correctly identifies the kind of item that can serve as a reason for action: the maxim or *logos* of an action, which expresses the agent's endorsement of the appropriateness of doing a certain act for the sake of a certain end.

At the same time, their view brings out one of the ways in which having a reason is an exercise of an agent's activity. On their view, the agent chooses not only the act, but also the purpose or end—he chooses the act for the sake of the end, but in doing so he chooses to promote or realize the end. Although his attraction to the end may be thrust upon him by nature, the decision to pursue the end is not. So choice on this view is a more fully active state than on the view that what we choose are mere acts, motivated by ends that are given to us. The agent does not just choose an act as a reaction to an end that is given him by his desire or even by his recognition of some external value. Since both the end and the means are chosen, the choice of an action is an exercise of the agent's own free activity.

But there is one last problem. Suppose someone objects that Aristotle and Kant's view does not actually solve the problem posed by the reflective structure of reasons. The Aristotelian or Kantian agent, the objector will say, is motivated by the nobility or moral worth of the whole action *rather than* by its content, by the end that it serves. I have still not shown that you can be motivated, as it were, in both ways at once. Nor (therefore) have I successfully shown that the agent is active in the way I've just claimed. On my theory of motivation, the agent's choice of the action is just a reaction to the goodness of the whole action, in the same way that, on the alternative theory, the choice of an act is just a reaction to the goodness of the end. So goes the objection.[22], [23]

---

enables it to perform its function. In a good maxim, the act and the end are related to each other in such a way that it can serve as a universal law (SN 3.3.5, pp. 107–8). I have also suggested that we might understand Aristotle's notion of the *orthos logos* in the same way—the parts are all related in a way that gives the action its nobility. See "From Duty and for the Sake of the Noble: Kant and Aristotle on Morally Good Action," Essay 6 in this volume, pp. 193–4.

[22] Notice that if this objection were correct, merely permissible action would not be possible, or at least there would be a difficulty about it, since in that case the action is judged to be "not bad" or "not ignoble" and that hardly sounds like a reason for doing it. The content of the maxim must play a role in motivation if permissible action is possible. The account I am about to give shows how permissible action is compatible with autonomy.

[23] Another way to put the objection, or at least a similar objection, is to wonder why "doing my duty" should not be regarded as a further end, to which the action as a whole serves as a kind of means. In this case the answer is to start the argument over, and to ask whether it is the fact that the action is a means to doing one's duty, or the agent's belief that the action is a means to doing his duty, that serves as the reason for doing it. We can only solve the problem by supposing that reasons have a reflexive structure, and to explain how that is possible, we have to come around once more to a view like Aristotle and Kant's—understood as I have presented it in the text.

This objection, I believe, is based on a fundamental misunderstanding of what it means to be motivated—a misunderstanding of the way in which reasons and actions are related. The objection assumes that a motivating reason is related to an action in the same way that a purpose is related to an act. The purpose is something separate from or outside of the act, for the sake of which one does the act. But the reason for an action is not related to an action in that way. So this brings us to the third question: how reasons and actions are related, or what it means to be motivated.

An essential feature of the view I have attributed to Aristotle and Kant is that the reason for an action is not something outside of, or behind, or separate from, the action. Giving a description or explication of the action, and giving a description or explication of the reason, are the same thing. The *logos* or maxim that expresses the reason is a kind of description of the action, and could be cited in response to the question: *what is he doing?* just as easily as it can in response to the question *why is he doing that?* Indeed—to make one last appeal to our ordinary practices—their view explains why in ordinary language these questions are pretty much equivalent. For the demand for justification can as easily take the form: *what are you doing?* or more aggressively and skeptically *what do you think you are doing?* as it can *why are you doing that?*[24] The reason for an action is not something that stands behind it and makes you want to do it: it is the action itself, described in a way that makes it intelligible.

I can best convey what I have in mind here by drawing your attention briefly to the middle player in the trio of items that we associate with the idea of reason—principles. The agent's *logos* or maxim is, as Kant puts it, his subjective principle. What exactly is a principle, metaphysically speaking, and what does it mean to say that an agent has one or acts on one? Some recent moral philosophers have been critical of principles, thinking of them as something like rules that function as deliberative premises. "I believe in the principle of treating people equally, and therefore I will show these particular people no favoritism, though they happen to be my relatives." And then it may seem as if there is an option to acting on principle, such as being moved by love or compassion or loyalty instead.

But I don't believe that, at least for a rational agent, there is any option to acting on principle.[25] To believe in a principle is just to believe that it

---

[24] Despite the apparent complexity of their view, the idea behind Aristotle and Kant's conception of what it means to have a reason is in one way simpler than that of their contemporary competitors. To have a reason is to be motivated by certain considerations, taking them to be appropriate grounds for motivation. To have a reason, in other words, is to *know what you are doing*.

[25] Actually, I believe that there is also a sense in which non-human animals act on principle: their instincts serve as their principles. See my "Motivation, Metaphysics, and the Value of the Self: A Reply

is appropriate or inappropriate to treat certain considerations as counting in favor of certain acts. Because that's what a principle is: a principle is a description of the mental act of *taking* certain considerations to count in favor of certain acts.[26] Suppose that Jack is tempted to take a trip to Chicago by the fact that it will help his mother, and he decides to act accordingly. The belief that the trip will help his mother does not cause him to act. Rather, he takes it to provide him with a reason for the action. We may represent this fact—his taking the fact that it would help his mother to count in favor of making the trip—by saying that it is his *principle*, his *logos* or maxim, to take a trip to Chicago in order to help his mother. So to say that he acts on principle is just to *record the fact* that he is active and not merely causally receptive with respect to his perception of the good-making properties of the action.[27] Jack's actively, self-consciously, taking the fact that it will help his mother to count in favor of making the trip *amounts to* his judging that the whole action is good. And his taking the fact that it would help his mother as a reason for making the trip, and in so doing judging that the whole action is good, is coincident with his *doing it*.[28] I don't mean that he doesn't think, he just acts: as I said earlier, reasoned action is above all self-conscious. What I mean is that the judgment that the action is good is not a mental state that precedes the action and causes it. Rather, his judgment, his practical thinking, is embodied in the action itself. That's what it means to say that the action is motivated and not merely caused. For a motive is not merely a mental cause. And an action is not merely a set of physical movements that happens to have a mental cause, any more than an utterance is a set of noises that happen to have a mental cause. An action is an essentially intelligible object that *embodies* its reason, the way an utterance is an essentially intelligible object that embodies a thought. So being motivated by a reason is not a reaction to the judgment that a certain way of acting is good. It is more like an announcement that a certain way

to Ginsborg, Guyer, and Schneewind," especially pp. 49–51, and *Self-Constitution: Agency, Identity, and Integrity*.

[26] The categorical imperative, in its universal law formulation, is in a way both descriptive of and normative for this act. It is descriptive insofar as the agent who takes end-E to count in favor of doing Act-A in effect makes "doing Act-A for the sake of End-E" her law, the law that governs her own action. It is normative insofar as it indicates what counts as performing this act well—namely, reflecting on whether that maxim is really fit to serve as a law. See note 5.

[27] For further discussion of the kind of activity involved in rational action, see "From Duty and for the Sake of the Noble: Kant and Aristotle on Morally Good Action," Essay 6 in this volume, especially p. 187.

[28] It is frequently argued that intentions must exist separately from actions because we often decide what we will do (and why) in advance of the time of action. I believe, however, that we begin implementing or enacting our decisions immediately, for once a decision is made, our movements must be planned so that it is possible to enact it, and that planning is itself part of the enacting of our decision. I thank Luca Ferrero for illuminating discussions of this issue.

of acting is good. The person who acts for a reason, like God in the act of creation, *declares* that what he does is good.[29]

[29] I would like to thank Charlotte Brown, Tamar Schapiro, and Ana Marta González for valuable comments on drafts of this essay. The essay was written for a series of lectures on Practical Reason at the Catholic University of America; the lectures in that series are forthcoming in *Studies in Practical Reason*, edited by V. Bradley Lewis, from the Catholic University Press. I also read it at a conference on contemporary Kantianism at the University of Navarra, at the meetings of the Danish Philosophical Society, at a conference on Kant at the University of Akureyri, and at the Graduate Student Conference at the Virginia Polytechnic Institute. I thank the audiences on those occasions. I would also like to thank audiences at the University of Virginia, the University of Illinois Urbana-Champaign, the University of California at Berkeley, the University of Oslo, and at the London School of Economics, and members of the Law and Philosophy Workshop Seminar at the University of Southern California, for helpful discussion. The arguments of section 4 are drawn from my 2002 Locke Lectures (*Self-Constitution: Agency, Identity, and Integrity*), and in that form were presented to an audience at Oxford, whom I also thank for discussion.

of acting is good. The person who acts for a reason, like God in the act of creation, realizes that when he does it is good.”

Part 3
Other Reflections

8

Taking the Law into Our Own Hands: Kant on the Right to Revolution

> If we place ourselves at the end of this tremendous process, where the tree at last brings forth fruit, where society and the morality of custom at last reveal *what* they have simply been the means to: then we discover that the ripest fruit is the *sovereign individual*, like only to himself, liberated again from the morality of custom, autonomous and supramoral.
>
> Nietzsche[1]

1. Taking the Law into Our Own Hands

Morality is unconditional and overriding. Its demands are uncompromising and its claims take priority over all others. Yet we can all think of situations in which, for reasons that seem to us honorable, unselfish, or conscientious, we would do things which morality seems to forbid. I want to ask how we can account for this fact.

There are two attempts to deal with the problem that, for obvious reasons, I will call skepticism and dogmatism. The skeptic denies that morality is unconditional and overriding. The dogmatist insists that it is, and argues that either the actions in question are not wrong, or, if they are, a good person just won't do them.[2]

---

[1] Friedrich Nietzsche, *On the Genealogy of Morals*, in *On the Genealogy of Morals and Ecce Homo*, p. 59.

[2] This use of the terms dogmatism and skepticism is of course borrowed from Kant. Kant characterizes the dogmatist as one who assumes "that it is possible to make progress with pure knowledge, according to principles, from concepts alone" (C1 B.xxxv). Dogmatism itself produces skepticism when dogmatic claims are found to be defeasible, or, as in the case of antinomy, when dogmatic arguments can be made on both sides of a question. The alternative is criticism, which calls into question reason's jurisdiction over the matter at hand; and *sometimes* ends by establishing only a more limited jurisdiction than reason had originally claimed. I leave the reader to judge for herself

Some skeptics and dogmatists are merely trying to domesticate the phenomena. The skeptic may have pretensions to being worldly and realistic, laughing at the ponderous claims of moralists. The dogmatist may simply be a moralistic prig. But there are serious and attractive versions of both views. The skeptic may think, as Bernard Williams does, that a life in which moral considerations can always override love and the cherished projects of a lifetime is not recognizably human.[3] The dogmatist may think that a suitably refined and sensitive moral theory will show us that the actions in question are not wrong after all, but, in the complex or terrible situations in which we are tempted to choose them, simply the right things to do.

A Kantian's job is to find the path between skepticism and dogmatism. In this essay, I try to construct an account of one category of cases in which a good person will do a terrible thing: cases in which she judges that, for moral reasons, she must take the law into her own hands. There are many such cases, but the one I will examine is the standout in the category: the case of the conscientious revolutionary. From Kant I will derive an account of this case that, unlike skepticism and dogmatism, preserves at least something of both of the thoughts with which I began. Morality is unconditional and overriding, and revolution is always wrong. Yet sometimes the good person finds she must rebel.

I have another motive for examining this category of cases. It is that human beings seem to find them profoundly interesting and somehow attractive. Literature and the movies are full of them. We are shown a good person who, rather than violate his own standards, submits to the unjust treatment of himself and others. He holds out against solicitations to rebel long enough to convince us that his honor is real. And then a moment finally comes when, breaking the rules he has set for himself, he takes up his weapons and fights. Fletcher Christian finally mutinies against Captain Bligh. Ransom Stoddard, who came to the west to bring it law, picks up his gun and heads to the street for a shootout with Liberty Valance.[4] Instead of feeling disappointed at their defection, these are moments that we find *thrilling*.

Neither skepticism nor dogmatism can give an adequate account of this fact. The skeptic thinks that the hero has awakened to a more realistic view

the extent to which these characterizations are apt for the work of this essay. Kant also characterizes dogmatism as despotic and suggests that skepticism, by contrast, is anarchic (C1 A.ix). In these terms, it is apt to characterize the two views about the nature of morality's rule over us which I am discussing here as skeptical and dogmatic.

[3] See, for instance, Williams's essays "Persons, Character, and Morality" and "Moral Luck," in *Moral Luck*.

[4] In the well-known story *Mutiny on the Bounty*, and in the movie, *The Man Who Shot Liberty Valance*, directed by John Ford. There are certain other popular characters whose appeal is certainly

of the role of morality in human life. The dogmatist thinks that the hero has arrived at a more sensitive and refined conception of what morality demands. Both see these stories as what are sometimes called "coming of age" stories, in which the hero advances to maturity. This seems to me to be wrong in every way. Although the heroes of these stories have not previously taken the law into their own hands, they are not morally immature characters who have finally seen what they ought to do. And it is important to us that they do what they do with a sense not of rightness but of profound loss and pain. If Fletcher Christian rebelled any earlier, we wouldn't admire and sympathize with him nearly as much as we do. The moments when someone arrives at a more sensitive view of what morality demands, or of its role in human life, are no doubt important and deeply formative. But they are not thrilling, like the moment when the hero takes the law into his own hands.

2. Kant on Revolution

Kant's attitudes towards revolution, both in his work and in his life, are notoriously paradoxical. In many of his published works, revolution is roundly condemned. In the *Metaphysical Principles of Justice*, Kant argues that "there is no right of sedition, much less a right of revolution" and concludes that "It is the people's duty to endure even the most intolerable abuse of supreme authority" (MPJ 6:320). In "On the Common Saying: 'This May be True in Theory, but it does not Apply in Practice,'" Kant says:

all resistance against the supreme legislative power, all incitement of the subjects to violent expressions of discontent, all defiance which breaks out into rebellion, is the greatest and most punishable crime in a commonwealth, for it destroys its very foundations. This prohibition is absolute. And even if the power of the state or its agent, the head of state, has violated the original contract by authorizing the government to act tyrannically, and has thereby, in the eyes of the subject, forfeited the right to legislate, the subject is still not entitled to offer counter-resistance. (TP 8:299)

---

related to that of the good person who takes the law into his own hands. For example, there is the hotdog cop, who uses irregular methods to catch bad guys. He doesn't take the law into his own hands on some particular occasion, but rather lives that way. Indeed, we are fascinated by the police in general, who, as Nietzsche points out, use all the same methods as criminals (*The Genealogy of Morals*, p. 82). Then there's the revenge film hero, who is, so to speak, *released* from the usual restraints of morality by a terrible crime committed against someone in his family. As we go down this list, a more deflationary account of the source of our pleasure becomes more plausible—the hero's plight serves merely to give us a kind of permission to enjoy the spectacle of violence wholeheartedly. But that's not what's going on in the cases mentioned in the text; and I think that an explanation of the phenomenon I discuss in the text should throw some light on the various pleasures we take in some of these stock figures.

And yet if a revolution succeeds, Kant thinks, the new government immediately becomes legitimate. In the *Metaphysical Principles of Justice* he writes:

if a revolution has succeeded and a new constitution has been established, the illegitimacy of its beginning and of its success cannot free the subjects from being bound to accept the new order of things as good citizens, and they cannot refuse to honor and obey the suzerain who now possesses the authority. (MPJ 6:323)

So even a regime newly established by an overthrow may not in turn be overthrown.

This may make it seem as if Kant were trying to defend quietism at any cost. And yet when Kant looked to history for a sign that would show whether the human race was making moral progress, he found encouragement in a phenomenon of his own day: the enthusiasm of the spectators of the French Revolution. In his essay "An Old Question Raised Again: Is the Human Race Constantly Progressing?" Kant writes:

The revolution of a gifted people which we have seen unfolding in our day may succeed or miscarry; it may be filled with misery and atrocities to the point that a sensible man, were he boldly to hope to execute it successfully the second time, would never resolve to make the experiment at such cost—this revolution, I say, nonetheless finds in the hearts of all spectators (who are not engaged in the game themselves) a wishful participation which borders on enthusiasm, the very expression of which is fraught with danger; this sympathy, therefore, can have no other cause than a moral disposition in the human race. (OQ 7:85)

Granted, it is the spectators, not the revolutionaries themselves, whose enthusiastic sympathy Kant thinks testifies to our moral nature. But if revolution is wrong, how can "wishful participation" in it be right? And we know that Kant himself was one of the most enthusiastic of these wishful participants. His personal obsession with both the French and the American Revolutions, his constant eagerness for the latest news from France, his persistent championship of the French Revolution even in the face of the Terror, won him the nickname "the Old Jacobin." Indeed, according to one report, "he said that all the horrors in France were unimportant compared with the chronic evil of despotism from which France had suffered, and the Jacobins were probably right in all they were doing."[5] Kant not only could sympathize with those aroused to violence by injustice; he could even cheer for them.

So here we have Kant's three views: revolution is unconditionally wrong; yet if it succeeds the government it establishes is a legitimate authority to which citizens owe their obedience; and, finally, our enthusiasm for the French

---

[5] Gooch, G. P., *Germany and the French Revolution*, p. 269.

Revolution, even our wishful participation in it, is an outward sign of the presence of a moral disposition in our nature, from which we may derive hope for our own moral progress. In what follows, I will try to show how this trio of views can make sense.

3. Justice and the Political State

Some background is necessary to my account. In the *Metaphysics of Morals*, Kant distinguishes two kinds of duties: duties of virtue and duties of justice (MM 6:218–221). Duties of justice are derived from the "Universal Principle of Justice" (MPJ 6:230), a restricted version of the categorical imperative. The Universal Principle of Justice tells us to act in a way that is compatible with the freedom of everyone according to a universal law (MPJ 6:231). Everyone is to have equal freedom of action, and the duties of justice are duties to avoid actions that violate that condition. According to Kant, the duties of justice are external duties. They are duties to perform or avoid certain outward acts. Insofar as a given action is regarded as a duty of justice, the duty is just to *do* it. The doctrine of right, in which the duties of justice are studied, is completely unconcerned about our motives. The sense in which the duties of justice are *duties* is cashed out entirely in terms of the fact that if you attempt to violate a duty of justice, others have the right to use force or coercion to stop you (MPJ 6:231). In the sphere of law and justice, "this is your duty" means "we have the right to demand this of you." This stands in sharp contrast to the sphere of ethics, which concerns the duties of virtue. There "this is your duty" means "insofar as you are autonomous, you demand this of yourself" (see MM 6:379–380).

Why is it permissible for others to force or coerce you to conform to the duties of justice? The Universal Principle of Justice in effect says that the *only* restriction on freedom is consistency with the freedom of everyone else. Anything that is consistent with universal freedom is just, and you therefore have a right to do it. If someone tries to interfere with that right, he is interfering with your freedom and so violating the Universal Principle of Justice. Violations of the Universal Principle of Justice may be opposed by coercion for the simple reason that anything that hinders a hindrance to freedom is consistent with freedom, and anything that is consistent with universal freedom is just. It follows that rights are coercively enforceable. Indeed, coercive enforceability is not something attached to rights; it is constitutive of their very nature (MPJ 6:232). To have a right just is to have the executive authority to enforce a certain claim. This in turn is the foundation of the executive or coercive authority of the political state.

Kant's political philosophy is a social contract theory, in obvious ways in the tradition of Locke. But the differences are important. In Locke's view, individuals have rights in the state of nature, and may enforce those rights. But when each person determines and enforces his own rights the result is social disorder. Since this disorder is contrary to our interests, people join together into a political state, transferring our executive authority to a government.[6]

Kant also believes that there is a sense in which we have rights in the state of nature. We have a natural right to our freedom (MPJ 6:237), and, Kant thinks, the Universal Principle of Justice allows us to claim rights in land and, more generally, in external objects, in property. Kant argues that it would be inconsistent with freedom to *deny* the possibility of property rights, on the grounds that unless we can claim rights to objects, those objects cannot be used (MPJ 6:246).[7] This would be a restriction on freedom not based in freedom itself, which we should therefore reject, and this leads us to postulate that objects may be owned. But unlike Locke, Kant argues that in the state of nature these rights are only "provisional" (MPJ 6:256). In this, Kant is partly following Rousseau. In contrast to Locke, Rousseau argues that rights are created by the social contract, and, in a sense, relative to it. My possessions become my property, so far as you and I are concerned, when you and I have given each other certain reciprocal guarantees: I will keep my hands off your possessions if you will keep your hands off mine.[8] Rights are not acquired by the metaphysical act of mixing one's labor with the land, but instead are constructed from the human relations among people who have made such agreements.[9] Kant adopts this idea, at least as far as the executive authority

---

[6] Locke, *The Second Treatise of Government: An Essay Concerning the Original, Extent, and End of Civil Government.* For the discussion of rights in the state of nature, see chapter 2; for our reasons for leaving the state of nature, see chapter 9.

[7] Why must things be property in order for us to use them? In the case of immediate consumables, it is of course true that by using them we make them our own—we make them part of ourselves in the most literal way, so that interfering with our use of them becomes in the most literal way interfering with ourselves. If we could not make them our own in this way, we could not use them. In the case of "the means of production" a simpler and more practical argument can be made—we cannot make *effective* use of them without some guarantee that they will be reserved for us exclusively during the time of use, since, for example, I cannot effectively grow corn in the same field where you are trying, at the same time, to grow barley. It is worth pointing out that this argument, if it works, does not establish the necessity of "private property" in any controversial sense; it establishes only that the means of production and action must be reserved to the exclusive use of certain individuals in certain times and places. This applies even to things owned communally—for instance, library books are reserved to particular patrons for specified amounts of time. Your right to the exclusive use of a book, for reading only, and for a certain length of time, still counts as a form of "property" in Kant's sense. In the same way, the means of production might be communally owned and "lent out" to particular users.

[8] Rousseau, Jean-Jacques, *On the Social Contract*, Book 1, chapter 9.

[9] Of course it may be argued that Lockean rights also depend on human relationships, because of the proviso that the laborer should leave "enough and as good" for others, which seems to substitute

associated with a property right is concerned. I may indeed coercively enforce my rights. But if my doing so is to be consistent with the Universal Principle of Justice, it cannot be an act of *unilateral* coercion. To claim a right to a piece of property is to make a kind of law; for it is to lay it down that all others must refrain from using the object or land in question without my permission. But to view my claim as a *law* I must view it as the object of a contract between us, a contract in which we reciprocally commit ourselves to guaranteeing each other's rights. It is this fact that leads us to enter—or, more precisely, to view ourselves as already having entered—political society.

In making this argument, Kant evokes Rousseau's concept of the general will. He argues that a general will to the coercive enforcement of the rights of all concerned is *implicitly* involved in every property claim.

Now, with respect to an external and contingent possession, a unilateral Will cannot serve as a coercive law for everyone, since that would be a violation of freedom in accordance with universal laws. Therefore, only a Will binding everyone else—that is, a collective, universal (common), and powerful Will—is the kind of Will that can provide the guarantee required. The condition of being subject to general external (that is, public) legislation that is backed by power is the civil society. Accordingly, a thing can be externally yours or mine [that is, can be property] only in a civil society. (MPJ 6:256)

It is because the idea of the general will to the reciprocal enforcement of rights is implicit in any claim of right that Kant argues that rights in the state of nature are only provisional. They are provisional because this general will has not yet been *instituted* by setting up a common authority to enforce everyone's rights. The act that institutes the general will is the social contract.

Kant concludes from this argument that when the time comes to enforce your rights coercively, in the state of nature, the only legitimate way to do that is by joining in political society with those with whom you are in dispute. In fact, you enforce your right by first forcing them to join in political society with you so that the dispute can be settled by reciprocal rather than unilateral coercion:

If it must be *de jure* possible to have an external object as one's own, then the subject must also be allowed to compel everyone else with whom he comes into conflict over the question of whether such an object is his to enter, together with him, a society under a civil constitution. (MPJ 6:256)

Suppose we are in the state of nature and we get into a dispute about rights. My goat has kids, and I take them to be mine because I was caring for the

for making agreements with others. But Locke seems to take it for granted that this proviso not only can be but also is met, whereas the relationships on which rights are built in the accounts of Kant and Rousseau are ones that people must actually enter into. See Locke's *Second Treatise*, chapter 5.

mother goat when they were born. However, one of them escaped, and you found it wandering around apparently unowned in the state of nature, took possession of it, fed it and cared for it for many years. Now we have discovered the matter, and each of us thinks she has a right to this particular goat. Since I think I have a right, I also think I may prosecute my right by coercive action. And you think the same. So what can we do? Perhaps I have a gun and you do not, so I can simply take the goat away from you. However, there are two ways to understand my action. One is: I am using unilateral force to take the goat away from you. Such an action would be illegitimate, a use of violence which interferes with your freedom. I cannot regard my action as an enforcement of my *right* without acknowledging that you have rights too, which also must be enforced. So if I am to claim that what I am doing is enforcing my right, I must understand my own action differently. The other way to understand the action is that I am forcing you to enter into political society with me. That gets us to the first step; the act of enforcing my right involves the establishment of a juridical condition (*rechtlicher Zustand*) between us and so establishes civil society. The second step, of course, is to settle the particular dispute in question in some lawful way.

This means that Kant's conception is different from Locke's in important ways. According to Kant a juridical condition—a condition in which human rights are upheld and enforced—can only exist in political society. And therefore existence in political society is not merely, as Locke had it, in our interest. It is a duty of justice to live in political society. That is to say, others have the right to require this of you, because that is the form that their authority to enforce their own rights takes. And you, reciprocally, have the right to require membership in political society of others with whom you might have such disputes. Since we will that our rights be enforced, reciprocal coercion, and therefore political society, can be seen as the object of a general will.

Kant does not take himself to be telling a historical story. He is answering a transcendental question: how is coercive political authority possible? His answer is that the idea of a general will to the reciprocal enforcement of rights is what makes coercive political authority possible. Governments are legitimate because human beings who live in proximity, who must therefore work out what their respective rights are, must form a general will. To put it another way, justice, which is the condition in which we have guaranteed one another our rights, only exists where there is government. Government, then, is founded on our presumptive general will to justice.

4. All Governments are Legitimate

Kant's account of the state, as I have just said, is transcendental: it is an account of how political authority is possible. But of course we need to know something more than that: we need to know when political authority is actual. Which regimes are legitimate governments, and which are mere Mafias ruling the people by main force? Kant's view is that *all* governments should be taken to be legitimate. That is, any regime's decisions are the voice of the general will of its people; and its procedures for making those decisions must be taken to be ones the people have agreed to.

Kant of course does not mean that all governments and all of their decisions are perfectly just. In fact, Kant thinks that his theory of the political state implies an ideal of the state that is not generally realized. The state must embody the general will of the people to the reciprocal enforcement of those rights which constitute the freedom of everyone. In order to do this, Kant argues, the state must be a republic, characterized by a constitution and by the separation of powers, in which legislation is carried on by representatives of the citizens. Although Kant has some negative things to say about "democratic" government, these must be understood in terms of his rather complex account of political authority. Kant asserts that, "legislative authority can be attributed only to the united Will of the people" (MPJ 6:313). This authority is then invested in a sovereign authority or ruler, which may be constituted by all, some, or one of the people (MPJ 6:338–339; PP 8:352), making the form of sovereignty democratic, aristocratic, or autocratic respectively. Members of the sovereign are citizens and must therefore be fit to vote (MPJ 6:314); Kant criticizes the autocratic form of sovereignty, which concentrates it in a single person's hands, because "none of the subjects are citizens" (MPJ 6:339). The sovereign is responsible for administering the government. If the sovereign "himself" carries out all three functions of government directly, the government is despotic; if, however, the sovereign adopts a constitution establishing legal and institutional forms through which it performs the three functions of government separately, then the government is republican.[10] A republican constitution,

---

[10] Following Rousseau, Kant argues that a republican constitution must provide for the separation of the three powers, since when they are united in one person the state is effectively despotic (MPJ 6:316–319; PP 8:352). Rousseau argues that legislation must be couched in general terms, while it is the business of the executive to apply the law to particular cases (see *On the Social Contract*, Book 2, chapter 4). This makes it easy to see why unification of the powers leads to despotism. Suppose we

Kant says, is the "one and only legitimate constitution" (MPJ 6:340) since it is "the only enduring constitution in which the law is autonomous and not annexed to any particular person" and in which therefore "each person receives his due peremptorily" (MPJ 6:341). In a republican constitution, that is, every person is bound by the law and so one's rights do not depend on anyone's (not even the majority's) will. And therefore:

Every true republic is and can be nothing else than a representative system of the people if it is to protect the rights of its citizens in the name of the people. Under a representative system, these rights are protected by the citizens themselves, united and acting through their representatives (deputies). As soon, however, as the chief of state in person (whether it be a king, the nobility, or the whole population—the democratic union) allows himself to be represented, then the united people do not merely *represent* the sovereign, but they themselves *are* the sovereign. (MPJ 6:341)

Once such constitutional forms are established, the united people no longer have to invest the sovereignty in any other "person," not even the collectivity of the whole people themselves. Instead the people govern themselves *directly* through their constitutional forms. Outwardly, of course, somebody must administer the functions of government, but those who do so are now regarded as magistrates who work for the people, not as sovereign authorities. The magistrate who runs the government may still be a "monarch," and Kant sometimes suggests that he thinks this is the best arrangement (PP 8:352–353). Yet it seems clear enough that this ideal requires that the magistrates be responsive to the demands of the people. For instance, Kant argues that the establishment of republican forms of government will bring war to an end, because a declaration of war will require "the consent of the citizens," who are unlikely to give it (PP 8:351). This result seems to depend on the idea that the citizens will have some actual influence on the political process. Thus Kant's ideal state appears to be most closely realized by our own modern constitutional "democracies." Legislation is to be carried on by more or less direct delegates of the citizens, while the other functions of government are to be separated from the legislative function and the magistrates who perform all

legislate by majority vote, and suppose that the majority would like to institute a majority religion as the official church of the state. In their capacity as legislators, they cannot name a particular religion, but they could make a law that, say, everyone is to practice the one true faith. It will be left to the executive to determine which faith that is. Under these circumstances, it is plausible to suppose that individual citizens would have reason *not* to vote for such a law—the same sorts of reasons that the parties in Rawls's original position have for upholding freedom of conscience (see John Rawls, *Political Liberalism*, pp. 310–15). But now suppose that the majority is also the executive, who will choose the one true faith. Then they can make the law in question with impunity. In this way the unification of the legislative and executive powers makes democracy degenerate into a form of despotism—the tyranny of the majority.

three functions are to understand themselves as representing the united will of the people.[11]

Why then does Kant think we must treat every regime, and all of its decisions, as the voice of the general will? To understand this, we need to consider Kant's responses to two possible challenges to the legitimacy of a government, one based on its history—on the illegitimacy of its origins—and the other on its present imperfections, as measured by the ideal.

Start with the historical challenge. I have already said that Kant is not proposing that there was an actual contractarian origin to the state. His social contract is a hypothetical or, perhaps better, a transcendental one, which explains how such things as governments are possible. Kant signals this by grounding the state in what he calls a "postulate." Earlier in the *Metaphysical Principles of Justice*, Kant had also grounded the possibility of property in a postulate. The notion of a postulate is introduced in the *Critique of Practical Reason*, in connection with Kant's account of practical religious faith. Suppose we have some rational concept, but we do not have theoretical grounds for assigning it "objective reality"—that is, for asserting that it could apply to any actual object. In some cases, we may nevertheless have practical grounds for doing so, based on the considerations that (1) moral practice is intelligible or possible only if we assume that this concept has objective reality, and (2) moral practice is absolutely obligatory. In the second *Critique*, this is our basis for assigning objective reality to God, Freedom, and Immortality, concepts that cannot be applied theoretically because their objects could not be part of the sensible world (C2 5:119–146).[12] In the *Metaphysical Principles of Justice*, Kant argues that both "property" (or right) and "government" are moral or normative, and so intelligible or rational rather than sensible or empirical, concepts. Empirically, all we can identify is *possession* in the one case and *ruling power* in the other: people have certain objects in their possession, or under their control, and some people rule over others. Yet it is essential for moral practice, as we have seen, that we treat some of these empirical relations as having normative force—that we treat some possessions as rightful property, and some cases of ruling power as cases of legitimate political authority. For we cannot have freedom without property rights, and we cannot have rights without government. The "Juridical Postulate of Practical Reason"

---

[11] In reconstructing Kant's complex account of these matters, I have draw on the discussion in Howard Williams, *Kant's Political Philosophy*, pp. 173–8.

[12] Kant argues that morality requires us to make the "Highest Good"—a state of affairs in which we all attain a virtuous disposition and happiness proportionate to that disposition—the end of our moral practice, and that we cannot conceive how such a state could be brought about unless God exists and we are immortal. We are therefore licensed to postulate that these things are so.

(MPJ 6:246) and the "Postulate of Public Law" (MPJ 6:307) establish the objective reality of rights and government respectively.

In contrast to the religious postulates, however, these postulates license us to assign their concepts to objects we encounter in the natural world. And in both cases, a problem springs from the fact that the concept invokes a kind of hypothetical history. Kant's account of the possibility of property follows the usual strategy of appealing to the legitimacy of an individual's taking first possession of some land in the state of nature, rightfully laying claim to an object hitherto unowned. The individual then of course has the right to transfer this property to others. This kind of story can make it seem as if the correctness of a property-claim depends on an object's entire history and ancestry. Ownership in an object must be the result of a series of legitimate transactions stretching all the way back to the beginning of human history, when someone took first possession of the land.

Suppose someone challenges my right to a book. I say it's mine, but he say it's not; it's stolen property. He doesn't mean that *I* stole it; but that there's an illegitimate move *somewhere* in its history. Imagine that a congress of Native Americans demands that immigrant Americans return all of the books made from paper made from American trees to them. They say: you stole the forests, and the forests were ours; so the paper is ours; and the books are ours. And of course they've got a point. If we traced the ancestry of the property each of us owns, it would be full of illegitimate transactions. No one would be found to be the legitimate owner of anything. The history of the human race is a history of war and looting and theft and violence, not a history of legitimate transactions. So here's what we do. We simply take it for granted that, generally speaking, what people now have is their property. And we try to ensure that, from here on in, transactions will be legitimate and just.[13]

Kant thinks that this is what we should do with governments too. We should take it for granted that the existing governments are legitimate representatives of the general will of the people who are ruled by them, as if they originated in social contracts. "One ought to obey the legislative authority that now exists regardless of its origin" (MPJ 319). Kant says in several places that it is criminal even to *research* the origin of a government if you do it with an eye to challenging its legitimacy (MPJ 6:318–319; 6:372). Now of course there is also an important difference between the two cases. Kant thinks that if a revolution succeeds, we should take it that the new government is legitimate.

---

[13] Kant does not say this directly, but he appeals to considerations of exactly this kind in explaining why in civil society we take long possession to establish a property claim (MPJ 6:292–293) and how we deal with cases in which someone has come into possession of stolen property (MPJ 6:302–303).

The policy of treating any extant political power as legitimate is an absolutely blanket one. But of course if a theft or a swindle succeeds, we do not take it that the new distribution of property is legitimate. We do trace ownership back in time, within limits. But there is also an obvious explanation of this disanalogy. When someone is accused of stealing property, there is a duly constituted authority, namely the state itself, to decide the case. So this kind of conflict can be handled in a just manner. But of course, after a revolution, there is no duly constituted authority to settle the question whether the old government or the new government is legitimate. The question which one is legitimate just is the question what the general will of the people is. And that, of course, can be settled only by consulting the true government, the voice of the general will, which is exactly what is at issue here.

Now we come to the second possible kind of challenge. Even if we don't deem governments illegitimate because of their histories, we might challenge the legitimacy of those that fall short of the republican ideal to which the idea of government points us. Kant also argues against doing this. In an appendix attached to later editions of *The Metaphysical Principles of Justice*, Kant quotes a reviewer, Friedrich Bouterwek, who among other things called it "the most paradoxical of all paradoxes" that "the mere Idea of sovereignty should necessitate me to obey as my lord anyone who has imposed himself upon me as a lord, without my asking who has given him the right to command me" (MPJ 6:371).[14] And Kant replies:

Every matter of fact is an object that is an appearance (of sense); on the other hand, that which can be represented only though pure reason and which must be included among the Ideas—that is the thing in itself. *No object in experience can be given that adequately corresponds to an Idea.* A perfect juridical [just] constitution among men would be an example of such an Idea. (MPJ 6:370; my emphasis)

The claim is that no existing government adequately corresponds to the idea of a government. And yet:

When a people are united through laws under a suzerain, then the people are given as an object of experience conforming to the *Idea in general* of the unity of the people under a supreme powerful Will. Admittedly, this is only an appearance; that is, a juridical constitution in the most general sense of the term is present. Although the [actual] constitution may contain grave defects and gross errors and may need to be gradually improved in important respects, still, as such, it is absolutely unpermitted and culpable to oppose it. If the people were to hold that they were justified in using violence against a constitution, however defective it might be, and against the supreme

---

[14] According to Kant himself, the review appeared in the *Göttingen Journal*, number 28, February 18, 1797.

authority, they would be supposing that they had a right to put violence as the supreme prescriptive act of legislation in the place of every right and Law. (MPJ 6:371–372)

There are two possible ways to understand this argument. One might read it, first, as a kind of slippery slope argument. Suppose that Kant is correct in saying that *no* extant government meets the ideal. If we then ask how close a government must come to the ideal before it counts as legitimate, there is no obvious place to draw the line. If we look for a minimum criterion of legitimacy, we find that the most natural one—universal adult suffrage—rules out nearly every "government" that has existed in the history of the world before the twentieth century.[15] So perhaps Kant thinks it is too dangerous to make such judgments.

This reading, however, does not sit well with the obviously Platonic character of the passage.[16] When Kant says that actual governments are only "appearances" he does not mean that they are not real. He means that they are imperfect participants, in the Platonic sense, in the form of justice, a form that is given by the ideal of the republic described earlier. When Kant contrasts autocracy, aristocracy, and democracy to the true form of government, he even calls them "those old . . . empirical forms of the state" in contradistinction to the "original (rational) form" which is the republic (MPJ 6:340). Kant is clearly confident that, despite their imperfections, we recognize these objects as governments, as imperfect approximations to a perfect form.[17]

In order to understand why, it helps to reflect that there is a kind of tension inherent in our very concept of justice: a tension between what I will call the procedural and the substantive elements of the concept. On the one hand, the idea of justice essentially involves the idea of following certain procedures. In the state, these are the procedures by which the three functions of government are carried out. In order to be just, any sort of decision, outcome, or verdict—any political judgment—must be the result of our *actually following* these procedures. That is a *law* which has been passed in form by a duly constituted legislature; this law is *constitutional* if (say) the supreme court says that it is; a person is *innocent* of a certain

---

[15] This criterion seems called for by Kant's account of citizenship as fitness for voting. Kant himself attempted to argue that some adults—apprentices, servants, and "all women"—could still count as "passive citizens" even though we are (rightly, according to Kant) not allowed to vote because of our "dependence" on others. But, in a textually rather unsteady moment, he also conceded that this is only legitimate if the laws chosen by the active citizens allow "everyone" to "work up" from a passive to an active status (MPJ 6:314–315).

[16] Kant himself associates his use of the terms "Idea" and "Ideal" with Platonic forms at C1 A313/B370 ff., and A568–569/B596–597; and, in the earlier discussion, he explicitly compares his own idea of a republic to Plato's (C1 A 316/B373).

[17] See Plato, *Phaedo* 74a–76a, and *Republic*, especially Books 2–4.

crime when he has been deemed so by a jury; someone is *the president* if he meets the qualifications and has been duly voted in, and so forth. These are all normative judgments—the terms I have italicized imply the existence of certain reasons for action—and the normativity of these judgments *derives from* the procedures that have established them.

On the other hand, however, there are many cases in which we have an independent idea of how these procedures ought to turn out. These independent criteria form our more substantive judgments—in some cases, of what is just, in other cases, simply of what is right or best. Perhaps the law is unconstitutional, though the legislature has passed it; perhaps the defendant is guilty, though the jury has set him free; perhaps the candidate elected is not the best person for the job, or even the best of those available, or perhaps due to the accidents of voter turnout he does not really represent the majority will. As this last example shows, the distinction between the procedurally just and the substantively just, right, or best, is a rough and ready one, and relative to the case under consideration. Who should be elected? The best person for the job, the best of those who actually run, the one preferred by the majority of the citizens, the one preferred by the majority of the registered voters, the one elected by the majority of those who actually turn out on election day . . .? As we go down the list, the answer to the question becomes increasingly procedural; the answer above it is, relatively, more substantive. We may try to design our procedures to secure the substantively right, best, or just outcome. But—and here is the important point—the normativity of these procedures nevertheless does not spring from the efficiency, goodness, *or even the substantive justice* of the outcomes they produce. The reverse is true: it is the procedures themselves that confer normativity on those results. The person who gets elected holds the office, no matter how far he is from being the best person for the job. The jury's acquittal stands, though we later discover new evidence that the defendant was guilty after all. And the normativity of the procedures themselves springs not from the quality of their outcomes but rather from the fact that we must have such procedures if we are going to form a general will. In order to act together—to make laws and policies, apply them, enforce them—in a way that represents, not some of us imposing our private wills on others, but all of us acting together from a collective general will—we must have certain procedures that make collective decision and action possible, and, normatively speaking, we must stand by their actual results.

This point has some weight in any collective decision—even when we make a decision, say, with a group of friends. But it applies most forcefully to cases of right and justice, to decisions backed by coercive authority. For if we reserve to ourselves the right to ignore the outcomes of such procedures when we believe them to be substantively wrong, then we are still in the state of nature. And this idea is reflected in our actual practice, leaving Kant aside, for it is a basic rule of citizenship, of living in accordance with the rule of law, that procedural judgments have a coercive normative force against which substantive ones have *no weight at all*. Your judgment that a law is stupid does not excuse disobedience; your conviction that the defendant is guilty does not justify a lynching; your belief that your candidate is the better man is no grounds whatever for a takeover.

When the substantive ideal that opposes the procedural outcome is also an ideal of justice itself, and not merely one, say, of efficiency or qualification, this gives rise to a tension. It's bad enough when the jury lets the guilty go free, but suppose you are sure they have convicted the innocent. The law passed by congress is not just stupid or inefficient or incoherent, but—you think—plainly unconstitutional; only the supreme court, called upon to decide the case, does not agree with you here. Where then does justice lie? When we are judging the very institutions of government themselves, this kind of tension can rise to the level of paradox, illustrated by a simple example. Suppose we are convinced that the idea that government should represent the general will of the people requires that some group of people, hitherto helplessly subjected to a powerful tyrant, be allowed to choose their own political institutions in a democratic election. And suppose that having been liberated from their tyrant and allowed to vote for their political institutions, they unanimously vote the democracy out, and their tyrant right back in again. Where now does justice lie? Shall we force upon these people a form of government they do not choose to have, in the *name* of respecting their general will?[18] We may be convinced, and for good reasons, that constitutional democracy is the best way for a people to express its general will. But the absence of democratic institutions cannot be taken as proof or even as evidence that a government does not represent the general will of its people.

"When a people are united through laws under a suzerain, then the people are given as an object of experience conforming to the Idea in general of the unity of the people under a supreme powerful Will" (MPJ 6:371–372). What makes a people unified is that there are procedures under which they are unified, procedures that make collective decision and action possible, and give

---

[18] Kant himself says, "Even if the sovereign were to decide to transform himself into a democracy, he would still be doing the people an injustice, because the people themselves might abhor this kind of constitution and might find that one of the other two was more advantageous for them" (MPJ 6:340). Of course Kant is talking here not about whether the state should be a republic, but about which of the three "empirical" forms it should take. The remark raises odd problems about whether Kant thinks there is *any* legitimate way for a state to change its basic form of government, but I leave those aside here.

them a general will. Kant's view is that wherever we see such an arrangement, we see an imperfect empirical realization of the form of justice, of the idea of a general will. If someone has enough authority to make and execute laws, and the people are living and acting and relating to one another under those laws, then that is their general will. The failure of their institutions to meet our more substantive ideals of justice is simply irrelevant.

It's worth pointing out that, in the international sphere, we accept this conclusion. Although we may agree with Kant that the modern constitutional democracy is the substantively best form of government, we do not think that this licenses us to impose it on other nations, or even to refuse recognition to those who neither have nor aspire to this ideal. It would, for the reasons just given, be not just wrong, but paradoxical, since the very idea embodied in the ideal of constitutional democracy is that government should be by the consent of the governed, or an expression of the general will. That idea demands that we recognize that the peoples of other nations must decide for themselves what kind of political institutions they will have.[19] If we are to recognize them as sovereign states at all, we must simply take it that their governments are expressions of their general wills.

To arrive at Kant's position you need only see that the individual subject, when considered only as a private individual with his own private ideas about what constitutes good government, is in exactly the same position as an outsider towards his *own* government.[20] He must acknowledge its procedures, as they stand, to be the expression of the general will, if he is to see his country as having a general will and so a government at all. And according to Kant he must see himself as living under a government because, as we saw earlier, it is our duty to live in political society.

5. Why There is No Right to Revolution

Since Kant thinks that any government represents the general will of the people, his argument against the right to revolution is an immediate, simple, conceptual one. He says:

For in order for the people to be able to judge the supreme political authority with the force of law, they must already be viewed as united under a general legislative

---

[19] When thinking about the terms on which we interact with other nations, as when thinking about the terms on which we interact with other people, it is important to distinguish two different issues: one is whether you disapprove of the way they go on, and the other is whether the way they go on prevents you from interacting with them on terms that are honorable in your own eyes.

[20] As a citizen, rather than merely as a subject, he is sometimes entitled to act on his own substantive views. For instance, they determine who and what he votes for. But the cases in which he is permitted in this way to act on his private views must be constitutionally defined.

Will; hence they can and may not judge otherwise than the present chief of state wills. (MPJ 6:318)

The point is plain. The government is the representative of the general will. But if *it* represents the general will, whatever it says is the voice of the general will. To revolt, where that means to oppose the decisions of the government, is therefore to oppose the general will. And to oppose the general will is to dissolve the juridical condition among human beings, and so to return to the state of nature. Revolution "is not an alteration of the civil constitution, but the dissolution of it" (MPJ 6:340). This is wrong, for, as we have seen, Kant thinks that living in political society is not, as Locke thought, a mere remedy for inconvenience, but instead is a duty of justice.

However paradoxical it seems, this argument has real force. If government exists by the general will, a revolution could only be legitimate if it in turn were in accordance with the general will. Otherwise, it is just a few lawless individuals making war against the nation. But we should ask how it could be established that a revolution *is* in accordance with the general will. Kant's argument shows how serious this problem is. The government contains agencies for both determining and interpreting what the general will is. Of course the people may decide that the government is not doing a good job of this. But this judgment can only be made by someone who has the right to speak for the people, and that right belongs to the government itself.[21] Therefore, the government can reform itself, but the people *as subjects* cannot reform the government.

The problem arises because the will of the people must be represented. A people cannot literally speak with one voice. They must speak through a representative who has their mandate. What makes the problem of revolution so acute is that what is in question here *is* who represents the people. And the people cannot literally speak with one voice about *this* any more than they can about anything else. Until we settle the question who represents the people the general will has no voice to speak with. So we cannot start with the will of the people; to know what the will of the people is, we must start with someone taken to be their representative, their voice. This can make it seem strangely arbitrary who we take to represent them. Kant's solution to this problem is to say that the representative of the people *just is* the extant government, whatever it is.

If we accept Kant's solution, a revolution is necessarily opposed to the general will and so it is illegitimate. To see this, imagine the best possible case for revolution. Suppose we have a small nation ruled by a single tyrant and his army. The revolutionary, hoping to establish legitimacy, assembles

---

[21] Hobbes makes essentially the same argument in *Leviathan*, chapter 18.

the entire population and takes a vote. Everyone except the dictator and his army votes for a new regime. If the dictator does not bow out, do the people have the right to revolt? The answer is no. In this country, the procedure for determining the general will is to consult the dictator, not to take a vote. Votes can only determine what the general will is where they are the duly constituted procedure for determining the general will. So for these people to revolt on the basis of this vote would be a raw act of the tyranny of the majority over the minority. The majority only represents the general will where it has been established that they do; and, in this case, it has not.

Kant's argument, as I've suggested, depends on a deeply procedural conception of the general will. Our general will, according to this argument, just is whatever follows from the procedures that make collective action possible, and so, in Rousseau's extravagant language, it can do no wrong.[22] Suppose we allow, instead, that there is such a thing as the general will, independently of our procedures, and that our procedures should be viewed as a fallible device for ascertaining it. Then we can allow, contrary to Kant, that the extant regime may not represent the will of the people and so may fail to be legitimate. Even so, we get the problem. It is still true that the people cannot speak as a people until they have a voice. A revolutionary who claims to be the representative of the people merely because of the spirit he senses among them or even because he has taken a favorable vote is misdescribing the situation. The people can only give their mandate through some duly constituted voice, through someone who has the right to represent them. If we admit the possibility that the extant regime does not represent the general will then there is *no way* to tell what the general will is. The general will has lost its voice, and there are only two ways to make it speak again. One is if the people arrive at actual unanimity—in which case, of course, there could be no need for revolution, since the people of a nation include its governors. The other is by the essentially arbitrary choice of a representative. So even if we grant the possibility that a government might be illegitimate, we can never say that the revolution is in accordance with the general will. Now all we have is a raw clash of arbitrary powers at war with each other in a world without justice. We have still not established that revolution is something to which there could be a *right*.

6. What Follows from the Fact that There is No Right to Revolution

Let's say Kant has made his case. There is no right to revolution. What follows?

---

[22] Rousseau, *On the Social Contract*, Book 2, chapter 3.

It follows from the fact that there is no right to revolution that there is a duty not to revolt. This duty is a duty of justice. It is important now to recall what this means. A duty of justice is a duty in the sense that others may coercively require your performance. To say that something is a duty of justice is to say that its violation is punishable. So the first thing that follows is that if you participate in a revolution, it fails, and you are caught, you may be punished. As Kant says, revolution is the "most punishable crime in a commonwealth, for it destroys its very foundations" (TP 8:299). So far, this is unproblematic. It would be extraordinary to believe that people may not be punished for revolting. Of course if people get out their guns and shoot at others and make mayhem in society they may be punished. The fact that their motives were political rather than venal may make us judge them less harshly as human beings, but for all that they may be punished.[23] The whole point of a government is to enforce people's rights in a way that is orderly and grounded in reciprocal coercion, rather than in a disorderly and unilaterally coercive way. Executive authority is supposed to be concentrated in a government; and so the idea of a government which is not allowed to enforce its own decisions is incoherent. As Kant himself points out, a right to revolution would involve a kind of contradiction, rather like the Liar's Paradox: "the supreme legislation would have to contain a stipulation that it is not supreme" (MPJ 6:320).[24]

There is also a second consequence, which follows from Kant's views about responsibility for actions and their consequences. Kant argues that one must do what the moral law demands, let the consequences be what they may. If you

[23] For Kant's own reflections on this point, see note 27 below.

[24] One standard response to this point is that it only shows that there cannot be a legal right to revolution, but not that there cannot be a moral right. Kant's system makes no use of any distinctive category of moral right; for him, a right is by definition the kind of moral claim that can legitimately be coercively enforced and so can be legalized. There are claims in Kant's system that it is tempting to identify with moral rights. Kant distinguishes duties of justice from duties of virtue on the grounds that the former are, and the latter are not, both legitimate and possible to enforce coercively. We *may not* force people to be virtuous because virtue is a matter of inner motives and attitudes, and your having a bad attitude towards me does not hinder my freedom. But we also *cannot* force people to do the duties of virtue, because we cannot control the motives from which they act. Yet one of the duties of virtue—the duty to respect others, seems to be a perfect duty and seems to establish a kind of claim, so that we might say that we have a moral right to the respect of others. This will not help us here, however. It is, though, related to what I take to be the most plausible grounds for claiming a "moral right" to revolution, namely, exclusion from full citizenship on arbitrary grounds. The most extreme case is that of slaves, but victims of apartheid, and Kant's so-called passive citizens (see note 15 above) may also plausibly claim that the general will is not their will, that they have been left outside of the commonwealth. So let me just say that the case of the conscientious revolutionary that I will shortly examine, the one I think morally interesting, is not that of someone who himself can plausibly claim to be excluded from the commonwealth, but rather someone who is part of the commonwealth but objects to its actions. One obvious reason why he might object is that some others are arbitrarily excluded.

do what is required of you, you are not responsible for the consequences. On the other hand, if you do something other than what the moral law demands, then you are responsible for the consequences. In the *Metaphysics of Morals*, Kant says:

The good or bad results of an action that is owed, like the results of omitting a meritorious action, cannot be imputed to the subject (*modus imputationis tollens*).

The good results of a meritorious action, like the bad results of a wrongful action, can be imputed to the subject (*modus imputationis ponens*). (MM 6:228)

In other words, if you do your perfect duties, you are not responsible for the results; if you do an imperfect duty, such as helping someone, you count as the author of the good result; and if you violate perfect duty and the results are bad, the consequences are on your head. In the *Lectures on Ethics*, Kant puts the point more simply:

If we do either more or less than is required of us we can be held accountable for the consequences, but not otherwise—not if we only do what is required, neither more nor less. (LE 59)[25]

Now the duties of justice are all perfect duties, and so, when you violate them, you are responsible for the results. Revolutionaries who are caught may be held legally liable not only for the crime of sedition but for the death, injury, and mayhem that result. But Kant makes it clear that this is not merely a legal point. He says that the consequences of violating a perfect duty should also be imputed to the agent by "his own conscience" (MM 6:431). So someone who undertakes to start or participate in a revolution must regard himself as responsible for the results. A revolutionary must see himself as the author of the loss of life and limb, the social disorder, and the suspension of the juridical condition that results from revolution.

Although this is a more controversial point, this too seems to me to be correct. Even those who are inclined to argue for a "right to revolution" cannot think that revolution is something to be undertaken lightly. Justice exists only where there is government; the revolutionary undertakes to destroy the government, and so undertakes to destroy justice. Of course his aim is to improve the juridical condition. He thinks that justice will rise revivified from its own ashes, like the Phoenix; he hopes to bring about a new and better system of justice, which will come closer to doing its job, which is guaranteeing freedom. As Kant says, revolutionaries undertake "to be unjust once and for all, in order thereafter to establish legal justice on a foundation

---

[25] For a further explanation of the basis and meaning of this view, see my "The Right to Lie: Kant on Dealing with Evil" (CKE essay 5), pp. 141–3.

that is so much more secure" (MPJ 6:353). But for however short a time, there will be a condition in which there is no justice. During this period, as a result of conditions the revolutionary himself has instigated or supported, lives will be lost, injuries sustained, property rights violated, careers interrupted and destroyed. During this period, the victims of these disasters will have neither recourse nor compensation. He may fail, and if he fails, all of this will have been for nothing. Surely the victims of social upheaval may rightly regard the revolutionaries as the authors of their injuries. And surely the revolutionary cannot just say: the consequences were not my fault, since I was doing what I had a right to do.

So far, we have two consequences. First, the conclusion that there is no right to revolution, in Kant's sense of a right, is unproblematic. Of course revolutionaries, if they fail or are caught in time, may be punished. The idea of a government that is not entitled to defend itself in this way makes no sense. But this is not merely a matter of what the law has to say, of whether there can be a legal right to revolution. Even from a purely moral point of view, a just revolution would have to be in accordance with the general will of the people, and we have seen that this is impossible. Either the government is the voice of the general will of the people, or there is no voice; in neither case can the revolutionary claim the mandate of the general will. So the revolutionary is doing something he has no right to do. And that means that all the consequences of the revolution are imputable to him. If he wins, his party becomes the legitimate government, and as such they are not legally answerable for their actions; and morally, then, he at least has an excuse. But if he loses, he is nothing more than a murderer and a thief. And this last should be not only in the government's eyes, but in his own.

But there is one consequence that does not follow. So far, I have said nothing that implies that there are no circumstances in which a good person would revolt.

7. When the Virtuous Person Revolts

More than any other philosopher in the tradition, Kant gives us an agent-centered moral philosophy. His primary question is not who shall we praise or blame, or which actions are right and which wrong. He has things to say about these questions, but they fall out of the discussion of what he takes to be the central question of moral philosophy: what must I do? So far, we have remained on the territory of duties of justice, and have discussed what we must say *about* revolutionaries and revolution. But we have not yet addressed the main question: should *we* ever revolt? Nor could we address that question, so long as we kept the discussion to the duties of justice. To approach this question we must turn to the doctrine of virtue, to ethics.

Again we will need some background. Earlier I said that the duties of justice are external duties. The sense in which they are duties is that we may legitimately be forced to do them. The duties of virtue, by contrast, are internal duties. The sense in which they are duties is that morality requires them of us, which is to say that we require them of ourselves. Duties of virtue are concerned with our motives and attitudes. They arise from the command that we should not only do certain things, but do them for moral reasons: in Kantian language, they command us to make duty itself the incentive of our action. As the constitutive aim of the duties of justice is the achievement of external freedom, so the constitutive aim of the duties of virtue is internal freedom: for through the cultivation of virtue we achieve the freedom of the will (MM 6:379–384).[26]

Kant believes that all human action is purposive (G 4:427; MM 6:381; MM 6:385; REL 6:4; REL 6:6–7 n.). This does not mean that we always act for the sake of some end in which we have taken a prior interest; but it does mean that we always act with some end in view. When we undertake an action, there is always some end to that action which we represent to ourselves as good. It does not have to be an end we are trying to bring about—it may be an end we wish not to act against, or wish to respect. In the moral case, for instance, we may simply see our action as expressing respect for humanity as an end in itself. Because morally good actions as well as others are purposive, Kant argues that the cultivation of virtue is achieved through the adoption of morally obligatory ends (MM 6:380–381; 384–385).

Kant thinks that there are duties, and so ends, that belong specifically to the territory of virtue: the pursuit of the happiness of others, and the cultivation of our own talents, powers, and character (MM 6:385–389). But ethics encompasses all of our duties. It is a duty of virtue to do the duties of justice from the motive of duty. In other words, justice itself is a virtue. And Kant says that the virtue of justice is possessed by one *who makes the rights of humanity his end* (MM 6:390).

In ordinary circumstances, this is the end we have in view when we carry out the moral duty to obey the law. If you keep your hands off your neighbor's property, even thinking he has more than his fair share; if you refrain from stuffing ballot boxes, even when that means the better candidate will lose; if you pay your debts, even when you could get away with not doing so, this is

---

[26] For discussion, see my "Morality as Freedom" (CKE essay 6), pp. 176–83.

because you care about the rights of others. The end you have in view is that their rights should be respected.

It is because justice is a virtue that there is an ethical duty, as well as a duty of justice, not to revolt. The just person respects the rights of humanity, and for this reason respects the government that enforces those rights, and the juridical condition that makes their enforcement possible. But it is by no means obvious that a person who makes the rights of humanity his end would never, under any circumstances, oppose the extant government. If this is correct, nothing in Kant's theory absolutely commits him to the view that a good person would *never* revolt. Nor, I believe, is this what he himself thought.[27]

Justice exists to preserve the rights and freedom of everyone: this is the idea, and the substantive ideal, of justice. But we all know that the procedures of justice may be used *against these very ends*. Apartheid South Africa horrified us more, perhaps, than more egregious despotisms, because of its outward forms of legality, its caricature of a modern western democracy. The same is true of America before the civil war. A master recapturing a runaway slave is brutal; but a court's ordering the slave's return is a mockery of justice. Women and children have often been returned to the legal custody of the very husbands and fathers who have abused them; Captain Bligh does not just beat his men, but does it with the Queen's authority. There is a special kind of horror associated with such cases. For in such cases the very language of rights, and the robes and wigs and forms and ceremonies with which we celebrate our will to form a general will, are used to corner the helpless. The agencies of justice are used to reinforce injustice; and what should be the recourse of the oppressed is the very tool of the oppressor. In such cases, justice is turned against itself, perverted; human rights need protection from the law itself.

Kant does not say this, of course, but he was keenly sensitive to the special kind of horror I am talking about here. This shows up, interestingly, in a footnote to the very section of the *Metaphysical Principles of Justice* in which Kant argues that revolution is always wrong. He says:

Of all the abominations involved in the overthrow of a state through revolution, the *murder* of the monarch is still not the worst, because it is possible to imagine that the people are motivated by the fear that, were he to remain alive, he might regain his

---

[27] Kant explicitly acknowledges the existence of conscientious revolutionaries in the course of a rather odd discussion of the morality of the death penalty at MPJ 6:333–334. People join rebellions both for honorable and for venal motives, Kant notices, and we might think that the former should be punished less severely than the latter. But applying the death penalty to all concerned achieves this, Kant argues, since "a man of honor would choose death and . . . the knave would choose servitude." The knave therefore *is* punished more severely.

power and give them the punishment they deserve; in that case, this deed would not be an act of penal justice, but only one of self-preservation. It is the *formal execution* of a monarch that fills the soul, conscious of the Ideas of human justice, with horror, and this horror returns whenever one thinks of scenes like those in which the fate of Charles I or Louis XVI was sealed. (MPJ 6:321 n.; my emphases)

Kant proceeds to examine the sources of this particular kind of horror. In the *Groundwork*, Kant had argued that since we cannot consistently will an evil maxim as a universal law, a person who acts wrongly cannot be doing *that*, but instead is making himself an exception to the law (G 4:424). Recalling these ideas, Kant argues here that to *get rid* of the ruler is to violate justice, and so to make yourself an exception to the law, but to *punish* the ruler (to executive the supreme executive) is to subvert justice—not just to make yourself an exception to the law, but actually to repudiate it, and so to make a kind of law of unlawfulness itself. In *Religion within the Limits of Reason Alone*, Kant distinguishes human evil, which consists in making yourself an exception to the law for the sake of satisfying some contingent interest, from the possession of a malevolent will, one that wills evil for its own sake, that wills evil as a law. Contrary to Augustine, Kant does not think that human beings choose evil for its own sake (REL 6:35). Yet here Kant argues that the execution of the monarch is like an exhibition of a malevolent will, because it presents an evil act in the outward forms of a lawful one. This is why we find it so horrifying.

Revolutionaries who formally execute a monarch perform an unjust act while dressed in the robes and wigs of justice; in so doing, they seem not just to ignore justice, but to mock it. But in cases of the sort I have mentioned, the state may seem to do this too. And then the just subject may find herself locked in exactly the sort of horror that Kant describes. When the very institutions whose purpose is to realize human rights are used to trample them, when justice is turned against itself, the virtue of justice will be turned against itself too. Concern for human rights leads the virtuous person to accept the authority of the law, but in such circumstances adherence to the law will lead her to support institutions that systematically violate human rights.[28] The person with the virtue of justice, the lover of human rights, unable to turn to the actual laws for their enforcement, has nowhere else to turn. She may come to feel that there is nothing for it but for her to take human rights under her own protection, and so to take the law into her own hands.

The decision to revolt would be a hard one to make because the person who loves the rights of humanity necessarily places a high value on the actual

---

[28] I owe this formulation to Andrews Reath.

procedures of justice as well as on the substantive ideal of protecting human rights. And, as I argued earlier, the procedures of justice are important not just because they approximate our substantive ideals, but because without such procedures there is no justice at all. Nor, of course, will the achievement of more substantive ideals be the result of the sacrifice. At the very best, revolution will bring only a closer approximation to the ideal. At the very worst, the result will be an extended period in which there is no justice at all, the rights of humanity are trampled underfoot, and a new excuse for tyranny will have been created. Short of that, there may be only marginal improvements, not obviously worth the ruined and ended lives we paid for it. The revolutionary risks this, and knows that she does, when she decides to revolt.

Two things make this decision different from most of the decisions which we make, at least as those are envisioned in Kantian ethics. The first is that the universalization test cannot serve as a guide when we make it. The imperfections of the actual state of affairs are no excuse for revolution—if they were, revolution would always be in order. It is the perversion of justice, not merely its imperfection, which turns the virtue of justice against itself. But the difference between imperfect justice and perverted justice is a matter of pure judgment. There is no criterion for deciding when imperfection has become perversion, when things have gone too far. If we turn for help to the Universal Principle of Justice, all it says is: do not revolt. The revolutionary cannot claim he has a justification, in the sense of an account of his action that other reasonable people must accept. That consolation is denied him. It is as if a kind of gap opens up in the moral world in which the moral agent must stand alone.

The revolutionary's stance, in fact, is one of paternalism towards a whole society, when paternalism, which after all is a kind of despotism, is what he hates the most. And this reminds us that revolution is only one case, the most vivid perhaps, in which good people take the law into their own hands. Another, much more common and familiar sort of case, is when we paternalize an adult human being who is engaged in some sort of self-destructive behavior. Most of us for instance would take action to prevent a suicide (at least unless the person was hopelessly ill and in great pain) even if we didn't think the person had simply gone crazy, but was really acting from his own choice. And many of us would be prepared to take action to prevent a close friend from going too far with self-destructive activities like abusing drugs. The structure of the problem we face in these cases is exactly the same as that of the problem faced by the revolutionary. When we see someone perverting or destroying the humanity or autonomy in his own person, our respect for his humanity or autonomy is turned against itself. Respect for his autonomy demands that we respect his right to choose. But if we respect his autonomy we cannot stand quietly by and watch while he destroys it. Like justice in an unjust state, his autonomy requires protection against itself. And so, like the revolutionary, the paternalist violates his respect for autonomy in order to save its object. Paternalists too take the law into their own hands. Here too, there is no way of deciding exactly when the moment has come, when things have gone too far. Morality cannot tell you when to leave the moral law behind, in order to make sure that the world remains a place where morality can flourish. In making this kind of decision, you are entirely on your own.

And this brings us to the second thing that makes this decision different from others. Since these decisions necessarily involve stepping outside of the law, they involve what Bernard Williams has called "moral luck."[29] For as Kant says, if you do more or less than the law requires, the consequences are on your head. The form of moral luck Williams describes exists in a case with these features: the agent does something that is, on the face of it, wrong, but may be justified by success. If the project fails, the agent will simply be wrong, and the consequences will be, in his own eyes and those of his victims, on his head. But if the project succeeds, he may at least be justified in his own eyes and in the eyes of outsiders, if not of those of his immediate victims. Williams thinks that the concept of moral luck is a notion inimical to Kantianism, but the case of the revolutionary has exactly this structure. Success makes the revolutionary, legally, the new voice of the general will, and, morally, one who has promoted the cause of justice on earth. In his own eyes and the eyes of the spectators this will justify him, though the victims of the revolution will still have a complaint. Failure, on the other hand, means that he has destroyed justice for nothing, that he is guilty of murder and treason, an assailant of the general will, and the enemy of everyone. Revolution may be justified, but only if you win.

Perhaps it will be doubted whether the view I have put forward could possibly be Kant's. Moral life in bad circumstances can be messy; Kant is often accused of denying this point. But I actually think it is a strength of his view that it allows us to see how one form of messiness arises—and that it does so without resorting to the pat explanation that we happen to be subject to an unsystematic plurality of duties which can of course conflict.[30] In the case of the conscientious revolutionary, the problem is not a conflict between different duties but rather the fact that a single duty, the duty to care for the

---

[29] See Bernard Williams, "Moral Luck," in his volume *Moral Luck*.

[30] An account that, to my mind, makes sense of the complexity of morality at the expense of depriving morality itself of sense. I am indebted to Tamar Schapiro for illuminating discussions of this topic.

rights of humanity, implodes when we try to act on it in an unjust world. But could Kant have recognized this? It is hard to know for sure, for the fact is that Kant never discusses the question whether the *ethical* duty not to revolt is always in place. His discussions of revolution are all concerned with the duty of justice, and it is, interestingly, the punishability of revolution that he always emphasizes. My view that he did recognize the possibility I've described here for the most part comes not from his published writings, but from what we know about his attitude towards the revolutions of his day. But there is one thing in the published writings that does support my claim. Listen again to part of the passage from "On the Old Question" where Kant praises the enthusiasm of the spectators of the French Revolution. Listen, in particular, to the way Kant imagines the deliberations of the would-be revolutionary himself:

The revolution of a gifted people which we have seen unfolding in our day may succeed or miscarry; it may be filled with misery and atrocities to the point that a sensible man, were he boldly to hope to execute it successfully the second time, would never resolve to make the experiment at such cost. (OQ 7:85)

Kant's revolutionary considers the prospects of success and views the costs of failure as his own. In this, he follows the pattern I have described.

8. Conclusion

The Kingdom of Ends is an ideal, not a goal. For the most part, our duty is to live as if it were real, not to bring it about that it is so. A Kantian doesn't paternalize every time a loved one makes a poor choice; a Kantian doesn't revolt every time the government makes a wrong decision. In the one case, respect for autonomy, in the other, respect for the rule of law, matter to her more than the content of the particular decisions that are made.

But in some cases, respect for autonomy, or respect for the rule of law, can be turned against themselves. When autonomy is used self-destructively, and law turns against the rights it is there to protect, morality ceases to give us clear guidance how to proceed. The claims of right remain clear, but the demands of virtue become ambiguous. In such cases, good people may do things that are, in one fairly clear sense, wrong.[31] A dogmatist may deny that a good person would ever do this; a skeptic may think such actions are unproblematic,

---

[31] What fairly clear sense? Not universalizable, certainly; but the more important point is what that shows: that such an action relates us wrongly to others. Almost any moral philosopher would grant that wrong actions relate us wrongly to others, of course, but I mean something different. I don't regard that as an incidental feature of wrong actions, a mere effect of the fact that the actions are wrong and therefore others don't want us to do them. I regard the way it relates you to yourself and others

showing only that morality is not unconditional after all. I believe that both views oversimplify our moral situation: the world is a less comfortable home for morality than they suppose. Skepticism and dogmatism are attempts to evade one of the most important facts about moral responsibility. The moral life can contain moments when responsibility is so deep that even a justification is denied us. The agent who can only save morality by violating its principles faces such a moment. At such moments the virtuous person may find that he must take morality itself under his own protection, and so take even the moral law into his own hands.

9. Afterword: Why We Find Revolution Thrilling

Earlier I claimed that the moment of revolution, though hard and full of pain for the revolutionary himself, is thrilling to the spectator. I also claimed that neither skepticism nor dogmatism could give an adequate account of that thrill. How should a Kantian account for it?

Kant, as we have seen, had his own explanation, detailed in the essay "On the Old Question: Is the Human Race Constantly Progressing?" There, Kant argues that revolutionaries of his day sought republican forms of government, the only form under which Kant thought real justice and peace could possibly be secured. With peace and justice would come enlightenment. The nations would be able to guarantee civil liberties, and spend money on education rather than on arms (IUH 8:26–28; CBHH 8:121). Enlightenment, the condition in which people think for themselves, leads to morality, the condition in which people live by the laws of their own autonomy (WE 8:35). Thus enthusiasm for the revolution can be understood as enthusiasm for the future of morality itself.

My explanation is different, though not incompatible with Kant's. If Kant is right, human freedom is autonomy and autonomy is morality. This makes human freedom a paradoxical thing. In everyday life, it consists to a surprising extent in having to do things. When we are dealing with evil, it consists to a tragic extent in having to put up with things. When faced with oppression, bullying, and heartbreaking unfairness, freedom can appear as helplessness; autonomy as a terrifying defenselessness. There's a real antinomy here, a natural dialectic that throws us into doubt about the nature and the value of our own moral capacity. Plato gave voice to this worry in the very earliest works of Western moral philosophy; Thrasymachus laughs at the just person as someone easily tricked into serving the interests of the stronger; Callicles argues

as *of the essence* of the morality of an action. See my "The Reasons We Can Share" (CKE essay 10), pp. 275–6 and 300–2; and SN 3.4.1, p. 114 n. 26.

that even self-government is merely a form of slavery.[32] Freud and Nietzsche recast the worry in more psychological terms. Morality is an expression of strength, the will to power, the aggressive instincts, turned inward. It is the magical transformation of masterfulness into self-mastery that makes us human. But morality is a form of weakness, for the will to power, the aggressive instincts, are eating us alive from the inside out, sapping our strength, making us herd animals, victims, sickly prey.[33] Autonomy gives life meaning, showing us that the world is ours to create; but autonomy is morality and morality leads to nihilism, for the good have no option but surrender.

The moment of revolution is a vindication of morality, and so of our humanity. We are the masters of our own self-mastery; in control of our self-control. Being human is not sapping our strength, for we still know when to fight. The revolutionary does not *become* strong and free when he picks up his gun. Instead, he proves to us that he's been free all along. It is because the laws of morality are his own laws that he is finally prepared to fight for them. The doubt created by the antinomy is dispelled. Revolution teaches us nothing but what we have known all along: that the good person and the free person are one and the same.[34]

---

[32] Plato, R 338 ff.; *Gorgias* 491–2.

[33] See Friedrich Nietzsche, *The Genealogy of Morals*, essay 2, and Sigmund Freud, in, for example, *Civilization and Its Discontents*, chapter 7.

[34] Versions of this essay were delivered at the Central Division meeting of the American Philosophical Association in the spring of 1991, where I had the benefit of a helpful and sympathetic commentary by Andrews Reath; at the Kantian Ethics Workshop in Chapel Hill in the fall of 1991, where I received challenging comments from Simon Blackburn; and at the Political Philosophy Colloquium in Princeton in the fall of 1995. I am grateful to the audiences at all three occasions for many illuminating comments and useful objections; I would like especially to thank Stephen Engstrom, Arthur Ripstein, and Avishai Margolit. I have benefited from discussing the issues of the essay with Charlotte Brown, Daniel Brudney, Peter Hylton, Arthur Kuflik, Tamar Schapiro, and Jay Schleusenser; and from written comments sent to me by Kenneth Westphal. The essay was completed while I was a Laurence S. Rockefeller Visiting Fellow at the University Center for Human Values in 1995–6; I am deeply grateful both for the time the Center provided me to finish the essay, and for the useful discussions of it I had with the Fellows there. But my primary debt, here as in everything that I write, is to the example and inspiration of my teacher, John Rawls.

9

The General Point of View: Love and Moral Approval in Hume's Ethics

1. A Problem in Hume's Moral Theory

1.1 *The General Point of View*

According to Hume, moral judgments are based on sentiments of approval and disapproval that we feel when we contemplate a person's character from what Hume calls "a general point of view" (T 3.3.1,581–582). Taking up the general point of view regulates our sentiments about a person in two ways. First, we view the person not through the eyes of our own interests, but instead through the eyes of our sympathy with the person herself and her friends, family, neighbors, and colleagues (T 3.3.1,582–584; T 3.3.2,601–602). We assess her in terms of the effects of her character on those with whom she usually associates, the people Hume calls her "narrow circle" (T 3.3.3,602). So, to use one of Hume's own examples, we approve of our enemy's courage, though it has deleterious effects on ourselves, because its effect on our enemy and her own fellow-citizens is a useful one (2E 5,216). Second, we judge her characteristics according to the usual effects of characteristics of that kind, rather than according to their actual effects in this or that case. As Hume puts it, we judge according to "general rules" (T 3.3.1,585).

These two regulating devices bring objectivity, in one sense of an overworked term, to our moral judgments. Judging in sympathy with a person's narrow circle and according to general rules, we are able to reach agreement about her character. We all approve and disapprove of the same characteristics, and as a result we come to share an ideal of good character. Our concepts of the virtues and vices in this way arise from the general point of view.

But Hume's account gives rise to a difficulty. Moral concepts and judgments are based on our moral sentiments, and our moral sentiments arise when we contemplate a person from the general point of view. The general point of view is a specially constructed perspective, or standpoint, from which we consider a person's character. But why do we contemplate a person from this special perspective in the first place? As I will put it, why do we take up the general point of view?

This question may be taken as a request either for an explanation or for a justification (or of course both), so let me clarify the sense in which I mean it. At one extreme, we might ask only for a psychological explanation of the fact in question: How does it come about that we take up the general point of view, and judge people's characters from it? What psychological forces impel us to do that? At the other extreme, we might ask the question with a fully normative aim, a philosopher's question. That is, we might ask not only how it comes about that we take up the general point of view, but also whether the judgments we make from it are authentically normative and if so why. Ought I really to approve those whom I am inclined to approve from the general point of view, or perhaps even try to be like them myself? What binds me to do that? Somewhere between these two extremes is what we might call a question of moral anthropology: that is, an explanatory question, but one that seeks an explanation why people *take* the ideas of virtue and vice to be normative. There is room for dispute about whether Hume intends to answer the fully normative question.[1] But I think there is no doubt that his explanatory aims extend to the question of moral anthropology. So I will put my point this way: Hume owes us an explanation *at least* of why we take up the general point of view, and of why we are inclined to *think* that the judgments we make from it are normative.

One answer that springs immediately to mind is a moral realist answer: we take up the general point of view in order to discover what moral virtues a person has, because that is the perspective from which (for some reason) his virtues can be seen. A slightly more sophisticated answer is that we take up the general point of view in order to make moral judgments.[2] But, as I am going to argue in more detail, neither of these answers will work. In Hume's theory, moral judgments are a *product* of the general point of view, and moral virtues and vices are, in turn, a product of moral judgments. As Hume himself says:

Take any action allow'd to be vicious: Willful murder, for instance. Examine it in all lights, and see if you can find that matter of fact, or real existence, which you call vice. In which-ever way you take it, you find only certain passions, motives, volitions and thoughts. There is no other matter of fact in the case. The vice entirely escapes you, as long as you consider the object. You can never find it, till you turn your reflexion into

[1] I argue that Hume does provide an answer to what I have here called "the fully normative question," SN 2.2.1–2.2.7, pp. 51–66.

[2] The second proposal is more sophisticated because it at least partly recognizes that on Hume's view virtue and vice depend on moral judgment rather than existing prior to it.

your own breast, and find a sentiment of disapprobation, which arises in you, towards this action. Here is a matter of fact; but 'tis the object of feeling, not of reason. It lies in yourself, not in the object. (T 3.1.1,468–469)

We deem, say, cowardice a vice *because* we disapprove of it, and that disapproval is a sentiment we experience when we view the character from the general point of view. So our employment of moral ideas results from our occupation of the general point of view. And this means that we cannot appeal to moral ideas in order to explain why we take up the general point of view in the first place. A creature who never viewed things from the general point of view would make no moral judgments, and for such a creature, there would be no virtues and vices. We cannot intelligibly say that such a creature would take up the general point of view *in order* to bring morality, of which he has no prior conception, into existence.

But this response shows that the question I am raising here is not just about an unresolved technical detail in Hume's account of moral judgment, a step missing from his general explanation. Asking why we take up the general point of view amounts to asking why, according to Hume, human beings operate with moral concepts and so are moral animals. The use of moral concepts is the result of a quite particular way of viewing people. Why do we view people in this particular way?

In the rest of section 1, I will explain this problem in more detail. In particular, I will explain how it is related to another question about Hume's theory, namely, why there is (or why we should think that there is—but I will not continue to add this qualification) a normative standard for love. In section 2, I will examine, and reject, Hume's explicit answer to the question why we take up the general point of view. Finally, in section 3, I will argue that Hume's theory of love contains the resources for a more interesting and plausible solution to the problem.

1.2 *Hume's Theory of Love*

The problem I have just described can be put in different terms, namely, as a problem about why there should be a normative standard for love. Before I can explain why this is so, we need to have a sketch of Hume's theory of love before us. Hume thinks of love as a passion, indeed, a simple impression or unanalyzable feeling (T 2.2.1,329). He tells us that just as the object of pride or humility is always the self, so the object of love or hate is always another. It is not terribly clear what could be meant by saying that a simple unanalyzable feeling has an object, but Hume seems to think that the object is an idea on which one's attention is focused when one is in the grip of the passion. In explaining what he means by saying that self is the object of pride and humility, Hume remarks: "Here [that is, on the self] the view always fixes when we are actuated by either of these passions" (T 2.1.2,277). A little later he says: "Pride and humility, being once rais'd, immediately turn our attention to ourself, and regard that as their ultimate and final object" (T 2.1.2,278); and again "Here at last, the view always rests, when we are actuated by either of these passions" (T 2.1.5,286). The order suggested here seems counterintuitive—we might suppose that a person has to be attending to the idea of herself *before* pride can be aroused. Hume rather surprisingly compares the way pride evokes the idea of self to the way hunger produces the idea of food (T 2.1.5,287). However that may be, the fact that love takes another for its object is what Hume calls an "original" feature of this passion. By "original" Hume means a feature that admits of no further explanation (T 2.1.3,280; T 2.1.5,286). Pride just does fix our attention on ourselves; love just does fix our attention on another.

Hume points out that the causes of pride and love must be different from their objects, since humility and hate, respectively, have the same objects, self and other. If the bare thought of yourself aroused pride just because you are its object, it would arouse humility for the same reason, and you would always feel both of these passions at the same time (T 2.1.2,277–278; T 2.2.1,330). The causes of love and pride are therefore different from their objects—they are, in fact, pleasant things that are associated with their objects. In the same way, the causes of hate and humility are unpleasant things that are associated with their objects. The mechanism by which love is produced is the notoriously obscure "double relation of impressions and ideas." Suppose that you have beautiful hair and I perceive this. The idea of your beautiful hair and the idea of you are related. Using Hume's own list of relations, we can specify this relation as contiguity because the hair is on your head or as causality because you grew it, say. In contemplating your beautiful hair, I feel pleasure, and all pleasant impressions are related by resemblance. Now Hume thinks of the passions themselves as impressions, which are either pleasant, painful, or mixed. Love is a pleasant impression, and so it is natural for my mind to move from the pleasure of contemplating your hair to the resembling pleasure of love. Since I move naturally from the idea of your beautiful hair to the idea of you, and naturally from the pleasantness of that idea to love, whose object is another, I fix the love on you (T 2.1.5,285–290; T 2.2.1,330–332). In this way, any pleasant thing associated with another person can cause you to love him.

However obscure Hume's account may be, its basic message is clear. Hume thinks that love is essentially pleasure in the thought of a person, caused by something pleasant about him. There are of course a number of objections we might make to this view, even apart from worries about how exactly the psychological mechanism is supposed to work. I sketch two of these, which concern the ontology of love, below. The third, which is important to my account, will get a section of its own.

First, we may object that love surely has something to do with caring about a person's welfare, and that the idea of taking pleasure in the thought of a person does not include or necessarily imply this important element of love. Hume is aware of this objection and he has a rather astonishing reply to it. He understands the objection to amount to the claim that love *just is* the desire of another's happiness, and so he thinks that it is amply defeated by the fact that we can sometimes find the two apart (T 2.2.6,367). Benevolence towards the beloved is indeed always associated with love when we happen to *think* about the beloved's happiness, Hume asserts, but we do not always do that. The connection between benevolence and love is therefore an original and so inexplicable causal connection, not essential to the passion of love (T 2.2.6,368). Nature might have made us so that love was always accompanied by malice, or so that it had no motivational tendencies at all. As it happens, love and benevolence go together in us. However odd this may sound, Hume's views make it necessary: if love is an unanalyzable feeling, the only way that it can be connected either to its object or to its characteristic motives is causally.

Second, we may protest, along with Aristotle and Kant, that love is not a passion or not merely a passion but rather something like a state of character or a condition of the will; or even that it essentially involves some sort of relationship with the beloved.[3] For Hume, love is just another experience. Pursuing this objection would take us too far afield, so I mention it only to say that I think that it is right, and lay it aside.

1.3 *The Grounds of Love*

A third objection, and the one most important for my purposes here, concerns Hume's attitude towards what I will call the "grounds" of love.[4] In ordinary language we may speak of loving someone "for" something, or of loving someone "because" of something. You might say that you love someone *for* his intelligence and sweetness, say, or that you love him *because* he is funny and brave. The idea of a ground of love appears to be subject to a normative

---

[3] For Aristotle's remarks on the ontology of love and friendship, see especially *Nicomachean Ethics* 8.1 1155a3; 8.2 1155b27–1156a1; 8.5 1157b25–1158a1; 9.5 1166b30–1167a1. In the first of these passages Aristotle declares friendship to be a virtue; but in the latter ones he suggests that it also essentially involves relationship. Kant's main discussions are found at MM 6:469–473 and LE 162–171 and 200–209. I discuss their views in my "Creating the Kingdom of Ends: Reciprocity and Responsibility in Personal Relations," CKE essay 7.

[4] Arthur Kuflik suggested the term "grounds" to me in a helpful discussion of this point.

standard: we use the phrases "you only love me for . . ." and "you only love me because of . . ." followed by, say, "my beauty" "my strength" or even something external like "my money" as a criticism or complaint about the character of someone's love. Significantly, people demand to be loved "for themselves," as opposed to something which they take to be incidental about themselves, with the suggestion that the best sort of love is that which is for the person himself. This idea is linked to the question which of the more specific grounds of love are appropriate or best. Those grounds that are most intimately or intrinsically connected to the person are supposed to be better, and the love based on them more authentic or superior. People sometimes complain about being loved only for their bodies, but usually only as a kind of joke about being loved only for their minds, and never about being loved only for their souls.[5]

I'm using the term "grounds" here not to avoid but rather to emphasize the obscurity of the *because* of love, which seems to fall somewhere in between the *because* of practical reason and the *because* of simple causality. The grounds of love do seem to have something in common with practical reasons. As I've just been saying, they are unlike mere causes, and like practical reasons, in that they can (sometimes) be right or wrong, or at least better and worse. And they tend, if not exactly to justify love, at least to make it intelligible in a way that goes beyond the intelligibility of mere successful mechanistic explanation. The grounds of love might be cited in an answer to the question "why do you love him?" where the questioner wants more than just an explanation of how your love came about. She wants to understand, as we say, *what you see in* your beloved. Yet the grounds of love do not quite seem to be practical reasons, and indeed seem to operate more like causes. To the extent that love is a passion, we do not decide to love on the basis of its grounds, for we do not *decide* to love at all. And, more obscurely, the kind of grounds that make love intelligible in the sense that they specify what we "see in" someone ("He's so funny, and kind, a great lover . . .") seem to compete for the same space (because _____) with two other kinds of grounds: first, grounds that make

---

[5] Harry Frankfurt has suggested to me that if you love somebody *for* something, then your love is conditional: you will cease to love him if he loses that attribute. We agree that this does not apply to loving someone "for himself." But that leaves open the question whether any attempt to specify or identify the essence of the "self" for which you love someone renders the love conditional: Frankfurt thinks that it does. So he thinks that what I am here calling the grounds of love should only be understood as causes. According to Frankfurt, you might be *drawn to* someone because he has certain virtues, for example, but once you love him you will do so even if he ceases to have those virtues. So you don't love him *for* his virtues. In the text I claim that Hume's idea of a cause is an attempt to capture the idea of a ground; Frankfurt, going the other way, would say that what I am calling a ground can only operate as a cause.

the love intelligible without specifying anything one "sees in" the beloved ("He's my brother") and, second, grounds that do not make love intelligible at all ("I always fall for these husky irresponsible types"). My point here is that citing the first of those things (what one "sees in" a person) looks almost like giving a reason, while citing the third (one's "type") seems hardly more than mentioning a cause of which one happens to be aware.[6] Perhaps somewhere along this continuum we have shaded away from grounds to mere causes. For all of these reasons, the notion we are dealing with is an obscure one, in need of more philosophical attention.[7]

The two questions I want to raise here are whether Hume intends his idea of a cause of love to occupy roughly the same space as that of a ground of love, and whether it can adequately do so. I think the answer to the first question must be yes. For one thing, if Hume wants his account to capture the idea of a ground of love at all, his only resource, given his theory, is to understand it in terms of causality. If love is a simple unanalyzable feeling, then the only way for it to be related to a person's attributes is causally, just as the only way for it to be connected to its object or to its characteristic motives is causally. For another, the fact that the cause is supposed to be something *pleasant* about the person suggests that Hume is looking for something that makes the love intelligible, for what it is we "see in" the person we love. Of course, I have already suggested that not every ground of love specifies what we see in the beloved; family relationships are an example of a ground that does not. Interestingly, Hume takes notice of the fact that we nearly always love our relations and everyday acquaintances, whether or not there is anything especially pleasant about them, as an apparent difficulty for his theory. He resolves it by arguing that familiarity is itself a source of pleasure (T 2.2.4,353). Human beings need company, since sympathetic connection is necessary to arouse and enliven the human mind, and familiarity increases

---

6 The fact that love has grounds suggests that it is neither a mere feeling (which might only have a cause) nor of course an action (which might be done for a reason), but something more like a reaction to a perception. As I mention in the text, you do not decide to love someone because he is kind and supportive, but neither do these attributes simply cause love in you in a mechanical way; rather, your love is a response to your awareness of him *as* kind and supportive. Thus there is something correct in Hume's account of the passions as "secondary impressions" (that is, impressions that are responses to other impressions). We might say that the passion of love is an intelligent, although not quite a rational, response; love can occur only in an intelligent creature that has some cognition of its world.

7 The nearest thing to the *because* of love, at least in cases where the love is made intelligible by the *because*, seems to be the *because* of psychoanalysis—for instance, when we explain a "Freudian slip." In this case too the ground makes the slip intelligible, as if the slip were a rational action, but the ground seems to operate not as a reason but rather as a cause, since the slip is not deliberate. Unfortunately, love and hate themselves are so often offered as the grounds of Freudian slips that this comparison is not very helpful in throwing light on the nature of this sort of *because*.

sympathy. Since you are familiar with the passions and sentiments of your acquaintance, your own passions and sentiments are more readily aroused by them, and this makes you find their company stimulating and therefore pleasant. Thus Hume wants to show us how even one of the apparently more "merely causal" occasions of love, family relationship, does nevertheless make the love intelligible. This suggests that Hume's notion of a cause of love is meant to coincide with what I have been calling a "ground" of love.

Whether it can do so adequately, of course, is another question. For, as I have already mentioned, the idea of a ground of love, although it does seem causal, also seems subject to a normative standard. At least for some kinds of love, some grounds are better than others. And if the cause of love is merely anything that makes you take pleasure in the thought of a person, how can the idea of a cause of love be subject to a normative standard? The solution to this problem, I will argue, is the key to explaining why we take up the general point of view.

1.4 *Love and Moral Approval*

I can now explain why the problem about why we take up the general point of view can also be understood as a problem about why there is a normative standard for love. It is clear that Hume thinks that virtue and vice are intimately related to love and hate, but he is a little unsettled about what exactly the relationship is.[8] In Hume's official account of love in Book 2 of the *Treatise*, virtue is identified as *one of* the "much diversify'd" causes of love, alongside such non-moral psychological attributes as wit, good sense, and good humor; physical attributes such as beauty and athletic ability; and external goods such as money and good family (T 2.2.1,330). According to Hume, love for a person can be caused by any of these things: indeed, a whole section of the *Treatise* is devoted to explaining "Our Esteem for the Rich

---

[8] Hume treats love and hate as if they were opposites, and on a footing. I think this is wrong, for reasons that emerge most clearly in connection with the issue of "grounds." Although love sometimes has grounds, and grounds are like justifications in the sense that they make love intelligible, yet there is a sense in which love does not seem to need a justification. Of course we might try to dissuade someone from the love of an unworthy object. But consider how odd it would be to say: "You have no excuse for loving him!" Whereas it does not seem odd at all to say that someone has no excuse for hating someone. And some might think that when hate does have a justification, or even when it has (good?) grounds, that makes it something else instead—resentment or indignation, say. These ideas may even be thought to lend support to those religious and moral traditions which hold that love is or ought to be the default position, so to speak, in our attitude towards others, whereas hate requires some special reason. But I do not mean here to put forward any developed views; rather I mean to bring out the obscurity of the topic, and some reasons for doubting the symmetry of love and hate. For the purposes of this essay, however, I will not quarrel with Hume's treatment of love and hate as simple opposites.

and Powerful" (T 2.2.5,357–365). Given the account we looked at in 1.2, it is clear why a person's virtues will be one of the causes of our loving him. As Hume says:

Pride and humility, love and hatred are excited, when there is any thing presented to us, that both bears a relation to the object of the passion, and produces a separate sensation related to the sensation of the passion. Now virtue and vice are attended with these circumstances. They must necessarily be plac'd either in ourselves or others, and excite either pleasure or uneasiness; and therefore must give rise to one of these four passions . . . And this is, perhaps, the most considerable effect that virtue and vice have upon the human mind. (T 3.1.2,473)

According to this view, virtue is one of the causes of love, and vice is among the causes of hate.

Yet at other times, Hume suggests an even more intimate connection between love and virtue. In Book 3 of the *Treatise*, Hume says that "these two particulars are to be consider'd as equivalent, with regard to our mental qualities, *virtue* and the power of producing love or pride; *vice* and the power of producing humility or hatred" (T 3.3.1,575). A few pages later he characterizes moral terms as "the terms expressive of our liking or dislike" (T 3.3.1,582). These remarks suggest that virtue is not just one of the many causes of love, but—at least "with regard to our mental qualities"—*the* cause of love. That is to say, the mental qualities for which we love people are *therefore* virtues. Of course, this idea coheres well with another notorious doctrine of Book 3, Hume's contention that there is no important distinction between moral virtues and natural abilities (T 3.3.4,606–614). One of his arguments for that contention is precisely that natural abilities, like moral virtues, give rise to love. He says:

Tho' we refuse to natural abilities the title of virtues, we must allow, that they procure the love and esteem of mankind; . . . and that a man possess'd of them is much more intitled to our good-will and services, than one entirely void of them. (T 3.3.4,607)

That last remark—that those with the natural virtues are "intitled to our good-will"—suggests yet another view of the relation between virtue and love that we also find in Hume's writings: namely, that virtue is what we *ought* to love people for, or, to put it more naturally, what makes people *worthy* of love, whether or not we in fact love them for it. Virtue, in the terms of the last section, is an appropriate ground of love.[9] After his description of

---

[9] In the opening passages of *An Enquiry Concerning the Principles of Morals*, Hume characterizes the moral skeptic (someone who denies the reality of moral distinctions) as committed to the view that "all characters and actions [are] alike entitled to the affection and regard of everyone" (2E 1,169–170).

the two regulating devices that constitute the general point of view, Hume remarks:

> But however the general principle of our blame or praise may be corrected by those other principles, 'tis certain, they are not altogether efficacious, nor do our passions often correspond entirely to the present theory. 'Tis seldom men heartily love what lies at a distance from them, and what no way redounds to their particular benefit; as 'tis no less rare to meet with persons, who can pardon another any opposition he makes to their interest, however justifiable that opposition may be by the general rules of morality. Here we are contented to say that reason requires such an impartial conduct, but that 'tis seldom we can bring ourselves to it, and that our passions do not readily follow the determination of our judgment. (T 3.3.1,583)

A similar passage occurs after another, later, summary of the general point of view. Hume says:

> And tho' the heart does not always take part with those general notions, or regulate its love and hatred by them, yet are they sufficient for discourse, and serve all our purposes in company, in the pulpit, on the theatre, and in the schools. (T 3.3.3,603)

These passages suggest that judgments of virtue are not judgments about what we *do* love people for, but judgments about what we *ought* to love people for. At the same time, and interestingly, both passages express skepticism about the extent to which our love is actually inspired by virtue.

In the first of the two passages I just quoted Hume mentions "reason" as the source of these objective judgments of the loveable, but he quickly corrects that. The passage continues:

> This language will be easily understood, if we consider what we formerly said concerning that *reason*, which is able to oppose our passion; and which we have found to be nothing but a general calm determination of the passions, founded on some distant view or reflection. (T 3.3.1,583)

This is just a reminder that the judgments that determine what we ought to love people for are not properly speaking judgments of reason, but rather calm sentiments felt from a general point of view, namely, the moral sentiments.

This reminder brings us to a fourth and final view of the relation of love and virtue found in Hume's writings, which is that moral approval itself is a *species* of love, specifically a calm form of love. This view is most clearly stated in a passage in Book 3 of the *Treatise* in which Hume says that moral approval and disapproval themselves are "nothing but a fainter and more imperceptible love or hatred" (T 3.3.5,614). We can love people for any quality that we find pleasant; but one of the main sources of our pleasure is sympathy with the pleasures of others. So, for instance, I may love you because you are kind to animals, and my sympathy with them makes me partake of the pleasure you give them. This kind of love may be more disinterested than some cases of more personal love, as when I love you because of your generosity to me. But it does not yet have the universal character of moral approval, for in itself, sympathy varies with our relations to those with whom we sympathize. For instance, resemblance may make me sympathize more strongly with women or academics than do I with men or plumbers, and the sympathy-based love I feel for those who help and champion other women or fellow academics may be stronger than the sympathy-based love I (also) feel for those who help and champion men or plumbers. Moral approval is a regulated version of this sympathy-based love. By taking the person's narrow circle as those with whom we are to sympathize, and using general rules, we fix the loveable qualities as those that are normally pleasant and useful to a person's narrow circle. This regulation of our sympathy makes a further difference: for while ordinary loves, both direct and sympathy-based, are generally counted among the violent passions (T 2.1.1,276), moral approval is a *calm* species of love, because it is, as Hume says in the passage above, "founded on [a] distant view or reflection."

Thus we find four slightly different accounts of the relationship between virtue and love in Hume's texts: first, that *virtue is one of the causes of love*; second, *that any cause of love*—or at least any mental attribute that is a cause of love—*is (therefore) a virtue*; third, *that a virtue is a quality that makes its possessor worthy of love*, or a quality for which we ought to love him; and, finally, *that moral approval is itself a species of love*. Though different, these accounts can be made coherent, if we suppose that Hume's view is as follows: when we view a person from the general point of view, we feel a particularly calm species of love or hate, which is moral approval or disapproval. The qualities that arouse these calm passions are the ones we call "virtues" and "vices." But these are not merely particular forms of love and hate, on a footing with our more personal and unregulated passions. Moral approval and disapproval are corrective of, and normative for, our more violent personal loves and hates. So, to take a fairly uncontroversial example, the prisoner who hates the judge who has condemned him, on account of the pain which the judge and her justice has caused him, has *a wrong feeling*. When the judge is considered from the general point of view, her justice is seen as a pleasant thing and causes love; and this love is normative for, and ought to be corrective of, the prisoner's more personal feelings. This view seems to be at work in passages like this one:

And tho' such interests and pleasures touch us more faintly than our own, yet being more constant and universal, they counter-ballance the latter even in practice, and alone are admitted in speculation as the standard of virtue and morality. (T 3.3.1,591)

To this extent, the general point of view is the point of view from which we ought to assess people, and the loves and hates it generates should govern our other loves and hates. And so the question why we take up the general point of view might be put this way: why should there be a normative standard for love? And why should that standard be provided by the general point of view?

2. Hume's Account of Why We Take Up the General Point of View

2.1 *Hume's Account in the Text of the Treatise*

Hume does provide his own answer to the question why we take up the general point of view, and in this section I will examine it. It may be divided into three related points:

(1) First, as I mentioned above, our sympathetic responses vary with our position with respect to others, and this varies for an individual over time, and among individuals. Hume says that in order to avoid the *contradictions* to which this would give rise if sympathy remained unregulated, we "fix on" the general point of view (T 3.3.1,581).

(2) The second point picks up on an idea that Hume inherits from Francis Hutcheson. Following Locke, Hutcheson believed that any simple idea must come from an impression of sense. Our idea of the morally good is a simple, unanalyzable idea, and the impression that gives rise to it is the sentiment of approval. Our capacity for this sentiment is therefore a kind of sense.[10] Following Hutcheson, in turn, Hume also characterizes the capacity for approval as a "moral sense." With that in mind, Hume supports his first point by observing that it is our practice "with regard to all the senses" to correct our judgments from fixed standpoints in order to eliminate contradictions (T 3.3.1,582).

Hume makes a similar, and I think more pertinent, comparison with the way we make judgments of beauty. Since the moral sense is concerned with what pleases us in characters, the idea of an objective standard of moral goodness is like the idea that there is an objective standard of beauty. Hume constantly reminds us of this connection by using phrases like "beauty and

---

[10] See Francis Hutcheson, *An Inquiry Concerning Moral Good and Evil*, pp. 261–70; and *An Essay on the Nature and Conduct of the Passions and Affections*, pp. 301–2 in D. D. Raphael's *British Moralists 1650–1800*, Volume 2.

deformity" to describe characters and "moral taste" to describe approval and disapproval (e.g. T 2.1.8,300; T 3.3.1,581; 2E 1,173; 2E 6,242). And as he points out:

In like manner, external beauty is determin'd merely by pleasure; and 'tis evid-ent, a beautiful countenance cannot give so much pleasure, when seen at the distance of twenty paces, as when it is brought near to us. We say not, however, that it appears to us less beautiful: Because we know what effect it will have in such a position, and by that reflexion we correct its momentary appearance. (T 3.3.1,582)[11]

(3) Third, in his most explicit remarks about why we fix on the general point of view, Hume frequently mentions the need for us to talk to each other about, and to come to some agreement upon, persons and characters. Here are some examples:

'tis impossible we cou'd ever converse together on any reasonable terms, were each of us to consider characters and persons, only as they appear from his peculiar point of view. (T 3.3.1,581)

Such corrections are common with regard to all the senses; and indeed 'twere impossible we could ever make use of language, or communicate our sentiments to one another, did we not correct the momentary appearances of things, and overlook our present situation. (T 3.3.1,582)

'tis impossible men cou'd ever agree in their sentiments and judgments, unless they chose some common point of view, from which they might survey their object, and which might cause it to appear the same to all of them. (T 3.3.1,591)

Besides, that we ourselves often change our situation in this particular, we every day meet with persons, who are in a different situation from ourselves, and who cou'd never converse with us on any reasonable terms, were we to remain constantly in that situation and point of view, which is peculiar to us. The intercourse of sentiments, therefore, in society and conversation, makes us form some general inalterable standard, by which we may approve or disapprove of characters and manners. And tho' the heart does not always take part with those general notions, or regulate its love and hatred by them, yet are they sufficient for discourse, and serve all our purposes in company, in the pulpit, on the theatre, and in the schools. (T 3.3.3,603)

So Hume cites, as the reasons we need to take up the general point of view, the need to avoid the contradictory judgments of unregulated sympathy, the need to stabilize all sensory judgments, and the need to converse on some agreed terms.

---

[11] A scenario: someone sighting Marilyn Monroe a couple of blocks away says "Now there is a beauti-ful woman," and his interlocutor replies "You think so? She just looks like a blob on the horizon to me."

But there is something deeply puzzling about all of these explanations, as we can see by taking them one at a time. First, why should the fact that your sympathy-based love of people varies over time, or the fact that it differs from mine, be regarded as a *contradiction*? Suppose that I like rye bread and you like wheat bread: that is not a contradiction. Nor is it a contradiction if you liked sweets as a child but have little interest in them now. Love, as Hume understands it, is the result of the pleasure we take in a person, either directly or from sympathy, but we do not in all cases expect to take pleasure in the same things at all times or to take pleasure in the same things as other people.[12] Why do we need to come to an agreement about whose character is good, if that is only an agreement about whom we find pleasing?

Next consider the argument that we do this with every sense. Take as a comparison the way we make judgments about what colors things are. Hume might say that when we make such judgments, we take up a certain point of view: say, we choose regular daytime sunlight as the perspective from which we answer the question "what color is it?" This, as Hume's account suggests, does enable us to converse about colors. If I described a thing by its color in regular daylight and you described it by its color at dusk we might have an unnecessarily hard time communicating about something we have to talk about. Suppose I want you to locate an object using a description I give of it, and its color is to be part of this description: then we need to be able to converse and agree about colors. So we fix on regular daylight as the obvious choice.

One problem with comparing this sort of regulating device to the moral point of view is that fixing on daytime sunlight doesn't seem to be the uniquely possible choice for regulating color language. Couldn't we have a language, for instance, in which people named things by the colors they are at dusk?[13] Leave aside, for the moment, the question whether this would be just as good as our actual method. Surely it matters more for the purposes of conversation that there be *some* shared point of view than which one we use. But it would be unwelcome to say that the general point of view that regulates moral language is one of many we might have constructed for the purpose. After all, we take the judgments we make from the general point of view to be normative; it is supposed to be the point of view from which we ought to regulate our loves and hates. The point of view from which we judge colors is normative in a thin sense: if, looking at a blue object at dusk, you say "it's purple," the conventions of our language allow me to say "No, you are mistaken." But nothing very important follows. I've corrected you on the linguistic usage and

---

[12] But see section 3.1.

[13] Wittgenstein discusses the possibility of such alternative ways of fixing terms in *Philosophical Investigations*, section 64, p. 31e.

nothing more. And the linguistic usage could have been otherwise, for we could have chosen a different point of view.

One may be tempted to block this objection by pointing out that our selection of a point of view for judging colors is not arbitrary. Daytime sunlight is the light in which we do most of our looking, and, even more importantly, it is the light in which we see best. By this of course I do not mean that it is the light in which we see the colors as they really are, but rather that it is the light in which we are able to make the finest color discriminations. We might say that the trouble with using dusk as a point of view for judging color is not that blue things look purple, but that blue and purple things look more like each other, that they are harder to tell apart. So at least we can say that sunlight is the *best* point of view for regulating color language.

Could a consideration of this kind be used to account for our choice of a point of view for judging beauty or character? Hume does appeal to such a consideration in the aesthetic case. One of the attributes of the good critic, as described in "Of the Standard of Taste," is an unusually refined and delicate sensibility, an ability to notice small distinctions, and to separate out, by his senses, the different elements that go into the composition of a work. And in defending this point Hume invokes the comparison to the senses: "It is acknowledged to be the perfection of every sense or faculty, to perceive with exactness its most minute objects, and allow nothing to escape its notice and observation."[14] Hume does not make any direct argument of this kind in the moral case. But perhaps we might argue on Hume's behalf that a person's narrow circle has a more refined sense of what his character is like, of the different elements that go into its composition.

But there would still be a problem about the normativity of the judgments we make from the general point of view. The fact that a certain perspective leads to more refined discriminations is sufficient to give color judgments all the normativity they require. All we need is to establish some convention about the point of view we will use for making these judgments; and the fact that sunlight enables us to make the most discriminations seems sufficient reason to favor it.[15] But in this case *all* that we are determining is how it is best

---

[14] "On the Standard of Taste," in *David Hume: Essays Moral, Political, and Literary*, p. 236.

[15] It is open to question whether this is the sort of case Hume had in mind when he talked about making these corrections for all of the senses. In "The Common Point of View in Hume's Ethics," Rachel Cohon reads Hume as having in mind the use of a shared point of view to correct for the effects of distance, thus bringing the case of sensory judgments closer to the case of aesthetic judgments. The idea is that when we see something far away we avoid concluding that it is small by taking up a fixed point of view. The difficulty with reading Hume that way, however, is that the normative standard for judging size is based on simple correctness—judgments of relative size are factual—so that comparison is less appropriate to the moral case than the one I discuss in the text.

to *talk*. It is true that some of Hume's remarks about moral concepts suggest that he thinks that in that case too all we are trying to do is determine how we should talk. I quote once more, for example:

And tho' the heart does not always take part with those general notions, or regulate its love and hatred by them, yet are they sufficient for discourse, and serve all our purposes in company, in the pulpit, on the theatre, and in the schools. (T 3.3.3,603)

Yet in the moral and aesthetic cases, more seems to be at stake, at least if the normative claims involved are to be taken seriously. Presumably we are determining the direction in which we should cultivate our tastes, who is entitled to our love and services, and what we ourselves ought to try to be like.[16]

In any case this leads us to Hume's final argument, which is about our need for conversations. Whether he has more in mind or not, Hume certainly does insist that we need to fix a point of view for judging characters in order to talk. But now we may ask: what is it we need to talk about here? If we had to have conversations about who was possessed of moral virtue, and come to an agreement about that, then we would need to fix a point of view for judging virtue. But if there were no normative standard applying to judgments of the pleasingness of people, there would be no moral virtue to talk about. And in general, the fact that we are pleased by different things seems to give us no difficulty in discussing them. If I say, "he's a good person" and you use a different standard of goodness from mine, then there may be room for confusion. But if I say "I like him," and you say "I don't," no confusion will arise. And I will not say "he's a good person," unless a shared standard exists. So this consideration can hardly show us why a shared standard has to exist.

So we are left still facing the problem I described at the beginning of the essay. Moral approval is a calm form of love that we experience when we view a character from a general point of view. But why do we view a character from the general point of view in the first place? Hume says that it is to avoid contradictions and enable us to regulate our judgments and our language. But if we ask "judgments about what?" we do not get a satisfactory answer. The answer cannot be that our judgments about *virtue* are contradictory until we take up the general point of view, since we make no moral judgments at all until after we take up the general point of view. We simply love and hate, and make judgments about whether or not we like people. And it is not, so far,

[16] Actually, I think that Hume's account gives rise to a problem about the normativity of aesthetic judgment as well. On Hume's view, questions of taste are settled by critics, who are distinguished among other things by their refined sensibilities. But Hume does not make it clear why the rest of us, who lack refined sensibilities, should like or try to like the things that those who have such sensibilities do.

obvious why we should expect to concur in our loves and hates, or regard it as a contradiction if we do not.

2.2 *The Felt Distinctness of Moral Sentiment: A Defense of Hume's Account*

In this section I examine and reject a possible defense of Hume's account, not one that he gives, but one that I think might naturally occur to some readers.[17] Hume argues that moral pleasure is characterized by a distinct phenomenological feel, different from the other pleasures we get from thinking about people. He makes this clear when he first argues that moral judgments are based on sentiments. He imagines an objector arguing that, if virtue and vice are determined by pleasure and pain, even inanimate objects, being pleasant and painful, would have virtues and vices. To this he replies that "under the term *pleasure*, we comprehend sensations, which are very different from each other, and which have only such a distant resemblance, as is requisite to make them be express'd by the same abstract term" (T 3.1.2,472). Not only can we distinguish, by phenomenological feel, the pleasure of drinking wine from the pleasure of surveying a good character, but, Hume adds, "Nor is every sentiment of pleasure or pain, which arises from characters and actions, of that *peculiar* kind, which makes us praise or condemn" (T 3.1.2,472).

The point may be extended. In those passages, Hume attributes a peculiar phenomenological feel to the pleasure we experience when we contemplate a good person's character. In passages I have already quoted, Hume also attributes a peculiar phenomenological feel to the love that immediately arises from that pleasure.[18] Indeed, as we have already seen, he sometimes characterizes approval as "nothing but a fainter and more imperceptible love or hatred" (T 3.3.5,614) and he speaks of this love as "a calm determination of our passions, founded on some distant view or reflection" (T 3.3.1,583). Both moral pleasure and moral love are distinguished from other pleasures and other loves by what I will call a "felt distinctness."

---

[17] Readers who are discouraged by the length of this essay will be glad to know that those who are not tempted by the defense of Hume I criticize in this section may skip it without losing anything essential to the main argument.

[18] Hume's account involves two distinctively moral sentiments—a pleasure we take in the character of the person to whom the virtue is attributed, and a love that is grounded in that pleasure. There is a certain unclarity in the text about which of these two things Hume has in mind when he talks about "moral approval." I don't think it matters very much, but I think he is best read as equating moral approval with the love that arises from the pleasure, as suggested by his own remark that approval and disapproval are fainter and more imperceptible forms of love and hate (T 3.3.5,614). Approval takes a person as its object, which suggests that it is a form of love; pleasure as Hume understands it has only a cause, not an object.

Two points about this felt distinctness are important here. First, Hume says that we experience it "only when a character is considered in general, without reference to our particular interest" (T 3.1.2,472). Second, despite the felt distinctness of moral sentiments, Hume observes that it is possible to confuse moral feelings with personal feelings. He says:

It seldom happens, that we do not think an enemy vicious, and can distinguish betwixt his opposition to our interest and real villainy or baseness. But this hinders not, but that the sentiments are, in themselves, distinct; and a man of temper and judgment may preserve himself from these illusions. (T 3.1.2,472)

That said, one may attempt to block my objection to Hume's account this way: moral feelings are characterized by a felt distinctness, a distinct phenomenological quality. "Virtue" is our name for whatever causes these particular feelings, the special feelings of pleasure and love that constitute approval. It is because we experience these *particular* feelings that we have something to talk about, namely virtue. We give the name "virtue" to whatever causes these particular feelings, just as we give the name "blue" to whatever causes certain visual sensations. And then we take up the general point of view to get rid of contradictions in our judgments about virtue just as we carry objects into the sunlight when we find ourselves disagreeing about which things are blue.

There are several objections to this solution. First, even if the feeling for virtue is distinct, it is not obvious why this should dictate that we try to arrive at an agreement about it. We have to arrive at agreements about colors because descriptions play a role in our practices—I ask you to bring me my blue sweater, for instance. The parallel in the case of judgments of value seems to be the practice of making recommendations. I might ask you to bring me a bottle of good champagne. But the practice of recommendation requires less agreement than the practice of description, and in cases where agreement cannot be found we can give up, or qualify the practice of recommendation. If this were not so, no one would ever suspect that there is such a thing as a "matter of taste."

Second, Hume says we experience this particular feeling "only when a character is considered in general, without reference to our particular interest" (T 3.1.2,472). If this means that we experience this feeling only when we view a character from the general point of view, it is obvious that our capacity for this feeling cannot explain *why* we adopt the general point of view. Unless there were some independent reason for taking up the general point of view, we might never have discovered our capacity for this particular feeling.

Someone may reply that perhaps saying that we experience this special feeling *only* when we take up the general point of view is overstating the case.

Hume's theory involves three sorts of love: personal love, sympathy-based love, and moral approval, which is sympathy-based love regulated by the general point of view. In the remark just quoted, Hume contrasts "considering a character in general" with viewing the person through the eyes of our own personal interest. Perhaps he thinks that not only moral approval, but *every* case of *sympathy-based* love results from considering a character in general, since sympathy-based love is a disinterested response to a person's characteristics. The pleasure that produces sympathy-based love therefore has the same felt distinctness as moral pleasure. Because of this special pleasure, we experience sympathy-based love as something different from ordinary love, but indistinctly: so we take up the general point of view in order to get the cause of sympathy-based love, namely character "considered in general," more clearly into view.

I think this is probably what Hume had in mind. But there are several problems with the suggestion, some of which are hard for me to describe without getting ahead of myself in my argument. The proposed solution depends on the idea that sympathy-based love is unlike personal love but like full-fledged moral approval in that it occurs when we consider a character in general. This, to my mind, involves both an overly moralized conception of sympathy-based love and an inadequately moralized conception of personal love. Sympathy-based love as we experience it before taking up the general point of view is a response to a person's characteristics, but it is not, like moral approval, a calm and disinterested response. This is not because it is inspired by thoughts about the lover's personal interests, but because it is affected by his personal resemblance and contiguity to the person with whom he sympathizes. Sympathy-based love can be as violent and as partisan as personal love. On the other side, it is a misconception of personal love to suppose it is a response to our own interests *rather than* to a person's character. Even in its personal form, love is a response to what someone is like, not just to his effects on oneself. As I will argue in section 3, personal love, however violent and partisan, must to some extent be a response to a person's character, or it is not love at all, but merely the valuing of a useful object. All of this being so, there is no good reason to believe that the sort of pleasure that causes sympathy-based love will be notably distinct from the sort of pleasure that causes personal love. And even if it were, the other point still stands: we have no more reason for expecting to agree about our sympathy-based loves than we have for expecting to agree about our personal loves. I will fill these ideas out in section 3.

In any case, there is an important objection to taking this line of defense. As we have seen, Hume's view is that certain basic passions and feelings are "original" in human nature, meaning that a phenomenologically distinct feeling is originally connected to a certain kind of cause or object.[19] But we do not have to posit a different *original* capacity for every passion and sentiment to which language gives a name, for some of them are modifications of others. One cause of this modification is *blending*, which results when one object gives rise to two passions. Respect, for instance, is not an original passion aroused in the face of respectable qualities, but rather a special form of love that results when the pleasing qualities in a person that cause the love also at the same time cause humility or fear in the lover (T 2.2.10,390). Again, Hume supposes that the special quality of erotic love results from the mixture of love with sexual appetite (T 2.2.11,394–396). Other causes of difference in our feelings lie in the circumstances which give rise to them. The violence of a passion is part of its felt character, and Hume acknowledges this to be influenced by the circumstances: whether the object of the passion is present and perceived, or absent and merely thought about, for instance. Dread, we might speculate, is not an original passion in human nature, but rather can be explained as fear muted by distance. Thus, Hume's view is that a small set of basic passions is modified into a larger set of different feelings by various forces.

This means that we may distinguish two possible views about the felt distinctness of the moral sentiments. One is that we are originally equipped to experience a sentiment with exactly this qualitative feel, a particular moral sentiment, originally connected to the view of a person's character that we get when we consider it "in general." The other is that the felt distinctness that characterizes the moral sentiments is caused by, or is a by-product of, the very fact that these sentiments are experienced when we consider a character in general.

This second possibility seems obviously to be the correct account of moral approval, since Hume says that moral approval is a species of love. The special phenomenological feel—the distinctive calmness—of this love *derives from* the fact that one loves from a disinterested and artificial, or at least rather abstract, point of view. Hume argues that we mistake both moral approval and prudential desire ("the general appetite for good, and aversion to evil, consider'd merely as such") for the operations of reason precisely because of the calmness of these passions (T 2.3.3,417). It seems natural to suppose that the calmness of these passions is *produced* by the fact that the object of prudence (one's own long-term good) and the cause of approval (a person's character) are abstract or conceptual objects. Neither of these objects is directly perceived: rather, they are inferred or constructed from long-term patterns of event and action. And presumably the same explanation should

---

[19] See for example the account of how pride is originally connected to the idea of self at T 2.1.5,287.

show that the sympathetic pleasure that causes moral approval gets its distinct character from the fact that it is caused by an abstract object that we must use reasoning even to conceive.[20] It is not surprising that these abstract objects produce only calm sentiments in us, especially when compared to the more palpable benefits that inspire today's pressing desire or make us welcome an enemy's cowardice.

There is also an important methodological reason for favoring the view that the felt distinctness of the moral sentiments derives from the fact that they are experienced when we take up the general point of view, rather than being the result of an original endowment of our nature. Hutcheson believed that moral approval is a sentiment whose felt distinctness is original; God simply implanted that particular sentiment in us as a response to benevolence. According to Hutcheson, morality springs from the fact that we experience the sentiment of moral approval; it is the capacity for this sentiment that makes us moral animals. But the fact that we experience moral approval does not admit of any naturalistic explanation; God simply installed the capacity for this particular sentiment in us. So if we ask Hutcheson why we are moral animals, his answer must ultimately be that God made us so. Hume's ambition, consonant with his anti-religious aims, is to give a naturalistic explanation of how moral feeling arises in us. We do not need a divine origin for moral approval if it can be explained in terms of the principles of natural psychology alone. If moral approval can be explained as a modification of love, produced by the fact that we take up the general point of view, then it can be explained naturalistically—provided, of course, that we can find a naturalistic explanation of why we take up the general point of view. In that case Hume's answer to the question why we are moral animals will appeal to natural features of our psychological make-up, not to divine provisions. But this naturalistic aim can be achieved only if the special characters of moral pleasure and moral love are the result of the fact that moral pleasure and moral love are modifications of natural forms of pleasure and love, modifications that are *produced* by the operations of sympathy and generality. If we must say that moral feeling is original, an implanted response to moral character as such, then Hume's attempt to give a completely naturalistic account of morality will have failed after all.

We can find support for the idea that the felt distinctness of moral sentiment is a product of the circumstances that give rise to it in the section on the natural abilities. There, Hume denies that there is just one moral sentiment.

---

[20] Hume himself stresses that the role of reason in moral judgment is to "pave the way" for approval or disapproval by giving "a proper discernment of its object," at 2E 1,173.

He imagines an opponent arguing that the feeling of approval aroused by the natural abilities is phenomenologically distinct from that aroused by the moral virtues. True, he says, but neither is there really exactly one phenomenologically distinct sentiment for all of the moral virtues:

Each of the virtues, even benevolence, justice, gratitude, integrity, excites a different sentiment or feeling in the spectator. The characters of *Cæsar* and *Cato*, as drawn by *Sallust*, are both of them virtuous, in the strictest sense of the word; but in a different way: Nor are the sentiments entirely the same, which arise from them. The one produces love; the other esteem: The one is amiable; the other awful: We cou'd wish to meet with the one character in a friend; the other character we wou'd be ambitious of in ourselves. (T 3.3.4,607–608)

There is a range of moral feelings, for the different virtues, in exactly the same way there is a range of different species of natural love. Clearly they are not all original, for if they were, then Hume would have failed in another way in his project of naturalizing Hutcheson's theory. For Hume also makes it clear that he wants to deny Hutcheson's thesis that there is only one virtue, benevolence, and that he wants to do it without bringing in a new explanation (that is, new original moral sentiments) for each new virtue. As he says:

It may now be ask'd in general, concerning this pain or pleasure, that distinguishes moral good and evil, *From what principles is it derived, and whence does it arise in the human mind?* To this I reply, first, that 'tis absurd to imagine, that in every particular instance, these sentiments are produc'd by an original quality and primary constitution. For as the number of our duties is, in a manner, infinite, 'tis impossible that our original instincts should extend to each of them . . . (T 3.1.2,473)

To explain the multiplicity of virtues naturalistically, Hume must argue that whatever is phenomenologically distinct about the different moral feelings derives from differences in their objects and circumstances. In the same way, to fulfill his naturalistic aim of explaining why we have moral sentiments in general, Hume needs to argue that *everything* that is phenomenologically distinct about moral feelings, everything that distinguishes moral approval from ordinary love, can be derived from the special circumstances in which it is felt.

In general, I think this throws doubt on the helpfulness of Hume's comparison of virtue to a secondary quality. Although color is (in a sense) produced by the perspective of creatures with a certain kind of vision, the differences between colors are not so produced, or not entirely so. They are based on something in the object. But if I am right, this is not true in the case of moral judgment. The felt differences between personal love, sympathy-based love, and moral approval (i.e. sympathy-based love regulated by the general point of view) result entirely from the perspective from which we view a person, not from anything in the person himself. If we take it that the distinctive calmness of moral approval is the result of the fact that the sentiment is produced from the general point of view, rather than from the special character of its object, then we must say that the general point of view *gives rise* to the distinction between ordinary love for a person and moral approval of him. And, accordingly, it gives rise to the difference in the "objects" of these two sentiments. Moral character would not exist if the general point of view did not. Since moral approval is a species of love, its object is simply a person. Blue is, or is based on, a special object of vision—certain surface properties of objects in the world. But virtue is not a special object of love. It is the object of a special love.

And so we are brought back once more to the original problem. If the idea of virtue arises from the general point of view, Hume must identify something that pressures us to occupy the general point of view. And that something cannot appeal, explicitly or implicitly, to the idea of virtue: that is, to the idea that there must be a normative standard for love. But Hume's own account of why we take up the general point of view seems implicitly to do this. There is no contradiction between my loving and your not loving the same person—unless we suppose that our loves ought to correspond. The fact that our loves are sometimes sympathy-based rather than based on our personal interests provides no special reason for us to expect them to correspond, for by Hume's own admission sympathy is in itself as variable as interest. So why should we suppose that our loves ought to correspond, unless we are already supposing that there is some normative standard governing our loves—a standard of virtue? There is no sense in saying that we take up the moral point of view in order to get its object more clearly into view, if that object has no existence prior to the adoption of the moral point of view. As for the needs of conversation, what exactly is it that we need to talk about, if it is not the person's virtues? The world has moral properties only when we view it from the general point of view. We do not, therefore, originally take up the general point of view in order to focus on, clarify, or come to an agreement about moral properties. Why then do we take it up?

3. A Proposed Solution

3.1 *Why We Need a Shared Point of View*

In this part of the essay I propose an answer to the question why we take up the general point of view, and why we take the judgments we make from the general point of view to be normative. This answer is not given in Hume's texts—his answer is the one I examined and found wanting above—but it is given in the terms of his theory, and I believe makes better sense of that theory than the one he explicitly gives.[21] The answer comes in three parts. In this section, I explain why we need *a* shared point of view for judging character, that is, why we need to come to some sort of agreement about what makes a character loveable.[22] In the next three sections, I will show how we are led to take up *the* general point of view, the point of view that consists of sympathizing with the person's narrow circle and judging according to general rules. In the penultimate section, I will turn to the question why judgments made from the general point of view are normative for love.

As we have seen, we need to identify some pressure to take up the general point of view that does not depend on the prior idea that there is such a thing as moral virtue, or, to put the same point another way, that does not depend on assuming in advance that there must be a normative standard for love. I believe that the pressure to take up *a* shared point of view can be explained on the basis of Hume's theory of sympathy. Hume sees sympathy as a mechanism whereby human beings (and other animals) tend to "catch" one another's sentiments. He models his account of the sympathy mechanism on his account of the mechanism that produces causal inference, so I will begin by reviewing that account here.

According to Hume, when two ideas are associated with each other, the mind moves naturally from one to the other. Such associations are produced by resemblance, contiguity in space and time, and causality, which in turn depends on custom or habit (T 1.1.4,11; T 1.3.7,97). If in your experience smoke has always been accompanied by fire, your mind will move naturally from the *idea* of smoke to the *idea* of fire. Now in Hume's theory sense impressions, beliefs, and mere ideas differ simply in the degree of their force and vivacity. Suppose you have a *sense impression* rather than a mere idea of smoke—you

---

[21] This is primarily an interpretive essay, but the interpretation I give is a constructive one. The view I assign to Hume is not his own expressed view. Neither is it my own view, since I do not accept Hume's account of moral judgment. It is, rather, a reconstruction that aspires to use the resources of Hume's own philosophy to answer questions I believe he deals with unsuccessfully in the text of the *Treatise*. Audiences who heard an earlier version of this essay sometimes expressed puzzlement about my own stance and the methodology it involves. Why reconstruct a view so that it makes better sense, if you cannot thereby make it into something you think correct? The answer is twofold. First, I am interested in seeing to what extent Hume's theory may be successfully reconstructed in its own terms, and in particular how much ethical work can be done from the essentially third-personal stance he assumes. See notes 30 and 32 for more on this point. Second, I think that there is something right about several aspects of Hume's theory as I construct it here, in particular about the complex relation between loving someone and thinking him good or virtuous which, as I will explain in section 3.5, I take it to imply.

[22] I'm using the phrase "shared point of view" to describe the species of which "the general point of view" is a member.

see or smell smoke, for instance. In this case, some of the force and vivacity that distinguishes your sense impression of smoke from a mere idea of smoke is transmitted by the associative connection, and imparted to the associated idea of fire (T 1.3.8,98–106). So you not only think of fire, but also have a lively and vivacious idea of it, which according to Hume amounts to believing that (somewhere in the vicinity of the smoke) there is fire. This is why when we see smoke we always believe that there is fire, and come to think there is a causal connection between them.

Sympathy in a similar way depends on the transmission of force and vivacity by associative connections. When I am exposed to your sentiments, whether by your words, your expressions, or whatever, I first form an idea of them. But you and I, or any two human beings, bear the important associative relation of resemblance—in particular, we are susceptible to the same basic range of sentiments (T 2.1.11,318). Hume also supposes that "the idea, or rather impression of ourselves is always intimately present with us, and that our own consciousness gives us so lively a conception of our own person, that 'tis not possible to imagine, that any thing can in this particular go beyond it" (T 2.1.11,317). Although the details of the process are a little obscure, Hume thinks that this liveliness is transmitted by resemblance to my ideas of the passions and sentiments of others. To have an enlivened idea of a passion amounts to having a faint version of that passion itself. So by this mechanism, I come to feel your cheerfulness, your sorrow, your resentment, and your love.[23] Furthermore, since according to Hume beliefs and judgments themselves are a species of sentiment, sympathy also causes us to "catch" one another's opinions and views.

As we have already seen, Hume emphasizes one role which sympathy plays in the formation of moral judgments. If someone hurts you, I experience your pain sympathetically, and this causes me to hate the person who hurt you. This kind of sympathy-based hate, when regulated by the general point of view, is moral disapproval itself. But sympathy plays another role in the formation of moral judgments, which Hume fails to emphasize. It follows from Hume's theory that any perceived difference in people's sentiments about an object will cause commotion and a sense of contradiction within the soul. As Hume himself explains:

Proud men are most shock'd with contempt, tho' they do not most readily assent to it; but 'tis because of the opposition betwixt the passion, which is natural to them, and that

---

[23] I can also feel these sentiments sympathetically when you don't feel them or when I have no direct evidence that you feel them but when I suppose they would be appropriate given your circumstances. The important thing is that the idea of your having the sentiment should arise in my mind as a result of my observing or thinking about you and your circumstances.

receiv'd by sympathy. A violent lover in like manner is very much displeas'd when you blame and condemn his love; tho 'tis evident your opposition can have no influence, *but by the hold it takes of himself, and by his sympathy with you.* (T 2.1.11,324; my emphasis)

When exposed to the vivid presentation of sentiments contrary to your own, you "catch" these sentiments, which then come into conflict with yours. Now we have something more like a contradiction, for now the two sentiments are both active *in you.* This, Hume thinks, and with some plausibility, explains the peculiar irritability that is produced in us when people express sentiments contrary to our own on matters about which we feel strongly. Just hearing someone say something you disagree with can set you amassing and rehearsing the arguments against it, even in the privacy of your own mind. Why should that be, unless the very expression of the unwanted opinion somehow pressures us towards entertaining and accepting it?[24]

If Hume is right, there is pressure on those who must endure one other's company to agree about *everything.* When you really like something, a movie, a popular book, a food—even things thought to be "matters of taste"—you urge your friends to try it. If they don't like it, this sets up a tension. Suppose that some exotic new flavor of ice cream is invented, and you think it is delicious. You bring a friend to the ice-cream parlor to try it, and she thinks it is revolting. This would be, for most people, slightly embarrassing, and that for both parties. Any difference of sentiment, however trivial, sets up a conflict or a tiny movement of estrangement that human beings find it difficult to endure. So on Hume's account the problem is not really to see why the loveable is not just a matter of taste like the flavors of ice cream. The problem is to see how we can possibly treat even the flavors of ice cream as a mere matter of taste.

In exactly this way, the force of sympathy pressures us to come to an agreement about the lovableness of people. So the second role sympathy plays

---

[24] While I think that the phenomenon Hume describes is real, I think that there would only be a contradiction, in the strict sense, if the same agent endorsed the two sentiments; and only a threat of contradiction if the same agent was tempted to do so. Hume conceives of belief in terms of the vividness, or force and vivacity, of an idea, not in terms of its active endorsement; to that extent, his account of belief renders it peculiarly passive. This may be because he takes as his paradigm sensory beliefs, which do seem to arise automatically in us. As we say, we cannot help but believe what is before our very eyes. Many philosophers think that logical arguments also operate on us by producing irresistibly vivid conclusions in the face of which we are passive, although I myself am inclined to doubt that: I think that in the case of an argument, the mental activity of arriving at the belief, working through the argument and putting the ideas together, is what constitutes the act of endorsement. Yet I think that Hume is right that the vivid expression of another's views sets up in us something like a pressure or temptation to endorse them; this is why our natural response is to fend them off by rehearsing the reasons and arguments against them. I discuss a related phenomenon, resulting from the publicity of language and the resulting capacity of people's words to make us entertain their thoughts, in SN 4.2.2–4.2.9, pp. 136–42.

in the production of moral judgment is that it is the source of the pressure to take up a shared point of view. Given the way sympathy works, it doesn't matter that my loving and your hating the same person is not logically speaking a contradiction or a disagreement. If I love where you hate, and we talk about it, I will receive your hate from the contagion of sympathy, and my both loving and hating, all at once, sets up an opposition within *my* soul. Furthermore, love is a pleasant sensation, naturally inclining me to benevolence towards its object; hate is a painful one, naturally inclining me to anger. So my ambivalent attitude will be accompanied by contrary motivations, and together these sentiments will cause a commotion within me that must be quieted. And of course the same is going to happen to you. There will be pressure on us, therefore, if we talk to each other about people, to come to share the same sentiments about them.

3.2 *How We Come to Take Up the General Point of View: A Preliminary Account*

It would be characteristic of Hume to suppose that we learn to take up the general point of view gradually and as the result of natural processes, rather than deliberately and all at once. I think he has something like this in mind: if sympathy pressures us to agree about people, it will also pressure us to move towards a shared standard which will make it possible for us to agree. Uncomfortable with our differences, I will try to see the person through your eyes and you will try to see him through mine. Enough of the resulting adjustments will lead to the formation of the general point of view. I express antipathy for the enemy general who has captured me, perhaps castigating him as ferocious. The soldier guarding me, finding this grating, reminds me of the inspiration and other benefits he and his fellow soldiers gather from the very attribute I have just criticized. Sympathy with members of the general's narrow circle presses me in the direction of admiring the attribute in question and so of admitting "courage" as a virtue, regardless of its effect on my own interests. Since it is the members of his narrow circle who are most likely to have sentiments about what a person does, it is from their point of view that such pressures and the attendant adjustments will most often be generated. Within the narrow circle, general rules will then produce pressures and adjustments of another sort. Today my father's prudence thwarts my desire, but how often have I been its beneficiary! Adjustments of these kinds become habitual whenever two people whose interests are at odds talk about some third person, or whenever I think about someone who affects me in different ways at different times.

And so we acquire the habit of looking at people from the general point of view.[25]

The story is not implausible, but it is incomplete. Why is my response in these cases a *personal* one—in Strawson's terms, a reactive attitude, in Hume's own terms, an indirect passion—at all?[26] Why do I respond to the person as such, rather than merely liking or disliking his action? Why not hate the sin but leave the sinner alone? And why does my reaction to the person focus on his *dispositions*, his ferocity or courage or prudence? In order to get a satisfactory account of this aspect of Hume's view, we must turn once again to Hume's theory of love.

3.3 *Character and the Object of Love*

Recall that according to Hume, the object of love, hate, pride, or humility, is a person. This is an original feature of these passions. Early in the section on pride and humility Hume tells us that:

'Tis evident, that pride and humility, tho' directly contrary, have yet the same OBJECT. This object is self, or that succession of related ideas and impressions, of which we have an intimate memory and consciousness. (T 2.1.2,277)

And the "other" that is the object of love or hate is another such self, or, as Hume says:

As the immediate object of pride and humility is self or that identical person, of whose thoughts, actions, and sensations we are intimately conscious; so the object of love and hatred is some other person, of whose thoughts, actions, and sensations we are not conscious. (T 2.1.1,329)

The self referred to here seems to be the bundle-of-successive-perceptions ("succession of related ideas and impressions") that Hume discusses in his famous section on personal identity (T 1.4.6,251–263). Yet in that discussion, Hume distinguishes between "personal identity, as it regards our thought or imagination, and as it regards our passions or the concern we take in ourselves" (T 1.4.6,253). This seems to suggest that the notion of the person as the object of pride or love is not the same as the notion of the person as a bundle of successive perceptions. And indeed we might wonder how another person can

---

[25] Charlotte Brown has pointed out to me that the account here coheres with the footnote at 2E 9,274–275, where Hume claims that "an untaught savage" judges people solely in terms of his own interest, while a civilized person has learned to judge in accordance with "enlarged reflections" and "general rules."

[26] See P. F. Strawson, "Freedom and Resentment," in *Freedom and Resentment and Other Essays*, pp. 1–25.

be the object of love, if the personhood of the other person is something of which we are essentially "not conscious" (T 2.2.1,329, quoted above). How do I attach the causes of my love (actions, beauty, money) to their objects (other selves) if those objects are inaccessible bundles of perceptions?

Hume suggests an answer in a passage in which he discusses the conditions under which we love or hate someone for his actions. He starts by asserting that we love and hate others for those qualities that are "constant and inherent in his person and character" (T 2.2.3,348). He continues:

But if the uneasiness proceed not from a quality, but from an action, which is produc'd and annihilated in a moment, 'tis necessary, in order to produce some relation, and connect this action sufficiently with the person, that it be deriv'd from a particular forethought and design. 'Tis not enough, that the action arises from the person, and have him for its immediate cause and author. This relation alone is too feeble and inconstant to be a foundation for these passions [love and hate]. It reaches not the sensible and thinking part, and neither proceeds from any thing *durable* in him, nor leaves anything behind it; but passes in a moment, as if it had never been. On the other hand, an intention shews certain qualities, which remaining after the action is perform'd, connect it with the person, and facilitate the transition of ideas from one to the other. (T 2.2.3,349)

That passage is the predecessor and exact parallel to another that occurs in the section on the liberty of the will. Here Hume is concerned to explain why the doctrine of necessity is essential for holding people responsible. We can hold people responsible for their actions only if we regard the people themselves as the causes of their actions; and we can do that only if we regard their actions as caused by their characters. Hume says:

Actions are by their very nature temporary and perishing; and where they proceed not from some cause in the characters and disposition of the person, who perform'd them, they infix not themselves upon him, and can neither redound to his honour, if good, nor infamy, if evil. The action itself may be blameable; it may be contrary to all the rules of morality and religion: But the person is not responsible for it; and as it proceeded from nothing in him, that is durable or constant, and leaves nothing of that nature behind it, 'tis impossible he can, upon its account, become the object of punishment or vengeance. (T 2.3.2,411)

Indeed, since as we have seen moral approval and disapproval are just calm and impersonal forms of love and hate, these two passages say exactly the same thing: we can love or hate a person for an action only if we can see it as proceeding from his character.

The problem Hume is addressing here is a familiar one. The idea essential to holding a person responsible for an action or loving him for it is that *he* should be its cause. But why should we regard him as the cause in any special way if he is just one of the places through which the causal chain leading to this action or event has passed? If I push you from behind, as a result of having been pushed from behind myself, you will cease to blame me as soon as you understand that that's what happened. But if I push you from behind, as a result of having been angered by the things I overheard you say, you will blame me. In each case, the causal chain passes through me, so what is the difference? Hume is perfectly well aware of this familiar puzzle, since he himself deploys it elsewhere to slyly suggest that God must be responsible for all of our wrongdoing (1E 8,99–103). Here, however, Hume seems to suppose that you may be regarded as *the* cause of your action, provided that the causal chain goes through your character. He seems here to gesture towards a conception of what we might now call agent-causation, and it is worth noting the comparison with Kant, who also thinks we must be the causes of our actions and their consequences in order to be held responsible for them. For Kant, agent-causation is achieved when the person is the first cause, the initiator of the causal chain. For Hume, agent-causation seems to be achieved when the person's character serves as a kind of filter in the causal chain, making the outcome turn out one way rather than another.

The lesson we should draw from these remarks is not that actions are a special case—that unlike the other grounds of love they cannot function as grounds unless we can trace them to a person's character. Rather, the important point here turns on the fact that nothing counts as an *action*, that is, as the sort of movement that can be the ground of love or praise, *unless* a person is its cause.[27] And if the person is the cause of the movement/action only if the movement/action can be traced to his character, then the person is, essentially, his character. Or at least we may regard someone as the author of actions and so as a person only insofar as we regard him as having a character.[28]

---

[27] Strictly speaking, it is not correct to say that the person is the cause of an action, since nothing not caused by a person (or an animal, by some sort of agent) could be an action. We should rather say that the person is the cause of an intentional movement, or something of that sort. In the passage from T 2.3.2,411 quoted in the text, Hume appears to lose track of this fact, and to entertain the idea of an agentless action. It is possible, however, to read the passage as employing that idea only as a *reductio*.

[28] The concept in terms of which we understand what it means to view a person as a person—call it the "personhood concept"—has a complex structure. On the one hand, it must identify something universal—something that all persons have in common. On the other hand, precisely because the person is the object of the indirect passions or reactive attitudes, it must be something that differentiates us from one another, in important, non-incidental ways. Love and hate, in particular, are supposed to be attitudes we have to particular individuals, and yet which are supposed to attach to their personhood rather than something more incidental about them. So the personhood concept must be something that, although universal, admits of non-accidental individuating features if we are to make sense of these ideas and feelings. Apart from textual considerations, the notion of character, since it is a

This provides Hume's answer to the questions I raised at the end of the last section: it explains why our response to an action must also be a response to the person, and also why the response to the person must be a response to his dispositions.

I don't mean to suggest that Hume mischaracterizes his own theory when he says that the object of love or pride is a "succession of related ideas and impressions" (T 2.1.1,277, quoted above), or a bundle of "thoughts, actions, and sensations" (T 2.2.1,329, quoted above). That is, I am not claiming that the character *rather than* the conscious self is the object of love or pride. Instead, I mean to spell out the implication of Hume's own assertion that an action "reaches not the sensible and thinking part" part of a person unless we can trace it to his character. The implication is that the person's character is the outward appearance or manifestation of his sensible or thinking part. In fact, this interpretation suggests a way Hume might deal with another problem in his account to which he does not pay sufficient attention. Even in the case of the ideas and impressions which succeed one another in *my own* mind, and of which I am introspectively aware, I need some way to distinguish those which are merely caused by the associative process from those which are thoughts that I actively think—ideas of which I am the active cause, the thinker, the author. It is to these that we must trace actions if we are to hold a person responsible for them, and find in them grounds for love or pride. On a Humean account of mental activity which mirrors his account of outward actions, the thoughts I think, as opposed to the ones I merely undergo, will be attributable to me only insofar as they can be identified as the products of my intellectual "character," the regular patterns in the way my own mind works. So the proposal I am making here is meant to bridge Hume's two notions of personal identity, at least if we suppose that by "personal identity . . . as it regards our passions or the concern we take in ourselves" (T 1.4.6,253), Hume means character. The conscious self that is the author of a person's own thoughts and actions and so would seem to be the proper object of pride or love cannot be identified, even by the person herself, independently of her character. To think of someone as a person we must think of her as having a character.[29]

<hr/>

universal feature of human beings but also differentiates us in essential ways, seems promising for the purpose. On this conception, character is what enables us to identify someone as a person in general, and his particular character is a manifestation of the inner thoughts and actions that make him *him*. You regard him as responsible when his actions proceed from his character; you regard him as loveable when he has a loveable character, and so on.

[29] There are some difficulties with this argument, which I cannot explain until the next section. See note 32.

To love someone, then, we must see her as a person. And to see her as a person is to see her as the cause of her thoughts and actions, and, more generally—as I will argue in the next section—as the cause of happiness and misery to herself and others. To regard someone as the cause of certain effects, as opposed to regarding her as a place through which the causal chain leading to those effects happens to run, we must regard her as having a character. Since the object of love or of moral approval is a person, and to see someone as a person is to see her as having a character, love and moral approval focus our attention on the person's character. With this idea in hand, we can explain both why we must assess people from the general point of view, and why the general point of view provides us with a normative standard for love.

3.4 *Character and the General Point of View*

As we have just seen, Hume supposes that we cannot view a person as the cause of her actions unless we view her as having a character. I have not yet said, however, exactly why Hume thinks this is so. The answer to this question is the key to the importance of the general point of view.

I have already described Hume's theory of causal inference. As the description makes clear, and as is well known, Hume thinks that we cannot make a causal inference without regular observation of the connection between two kinds of events. It is only if smoke is *regularly* accompanied by fire that the customary association between these two ideas is set up, which eventually enables us to make the judgment that smoke and fire are causally connected. Furthermore, Hume argues that the necessary connection between these two events does not exist, or rather is not known to exist, "out there" in the world. Instead, causal connection consists simply in this: that when you perceive smoke, you always believe there is fire. Causal connection exists in the eye of the beholder.

Now this means that no one can form an idea of you as a cause—that is, as having certain characteristic dispositions—without *regular* observation of what you do. Your character is a form of causality, but causality is in the eye of the beholder. You are a cause when others infer your future conduct from your past conduct. But only certain people observe you with sufficient regularity to see you as the cause of anything. These people are *the members of your narrow circle*. Therefore your character is something that *exists* in the eyes of your narrow circle. It is something that is constructed from their point of view. This means that to see you as having a character is *essentially* to take up the point of view of your narrow circle towards you.[30]

---

[30] Elsewhere I have argued that according to Kant and Plato, persons are self-constituting, and in particular, that we constitute ourselves as agents by acting in accordance with justice, in Plato's

To support this, I want to draw your attention to something strange Hume says in both of the texts I quoted earlier, in which Hume argues that we cannot connect an action to a person unless it springs from his character. In the passage about love, Hume complains that an uncharacteristic action, "neither proceeds from anything durable in him, *nor leaves any thing behind it*" (T 2.2.3,349; my emphasis). In the passage about necessity, Hume says that an uncharacteristic action "proceeded from nothing in him that is durable or constant, and *leaves nothing of that nature behind it*" (T 2.3.2,411; my emphasis). He also says the action fails to *infix* itself upon the person. Now what does Hume mean by saying that an action "leaves something behind it"? The answer is that if it is a characteristic action it forms part of the pattern of constant conjunction that will eventually lead the members of your narrow circle to expect certain sorts of actions from you. What it leaves behind is a sort of trace in the minds of your narrow circle, a contribution to their tendency to make certain inferences about you. Hume confirms this at the end of the passage on love when he says:

On the other hand, an intention shows certain qualities, which remaining after the action is perform'd, connect it with the person, *and facilitate the transition of ideas from one to another.* (T 2.2.3,349; my emphasis)

In that sense, the action leaves behind a trace that forms a part of your character.

This conclusion may be reinforced, I think, by some reflections about the general nature of the virtues as Hume sees them. Consider this list of Humean virtues: justice, benevolence, courage, prudence, magnanimity, cheerfulness. Of what genus are these species? Certainly, they generally bear on our actions, and are displayed in them, but in a wide variety of ways. Some of them, like benevolence, motivate us directly to actions: benevolent people regularly do kind or helpful actions. Others, like justice, motivate us to a general policy of cooperation with the social system rather than to certain particular actions. Courage is not directly a motive at all, but rather is what is sometimes called

account, or on the categorical imperative, in Kant's (in "Self-Constitution in the Ethics of Plato and Kant," Essay 3 in this volume). In this section and the last, I argue that, according to Hume's view, persons are *socially* constituted, and in particular that we constitute someone as an agent by viewing him from the general point of view. As I read them, all three philosophers are concerned with the question what is required before a person may be regarded as the cause of his actions (or rather, since nothing without an author can *be* an action, of his intentional movements). All three think morality is essentially involved in the constitution of an agent: Plato and Kant think that to successfully constitute yourself as the cause of your actions you must act morally, while Hume thinks that to constitute another as the cause of his actions is to view him from the general (moral) point of view. Hume's view therefore provides a rather exact third-personal analog, as well as a helpful third-personal supplement, to the Kantian/Platonic view I think correct.

an "executive" virtue. But "courageous" also characterizes the way a person reacts to things—to sudden alarms or bad news, say. I suppose magnanimity can motivate you to heroic actions, but it seems to be more a matter of personal style. Cheerfulness has little to do with action, although it does show up in one's outward demeanor. In short, the character traits that we call virtues and vices don't have a single common structure. Certainly, they are not all motives, as Hume sometimes misleadingly suggests.[31]

What they do have in common is this. They are dispositions that we pick out as such only because of their regular connection to the happiness and misery of people; they are the kinds of things a person's narrow circle would be apt to find salient or important about him. We do not first discover that there is such an attribute or disposition as, say, courage, and then on further observation discover that on the whole its effects are useful or pleasant. Instead, we pick out courage as a disposition by noticing a certain regular way of being useful or pleasant. We might say that character traits are essentially normative dispositions, not natural dispositions about which we make normative judgments. A person has a character exactly insofar as she is the cause of happiness and misery to herself and her regular associates, that is, to her narrow circle.[32] Character is a normative notion all the way down.

We can now see why the general point of view is essential. To view someone through the eyes of love or hate is to respond to him as a person. To respond to him as a person is to view him as having a character. To view him as having a character is to view him as a cause, that is, a regular source, of happiness and misery to himself and others. And to view him as such a cause is to view him

[31] For instance, Hume says, "when we praise any actions, we regard only the motives that produced them" (T 3.2.1,477). Hume's list of the virtues does not support this remark, since, for example, we may praise an action for its courageousness.

[32] In her essay, "Hume and Responsible Agency," Charlotte Brown argues that Hume's arguments identifying action with what springs from character fail to capture the notion of responsible agency needed to support the reactive attitudes or indirect passions. As Leonard Katz also pointed out to me in a discussion of this essay, Hume really shows only that we respond to the person as a cluster of dispositions, and see the action as a product of those dispositions. The problem is that we do this even with ordinary objects—Katz's example is a hero with a favorite sword, which he characterizes as light, well-balanced, sharp, etc. Of course to the extent that the hero regards the sword as a favorite, and uses the dispositional terms to express his favor, the hero does take up a quasi-personal attitude towards the sword. But he does not therefore hold the sword *responsible* for its effects. The root of the problem, I think, is this: the view of an object as a cluster of dispositions does enable us to assign certain effects to that object, and so to regard the object as *the cause* of certain normatively important states and events. But it does not, as Hume suggests in the passages quoted in the last section, "reach the sensible and thinking part" in the way needed to support moral responsibility. To hold someone responsible, we must see him as a fellow subject of deliberation, not merely as a cluster of dispositions. If Hume's argument is to work it therefore needs more shoring up at this point. In my view we run up against the limits of Hume's third-personal approach here—we will never be able to reach "the sensible and thinking part" in the needed sense working only with Humean resources.

through the eyes of his narrow circle, that is, from the general point of view. A person's character, his personhood, is constructed from the general point of view. Thus the pressure to take up the general point of view is built into the original connection between love and its object, a person.

3.5 *Why the Love of Character is Normative for Love*

We are now in a position to explain why moral approval, or love regulated by the general point of view, is—or seems to us to be—normative for love in general. I begin with a preliminary point. Recall that according to Hume's account of love, you *can* love a person for anything pleasant with which you can associate him (T 2.2.1,331–332). You can love a person for his wealth, his fine clothes, his cheerful disposition, or his virtues. You can even love him because his crimes redound to your benefit. In all of these cases Hume insists that the person is the *object* of love, while the *cause* of love varies. But moral approval, the standard of virtue, is love grounded in a person's character. So the normativity of moral approval carries with it the thought that we *ought* to love people for their characters. And according to Hume a person as such *is* his character. (Or to put it more accurately we can only see someone as a person by viewing him as having a character—but I will not continue to add this qualification.) So the normativity of moral approval is naturally connected to a commonplace thought which Hume's separation of cause and object makes it hard even to formulate, namely, that we ought to love people for *themselves*.

Let me say something about the difficulty I just referred to. As we saw, Hume argues that the causes of pride, humility, love, and hate must be different from their objects, because if you could love a person just because he was him, and also hate him just because he was him, you would always do both at once. So it must be because of something *about* the person that you love or hate him. This argument seems to force Hume to treat both a person's virtues and, say, his good looks, or even his wealth, as "something about the person" and to that extent as on a footing. And this in turn makes it difficult for Hume even to formulate the colloquial distinction between loving someone for himself and loving him for an incidental reason.

But if moral love is the love of character, and character is the person himself, then moral approval is the one form of love in which cause and object come together, and we can say that you love the person for himself. As we've also seen, Hume suggests that this form of love is normative for love in general—that we feel that we ought to "regulate [our] love and hatred" (T 3.3.3,603) by the standard of virtue which moral approval provides. Our question is why moral approval seems to be normative for love in this way.

To see why, recall Hume's somewhat surprising theory of what it means for a passion to have an object. The object of a passion is an idea on which the mind becomes fixed when one is in the grip of the passion. This means, by Hume's own account, that the sentiment of love focuses our attention on the *person*. If we take this to mean focusing our attention on the person *as such*, and if the person as such is his character, then Hume's view should be that love itself, by the very nature of the passion, tends to focus our attention on a person's character.

With that in mind, we can reconstruct Hume's view as follows. The object of love is a person, and as we have seen that means that when you feel love for a person, your mind fixes its attention on the person herself. You focus your attention on *her*. Since a person is essentially a being with a certain character, love makes you think of her character. Once you think of her character, it is bound to strike you as pleasant or painful, depending on whether the person is in general a cause of happiness or misery to the members of her narrow circle, because of your sympathy with them. And that pleasure or pain will then inspire you with love or hate—a new love or hate, so to speak, in addition to the one that drew your attention to her personhood or character in the first place. Since love focuses your attention on her character, there is pressure *built into the nature of love itself* to take character for at least one of its causes or grounds as well as for its object. There is pressure, that is to say, to love the person for herself. But if I hate someone for her character, while loving her, say, because her crimes redound to my benefit, there is going to be a conflict, and an instability, in my own attitude. For my love draws my attention to her character, and if I hate her whenever I think of her character, that is, whenever I think of her *as a person*, then it is hard to see how my attitude toward her can continue to *be* love.

This doesn't mean that character is the only proper ground of love. We do not need to foist on Hume the view that we love people (or even should love people) only because they are good. Beauty, for instance, might be what draws your attention to someone in the first place, and might remain a considerable part of the cause of the pleasure that you take in her. But if what you feel for her is love, not mere aesthetic appreciation, then the love will turn your mind to her personhood, her character. If her character is loveable, then what you are loving is *a beautiful person*. Better still, although here we get beyond Hume's text, you might come to see her beauty as an expression or emanation of her character—her smile as gracious, her expression as gentle, and so on.[33]

---

[33] Certainly this works in reverse—we like the looks of almost everyone we really care for, whether conventionally beautiful or not, because we see the person *inhabiting* his looks.

But if you don't come to take some pleasure in her character too, if you are indifferent to it or have a distaste for it, your attitude cannot remain, in any stable way, the passion of love, for that passion constantly draws your attention to her character, and makes you think about and respond to her character. You might of course retreat to a merely aesthetic appreciation of her as a beautiful object, but then your attitude is no longer love. The love of a bad person is not therefore impossible, but someone who loves a bad person will be driven to try to find, and to cling to, traces of goodness or greatness in her character. For a parallel reason, there will be an instability in hate grounded in an incidental attribute, where its object has a good character, or is not known to have a bad one. To quote Hume again, but with a slightly different reading:

It seldom happens, that we do not think an enemy vicious, and can distinguish betwixt his opposition to our interest and real villainy or baseness. But this hinders not, but that the sentiments are, in themselves, distinct; and a man of temper and judgment may preserve himself from these illusions. (T 3.1.2,472)

On the present interpretation, we make this kind of error not merely because the sentiments of approval and disapproval resemble those of personal love and hate, but because approval and disapproval are normative standards that arise from the very nature of love and hate. Love needs to idealize its object, and hate either to vilify or depersonalize it.

It is one of the merits of this account that the normative standard that results is an internal or constitutive standard for love or hate.[34] An internal standard is one that arises from the nature of the object to which it applies, rather than being imposed upon it from the outside. The advantage of internal standards is that their normative force is unquestionable. If I say "bake a cake, and make it taste good" and you ask why you should make it taste good, we will think you don't know what baking cakes is all about. But if I say "bake a cake, and make it ten feet high," and you ask why you should make it ten feet high, your question seems perfectly in order. External standards give rise to further questions, and leave room for skeptical doubt. But we do not need to know why cakes should taste good, knives should be sharp, or works of philosophy should be illuminating. Of course not every cake does taste good, not every knife is sharp, and not every work of philosophy is illuminating. But it is the very nature of such objects to aspire to meet these standards. And in

---

[34] I have discussed the idea of an internal (or "constitutive") standard elsewhere. See "The Normativity of Instrumental Reason," essay 1 in this volume, especially pp. 61–2; and "Self-Constitution in the Ethics of Plato and Kant," essay 3 in this volume, especially pp. 110–13. Some of the discussion here is lifted from the first of those essays.

the same way, we might say that on Hume's account, love by its very nature aspires to be the love of character, to find its ground in the person himself.

Although this is a strong conclusion, the examples given above make it clear that we are not driven to the even stronger conclusion that a love grounded in something other than character is not really love at all. Or rather, the sense in which we might say that such a love is "unreal" is a special sense. Certainly, we do sometimes say that someone who loves another only for his beauty or his rank or his money "does not really" love him. In other moods, however, we might be inclined to describe the same situation not by denying the reality of the love, but rather by asserting that there is something inherently defective about it. Hume's theory can accommodate both of these thoughts, for there is a class of objects for which the "inherently defective" and the "not real" tend to coincide. And these are precisely those objects which are subject to an internal standard, objects which have a norm built into their nature. Take for instance "reason" or "art." We can, and do, equivalently say "that's a terrible reason" and "that's no reason at all" or, again, "that's bad art" and "that's not art." It is in just this way that we waver between "that's not really love" and "that's a poor sort of love" when someone fails to love another for herself. "Poor" and "unreal" coincide in this case, because love, like reason and art, has a norm built into it. So when we say that on Hume's account you should love a person for his virtues, because this is what it means to love him for himself, we are not talking about some moral standard applied to love from on high. Rather, the idea is that love itself aspires to respond to people as moral agents.

4. Conclusion

We are now in a position to answer the question from which we began. Why do we take up the general point of view when we think about and respond to people? The answer has two parts. First, the pressure to take up some shared point of view, and form a common standard for judging people, comes from sympathy between those who respond to, and assess, a person. Sympathy ensures that any difference of sentiment about a person is internalized by those who perceive that difference, and the resulting internal commotion and ambivalence leads us to seek a point of view from which we can form a shared standard. Second, the particular features of the point of view we arrive at—the fact that we judge from the standpoint of the narrow circle, and in accordance with general rules—arise from the fact our responses to people are indirect passions or reactive attitudes, responses of love and hate. Love and hate focus our attention on their proper object—a person, considered as such, therefore considered as having a character. To have a character is to be the cause of your actions, and more generally of happiness and misery, to yourself and those around you. And given Hume's theory of causation, your character quite literally exists in the eyes of your narrow circle. This means that love and hate pressure us to view a person through the eyes of her narrow circle. When we view someone through the eyes of her narrow circle, sympathy is again operative, causing us to love or hate the person in sympathy with them. The resulting calm passions are moral approval and disapproval. Although calmer than ordinary love, moral approval exerts a normative pressure on our ordinary loves, for any form of love turns our attention to the person's character, and to approve of a person's character is to love her for herself.

We take up the general point of view because that is the point of view from which others appear to us *as persons*. If love and sympathy did not impel us to view the world from the general point of view, our fellow human beings would just be so many useful or dangerous objects to us. According to Hume, it is only when we view the world from the general point of view that the moral world—the world composed of *people* who have *characters* and perform *actions*—comes into focus.[35]

---

[35] In writing this essay, I have benefited from working through Rachel Cohon's "The Common Point of View in Hume's Ethics," which presents different answers to some of the same questions. I am grateful to audiences at the University of Kentucky, the University of Michigan, New York University, and Tufts University for responses to an earlier version of this essay. Jay Schleusener and James Chandler commented on a still earlier version, and I thank them especially for discussions of the concept of character in the eighteenth century. Charlotte Brown and Arthur Kuflik read and commented helpfully on various drafts, and I am obligated to them as well as to Harry Frankfurt for interesting discussions of love and its relationship to morality.

10

Realism and Constructivism in Twentieth-Century Moral Philosophy

1. The Origins of Moral Realism

The story I'm going to tell is a story about the moral and political philosophy of the twentieth century, but it begins a little earlier. I date it from 1706, the year that Samuel Clarke published his *Discourse Concerning the Unchangeable Obligations of Natural Religion*.[1] This work contains the first clear statement of the position we have come to know as moral realism. I start there, because the vicissitudes of moral realism in the twentieth century, and the need to put it behind us in the twenty-first, is what I want to talk about in this essay.

By moral realism, I do not mean the view that propositions employing moral concepts may have truth values. That, as I will argue in due course, is a point on which realists and constructivists can agree.[2] Moral realism, rather, is a view about *why* propositions employing moral concepts may have truth values. Since articulating this view will be a large part of the work of this essay, I will only try to gesture at it in a rough and ready way here. Moral realism, then, is the view that propositions employing moral concepts may have truth values because moral concepts describe or refer to normative entities or facts that exist independently of those concepts themselves.[3] We have the concepts

---

[1] The Boyle Lectures, 1705, first published in London in 1706. Selections are available in D. D. Raphael, *British Moralists 1650–1800*, volume 1. References to Clarke will be to this edition.

[2] The ancestor of what I say here is my discussion of distinction between procedural and substantive realism in SN 1.4.4–1.4.9, pp. 34–47.

[3] We may understand "normative entities or facts" capaciously here. Some contemporary realists who ground moral judgment in reasons like to say that they are not committed to the existence of anything like Platonic forms: they are only committed to the existence of irreducibly normative facts about what is a reason for what. I include "facts" to accommodate them. Indeed the view I am about to discuss in the text, Samuel Clarke's view, also seems to be about facts rather than entities: facts about what makes what fit. Once facts are included, however, naturalistic realists may then wish to add that the facts in question may supervene on natural facts, say about pleasure or desire, which can be used to explain our moral views and practices in a systematic way. I mean to

in order to describe or refer to those facts. Seen this way, moral realism is a view about why we have moral concepts, one that I will argue is mistaken.

Moral realism was first articulated as a reaction against another theory, the theory of Thomas Hobbes.[4] Hobbes had argued that morality is the solution to a problem. To see what the problem is, we need only consider what human life would be like if there were no morality; and to consider that, we need only reflect on the facts of human psychology. According to Hobbes, human beings are driven by an insatiable appetite for power, which is in turn fueled by a kind of bottomless insecurity. Whatever resources we may obtain in order to satisfy our appetites and protect ourselves from others, it turns out that we need more resources still in order to protect the first ones. Hobbes envisioned a "state of nature," a sort of pre-moral condition in which the consequences of our psychology are allowed to work themselves out freely. In a state of nature, each person would try to dominate and if possible to enslave everyone else around him, because this would be the only security for his position in a world where everyone else would be doing the same thing. This would lead to that miserable condition that Hobbes called a "war of all against all," in which, as he famously tells us, the life of a human being would be "solitary, poor, nasty, brutish, and short."[5]

In order to alleviate this condition, Hobbes thought, human beings would be motivated to make a contract with one another, in which we give up our power and freedom to a sovereign who would be able to enforce laws that would make life tolerable. When the sovereign is placed in authority and the laws are enforced, not only the political state, but also moral obligation, comes into existence. Reason itself tells us *which* laws we must follow in order to bring about conditions of peace and security among human beings. But Hobbes thought that until the sovereign can enforce these laws and make sure that nearly everyone obeys them, no one can be *obligated* to obey them. To obey moral laws all by yourself would just make you the victim of your more ruthless neighbors. In the state of nature, Hobbes therefore said, the notions of right and wrong have no place.[6]

One might take Hobbes to be pointing out just how deeply rooted in human nature morality must be. But Samuel Clarke took Hobbes to be attacking what Clarke called "the real difference" between good and evil.[7] Given the relations between things, Clarke tells us, certain actions are by their very nature fit or

---

include this too. What is essential to a realist position is the view that propositions employing moral concepts have truth value because they track certain independent facts which explain our use of moral concepts.

[4] In *Leviathan*.   [5] *Leviathan*, p. 76.   [6] Ibid., p. 78.
[7] Clarke, Boyle Lectures, p. 194.

unfit to be done. Given that God is superior to us, for instance, it is fit that we should worship Him. And given the relations between people, it is fit that we should promote the good and be faithful to our contracts, that we should treat one another justly, that we should rescue the endangered, and so on.[8] All these things are fit "in themselves." How do we know this? Clarke tells us that:

These things are so notoriously plain and self-evident, that nothing but the extremest stupidity of mind, corruption of manners, or perverseness of spirit, can possibly make any man entertain the least doubt of them.[9]

In fact, Clarke continues:

it might . . . seem altogether a needless undertaking, to attempt to prove and establish the eternal difference of good and evil; had there not appeared certain men, as Mr. Hobbes and some . . . others, who have presumed . . . to assert . . . that there is no such real difference originally, necessarily, and absolutely in the nature of things.[10]

And so begins the most frequently recurring theory of the modern period. In the eighteenth century, moral realist positions were defended by John Balguy against the moral sense theory of Francis Hutcheson,[11] by Richard Price against the sentimentalist views of both Hume and Hutcheson,[12] and by Thomas Reid against Hume.[13] In the nineteenth century realism was defended by William Whewell against the utilitarianism of Paley and Bentham.[14] In the twentieth century realism was first defended by G. E. Moore against the utilitarianism of Mill and Sidgwick as well as against what Moore called the "metaphysical ethics" of Kant.[15] Moore took up a realist position about the Good but not, at least as he was understood by his successors, about the Right, so his admirer W. D. Ross then took up the realist cudgels against Moore himself.[16] H. A. Prichard, with even more temerity than the rest of this crowd, leveled volleys of realist ammunition against Plato and Aristotle.[17] Later in the century, naturalistic realists like Peter Railton and David Brink took on the emotivists and other so-called "non-cognitivists," while Thomas Nagel took on John Mackie and Gilbert Harman.[18] And in a book that was already in progress as

---

[8] Clarke, Boyle Lectures, pp. 193–4.   [9] Ibid., p. 194.   [10] Ibid., p. 194.

[11] Balguy, *The Foundation of Moral Goodness*. Selections are available in D. D. Raphael, *British Moralists 1650–1800*, volume 1.

[12] Price, *Review of the Principal Questions and Difficulties in Morals*, London, first published 1758. Selections are available in D. D. Raphael, *British Moralists 1650–1800*, volume 2.

[13] Reid, *Essays on the Active Powers of Man*. Selections are available in D.D. Raphael, *British Moralists 1650–1800*, volume 2.

[14] Whewell, *The Elements of Morality*.

[15] Moore, *Principia Ethica*, Cambridge: Cambridge University Press, 1903.

[16] Ross, *The Right and the Good*, Oxford: Clarendon Press, 1930.

[17] Prichard, *Moral Obligation* and *Duty and Interest*.

[18] Nagel, *The View from Nowhere*, chapter 8.

the century turned, Derek Parfit is defending a realist position against, among other people, Christine Korsgaard.[19]

Perhaps it would be best for the honor of our subject if we could conclude that such an army of defenders is a sign that moral realism is the correct position. But I want you to notice all of the "againsts" in the list I just presented, because I think they are no accident. Moral realism seems to owe its perennial reappearance to its reactive character rather than to its truth. It reappears in the wake of almost every attempt to give a substantive account of our moral nature. This might make us suspect that many realists share Samuel Clarke's view that it would not be necessary to defend ethical reality, if only philosophers would stop trying to explain it. But what, more precisely, is the realist reacting against?

Clarke thought that Hobbes's theory could not really explain obligation. For Hobbes says that obligation springs from the social contract, and, if that is right, how are we to explain the obligation to be faithful to the social contact itself? *That* obligation cannot come *from* the contract. So according to Clarke, Hobbes faces a dilemma. On the one hand, Hobbes could admit that being faithful to the social contract is fit and reasonable in itself. But in that case he may as well admit that other morally required actions are fit and reasonable in themselves too, and therefore do not depend for their obligatory character on the social contract. On the other hand, Hobbes could insist that being faithful to the contract, and the other things the sovereign compels us to do, are not fit and reasonable in themselves. In that case, what we call "moral obligation" is really just the exercise of arbitrary power, on the part of either God or a sovereign.

Clarke's eighteenth-century successor, Richard Price, found the exact same difficulty in moral sense theory. Hutcheson had argued that human beings are equipped with a "sense" that gives rise to responses of approval and disapproval. We have a natural tendency to take a particular kind of pleasure in the contemplation of benevolent action, and as a result of that particular pleasure we deem benevolent action to be virtuous. The moral sense does not discern a moral quality that is already there; rather, it confers a moral quality, a virtuousness, on the action it approves of, just as the Hobbesian sovereign confers an obligatory character on the actions required by his laws. So the moral sense is after all only a sort of internalized sovereign, and can no more obligate us, according to Price, than a real external sovereign can. The moral sense, like a sovereign, can bully us, but nothing outside of the character of the action itself can make it obligatory. If an action is not intrinsically *right*, Price insists, then it cannot be obligatory. Right and obligatory *mean* the same thing,

---

[19] Parfit, *Rediscovering Reasons*.

and since rightness cannot coherently be conferred on an action from outside, neither can obligatoriness. Price thinks this shows "that virtue, as such, has a real obligatory power antecedently to all positive laws, and independently of all will."[20] And this has a further implication. Price says:

As to the schemes which found morality on self-love, on positive laws and compacts, or the divine will; they must either mean, that moral good and evil are only other words for *advantageous* and *disadvantageous*, *willed* and *forbidden*. Or they relate to a very different question; that is, not to the question, what is the nature and true account of virtue; but, what is the subject-matter of it.[21]

Things should be starting to sound familiar now, for the argument I have just quoted from Richard Price's 1758 *Review of the Principal Questions and Difficulties in Morals* is exactly the same argument that we find in G. E. Moore's *Principia Ethica* a century and a half later. Non-normative words, Price insists, cannot just be "other words" for normative ones. It may turn out that what is advantageous, or what is willed by God or commanded by a sovereign, gives us the content or "subject matter" of ethics, but, Price tells us, it cannot be what "virtuous" or "obligatory" *means*.

2. Realism in the Twentieth Century

The predominant ethical theory when Moore wrote was of course utilitarianism. This was Moore's target, and he took aim at it by arguing that "good" does not *mean* "pleasant." In fact, he argued, any attempt to define "good" falls afoul of the (misnamed) "naturalistic fallacy"—the fallacy of believing that "good" can be defined in any naturalistic or indeed any non-normative terms.[22] When we say that something is good we are saying something normative—we are implying that it ought to be brought about or pursued. But Moore argued that for any natural or metaphysical quality put forward as the essential characteristic of the good, it is an open question—an intelligible question, worth asking—whether things with that characteristic really ought to be brought about or pursued. "Good" is therefore indefinable, Moore argued, and, as a corollary to that, value must be understood as an intrinsic rather than a relational property. That is, because the good cannot be defined

---

[20] Price, *Review of the Principal Questions and Difficulties in Morals*, p. 162.

[21] Price, *Review of the Principal Questions and Difficulties in Morals*, p. 133. Even Clarke's extremely vague gesture towards deriving the fitness of actions from the relations between things comes in for an implied criticism from Price: "the term *fit* signifies a simple perception of the understanding." Price, p. 161.

[22] The "naturalistic fallacy" is misnamed because Moore believed that his argument showed not only "naturalistic" definitions of "good" but also "metaphysical" ones to be impossible.

relationally as that which someone desires or that which someone enjoys or as that which someone wills, it must be intrinsic to its object. Of course it might be *true* that the good is pleasure, or the desirable, or what someone wills. But—and now Moore might have put his point in Price's exact words—that is a question of the subject matter of ethics, not a question of what Price called the "nature and true account" of the good. Although utilitarianism and hedonism were the most famous targets of his argument, Moore himself thought the argument just as effective against other theories. Egoism, evolutionary ethics, and the so-called "metaphysical ethics" of Kant are all equally guilty of the supposed "fallacy."

In fact Moore's argument was unoriginal. Not only earlier realists like Richard Price, but also nearly everyone in the modern period who considered the question of definitions agreed that normative words could only be defined in terms of other normative words.[23] Indeed moral sense theorists such as Hutcheson considered this to be one of the strongest arguments in their favor. If normative terms cannot be defined then they must denote simple ideas, and according to the Lockean psychology these empiricist philosophers accepted, simple ideas can only come from sense, not from reason. Richard Price appreciated the force of this argument, and saw that to meet it, he had to undermine the empiricist assumption that underlies it. Price's book therefore opens with an attempt to show that reason *can* be the source of simple ideas. It was Price, in this connection, who brought into prominence the fateful idea that we know ethical truths by "rational intuition."[24] But Moore's attack on the definability of goodness had more impact than Price's because of the way it intersected with broader trends in philosophy that were destined to change the shape of the subject.[25]

The period starting in the late nineteen thirties and forties was the age of what we might call "high" analytic philosophy. One of the things it brought with it was a slight change in the emphasis of empiricism. The empiricists of the eighteenth century saw their debate with the rationalists as a debate about the intellectual sources of our concepts or "ideas"—whether we get our ideas from reason or from sense experience and sentiment. In the early twentieth century empiricism shifted from a view about the sources of our concepts to a view about their contents, about how they are to be analyzed. It is an interesting question how those two ideas are related—whether a concept can come from

[23] See the selections from Cudworth, in D. D. Raphael, *British Moralists*, volume 1, p. 106; from Hutcheson, in Raphael 1, pp. 295–6, 305; from Price, in Raphael 2, pp. 141, 161; and from Reid, in Raphael 2, p. 271.
[24] Price, *Review of the Principal Questions and Difficulties in Morals*, p. 142.
[25] Not accidentally, because Moore himself was one of the founders of analytic philosophy.

experience without being analyzable in terms of experience. The twentieth-century emotivists who claimed Hutcheson and Hume for their philosophical ancestors assumed, without much argument, that it follows from the view that moral concepts come from sentiment that moral judgments may be analyzed as the mere expression of sentiments. As I have just pointed out, Hutcheson at least would have rejected this idea, and the non-cognitivism that goes with it, since Hutcheson did not think that moral concepts and judgments can be analyzed at all. But, as the case of Richard Price shows, the realists already had some tendency to interpret any account of why and how human beings use moral concepts as a reductivist account of what those concepts mean. The shift in the emphasis of empiricism cemented that tendency.

And of course it had more alarming implications still. According to the "verificationist" theory of meaning popular among logical empiricists, a concept's content is given by the way its application would be empirically verified, by the experiences we would use to tell whether the concept applies or not. This view raised important questions about moral language, for it looks as if the applicability of moral concepts, of good and bad and right and wrong, cannot be empirically verified. Under the influence of verificationism, many early twentieth-century philosophers came to doubt whether moral concepts had what they called "cognitive content" at all. This is one philosophical expression of the famous Fact/Value distinction, and it sparked a debate about what the function of moral language is, if it is not to report facts about the world. Various "non-cognitivist" proposals about the nature of moral language were explored. Prescriptivists held that moral language is essentially prescriptive or imperative. Emotivists held that moral language is used to express our approval and disapproval of actions, and that moral judgments are no more true or false than cheering or booing are true or false. By the 1950s, this view was the prevalent moral theory in the United States.

All of this sharpened up the debate between the realists and everybody else. Now the alternatives appeared to be either having or lacking cognitive content, where having cognitive content meant being descriptive of some possible object of experience. If one filled in the content of moral concepts with some item that is a possible object of experience—say, pleasure—then one ran afoul of the naturalistic fallacy. If one filled it in with some non-natural object of intuition, like Moore's intrinsic values, then one ran afoul of the scientific conception of the world. This seems to leave ethics in a real bind, and it resulted in extensive debates both about verificationism, and about whether the naturalistic fallacy is indeed a fallacy. I'm not interested in rehearsing those debates here. What is important for my purposes is this: even when what we might call the verificationist element in verificationism was dropped—that is, even when philosophers reclaimed the intelligibility of propositions that cannot be verified through the empirical sciences—one element in the verificationist picture was retained. That element is the idea that it is the function of all of our concepts, or anyway all of our authentically cognitive concepts, to describe reality.

We must go carefully here. In calling this into question, I don't mean to deny that there is a sense in which all of our concepts—that is, all of the concepts we have any business using—can be used in propositions that do in fact describe reality, in the sense that they are capable of being true or false. Rather, I mean to call into question the idea that this is what all of our concepts are *for*—that their cognitive job, so to speak, is to describe reality. So long as we retain that idea, it will continue to appear that moral realism is the only possible alternative to relativism, skepticism, subjectivism, and all of the various ways that ethics might seem hopeless. And so long as moral realism appears to be the only alternative to these skeptical options, the need to show that moral truth is as solid, as real, as objective, as scientific truth—and also that it is objective *in the same way* as scientific truth—will seem pressing. This was our situation in the early and middle years of the twentieth century.

I am aware that what I have said about the function of our concepts will seem vague until I articulate an alternative function. I intend to do that presently, but first I want to notice that from the start there was already a problem with the distinction between cognitivism and non-cognitivism in ethics. The distinction suggests that a moral judgment either articulates a description of some fact or is a disguised version of some alternative use of language—either expressive or prescriptive. But where does this leave theories like Aristotle's and Kant's, according to which moral judgments are the conclusions of practical reasoning? A conclusion of practical reasoning is not obviously a description of a fact about the world, but it hardly seems like some sort of emotional expletive, either. Where do these theories fit?

I believe that the answer is that they *don't* fit, but unfortunately this may not be obvious, because the issue raises a further question about the principles of practical reason themselves. We may say that it is true that an action is right just in case it accords with the categorical imperative, for instance, but what then are we to say about the categorical imperative itself? When we ask about the status of the principles of practical reason, the question of cognitivism and non-cognitivism seems to come up once more. For instance one may suppose that the principles of practical reason must be self-evident truths known by intuition, and then Kant will come out looking like a traditional rationalistic realist. This is not just a fantasy—this is how Kant was actually read by many late nineteenth- and twentieth-century philosophers, especially in Britain. Sidgwick and Mill, who read Kant this way, will serve as sufficiently distinguished examples.

Alternatively, someone who takes seriously Kant's thesis that moral laws are the laws of autonomy, legislated by the agent's own will, may read him, as Hare sometimes seems to do, as a prescriptivist and so a non-cognitivist. So although practical reason theories might at first seem to fall between the cracks, there are ways of making them fit the mold.

I will come back to the question how practical reason theories, or at least Kant's theory, should be understood. What I want to do now is articulate a contrast between the theory of normative concepts that I believe stands behind the debate between the cognitivists and the non-cognitivists, and another theory of normative concepts which I take to be a genuine alternative. I call this alternative, in deference to prevailing usage, constructivism. In order to articulate the contrast, I'm going to compare arguments from two of the giants of twentieth-century moral philosophy, Bernard Williams and John Rawls. Both of these arguments concern a favorite twentieth-century theme—the implications of the diversity of ethical opinion. It's going to be necessary for me to spell these arguments out in some detail. But what I am asking you to be interested in for the purposes of this essay is not their particular success, but rather the conception of moral concepts and along with it of moral philosophy that lies behind them.

3. Case Study One: Bernard Williams[26]

Williams is certainly not a moral realist, so his position here as its spokesman may occasion some surprise. I choose him for two reasons: first, because I think his attempt to articulate the idea behind realism is unrivalled in its clarity, and second, because of a realist assumption that I think in the end still haunts his own account of moral objectivity. In *Ethics and the Limits of Philosophy*, Williams argues that there is a contrast between the kind of objectivity we can hope to find in science and that which we can hope to achieve in ethics. He frames this contrast in terms of convergence, that is, in terms of what might lead us to the best kind of agreement about the judgments in question. In science, the ideal form of convergence would be this: we come to agree with one another in our scientific judgments because we are all converging on a description of the way the world really is. In ethics, Williams thinks, this sort of convergence is unavailable, and so another must be found.[27]

---

[26] This discussion is largely extracted from my *The Sources of Normativity* 2.3.1–2.3.9, pp. 67–78.
[27] Williams, *Ethics and the Limits of Philosophy*, p. 136.

Williams's account of realism emerges when he explains what he means by "the way the world really is." One thing we might mean in talking about "the way the world really is" is whether we have applied our concepts correctly. If we say the sky is blue on a day when it is blue then we have done that. But we can also query our conceptual scheme itself. We can ask whether it is the correct one or the best one or something along those lines. Since science leads us to modify our conceptual scheme, and we think of these modifications as improvements, it seems as if some such question must be in order. Williams supposes that the improved scheme is improved in the sense that it comes closer to describing the way the world really is.

Williams proposes that we can capture the notion of "the way the world really is" by formulating a kind of limiting conception which he calls "the 'absolute conception' of the world."[28] The idea involves a contrast between concepts that are more and less dependent on the particular perspective from which we view the world. For instance, we use color concepts because we see in color, so color concepts are dependent on our own particular perspective. The concept of a certain wavelength of light is supposed to be less dependent on our perspective.

Williams associates two other properties with a concept's greater independence from particular perspectives. First, our use of concepts which are more dependent on our own perspectives will be both explained, and justified, in terms of a theory that employs concepts which are less dependent. So, for instance, our use of color concepts might be explained by a theory of vision that employs wavelength concepts. Relatedly, this theory will also *justify* our belief that color vision is a form of *perception*, that is, a way of learning about the world, by the way that it explains it.[29] Color vision is a way of learning about the world because it gives us information about wavelengths, or something yet more ultimate, which we take to be part of reality. Second, the more independent of our own perspective a concept is, the more likely it is that it could be shared by other rational investigators who were unlike us in their ways of learning about the world. Suppose that there are rational creatures on some other planet who cannot see colors but can hear them. They could not use color concepts but they might be able to use wavelength concepts. The more independent concepts are more shareable.

Williams thinks that the nearest thing we have to a conception of "the way the world really is" is the conception of the world that is maximally independent of our own perspective. And he thinks that if we and the alien

---

[28] Ibid., p. 139.   [29] Ibid., p. 149.

investigators began to converge on such a conception (and of course to agree on which judgments are correct within it) then we would have reason to believe we were converging on the absolute conception. This would be the best case of convergence for science. Our theories would come to converge with the theories of other investigators because all of us were converging on a description of the way the world really is.

Now consider what the parallel would be in ethics. Here Williams first deals with a possible objection, namely, that there is nothing analogous to perceptual judgments in ethics. Seeing the facts is one thing, and evaluating them in a certain way is another. To counter this objection, Williams appeals to the existence of what he calls "thick" as opposed to "thin" ethical concepts. Thin ethical concepts—like right and good and ought—do not appear to be world-guided, in the sense that their application does not appear to be guided by the facts. (Notice the echo of verificationism here.) But thick ethical concepts—Williams's examples are coward, lie, brutality, and gratitude—are world-guided and action-guiding at the same time.[30] Only an action that is in a particular way motivated by fear can be called cowardly, and yet to call an action cowardly is to suggest that it ought not to be done.[31]

Of course a prescriptivist or emotivist or a latter-day expressivist has his own account of these concepts. He thinks that their world-guidedness is one thing and that their action-guidingness is another. To say that an action is cowardly is simply to denigrate an action motivated by fear. The difficulty with this analysis, according to Williams, is that it suggests that it would be possible to use a thick ethical concept with perfect accuracy even if you were completely incapable of appreciating the value that it embodies. Williams thinks this is implausible. He does not mean that we can only use an evaluative concept when we ourselves actually endorse the value in question. But he thinks we can apply such concepts only by entering imaginatively into the world of those who have the relevant values, not merely by applying a set of factual criteria.[32] We have to see the world through their eyes. This makes it natural to think of judgments employing thick ethical concepts as a kind of perceptual judgment, for they are a sort of lens through which we view the world. And that in turn

---

[30] Williams, *Ethics and the Limits of Philosophy*, pp. 140–1.

[31] Williams says that thick concepts often provide reasons for action (or refraining) but of course in one way this is not true of "cowardly." To say that an action is cowardly is to suggest that there is a reason not to do it, but not to mention what that reason is. Something in the situation is worth overcoming human fearfulness for, but the term doesn't tell us what. This is because courage is a so-called executive virtue. Williams's other examples suggest more directly why the action shouldn't be done, but they are still not strictly speaking action-guiding. One does not avoid an action because it is brutal, for instance. One avoids it because it will hurt someone.

[32] Williams, *Ethics and the Limits of Philosophy*, pp. 141–2.

makes it natural to think that, like other perceptual judgments, they may be a kind of knowledge.

I say that the sky is blue, and my visitor from Mars says that it makes a humming noise. Are we agreeing? Certainly we don't *mean* the same thing, since I am talking about how the sky looks and he is talking about how it sounds. Yet when we reflect on these views we find that the things we both say have implications expressible in terms of a more absolute concept, that of wavelengths. And when we look at those implications our judgments are found to converge. Here we find grounds for confidence that both of our perceptions are guiding us rightly: they are ways of knowing about the world.

To get the parallel in ethics, we would have to compare judgments made in alternative sets of thick ethical concepts. One person says that lying is sinful and another says it is dishonorable. They do not appear to *mean* exactly the same thing. But we might take both of their remarks to have implications describable in terms of what *we* think is a more absolute concept—that lying is *wrong*—and here we find that they converge. This would be evidence that their moral perceptions are guiding them rightly, and are ways of knowing about the moral part of the world. On the other hand, suppose what is in question is avenging an insult. The first person thinks it is sinful to avenge it, while the second thinks it is dishonorable not to. Does this imply any disagreement, in particular a disagreement about whether avenging an insult is, in our sense, morally wrong? Williams does not think so, and this is partly because there is a world-guided side to the idea of something's being dishonorable. The second person may indeed be dishonored—he may be personally diminished, in his own eyes and those of his community—if he does not stand up for himself. Williams thinks that facts of this kind should make us doubt whether the two people are using concepts that converge on what is morally wrong, and so should also make us doubt whether "morally wrong" is a more absolute concept after all—that is, doubt whether it describes some reality.

Instead Williams proposes a different way in which we might think about differences in ethical beliefs. He suggests that we should see the values of a culture not as their best approximations of the truth about right and wrong, but rather as a kind of *habitation*—although, as he emphasizes, and this is a point I will come back to—*not one that they have built*. Their values form a part of the structure of the social world in which they live. This does not mean that we cannot make any evaluative judgments about a culture's values. We can ask whether the social world that is made of those values is a good place for human beings to live. A theory of human nature, drawing on the resources of the social as well as the physical sciences, could guide our reflections about what conduces to human flourishing. Psychoanalytic theory, for instance, could guide our views about whether a social world structured by certain values was mentally healthy or not. Williams proposes that if we did find that a social world promoted the best life or at least a flourishing life for human beings, this would justify the values embodied in that social world.

I have two reasons for placing this argument before you. First, I want you to consider Williams's very clear articulation of the idea of realism, and of what moral realism would be if we had it. The values of different cultures would represent their attempts to discern the moral part of reality, perhaps through the lens of some more perspectival concept. Second, I am interested in what the kind of objectivity Williams does suppose ethics might have has in common with scientific objectivity as he conceives it. This is the one piece of realism that I mentioned earlier as still haunting Williams's account, and it comes out clearly when Williams draws his conclusion. He argues that only one ethical belief might be objectively true in the ordinary, scientific, sense, namely, the belief that a certain sort of social world was the best one for human beings to live in. And then he says:

other ethical beliefs would be true only in the oblique sense that they were the beliefs that would help us to find our way around in a social world which . . . was shown to be the best social world for human beings.[33]

Williams thinks that scientific beliefs are objective in the sense that they approximate as closely as possible to a representation of "the way the world really is." Such beliefs help us find our way around in the natural world. So when Williams goes looking for some remnant of objectivity in ethics, he looks for the world that ethical beliefs would help us to find our way around in. Theoretical beliefs constitute a kind of map of the natural world, and ethical beliefs constitute a kind of map of the social world.[34] To be knowledge, a belief must help you find your way around in some world, he seems to think, and to do that, it must represent that world. It must describe some kind of reality.

---

[33] Williams, *Ethics and the Limits of Philosophy*, p. 155.

[34] The argument of this essay could give the reader the impression that I think a realist account is appropriate for science but not for ethics. This is the right moment to signal that that is not my view. But I do think that theoretical concepts have, as I suggest in the text, something like a map-making function: they enable us to find our way around. That should not be confused with a descriptive function; the qualities of a good map are by no means the same as the qualities of a good description. What is necessary for my argument is not "realism for scientific concepts, a different function for ethical ones," but rather "concepts that enable us to find our away around in the world versus concepts that enable us to solve practical problems."

4. Against the Model of Application

I think that this view of the relations between science and ethics represents a rather deep confusion about the difference between knowledge and action—something almost amounting to a failure to tell them apart. One way to articulate this admittedly difficult thought is by the metaphor I have just used. If to have knowledge is to have a map of the world, then to be able to act well is to be able to decide where to go and to follow the map in going there. The ability to act is something like the ability to *use* the map, and that ability cannot be given by *another map*. (Nor can it be given by having little normative flags added to the map of nature that mark out certain spots or certain routes as good. You still have to know how to use the map before the little normative flags can be of any use to you.) To put the same point another way, goodness in action cannot just be a matter of applying our knowledge of the good—not even a matter of applying our knowledge of what makes action itself good. This is because the ability to apply knowledge *presupposes* the ability to act.

Let me try to make this last point in a less metaphorical way. Suppose we agree that ethics is about what makes action good. For now I intend that phrase—"what makes action good"—to be neutral between consequentialist, virtue-theoretic, and deontological accounts of what makes an action good. Whatever their differences, the proponents of all of these accounts have to agree that one thing that makes an action good is conformity to the principle of instrumental reason, or what Kant calls the hypothetical imperative. An action that does not succeed in achieving its end is a failure, after all, but a movement that does not even succeed in aiming at an end doesn't succeed in being an action at all.

Now a realist account of the normativity of the instrumental principle is incoherent. For think how that account would have to work. The agent would have to recognize, as some sort of eternal normative verity, that it is good to take the means to his ends. How is this verity supposed to motivate him? The obvious way to understand how facts motivate us is by means of a kind of extension of the instrumental principle itself. Philosophers have long acknowledged that the instrumental principle naturally extends to what is sometimes called "constitutive reasoning"—to use Williams's example, your end is an entertaining evening, and you choose dinner and a movie as what will constitute that end. The same line of thought extends the instrumental principle even further to cover the role of *judgment* in action quite generally. Your end is to have a cup of coffee and you choose *this* cup of coffee as what constitutes your end. But this cannot be how we employ the instrumental principle itself. We would have to say that an agent's end is to do a good action, and that he sees that an action conforming to the instrumental principle is good. Taking the means to his ends is therefore *itself* a means to his end of doing a good action, and he chooses to conform to the instrumental principle under the influence of—the instrumental principle itself. The point is that the instrumental principle cannot be a normative truth that we *apply* in practice, because it—or its natural extension to cover the case of judgment—is essentially the principle of application itself, that is, it is the principle in accordance with which we are operating when we apply truths in practice.[35]

But the realist picture in fact works no better for moral principles than it does for the principle of instrumental reason. For even if we know what makes an action good, so long as that is just a piece of knowledge, that knowledge has to be applied in action by way of another sort of norm of action, something like an obligation to do those actions which we know to be good. And there is no way to derive such an obligation from a piece of knowledge that a certain action is good. A utilitarian thinks an action is good because it maximizes good consequences and a virtue theorist thinks it is good because it is kind or brave. But how is it supposed to follow that it is to be done?

Now a classical utilitarian (or, for that matter, an intuitionist) might argue that I am ignoring the obvious. An agent is obligated to perform an action when there is a rule specifying that actions of that kind are to be performed. The classical utilitarian, for example, thought there was such a rule, the principle of utility. It is because of the existence of this rule that we characterize actions as obligatory or forbidden. But the trouble with that strategy is that it leaves us with two problems, which in the end come to the same thing. First, it does not tell us why there is such a rule. Nor, if this is a different question, does it tell us why we should conform to the rule. We seem to be caught on the horns of a dilemma when we confront this question: are we obligated to obey the rule? If one is obligated to obey the rule, then the notion of obligation must be prior to the existence of the rule. We cannot explain obligation in terms of the rule, as something that arises from it. On the other hand, if we are *not* obligated to obey the rule, then it seems we may permissibly ignore it, and so we have not after all explained why the actions it directs are obligatory. This is really a variant of the same problem that Clarke found in Hobbes, but I am now claiming that it also holds for any view that makes the goodness of action

---

[35] This is a version of an argument that also appears in "The Normativity of Instrumental Reason," Essay 1 in this volume, pp. 53–4.

an item of knowledge. The knowledge itself, being something external to the will, is just a kind of sovereign.

The problem rests in thinking of the rules that define the obligatory and the forbidden as standards we *apply* when we are deliberating about what to do. Standards of goodness for things other than action do work this way. Having decided, say, that you are going to buy a car, you then ask yourself what makes for a good one, or perhaps what makes for a good one in your own case. But these standards exert their normativity, if they do so at all, through action itself. Possession of a good car is the object, and if one is successful the product, of the action. But the performance of a good action cannot intelligibly be the object and product of action itself. And it is a related fact that in the case of things other than action, you don't absolutely have to apply the standards of goodness. Usually you have the same reason for choosing a good X (or a good X for you) that you have for choosing an X. But it is at least imaginable that you might just *pick* an X without reference to its goodness, like someone who is asked to pick a number from one to ten or someone randomly picking a cookie from a passing tray. Evaluative standards, taken by themselves, do not obligate. If we think of rules of action as something we may or may not *apply* when we deliberate about what to do, then either we are obligated to apply them or we are not. In neither case, as I have argued, can obligation be derived from the existence of a rule of action. So it is not just the principle of instrumental reason that gives rise to the problem.

Nor can we solve the problem by omitting the talk of rules and just saying that the goodness of action is directly normative for the agent. So long as the fact that the action is good is supposed to be a piece of knowledge that the agent applies when she acts, the same problem will arise. The argument I am making now is, in a way, the ultimate extension of the open question argument. If it is just a fact that a certain action would be good, a fact that you might or might not apply in deliberation, then it seems to be an open question whether you *should* apply it. The model of applied knowledge does not correctly capture the relation between the normative standards to which action is subject and the deliberative process. And moral realism conceives ethics on the model of applied knowledge.

5. Case Study Two: John Rawls

But if moral philosophy is not the search for some sort of knowledge that we might apply in action, what else can it be? What other model is available to us? We can find an alternative model in the work of John Rawls. Rawls, following

Kant, treats the problems of political philosophy as problems that are practical all the way down.

Rawls, like Hobbes before him, thinks that justice is the solution to a problem.[36] Political philosophers have long been aware that there is a kind of paradox at the very heart of liberalism. The paradox emerges most starkly if you imagine someone trying to argue in favor of instituting liberal policies in a nation whose culture and beliefs are not liberal. Anyone who wanted to argue that liberal policies should be instituted in such a society would face an intractable problem, for it is an essential tenet of liberalism that political policies should be acceptable in the eyes of the people who are governed by them. If liberalism is the doctrine that you can't push people around in the name of what you think is right, then liberals themselves are committed to the view that *they* can't push people around in the name of the doctrine that you can't push people around in the name of what you think is right. To put the point more simply, we cannot tyrannize over others in the name of liberalism and still be consistent liberals.

Now Rawls is not, in this sense, trying to justify the liberal state. That is, he is not trying to give arguments that would show that there are grounds for forcing a liberal regime on an illiberal population. But he is concerned about a parallel problem that arises when we try to justify policies *within* the liberal state, for even within the liberal state, we must use the coercive mechanisms of the state to enforce liberal policies. Since liberalism claims that political policies are justified only when they are acceptable in the eyes of the citizens, we must be able to offer reasons in support of these coercive policies that are acceptable to all the citizens. Suppose, for instance, a society contains a majority and a minority religion, and suppose the majority wishes to get their church accepted as the official state church. What reasons can they offer for this? They might say, "Our religion should be the state religion, because our religion is the one true faith." This is not a reason that the minority can reasonably be expected to accept. So in a liberal society, this will not be accepted as a good reason for coercive action. It does not meet the standard of "public reason."

Of course the majority are not just going to *insist* that theirs is the one true faith. They have certain arguments for their view—metaphysical, theological, and historical arguments—and they can marshal these and try to convince the minority that they are right. But the minority also has these kinds of arguments, and we may suppose that when all is said and done the disagreement remains.

---

[36] This discussion is extracted from "Rawls and Kant: On the Primacy of the Practical," in the *Proceedings of the Eighth International Kant Congress, Memphis 1995*, pp. 1165–73.

In a modern society, people may hold different philosophical, theological, and metaphysical doctrines, and with them different conceptions of a good life, which are all "reasonable" in the sense that they need not involve any obvious error or craziness. In the face of this fact it is inconsistent with liberalism to justify political policy on metaphysical or theological grounds, since such grounds may not be acceptable to all.

But of course it follows from this that we cannot justify liberal policies *themselves* on controversial metaphysical or philosophical grounds. For instance, in explaining to the majority why we must honor freedom of religion, we cannot consistently appeal to Kant's theory that autonomy is the supreme moral value or to Mill's arguments for the consequentialist value of open discussion and experimental living. These may be excellent reasons for believing in freedom of religion; but they do not meet the criterion of being acceptable in the eyes of everyone. But this seems to leave us at a loss. So there is the problem: how are we to give reasons that everyone can accept, in a society where people derive their reasons from radically different conceptions of the good?[37]

Now before we go on, I want you to consider the parallel between this problem and the one that confronts Kant in the opening argument of the third section of the *Groundwork*, when he is explaining the foundation of the categorical imperative (G 4:446–447). Kant begins by defining a free will as a causality that is effective without being determined by any alien cause. Anything outside of the will counts as an alien cause, including the desires and inclinations of the person. The free will must be entirely self-determining. Yet, because the will is a cause, it must act according to some law or other: a lawless cause, Kant thinks, is a kind of contradiction.[38] Alternatively, we may say that since the will is practical reason, it cannot be conceived as acting and choosing for no reason. Since reasons are derived from principles, the free will must have a principle. But because the will is free, no law or principle can be imposed on it from outside. Kant concludes that the will must be autonomous: that is, it must have its *own* law or principle. But now we have a problem: for where is this principle to come from? If it is imposed on the will from outside then the will is not free. So the will must adopt a principle for itself. But until the will has a principle, there is nothing from which it can derive a reason. So how can it have any reason for adopting one principle rather than another?

[37] This problem is much more clearly in focus in *Political Liberalism* than it was in Rawls's earlier book, *A Theory of Justice*, and the modifications in the way Rawls presents his view in the later work are largely due to his increased appreciation of its depth and difficulty. Nevertheless, as I am about to argue and as Rawls himself believes, the strategy of the argument in *A Theory of Justice* does provide for its solution.

[38] For an explanation of why Kant thinks this, see my "Self-Constitution in the Ethics of Plato and Kant," Essay 3 in this volume, pp. 120–4.

And indeed the problem is in a way even worse than that. For it looks as if the free will, by imposing some principle upon itself, must restrict its own freedom in some arbitrary way.

These two problems, Kant's and Rawls's, have the same structure. In both cases what we are looking for is principles themselves, for we need reasons, ways of choosing and justifying our actions or our policies, and reasons are derived from principles. Yet the very structure of the situation seems to forbid us to choose any *particular* principles. The liberal's need to avoid compromising the freedom of the citizens by forcing a particular conception of the good on them parallels the free will's need to avoid adopting a principle that will compromise its own freedom. In each case, it looks as if the choice of any particular principle will represent an act of arbitrary power. In Rawls's construction of his problem, it looks as if the choice of any particular principle of justice must be based on an arbitrary preference for one conception of the good over others. In Kant's construction of his problem, it looks as if the choice of any principle for the will must involve an arbitrary restriction of the will's freedom. And the solutions proposed by Kant and Rawls take a parallel form.

Kant's solution goes like this: The categorical imperative, as represented by the Formula of Universal Law, tells us to act only on a maxim that we could will to be a law. And *this*, according to Kant, *just is* the law of a free will. To see why, we need only compare the *problem* faced by the free will with the *content* of the categorical imperative. The problem faced by the free will is this: the free will must have a law, but because the will is free, it must be its own law. And nothing determines what that law must be. *All that it has to be is a law.* Now consider the content of the categorical imperative, as represented by the Formula of Universal Law. The categorical imperative merely tells us to choose a law. Its only constraint on our choice is that it have the form of a law. And nothing determines what that law must be. *All that it has to be is a law.* Kant concludes that the categorical imperative *just is* the law of a free will. It does not impose any external constraint on the free will's activities, but simply arises from the nature of the will. It describes what a free will must do in order to be a free will. It must choose a maxim that it can regard as a law.[39]

Rawls's solution to his problem can be put in parallel terms. Rawls's two principles of justice tell us that all citizens must have equal basic liberties, and that our society must otherwise be designed so that everyone has as large a share of primary goods as possible, with which to pursue his or her own

---

[39] I defend this interpretation of Kant's solution at greater length in my essay "Morality as Freedom," CKE essay 6.

conception of the good.[40] And *these*, Rawls might say, *just are* the principles of justice for a liberal society. To see why, we need only compare the *problem* faced by a liberal society with the *content* of Rawls's two principles of justice.[41] Echoing Rousseau, we might say that the problem faced in the original position is this: to find a conception of justice which enables every member of society to pursue his or her conception of the good as effectively as possible, while leaving each member as free as he or she was before.[42] The content of Rawls's two principles simply reflects this conception of the problem. So Rawls's two principles simply describe what a liberal society must do in order to *be* a liberal society, just as Kant's principle describes what a free will must do in order to *be* a free will. Rawls's principles are derived from the idea of liberalism itself, in the same way Kant's categorical imperative is derived from the idea of free volition.

In Kant's argument we arrive at the categorical imperative by thinking about the problem faced by a free will, just as in Rawls's we arrive at the principles of justice for a liberal society by thinking about the problem faced by a liberal society. In each case, in fact, a sufficiently detailed and accurate description of the problem actually yields the solution. And you should notice one implication of this—the categorical imperative is not a rule one *applies* in deliberation. We arrive at the categorical imperative by thinking about *how* a free will must deliberate: it must do so by choosing a law for itself. The categorical imperative is a principle of the *logic* of practical deliberation, a principle that is constitutive of deliberation, not a theoretical premise that is applied in practical thought. And one might also say that Rawls's principles are a development of the *logic* of liberalism.

6. Constructivism

Kant and Rawls are constructivists: I will now try to articulate what this means. Practical philosophy, as conceived by Kant and Rawls, is not a matter of finding knowledge to apply in practice. It is rather the use of reason to solve practical problems. The concepts of moral and political philosophy are the names of

---

[40] This is a deliberately general statement of Rawls's two principles, which he states with increasing specificity as he develops his view. For more exact formulations, see *A Theory of Justice*, section 46, and *Political Liberalism*, pp. 5 and 271.

[41] For the idea of constructing a solution from the "original position," see *A Theory of Justice*, section 4, and *Political Liberalism*, pp. 22–8.

[42] Rousseau says that the problem solved by the social contract is to "Find a form of association which defends and protects with all common forces the person and the goods of each associate, and by means of which each one, while uniting with all, nevertheless obeys only himself and remains as free as before." Quoted from p. 148 of *On The Social Contract*, in *The Basic Political Writings of Jean-Jacques Rousseau*.

those problems, or more precisely of their solutions. This is made clear by the way Rawls employs the concept/conception distinction in *A Theory of Justice*.[43] There, the *concept* of justice refers to the solution to a problem. The problem is what we might call the distribution problem: people join together in a cooperative scheme because it will be better for all of them, but they must decide how its benefits and burdens are to be distributed. A *conception* of justice is a principle that is proposed as a solution to the distribution problem, arrived at by reflecting on the nature of the problem itself. The concept *refers* to *whatever solves the problem*, the conception proposes a particular solution.[44] The normative force of the conception is established in this way: if you recognize the problem to be real, to be yours, to be one you have to solve, and the solution to be the only or the best one, then the solution is binding upon you.

The same structure is clear in Kant's argument. There the problem is the one set by the fact of free agency. It is nothing less than the problem of what is to be done. And Kant thinks that just by reflecting on the nature of that problem, we can arrive at the categorical imperative. The move from a negative to a positive conception of freedom in Kant's argument parallels the movement from concept to conception in Rawls's. Negative freedom is the name of a problem: what shall I do, when nothing determines my actions? Positive freedom proposes a solution: act on a maxim you can will as a universal law.

So according to constructivism, normative concepts are not (in the first instance—a caveat I will explain below) the names of objects or of facts or of the components of facts that we encounter in the world. They are the names of the solutions of problems, problems to which we give names to mark them out as objects for practical thought. The role of the concept of the right, say, is to guide action: the role of the concept of the good might be to guide our choice among options, or of ends. The "thinness" of these concepts, to use Williams's language, comes from the fact that they are, so far, only concepts, names for whatever it is that solves the problems in question. We need *conceptions* of the right and the good before we know how to apply the concepts. The task of practical philosophy is to move from concepts to conceptions, by constructing an account of the problem reflected in the concept that will point the way to a conception that solves the problem. To produce a constructivist account

---

[43] This discussion is extracted from SN 3.4.1–3.4.3, pp. 113–16.

[44] When we think of the subject this way, we will not be inclined to think that there is a difference between doing "meta-ethics" and doing "normative" or practical ethics. The attempt to specify the meaning and reference of an ethical concept will point fairly directly to practical ramifications. This represents another way in which constructivists break with the platitudes of twentieth-century ethics—and return to the more substantive ethical theorizing of the past.

of the right or the good is to ask: is there some feature of the problem itself, or of the function named by the concept, that will show us the way to its solution? The feature of the problem of liberal justice that shows us the way to its solution, according to Rawls, is that a liberal society must respect the freedom of its members while enabling them to pursue their conceptions of the good. The feature of the problem of free action that shows us the way to its solution, according to Kant, is that free action must be determined by the agent herself.

It may seem at first glance as if on a constructivist account there is something very special about the moral or normative domain. All of our other concepts, one might think, name things in the world, or perhaps things which track things in the world, while ethical concepts gesture at practical problems and their solutions.[45] But even leaving aside the question whether this is a correct account of our scientific concepts, the idea that some of our everyday concepts refer to the solutions to problems is perfectly familiar. To see this, consider artifact concepts—consider, for example, the concept of "chair." Why do we have the concept of chair? Certainly not because it would form part of the absolute conception of the world, for those alien investigators with whom we are to share that conception might, for all we know, be oval creatures who swim through their environment like fish, and never sit down. We have the concept of "chair" because the physical construction of human beings makes it possible, and occasionally necessary, to sit down. So the concept of chair is functional; a chair is something that plays a certain necessary role in human life, and the conception of chair is filled out by asking what sorts of things can properly fill that role. The person who first came up with a conception of chair probably was also the first who constructed an object—a chair—to fit that concept, and so to solve the human problem that it represents. To this extent constructivism makes moral concepts like the concepts of artifacts. This doesn't make them arbitrary or relative, for there are kinds of artifacts—"chair" is an example—that all human beings in all human cultures have some version of, and that have to have certain features given the problems that they solve. Williams, you may recall, said that the values of a culture are "part of their way of living, a cultural artifact they have come to inhabit (though they have not consciously built it)."[46] But why shouldn't we consciously build our social world, or our political societies, or for that matter our practical identities? This, according to a constructivist, is what practical philosophy is all about.

---

[45] But see note 34.   [46] Williams, *Ethics and the Limits of Philosophy*, p. 147.

And of course none of this means that moral language doesn't admit of truth and falsehood, any more than it means that artifact language doesn't admit of truth and falsehood. For the correct conception of a concept will be a guide to its correct application, and when a concept is applied correctly, what we get is truth. But what makes the conception correct will be that it solves the problem, not that it describes some piece of external reality. Rather, as the term "constructivism" suggests, our use of the concept when guided by the correct conception *constructs* an essentially human reality—the just society, the Kingdom of Ends—that solves the problem from which the concept springs. The truths that result describe that constructed reality.

It is important to note one feature of constructivist theories. Theories will vary in how extensively constructivist they are, because different normative "objects" are constructed in different constructivist theories. Rawls constructs the principles of justice. In doing so he takes certain other normative notions for granted. The parties in Rawls's "original position" choose with a view to what will be *best* for them, but under constraints of information, the veil of ignorance. The notion of what is "best" for someone is also a moral or normative notion, and it, or rather the notion of "good" upon which it is based, is not constructed, according to Rawls.[47] In T. M. Scanlon's theory, to take another example, moral principles are constructed; the problem they solve is one of justifiability. Scanlon, in constructing moral principles, asks which principles people might reasonably reject. The notion of reason is also a normative notion, and Scanlon does not think that it is a constructed notion.[48] So there is a question about how "deep" constructivism can go. Can even our own most basic reasons themselves be constructed? Kant's view, as I understand him, and as I have sketched his view in this essay, is that they can. To put it in my own terms, when an agent determines whether she can will a maxim as universal law, she is determining that she can endorse a certain consideration in favor of doing something and therefore can treat it as a reason. This constructed normative "object" is then available for use in other constructions. If this sort of Kantian argument doesn't work, then constructivism cannot go "all the way down." I of course think that it can.

7. Conclusion

And now I will conclude with a bit of a twist. In this essay I've contrasted two theories of normative concepts and their function. I've identified, as the basic

---

[47] At least this is Rawls's view in *A Theory of Justice*. See section 68.
[48] See T. M. Scanlon, *What We Owe to Each Other*, p. 17.

assumption behind the realist model, a general view of our concepts—that view that the function of a concept is to describe a piece of reality. I've suggested in opposition to this that some of our concepts—including justice, right, and good—are essentially names that refer to the solutions to problems. Now the objection inevitably arises: shouldn't we be asking which of these two theories of our normative concepts *is true*? But we don't have to ask that question, for considered in one way, constructivism and realism are perfectly compatible. If constructivism is true, then normative concepts may after all be taken to refer to certain complex facts about the solutions to practical problems faced by self-conscious rational beings. Of course it is only viewed from the perspective of those who actually *face* those problems in question that these truths will appear normative. Viewed from outside of that perspective, those who utter these truths will appear to be simply expressing their values.[49] Realism and expressivism are both true in their way. But establishing that realism is true in *that* sense is not the *end* of moral philosophy, in either sense of "end": it is only the *beginning*.

The important difference between realism and constructivism rests then not in which one is true, but in how they orient us towards the tasks of practical philosophy. The moral realist thinks of practical philosophy as an essentially theoretical subject. Its business is to find, or anyway to argue that we can find, some sort of ethical knowledge that we can apply in action. According to constructivism, the only piece of knowledge that could be relevant here is knowledge that the problems represented by our normative terms are solvable, and the only way we can find out whether that is so is by trying to solve them. So for the constructivist practical philosophy is a practical subject. Its business is to work out solutions to practical problems.

For much of the twentieth century, just as for the three centuries or so that preceded it, philosophers remained in thrall to the view that the function of all human concepts, and perhaps of all conceptual inquiry, is to describe the world. This, in my view, amounts almost to thinking that the function

[49] I haven't said much in this essay about expressivism, our latter-day form of non-cognitivism. So I cannot adequately develop the ideas I am about to voice here. Expressivism, I believe, is like realism also true after all, and also in a way that makes it boring. From the descriptive and explanatory perspective that is appropriate to scientific or perhaps in this case social-scientific inquiry, those who use normative language will appear to be simply expressing their values. When you are not in the grip of practical problems that provide standards for their own solutions, the truth and falsehood of statements employing concepts that embody those problems must be elusive. The trouble with expressivism is that it describes moral language from the outside, as if we were not ourselves the creatures who face practical problems, but only someone else making anthropological observations about them. Behind that stance is the idea that so long as we are reasoning we must remain at this anthropological level, and behind that view is the same error that animates moral realism—the view that the business of cognition is describing the world.

of human life is to describe the world, and if that's right, it is clear enough
what is wrong with realism. Rawls's work in one way broke new ground, but
in another way simply followed the lead of Hobbes and Kant, in thinking
that philosophy can be practical, or to put the same point another way, that
practice itself can be reflective. And after all, it is no accident that we still read
Hobbes and Kant, while we have forgotten Clarke and Price and Whewell,
just as the philosophers of the future will still be reading Rawls when they
have forgotten G. E. Moore. For it is in this practical conception of moral and
political philosophy that both our significant historical achievements and our
hopes for making progress in the future can be found.[50]

[50] This essay was originally written for the meetings of the Australian Association of Philosophy
in the year 2000, and then revised for the American Philosophical Association's Special Sessions on
Philosophy in America at the Turn of the Twentieth Century in 2001. I'd like to thank the audiences on
both occasions, as well as the audiences at the Harvard/MIT Graduate Student Philosophy Conference
and at Cornell University in spring 2002. I owe a special debt to Jay Wallace for his commentary at the
American Philosophical Association and to Nicholas Sturgeon for comments written when I delivered
the paper at Cornell. And I'd like to thank Charlotte Brown and Arthur Kuflik for comments on the
early draft version.

Bibliography

Annas, Julia. "Aristotle and Kant on Morality and Practical Reasoning," in *Aristotle, Kant and the Stoics: Rethinking Happiness and Duty*. Edited by Stephen Engstrom and Jennifer Whiting. Cambridge: Cambridge University Press, 1996.

Aristotle. *The Complete Works of Aristotle: The Revised Oxford Translation*. Edited by Jonathan Barnes. Princeton: Princeton University Press, 1984. *NOTE: In quoting from this edition I have deviated from the translation in two ways: I have always translated "ergon" as "function" rather than "work," and I have always translated "arete" as "virtue" rather than "excellence."*

Audi, Robert. "Moral Judgment and Reasons for Action," in *Ethics and Practical Reason*. Edited by Garrett Cullity and Berys Gaut. Oxford: Clarendon Press, 1997.

Augustine, Saint. *Confessions*. Translated by R. S. Pine-Coffin. Harmondsworth: Penguin Books, 1961.

Austen, Jane. *Emma*. Oxford: Oxford University Press, 1990.

Balguy, John. *The Foundation of Moral Goodness*. London: John Pemberton, 1728–9. Selections from this work may also be found in *British Moralist 1650–1800*, edited by D. D. Raphael. Indianapolis: Hackett Publishing Company, 1991.

Broadie, Sarah. *Ethics with Aristotle*. New York: Oxford University Press, 1991.

Broome, John. "Does Rationality Give Us Reasons?," *Philosophical Issues* 15 (2005): 321–7.

Brown, Charlotte. "From Spectator to Agent: Hume's Theory of Obligation," *Hume Studies* 20 (1994): 19–35.

_____ "Is Hume an Internalist?," *Journal of the History of Philosophy* 25 (1988): 69–87.

_____ "Hume Against the Selfish Schools and the Monkish Virtues" (unpublished).

_____ "Hume and Responsible Agency" (unpublished).

Butler, Joseph. *Fifteen Sermons Preached at the Rolls Chapel* (1726). The most influential of these are collected in Butler, *Five Sermons Preached at the Rolls Chapel and a Dissertation upon the Nature of Virtue*. Edited by Stephen Darwall. Indianapolis: Hackett Publishing Company, 1983.

Clarke, Samuel. *A Discourse Concerning the Unchangeable Obligations of Natural Religion, and the Truth and Certainty of the Christian Revelation*, The Boyle Lectures, 1705. Selections in *British Moralists 1650–1800*. Edited by D. D. Raphael. Indianapolis: Hackett Publishing Company, 1991.

Cohon, Rachel. "The Common Point of View in Hume's Ethics," *Philosophy and Phenomenological Research* 57 (1997): 827–50.

Freud, Sigmund. *Civilization and Its Discontents*. Translated by James Strachey. New York: W. W. Norton and Co., 1961.

Gibbard, Allan. *Thinking How to Live*. Cambridge, MA: Harvard University Press, 2003.

Ginsborg, Hannah. "Korsgaard on Choosing Non-Moral Ends," *Ethics* 109 (1998): 5–21.

Glassen, P. "A Fallacy in Aristotle's Argument about the Good," *Philosophical Quarterly* 66 (1957): 319–22.

Gooch, G. P. *Germany and the French Revolution*. New York: Russell and Russell, 1966.

Hardie, W. F. R., *Aristotle's Ethical Theory*. Oxford: Clarendon Press, 1968.

Herman, Barbara. "Making Room for Character," in *Aristotle, Kant and the Stoics: Rethinking Happiness and Duty*. Edited by Stephen Engstrom and Jennifer Whiting. Cambridge: Cambridge University Press, 1996.

_____ *The Practice of Moral Judgment*. Cambridge, MA: Harvard University Press, 1993.

Hill, Thomas, Jr. *Dignity and Practical Reason in Kant's Moral Theory*. Ithaca: Cornell University Press, 1992.

Hobbes, Thomas. *Leviathan*. Edited by Edwin Curley. Indianapolis: Hackett Publishing Company, 1994.

Hume, David. *A Treatise of Human Nature*. Second edition edited by L. A. Selby-Bigge and revised by P. H. Nidditch. Oxford: Clarendon Press, 1978.

_____ *Enquiry Concerning Human Understanding*, in *David Hume: Enquiries Concerning Human Understanding and Concerning the Principles of Morals*. Third Edition edited by L. A. Selby-Bigge and revised by P. H. Nidditch. Oxford: Oxford University Press, 1975.

_____ *Enquiry Concerning the Principles of Morals*, in *David Hume: Enquiries Concerning Human Understanding and Concerning the Principles of Morals*. Third Edition edited by L. A. Selby-Bigge and revised by P. H. Nidditch. Oxford: Oxford University Press, 1975.

_____ "Of the Standard of Taste," in *David Hume: Essays Moral, Political and Literary*. Edited by Eugene F. Miller. Indianapolis: Liberty Classics, 1985.

Hutcheson, Francis. *An Essay on the Nature and Conduct of the Passions and Affections*. Selections in *British Moralists 1650–1800*. Edited by D. D. Raphael. Indianapolis: Hackett, 1991.

_____ *An Inquiry Concerning Moral Good and Evil*. Selections in *British Moralists 1650–1800*. Edited by D. D. Raphael. Indianapolis: Hackett Publishing Company, 1991; and in *British Moralists*, ed. L. A. Selby-Bigge. Oxford: Clarendon Press, 1897; reissued in Indianapolis: Bobbs-Merrill Library of Liberal Arts, 1964.

Irwin, Terence H. "Kant's Criticisms of Eudaemonism," in *Aristotle, Kant and the Stoics: Rethinking Happiness and Duty*. Edited by Stephen Engstrom and Jennifer Whiting. Cambridge: Cambridge University Press, 1996.

_____ "The Metaphysical and Psychological Basis of Aristotle's Ethics," in *Essays on Aristotle's Ethics*. Edited by Amélie Oksenberg Rorty. Berkeley: University of California Press, 1980.

_____ Notes to the *Nicomachean Ethics*. In *Nicomachean Ethics*, translated by Terence Irwin. Indianapolis: Hackett Publishing Company, 1985.

Kant, Immanuel. "An Old Question Raised Again: Is the Human Race Constantly Progressing?" Translated by Lewis White Beck in *Kant On History*. Edited by Lewis White Beck. New York: Macmillan Library of Liberal Arts, 1963.

___ *Anthropology from a Pragmatic Point of View*. Translated by Mary Gregor. The Hague: Martinus Nijhoff, 1974.

___ "Conjectures on the Beginning of Human History," in *Kant's Political Writings*. Second edition translated by H. B. Nisbet. Edited by Hans Reiss. Cambridge: Cambridge University Press, 1991.

___ *Critique of Practical Reason* (Cambridge Texts in the History of Philosophy). Translated and edited by Mary Gregor with an Introduction by Andrews Reath. Cambridge: Cambridge University Press, 1997.

___ *Critique of Pure Reason*. Translated by Norman Kemp Smith. New York: Macmillan, St Martin's Press, 1965.

___ *Ethical Philosophy*. Translated by James Ellington. Indianapolis: Hackett Publishing Company, 1981.

___ *Groundwork of the Metaphysics of Morals* (Cambridge Texts in the History of Philosophy). Translated and edited by Mary Gregor with an Introduction by Christine M. Korsgaard. Cambridge: Cambridge University Press, 1998.

___ "Idea for a Universal History with a Cosmopolitan Purpose," in *Kant's Political Writings*. Second edition translated by H. B. Nisbet. Edited by Hans Reiss. Cambridge: Cambridge University Press, 1991.

___ *Lectures on Ethics*. Translated by Louis Infeld. Indianapolis: Hackett Publishing Company, 1980.

___ "On the Common Saying: 'This May Be True in Theory but It Does not Apply in Practice'," in *Kant's Political Writings*. Second edition translated by H. B. Nisbet. Edited by Hans Reiss. Cambridge: Cambridge University Press, 1991.

___ *Perpetual Peace*. Translated by Lewis White Beck in *Kant On History*. Edited by Lewis White Beck. New York: Macmillan Library of Liberal Arts, 1963.

___ *Religion within the Limits of Reason Alone*. Translated and edited by Theodore M. Greene and Hoyt H. Hudson with an Introduction by John R. Silber. New York: Harper Torchbooks, 1960.

___ *The Metaphysical Elements of Justice*. Translated by John Ladd. New York: Macmillan Library of Liberal Arts, 1965.

___ *The Metaphysics of Morals* (Cambridge Texts in the History of Philosophy). Translated and edited by Mary Gregor with an Introduction by Roger J. Sullivan. Cambridge: Cambridge University Press, 1996.

___ "What is Enlightenment?" Translated by Lewis White Beck in *Kant On History*. Edited by Lewis White Beck. New York: Macmillan Library of Liberal Arts, 1963.

Kenny, Anthony. *Action, Emotion, and Will*. London: Routledge, 1963.

Korsgaard, Christine M. *Creating the Kingdom of Ends*. New York: Cambridge University Press, 1996.

___ "Fellow Creatures: Kantian Ethics and Our Duties to Animals," in *The Tanner Lectures on Human Values*. Edited by Grethe B. Peterson, Volume 25/26. Salt

Lake City: University of Utah Press, 2004; and on the Tanner Lecture website at <www.TannerLectures.utah.edu>.

Korsgaard, Christine M. "Motivation, Metaphysics, and the Value of the Self: A Reply to Ginsborg, Guyer, and Schneewind," *Ethics* 109 (1998): 49–66.

——— "Rawls and Kant: On the Primacy of the Practical," in *The Proceedings of the Eighth International Kant Congress*. Edited by Hoke Robinson. Milwaukee: Marquette University Press, 1995.

——— *Self-Constitution: Agency, Identity, and Integrity*. Oxford: Oxford University Press, 2009.

——— *The Sources of Normativity*. Cambridge: Cambridge University Press, 1996.

Locke, John. *The Second Treatise of Government: An Essay Concerning the Original, Extent, and End of Civil Government*. Edited by C. B. Macpherson. Indianapolis: Hackett Publishing Company, 1980.

McDowell, John. "Deliberation and Moral Development in Aristotle's Ethics," in *Aristotle, Kant and the Stoics: Rethinking Happiness and Duty*. Edited by Stephen Engstrom and Jennifer Whiting. Cambridge: Cambridge University Press, 1996.

Mackie, John. *Ethics: Inventing Right and Wrong*. Harmondsworth: Penguin, 1977.

Mill, John Stuart. *Utilitarianism*. Edited by George Sher. Indianapolis: Hackett Publishing Company, 1979.

Mineka, Francis E. and Dwight N. Lindley, editors. *The Later Letters of John Stuart Mill, 1849–1873*. Toronto: University of Toronto Press, 1972.

Moore, G. E. *Principia Ethica*. Cambridge: Cambridge University Press, 1903.

Nagel, Thomas. "Aristotle on Eudaimonia," *Phronesis* 17 (1972): 252–9. Reprinted in *Essays on Aristotle's Ethics*. Edited by Amélie Oksenberg Rorty. Berkeley: University of California Press, 1980.

——— *The Possibility of Altruism*. Oxford: Clarendon Press, 1970. Reprinted in Princeton: Princeton University Press, 1978.

——— *The View from Nowhere*. New York: Oxford University Press, 1986.

Nietzsche, Friedrich. *On the Genealogy of Morals*. Translated by Walter Kaufman and R. J. Hollingdale. In *On the Genealogy of Morals and Ecce Homo*. Edited by Walter Kaufman. New York: Random House, 1967.

——— "The Twilight of the Idols," in *Twilight of the Idols and The Anti-Christ*, translated by R. J. Hollingdale. Harmondsworth: Penguin Books, 1968.

Nozick, Robert. *Philosophical Explanations*. Harvard: The Belknap Press, 1981.

Nussbaum, Martha. *Aristotle's De Motu Animalium*. Princeton: Princeton University Press, 1978.

O'Neill, Onora. *Constructions of Reason: Explorations of Kant's Practical Philosophy*. Cambridge: Cambridge University Press, 1989.

Parfit, Derek. *Reasons and Persons*. Oxford: Clarendon Press, 1984.

——— *Rediscovering Reasons*. In manuscript, to be published by Oxford University Press.

Plato. *Plato: Complete Works*. Edited by John M. Cooper. Indianapolis: Hackett Publishing Company, 1997.

Price, Richard. *Review of the Principal Questions and Difficulties in Morals*, selections in *British Moralists 1650–1800*. Edited by D. D. Raphael. Indianapolis: Hackett Publishing Company, 1991.

Prichard, H. A. *Moral Obligation* (1949) and *Duty and Interest* (1929). Oxford: Oxford University Press, first published together in 1968.

Railton, Peter. "On the Hypothetical and Non-Hypothetical in Reasoning about Belief and Action," in *Ethics and Practical Reason*. Edited by Garrett Cullity and Berys Gaut. Oxford: Clarendon Press, 1997.

Raphael, D. D., editor. *British Moralists 1650–1800*. Indianapolis: Hackett Publishing Company, 1991.

Rawls, John. *A Theory of Justice*. Cambridge, MA: Harvard University Press, 1971; 2nd edition, 1999.

_____ *Political Liberalism*. New York: Columbia University Press, 1993.

Raz, Joseph. *Engaging Reason*. Oxford: Oxford University Press, 1999.

Reid, Thomas. *Essays on the Active Powers of Man*. Edinburgh: 1788.

Rorty, Amélie Oksenberg. *Essays on Aristotle's Ethics*. Berkeley: University of California Press, 1980.

Ross, W. D. *The Right and the Good*. Oxford: Oxford University Press, 1930.

Rousseau, Jean-Jacques. *On the Social Contract*, in *The Basic Political Writings of Jean-Jacques Rousseau*. Translated by D. A. Cress. Indianapolis: Hackett Publishing Company, 1987.

Scanlon, T. M. *What We Owe to Each Other*. Cambridge, MA: Harvard University Press, 1998.

Schneewind, J. B. "Kant and Stoic Ethics," in *Aristotle, Kant and the Stoics: Rethinking Happiness and Duty*. Edited by Stephen Engstrom and Jennifer Whiting. Cambridge: Cambridge University Press, 1996.

Selby-Bigge, L. A. *British Moralists*. Oxford: Clarendon Press, 1897; reissued in Indianapolis: Bobbs-Merrill Library of Liberal Arts, 1964.

Sidgwick, Henry. *The Methods of Ethics* (7th edition). Indianapolis: Hackett Publishing Company, 1981.

Smith, Michael. "A Theory of Freedom and Responsibility," in *Ethics and Practical Reason*. Edited by Garrett Cullity and Berys Gaut. Oxford: Clarendon Press, 1997.

Strawson, P. F. *Freedom and Resentment and Other Essays*. London: Methuen, 1974.

Velleman, David. "Deciding how to Decide," in *Ethics and Practical Reason*. Edited by Garrett Cullity and Berys Gaut. Oxford: Clarendon Press, 1997.

_____ *Practical Reflection*. Princeton: Princeton University Press, 1989.

_____ *Self to Self*. Cambridge: Cambridge University Press, 2006.

_____ *The Possibility of Practical Reason*. Oxford: Clarendon Press, 2000.

Whewell, William. *The Elements of Morality*. Cambridge: 1845.

Whiting, Jennifer. "Self-Love and Authoritative Virtue: Prolegomenon to a Kantian Reading of *Eudemian Ethics* 8.3," in *Aristotle, Kant and the Stoics: Rethinking Happiness and Duty*. Edited by Stephen Engstrom and Jennifer Whiting. Cambridge: Cambridge University Press, 1996.

Wilkes, Kathleen V. "The Good Man and the Good for Man in Aristotle's Ethics," *Mind* 87 (1978): 553–71. Reprinted in *Essays on Aristotle's Ethics*. Edited by Amélie Oksenberg Rorty. Berkeley: University of California Press, 1980.

Williams, Bernard. *Ethics and the Limits of Philosophy*. Cambridge, MA: Harvard University Press, 1985.

—— *Morality: An Introduction to Ethics*. New York: Harper Torchbooks, 1972.

—— *Moral Luck*. Cambridge: Cambridge University Press, 1981.

—— *Problems of the Self*. Cambridge: Cambridge University Press, 1973.

Williams, Howard. *Kant's Political Philosophy*. New York: St Martin's Press, 1983.

Wittgenstein, Ludwig. *Philosophical Investigations*. Translated by G. E. M. Anscombe. New York: Macmillan, 1971.

Wood, Allen. "Self-Love, Self-Benevolence, and Self-Conceit," in *Aristotle, Kant and the Stoics: Rethinking Happiness and Duty*. Edited by Stephen Engstrom and Jennifer Whiting. Cambridge: Cambridge University Press, 1996.

Sources

"The Normativity of Instrumental Reason" was first published in *Ethics and Practical Reason*, edited by Garrett Cullity and Berys Gaut. Oxford: Clarendon Press, 1997: pp. 213–54. It is reprinted here by permission of the publisher.

"The Myth of Egoism" was first published by the University of Kansas as the Lindley Lecture for 1999, and is reprinted here with the permission of the University of Kansas.

"Self-Constitution in the Ethics of Plato and Kant" was first published in *The Journal of Ethics* 3 (1999): 1–29. It is reprinted here by permission of the publisher.

"Aristotle's Function Argument" is published here for the first time. © Christine M. Korsgaard 2008.

"Aristotle on Function and Virtue" was first published in the *History of Philosophy Quarterly* 3/3 (July 1986): 259–79, and is reprinted here by permission of the publisher.

"From Duty and for the Sake of the Noble: Kant and Aristotle on Morally Good Action" was first published in *Aristotle, Kant, and the Stoics: Rethinking Happiness and Duty*, edited by Stephen Engstrom and Jennifer Whiting. New York: Cambridge University Press, 1996, pp. 203–36, and is reprinted here by permission of the publisher.

"Acting for a Reason" is forthcoming in *Studies in Practical Reason*, edited by V. Bradley Lewis, from the Catholic University Press. © Christine M. Korsgaard 2008.

"Taking the Law into Our Own Hands: Kant on the Right to Revolution" was first published in *Reclaiming the History of Ethics: Essays for John Rawls*, edited by Andrews Reath, Barbara Herman, and Christine M. Korsgaard. New York: Cambridge University Press, 1997, pp. 297–328, and is reprinted here by permission of the publisher.

"The General Point of View: Love and Moral Approval in Hume's Ethics" was first published in *Hume Studies* 25/1 & 2 (April/November 1999): 1–39, and is reprinted here by permission of the publishers.

"Realism and Constructivism in Twentieth-Century Moral Philosophy" was first published in *Philosophy in America at the Turn of the Century*. APA Centennial Supplement to *The Journal of Philosophical Research*. Charlottesville, Virginia: The Philosophy Documentation Center, 2003, pp. 99–122, and is reprinted here by permission of the publishers.

Index

normativity, *see* action, goodness or
badness of; constitutive (internal)
standards and principles; justice,
procedural vs. substantive; practical
reason, empiricist account of;
practical reason, rationalist/realist
account of; rationality, descriptive
vs. normative senses of; reason
Nozick, Robert, 132, 151–2 n. 1, 214 n .9
Nussbaum, Martha 131 n. 2, 135 n.

O'Neill, Onora, 62–3 n. 60
obligation (sometimes mentioned as
"duty" or "requirement"), 7, 12,
184–5, 212–13, 305–6, 316–17, *see also*
action, goodness or badness of;
categorical imperative; noble (as a
motive: *to kalon*); duty, acting from
obligatory ends, 220, 255

pain, *see* pleasure
Paley, William, 304
Parfit, Derek, 29, 30 n. 8, 305
particularistic willing, impossibility
of, 120–4
passions and emotions
Aristotle and Kant's different attitudes
towards, 18–19, 176, 197–205
Aristotle's account of how they are
related to rational activity, 17–18,
153–73
Aristotle's account of passions as
perceptions of the good, 18, 18–19,
170–3, 156, 201–5
Hume's theory of, 265–70, 279–89
Hume on the calm passions, 37, 38, 44,
272–3, 279, 282–3
passions as secondary impressions,
according to Hume, 269 n. 6
sense in which they have grounds rather
than mere causes, 267–70, 297–300
sense in which they have objects, 265–6
relation to reason, in the Combat and
Constitutional Models of the
soul, 100–3, 110
see also desire; pleasure and pain;
sympathy
paternalism, 258–9
Penner, Terry, 153 n. 3, 173 n. 15
perception, 2, 61 n. 56, 207, 311, 313
Aristotle's conception of, 204 n. 29

as one of the three forms of life, in
Aristotle, 132, 142, 153
Hume, on the use of the general point of
view for making sensory
judgments, 274–9
as the ground of belief and action 3–5
pleasure as a perception of the good, 18,
18–19, 156, 170–3, 201–5
permissibility, 12, 184–5, 212, 225, 226
n. 22
personal identity, *see* identity
Plato
on action, 13–14, 101–9, 111, 112,
on the metaphysics of activity, 9
on bad or defective action, 110–13,
114–17
on the city/soul analogy, 101–9
on the Constitutional Model of the
soul, 101–9
on defective types of soul, 115–17, 118
on evil, 261–2
on the function argument, 129, 131,
144–5, 150, 153
on ideas, 246
on justice, 13–14, 21, 60 n. 53, 67, 105–6,
108–9, 118–19
on the unjust person's incapacity for
effective action, 102, 108–9, 117
compared with Kant, 14, 110–17, 119–20,
125–6, 246
on the commensurability of pleasure, 43
n. 26
on self-constitution, 13–14, 108, 294–5
n. 30
on tyranny, as a condition of the
soul, 66 n. 66, 117
on virtue, 103, 158, 202–3 n. 26
pleasure
pleasure as a perception of the good, 18,
18–19, 156, 170–3, 201–5
connection to happiness, 99 n. 27, 131
relation to virtue, in Aristotle's
account, 156, 158, 164–73, 176,
197–204
Hume's account of, 266, 279
relation to love, in Hume's
account, 266, 269–70, 272–3
political legitimacy, 241–9
political state
as an agent, 13–14, 20, 104–8, 248–9, *see
also* general will